THE WAY WE LIVE NOW

RICHARD HOGGART

Chatto & Windus
LONDON

First published in 1995

1 3 5 7 9 10 8 6 4 2

Copyright © Richard Hoggart 1995

Richard Hoggart has asserted his right under the Copyright,
Designs and Patents Act, 1988, to be identified as the author
of this work.

First published in Great Britain in 1995 by
Chatto & Windus Limited
Random House, 20 Vauxhall Bridge Road,
London SW1V 2SA

Random House Australia (Pty) Limited
20 Alfred Street, Milsons Point, Sydney
New South Wales 2061, Australia

Random House New Zealand Limited
18 Poland Road, Glenfield
Auckland 10, New Zealand

Random House South Africa (Pty) Limited
P O Box 337, Bergvlei, South Africa

Random House UK Limited Reg. No. 954009

Papers used by Random House UK Limited are natural, recyclable
products made from wood grown in sustainable forests. The
manufacturing processes conform to the environmental
regulations of the country of origin

A CIP catalogue record for this book
is available from the British Library

ISBN 0 7011 6501 4

Printed in Great Britain by
Mackays of Chatham PLC, Chatham, Kent

To my grandchildren,
with love

Contents

Acknowledgments   x
Introduction   xi

PART ONE: RELATIVISM TO OPPORTUNISM

1 Riding Relativism's Wave   3
   i Them and Us   4
   ii Just Us – or Just Them   6
   iii Mary and Martha   11

PART TWO: ASPECTS OF THE DOMINANT MOOD

2 Distortions of Education   21
   i The Climate   22
   ii Schools   26
   iii Further Education: the Cinderella   37
   iv Higher Education: the Universities   40
   v Adult Education Today   49

3 The Arts: Intellectual, Artistic and Academic Relativism   55
   i The Peculiar Debate; Communitarian Art   55
   ii Reading   65
   iii Literary Essences   75
   iv Academic Responses: Meaning and Modern Theory   82
   v Literary Influences   88

4 Angles on Mass and Popular Culture   96
   i Characteristics of Mass Culture   97
   ii Elements of Popular Culture   102

5 The Betrayal of Broadcasting   114
   i The Public Service and Professionalism   114
   ii Radio   126

iii Television 133
iv Broadcasting and the Arts 138
v The 1990 Broadcasting Act and After 144
vi Conclusion 152

6 Misuses of Language 157
  i Linguistic Tics 158
  ii Dodging Reality and Judgment 160
  iii Language and Ideology 163
  iv Hospital Kindly Gentility 166
  v Embarrassed by the Words 167

7 Ways of Looking: Compass Bearings in a Wide-Open
  Society? 172
  i The Need for a Discipline 172
  ii Where Did It All Begin? 174
  iii Theory? Naturally 177
  iv Elements of Cultural Reading 179
  v Some Rules of Thumb 182
  vi Instances of Surprise 189

PART THREE: GRIT ON THE FLYWHEEL

8 Home Thoughts: Old-Style Checks and Balances 193

9 From Class to Status: Resistance by Transference 198
  i The Survival of Class? 198
  ii Status and Life-Style 202
  iii Piggybacks, Partial Profiles and Emotional Energy 209

10 Patrons and Sponsors 213
  i Why Give at all – in an 'Open' Society? 214
  ii Class, Education, the Arts; and Public Duty 218
  iii Grass-roots, 'Ethnic Arts' and Their Claims 223
  iv Confused Alarms of Struggle and Fight 224
  v Patronage and Sponsorship 226
  vi Who Should Get What, and How? 231
  vii Spreading Your Arts Abroad 237

11 Effects of Mass Media: Kinds of Censorship –
  a Baker's Dozen 243
  i Counterweights and Contradictions Again 244
  ii Effects, Broadcasting and Elsewhere 246

Contents

iii Kinds of Censorship 249
iv 'Am I My Brother's Keeper?' 266

12 Ancestral Voices: Myths and Mottoes to Live By 268
   i Deep Springs 268
  ii Sophisticated Memories 273
 iii Three Types of Aphorism 275
 iv Walking on the Water 278

PART FOUR: WHO NEEDS A CLERISY?

13 Democratic Representations and Democratic Spirits 283
  i Confrontation, Consensus and Cohesion 285
 ii Jude and His Kind 296

14 Diverse Voices, and Opinion-Formers 300
   i A Mixed Bunch, Mainly Official 302
  ii Reviewers; and Some Critics 305
 iii No Committees, Please, We're English 311
 iv Jobs for Intellectuals? 312

PART FIVE: A SUMMING-UP; AND A VERY QUALIFIED
PROSPECTUS

15 Where are We, and Where Do We Go from Here? 321
   i Relativism Rampant 321
  ii Old Strengths 329
 iii New Opportunities 332
 iv What to Do About It? or: Let's Put Out the Lights and Go
    to Sleep? 335

Index 341

Acknowledgments

Many people have helped, to a greater or lesser degree, to get this book into shape. Any errors of fact or judgment which remain are mine. So, my thanks to: Richard Beck, Geoffrey Goodman, Stephen Hearst, Muriel McNaughton, John Miller, Michael Orrom, Sue Rose, Roy Shaw.

Catharine Carver was, as she has been for many years, a cherished supporting presence.

Jenny Uglow was a splendidly perceptive, and much needed, editor. I am very grateful to her and to all others at Chatto & Windus.

I am also greatly indebted to Michael Shaw of Curtis Brown for his encouragement and help.

Last, my warmest thanks to all members of the family; most of all, to my wife, Mary.

Much use has been made of quotations from other writers, most of them long dead, some happily alive. The passages from the latter do not exceed the conventionally accepted length for quotations in studies of this kind. References are given within the text except for a few which have escaped my notes. I would be very grateful for information about these and will include them in any later printing. Meanwhile, I am grateful also to all the authors and publishers concerned and in particular to: Allen Lane/The Penguin Press (and M. A. Screech), the Arts Council of England, Batsford, *Blackfriars*, Blackwell, Bloodaxe, Bloomsbury, Broadcasting Research Unit, Cambridge University Press, Chatto and Windus, Faber and Faber, Harper, HMSO, Merlin Press, Oxford University Press, Penguin Books, PEP, Polity Press, Routledge, *Stand*, Zwan/Pluto. And to the executors of: W. H. Auden, T. S. Eliot, E. M. Forster, C. S. Lewis, George Orwell, Herbert Read, I. A. Richards, E. P. Thompson, G. M. Trevelyan, Raymond Williams.

Introduction

Long essays are rather like sizeable pieces of fretwork. Each is put together with loving care over quite a long time. The fretwork is shown to friends in the local Carpentry Club. The essays are offered to journals of small but, it is hoped, relevant circulation. Both creations then lie about the house or are put to rest in the attic; for years.

Eventually you gather them together, find a sort of order if you can and send them out to a wider world. It is more than a dozen years since I published a book of collected essays, and a good many have been written in the interim. When I read them through again I realised for the first time that the things I had been writing about were related in a way I hadn't fully recognised. Teased, I sat before them for a long while, tracked back to even earlier writings, and began to see a shape behind the recurrent interests, a shape which seemed interesting in itself and so, after a great deal of rewriting and new writing, one which might make a coherent full-length book.

The shape was determined by a not fully conscious drive which lay behind and linked most of the subjects: education, the arts, broadcasting and the other mass media, changes in language and changes in the general culture, especially in attitudes to class; the nature of 'Englishness' and the place of intellectuals in English life.

All these subjects were, it gradually became clear, held together, underneath, by a range of secular movements running through the century. They were, mainly: the decline of authority, the rise of relativism and of its siblings such as populism (the word 'pluralism' was avoided as suggesting diversity and openness; 'relativism' works the other way), and the dangers relativism and populism present to democracy. These and a half-dozen others form the recurrent key-words of the argument. The processes they indicate, gathering pace since the end of the last war and especially from the Sixties, have been accelerated by technological advances. They have been exploited, for their own purposes and not altogether consciously, by the Conservative governments of the last decade and a half.

No earlier writing is included in its original form: the structure is new, most of the writing is new; but where for the wholeness of the argument a solid passage from an earlier essay seemed to be needed more or less as it stood, it has been incorporated.

I said 'English' and 'Englishness' above where 'British' might have been expected. That is deliberate. I am not competent to say where Scottish or Welsh or Northern Irish cultures are the same as English and where different. Is it certain that there is such a thing as 'British' culture? There is an administrative and political unity which has lasted over centuries and so shares much history and responses to it. But when Eliot, Orwell and Lawrence talk about the culture of the biggest part of these islands, they say 'English' and seem to believe they are pointing to a network of attitudes which they find central to the English, not all of which they would wish to father on the Scots or Welsh or Northern Irish. I share that view. But there is no need to be pedantic here. I have sometimes used 'British', if it seemed to come naturally.

This book is exceptionally full of quotations from writers over several centuries (some I have used before, being particularly fond of them). That too is deliberate. When you write on these themes, apt and often moving passages flood in, from the simplest hymns to the grandest organ-music of great poetry. Why should they be repressed? Especially since one of the book's themes is the continuity of English attitudes, the extent to which writers separated by hundreds of years have reflected on the nature of their Englishness and its relation to the main issues in human experience at all times and places, not just in this small island. A related theme is the neglect of that inheritance, the forgetting of history in preference to what I call 'living in the successive present'. So a main element in what should be our sense of ourselves – access to the insights which creative writers uniquely offer – is often missing from our minds. In view of these considerations the inclusion of this large number of quotations from the great dead and the more thoughtful among the living seems to need no justification. I have included many anecdotes simply because they seemed to stand for more than themselves. So names and places could have been distracting and have not been given.

In the early part of the last century Carlyle gave us the phrase 'The Condition of England' (and many other beauties, such as 'the cash-nexus'). We are all still in his debt. There followed the 'Condition of England' novels of Disraeli, Kingsley, Charlotte Brontë, Mrs Gaskell and Dickens. We are in their debt too.

Trollope is greatly liked and greatly read today, but often for reasons which undervalue his moral penetration into individuals and into society. His *The Way We Live Now* is one of the best antidotes to that. The use of that title is a form of salute.

A! Fredome is a noble thing!
Fredome mayse man to haiff liking.

John Barbour, *The Bruce*, 1376

Increased means and increased leisure are the two civilisers of man.

Benjamin Disraeli, speech, 1872

I favour ... politics not as the technology of power and manipulation of
cybernetic rule over humans, or as the art of the useful, but politics as
practical morality, as service to the truth, as essentially human and
humanly measured care for our fellow humans. It is an approach which,
in this world, is extremely impractical and difficult to apply.

Václav Havel, *Living in Truth*, 1989

PART ONE

Relativism to Opportunism

It is characteristic of the intellectual life of our culture that it fosters a form of assent which does not involve actual credence.
Lionel Trilling, *Beyond Culture*, 1965 (true of the personal
life too)

There is no such thing as Society. There are individual men and women, and there are families. And no government can do anything except through people, and people must look after themselves. It's our duty to look after ourselves and then to look after our neighbour.
Margaret Thatcher, *Woman's Own*, 31 October 1987 (a
statement untrue to much in the English spirit)

CHAPTER ONE

Riding Relativism's Wave

[The concept of post-modernism] proclaimed the end of the exploration of the ultimate truth of the human world or human experience, the end of the political or missionary ambitions of art, the end of dominant style, of artistic canons, of interest in the aesthetic grounds of artistic self-confidence and objective boundaries of art.

Zigmunt Bauman, *Legislators and Interpreters*, 1992

This is a surf-riding phase in British life. The wave of relativism – the obsessive avoidance of judgments of quality, or moral judgment – has risen higher then ever before (as in all prosperous societies). Here, since 1979, one political party has with much success ridden that wave.

For more than a century, and most rapidly in the last half-century, the powers of Authority, whether lay or religious, have been eroded. The remaining power of the Roman Catholic Church in some areas – much of Eire, some parts of England – is no more than the inevitable exception.

Those guiding authorities having lost their power (which is to the good), something had to take their place: no society can tolerate a vacuum. It can now with hindsight be seen that forms of relativism would take their place; and that that transformation would be vastly accelerated, in commercial democracies, by greater and more wide-spread prosperity, the urge to sell everything from clothes to notions, and so the need to persuade; which is where the other main technical force, the technology of mass communications, increasingly comes to the front.

The second phase of change has had a shorter life, and is a remark-able example of how a political party can ride the waves of change for its own purposes: partly consciously, partly unconsciously. This is the record of successive Tory governments from the end of the Seventies to the moment of writing. They have managed by an extraordinary trick of juggling to combine the exploitation of relativism with new forms of authoritarianism, of populism with privilege.

i THEM AND US

As to the sense of Authority, religious or secular, where is the watershed? Perhaps at the end of the last war, there or thereabouts. Which means that almost all those under fifty would not easily appreciate the strength of that sense of 'Them' and 'Us' which so powerfully influenced their parents' lives, unless they were better off than most; and whether they accepted that background or resented it.

That sense differed in strength according to class, and intensified as you moved down the social scale. Working-class people felt it most; it follows that the movement into relativism affected them most; they had more to shake off; the change 'liberated' them more than other groups. Which is why the American sociologist Edward Shils could say that the most important cultural change of the second half of the twentieth century was 'the entry of the working class into society': spending for pleasure, not simply to survive; being evident, inescapable, making their own kinds of noises.

Before the war most 'respectable' working-class families in their own big-city districts went to church or chapel, some regularly, the majority only on family 'state occasions' or habitual community anniversaries: baptisms, marriages, deaths, Christmas, New Year and perhaps Easter and Whitsuntide. Most children were sent to Sunday School or its equivalent, and not only so that their parents could make love undisturbed, unhurriedly and without the tiredness of the working week. You were sent because that was the right thing to do. Even though most parents did not attend except on those state occasions, enough did to make congregations better than meagre. In a typical such area today, or what remains of it, four or five chapels will have been merged into one, and that one will be lucky to have a regular congregation of above fifty. Depopulation is the least important cause of that decline.

There might have been a couple of streets of Irish people, descendants of the 'navvies' who had come here well over a century before, to work on the canals and then the railways. They went to at least one Sunday Mass. A minority of the English went to the local parish church; they were C. of E. as habitually as they were deferential Tory voters; they assumed that some people were our natural rulers, that the Church of England was indeed the Tory Party at prayer. Of the others, those who regularly worshipped went to a Nonconformist chapel – Baptist, Congregationalist, Methodist or Primitive Methodist. They were always aware of the chapel up near the main road and of the minister who, when he bobbed round during a crisis, easily assumed a tutelary role – as a fairly minor member of Them.

The local 'Panel' doctor was regarded as a slightly superior member of the company of Them; about equal if not slightly above the Church of England vicar. He expected to be listened to and felt free to offer firm advice about drinking and smoking, as well as the care of the child's chest. No doubt many GPs act like that today, but they do so from a less securely elevated position.

Then there were the Board of Guardians 'visitors', if the home was drawing benefit from that local Board, the School Attendance Officer, the dreaded Means Test Inspector and the local bobbies. Beyond all those, up in imposing buildings in the centre of town, was the top tier of Them: the local authorities who controlled all the public services – education, social work, council rents, the police; and the magistrates – the Bench who, except for an occasional Trade Union official, were rarely from your class. The most shadowy outer penumbra of Them contained the government in London. They were little thought of and then usually with suspicion and wariness; they came from a different world; the local representatives of Them were enough to be going on with.

Inevitably, attitudes towards Them were complex. You knew their powers but would not easily show actual deference; you might act bloody-mindedly if you came up before them for some lapse or another, but you did not take them for granted. You had a sense of these others in power who had to be treated cautiously rather than fearfully. You didn't often say: 'What They ought to do is . . .' as if you were accusing them of falling down on some duty they owed to you; you did not have or want that kind of relationship. But you knew that 'if it came to it, They can make things worse for you'.

No doubt people on Social Security today cannot avoid a sense that there is a group of Them keeping on eye open for abuses; plus the staff of the Social Services Departments allotted to trying to help. Yet it is unlikely that the web, the network, of Them is as complicated as it used to be, even for very poor people; and unlikely, even there, that attitudes towards Them are unchanged. Although many people live below the 'poverty line', for many others the possession of at least adequate money to manage on, plus the general decline across all parts of society of the sense of deference, is a major change; the social world is far more horizontal and diffused.

The pattern of authority-consciousness in slightly higher social groups was inevitably different; but a form of it was there. It too has relaxed, though – as with working-class people – it has lingered longer in those over fifty, especially with some not very high up, who gratefully felt themselves to be the NCOs of the authority-pattern; that allowed them to look not only up but also down.

Among younger people in the secure middle classes the outcome has been much the same as for working-class young people. The sense of external authority (and often of parental authority) has virtually gone; there are hardly any injunction-givers, finger-waggers, these days.

It would be wrong-headed, short-sighted and probably mean-spirited to regret these changes as a matter of principle. One *can* retain the right to regret some of their manifestations; not to do so would be to assume – and that is common today – that all social changes are, simply by happening, self-validating, to be accepted without question. Much of the old style of authority was mistakenly assumed and adopted, born of the disadvantages of others. Some of it was wrongly applied, the petty authoritarianism of petty people in positions of petty power. Some of it based itself on fear, religious or secular.

ii JUST US – OR JUST THEM

The Authorities, then, have almost all gone. The contemporary ground-level is relativism. It is an amenable ground for those societies which, though not uniformly prosperous, are generally well-off to a degree which most other nations are not; those technologically advanced societies, 'open democracies', capitalist, operating ever more elaborate communication systems; consumer-driven and so run by means of persuasions of all kinds, at all levels and depths.

Such societies need relativism; it is the perfect soil for their endless and always changing urges. A society of beliefs, of different beliefs, divides, splits people into majorities and, worse, awkward minorities. Some well-heeled minorities can by now be addressed with profit. But that specialised provision is inextricably related to the fact that others, the great body of people, are more and more led towards having undifferentiated, shared, but always changing tastes.

Utterances characteristic of this overall climate can be met any day

6

and everywhere, in shops, trains, pubs and clubs; and in Cabinet Ministers. All are pronounced as matters of obvious common sense. A Cabinet Minister is asked, apropos of the concept of the Public Service in broadcasting, about the exact definition of a public service, the public interest. With no apparent sense of hedging, he replies that, like so many other matters, such a concept 'has to be redefined in and for each generation'. So what's the definition of honesty for this generation? This year? This month? Why should any particular definition be accepted at any one time by any individual, or shared at any one time by any group?

It follows that relativism also implies levelling, the belief – if belief it is; more likely it is an assumption – that with a few obvious exceptions all are equal in all things and so all views are of equal worth. We should not have to note, but perhaps it is necessary as an agreed proper marker, that in some important respects we should indeed be thought of as equal: before God, if we recognise one; before the law; and before others – that in these things we are all initially worthy of respect. After that, the lines divide: we are not equal in beauty or sporting ability, or in the talents needed to become a pop star; or in intelligence; or, hardest of all, in virtue.

It is of the essence of a true democracy that people should be respected individually, not simply collectively. It is also of the essence of a democracy that differences and distinctions are recognised and, where relevant, honoured. A democracy should be above all a *thoughtful* type of society, in these and other respects.

Anything less than that set of basic precepts demotes a democratic to a populist state; populist states are by nature thoughtless rather than thoughtful. Those who work the levers of power and persuasion need, above all else, to be accepted, to be liked, to be seen as having the truth within them; they have to 'manufacture consent'. All playing-fields are level and all compasses point in the same direction, towards the same fallacious Shangri-La.

In such a society those on the Right politically can move happily. They know that, behind the slogans and the blokishness, most levelling is bogus, that 'the masses' will not invade their clubs, seek to marry their daughters, travel first-class or have access to a range of other privileges.

Many active on the Left accept the same framework either because it allows them, as it allows those on the Right, to flatter people low down in the heap, or because they are muddled enough actually to believe that all really are equal in every possible sense (apart, of the exceptions noted above, from beauty, and sporting and pop stars' talent; intelligence and virtue are less happily accommodated, maybe positively rejected from membership in this category). Otherwise all are equal. In particular, all opinions are as good as all others; therefore head-counting will produce the 'right' answer on every conceivable issue.

To sum up so far; relativism leads to populism which then leads to levelling; and so to reductionism, to quality-reductionism of all kinds – from food to moral judgments. There are no varying perspectives, no changes of level, no goals, no aims outside this sequence; except the aim of being so far as possible like everyone else; or apparently so, for the sake of rubbing along. Even those who have proved to be exceptional in the accepted way – pop stars and sports stars – have to act on the required occasions as if they are just ordinary blokes; even though their styles of life outside such occasions are wildly unordinary. That too is not only accepted but wished for; the exceptional bloke is at bottom ordinary but also fascinatingly unordinary – as he turns up from time to time at his ordinary childhood home in his exceptional Rolls-Royce. Such individuals are not usually the focus of envy; they are liked as they are, in their exceptionalness of gifts, their apparent ordinariness of manner before their fans, and their manifestly unordinary styles of life in all else.

That sequence – relativism to populism to levelling to reductionism – leads in technically sophisticated capitalist societies to concentration. Here the powerful links of relativism to consumerism become clear. So as to make economies of scale and enhance profits, consumerism must persuade people to allow themselves to be seen as, to come to see themselves as, a single body with shared tastes, small to large. 'You can have the Model T in any colour – so long as it's black.' It was not accidental that that first Fordism became so emblematic. It was an early, unabashed, apparently paradoxical but actually straightforward statement of the populist/reductionist ethos. Since it was about making objects cheap, not ideas, it was not very important.

Relativist-consumerism is also by nature jerky; it cannot rest. Once it has its mass clientele and its methods of mass production it must move those masses quickly and often, or the machines will seize up and the whole process threaten to collapse. The articles produced must themselves enter and leave at faster and faster intervals like cream crackers on a conveyor-belt – a 'new' new car each year, a

8

'new' model of camcorder, a 'new' set of interests and notions – even if almost all of those changes are, are forced to be, marginal and cosmetic. They can be sufficient to still the itch for change in us. This is a world of short breaths and short distances, more a matter of spinning round in grooves than of taking off into the high blue yonder.

Hence the yearly, monthly, weekly stunts, the unceasing search for the newly fashionable, the unmistakably modish approach to all things concerning taste; and to opinions. The race goes round and round itself; notion-guessing is a limited and limiting game. The most obvious instance of this is found in the Sunday papers of all kinds. By the alchemy of modishness the same person, the same evanescent fashion, the same subject, the same scandal, the same would-be-intellectual quirk, have caught the attention of almost all the columnists and personality-paraders in the same week. As always, language is a main carrier. 'The flavour of the month' is both an example of that and an apt comment on it. Many other phrases catch something of the feel of the time; and all pass away sooner or later, usually sooner.

Here is yet another paradox. The relativist-consumerist society is, yes, entirely committed to endless change. From another angle it is also committed to keeping things as they are. It is committed to change in things which do not greatly matter, to unimportant tastes and weightless opinions. It is committed to not having change – which would be the renewed recognition of their importance – in attitudes to some things which do matter, to those things which might rock the consumerist boat, to critical judgments and steadiness of purpose. It believes in what will later be described as the 'stay as sweet as you are' syndrome. One is urged not to entertain the thought that some things and some attitudes might conceivably be more worthwhile than others. For to take such a line is to welcome change in *significant* ways, is to judge and dismiss certain things, to say: 'Come off it. That's rubbish.' Where would that sort of thing end? For a start, it's bad for trade.

A further paradox. The exploiters use the 'stay as sweet as you are' line of persuasion because it suits their purposes. Once again, some people on the Left also use it; for example, those who oppose all forms of 'correct' speech and insist that any kind of speech, no matter how unclear and hence unintelligible it may be outside its local area, is unqualifiedly acceptable and suitable for all purposes. They thus trap those they would wish to release. An intended release into 'bourgeois ways' and 'the consumer society'? Certainly not. There may be good intentions here, not a wish to exploit. But the short-circuiting of thought has produced an unmeant and undesirable alliance; a dubious apparent congruity.

Hence, as in so much, the only standard is the echo back. If the roar of the crowd comes back, that is success, and so unanswerably right and good. This is the numbers game, a substitute for judgment, the refusal to tangle with 'better' and so with 'worse'. In this world there can be no 'worse', only failure by numbers; there can be no 'better', only the jingle of the cash registers and the number-crunching of the pollsters.

The mutations do not occur only in directly commercial affairs; they have to spread into institutions which should move to other music, to that idea of 'the public service', to the assumption that not all services or initiatives can have their worth measured by profit or numbers or even popular success. Historically, such institutions have had criteria for achievement which are less tangible, more difficult to discern. These criteria you may recognise and respect – if you do finally see them straight; and that is not easy.

Obvious and outstanding examples are the National Health Service, the teaching profession, the Fire Service, the Social Services and the Public Libraries. They all place professional and human satisfaction from public service before the size of wage or salary, or the acquisition of bonuses for aggressive salesmanship. All are under attack, tactically by being asked to prove their achievements according to irrelevant and spuriously 'objective' weights and measures ('performance indicators'), strategically by seeing the very idea of the public service cut away beneath them.

Relativism has had many complex offspring; 'post-modernism', for instance. But the trend which runs from relativism-to-populism-to-levelling-to-reductionism-to-consumerist-concentration finds its lowest level in opportunism; and that cluster leads straight into the main characteristics of the British governments of the last couple of decades. Here the secular trend meets the opportunist application.

It is easy to see why those impulses have been given the label 'Thatcherism'; there is some justice in that. But it gives the lady too much credit, makes her too much the initiating spirit. She welcomed them, she sensed (rather than analysed) how they might be used. But she was more a symptom than a cause, more carried along by those forces than their avatar. She had the force and the determination to make use of them; she lacked the vision to see their limitations; she was a dominant Party leader but not a stateswoman. Her acolytes were, as she was at bottom, more ridden than riding; the underlying process preceded them and will, more's the pity, outlast them.

iii MARY AND MARTHA

What is false in the science of facts may be true in the science of values.
George Santayana, *Interpretations of Poetry and Religion,*
1900

[High taxes] rob people of the chance to make the moral choice to assist others.
Conservative Cabinet Minister, 1994 (a revised definition of robbery)

No one would have remembered the Good Samaritan if he'd only had good intentions. He had money as well.
Margaret Thatcher, *television interview,* 1980

To commit violent and unjust acts, it is not enough for a government to have the will or even the power; the habits, ideas and passions of the time must lend themselves to their committal.
Alexis de Tocqueville, *Democracy in America,* 1835–40

Whoever could make two ears of corn or two blades of grass grow upon a spot of ground where only one grew before, would deserve better of mankind and do more essential service to his country than the whole race of politicians put together.
Jonathan Swift, *Gulliver's Travels,* 1726

So Mrs Thatcher's first government rode in on a wave, with more than one wind behind it. After a time people tire of even the best government. 'A change is as good as a rest,' we all sententiously observe at due moments. 'Change for change's sake' is less a critical phrase than a statement of a conventionally agreed fact of life. So is the vague but recurrent feeling that the grass is always greener on the other side of the hill.

In 1979 there were some solid grounds to encourage such feelings. The Labour government was in a mess. Inflation was very high. The 'winter of discontent' had upset many otherwise loyal Labour voters and more waverers. There was a general feeling that the Trade Unions had too much say; and that some unions were being run at the shop-steward level, wildly, as laws unto themselves. Restrictive practices, overmanning, and a not universal but quite common refusal by the unions to face the danger the country was in, all added to the sense of fed-up-ness.

The behaviour of a few Labour-run local councils – such as Liverpool and Lambeth, especially incurring excessive, politically driven expenditure – was plainly out of order, a mixture of bone-headed ideology and petty corruption. You did not need to read the right-wing press to recognise these things.

The mass media had a field day: with scenes of rotting rubbish piled in the streets for days on end, refusals by union activists to bury the dead, shots of snarling NHS ancillary workers picketing their own hospital services. It was all, of course, exaggerated by that same right-wing press; but the list of ills was long and not to be brushed aside by conspiracy theories. If ever a government had given signals to ordinary voters that it was time for a change, this was it.

*

No government is voted in without touching some deep nerves in a country's habitual nature. In 1979, even more than usually, that change had to be towards a set of radically different attitudes. Not foreign or unusual or outlandish attitudes; simply attitudes from another facet of the collective English character. Like many other national psyches, like many individuals, that 'national character' contained contradictions, and leaned towards one or the other side at different times, according to public and private mood.

On this occasion, the Martha side took over from the Mary (well, from what at that unhappy time could still be seen of Labour's Mary-ist approach). As always, idioms carry attitudes. The Martha side of the English character expresses itself in such phrases as 'you must live within your means', 'cut your coat according to your cloth', 'pay your way', 'don't spend what you haven't earned', 'be beholden to no one', 'stand on your own two feet', 'cleanliness before godliness', 'don't kill with kindness'. 'Unto every one that hath shall be given . . . but from him that hath not shall be taken away even that which he hath.'

Most of these are, within limits, admirable guidelines if a bit purse-lipped and so quickly purse-proud. Not surprisingly, Kipling made himself one of their celebrators: 'the Sons of Martha favour their Mother of the careful soul and the troubled heart . . . They do not preach that their God will rouse them a little before the nuts work loose. – They do not teach that His Pity allows them to leave their job when they damn-well choose' ('The Sons of Martha'). Fair, in many respects; but over-generous. Others of Martha's assumptions include that there is only a limited amount of goods and things of value in our world and that they have to be earned and then duly apportioned, or more will mean worse, dilution; resources do not grow by being used or planted around. The Martha spirit is therefore practical, Ricardian, hates hire purchase, works hard. It clearly has at its best some strong virtues, notably reliability and probity. It can produce redoubtable civil servants, especially for the Treasury; and good ships'-engineers.

If those qualities are unleavened by imagination, they can become rigid, in need of Arnold's 'a shade more soul'. They can then show a mean streak. Here is a fairly recent small example: when Neil Kinnock was made a European Commissioner in 1994, almost all the press concentrated, and knew they would find a response, on the 'huge' salary he would receive. That salary was well below what British commercial tycoons were awarding themselves each year; and by European top-executive standards, which determined the sum, was not particularly large. Little attention was paid to the duties of the post; the nag about money dominated.

Another mean streak and also a cock-eyed one. The Secretary of State for Social Security will harp on and on, especially to meetings of Party members, about 'DHSS scroungers'. One such Minister adapted Gilbert and Sullivan so as to prove his determination to root out the malingerers: 'I've got a little list. They'll none of them be missed'. Little is said about the many now on inadequate pensions and allowances; even less about the City fiddlers and tax-dodgers, the mini-Maxwells and today's Melmottes, those who 'live in riot and luxury on the plunder of the ignorant, the innocent' (Cobbett, *Political Register*, 1866).

The Martha spirit on its much less admirable side intones that as to criminals we must 'condemn more and understand less'. It is inclined to be vengeful (especially towards the 'work-shy' – a favoured word from its battery of dismissive epithets), bitten-in, lacking in charity, suspicious, fearful of being conned, self-righteous. It does not approve of minimum wage-levels or of improvements in the lot of part-time workers, or of the need to provide accessible housing for the poorly paid or homeless. It is more often chauvinistic and nationalistic than patriotic. On one side it tends to the narrowly puritan and prim. But it is intensely money-conscious and so will enact legislation which, whilst being restrictive to would-be political refugees, will give relaxed terms for entry to those who can bring an enormous dowry.

When Mrs Thatcher, newly elected and standing before Number 10 Downing Street, quoted (courtesy of her speech-writer Ronald Millar) St Francis on charity and the like, many people could not believe their ears. This from the head of a government which seemed likely to have – and bore out the expectation – no sense at all of what the social historian Richard Titmuss nicely called 'Humanistic accounting'.

The outgoing Labour government was on its knees. But in principle – and that is what most matters: first-order principles, not second-order convictions; those always end in expediency – in principle Labour, Socialism, is a creed of Mary not Martha. It believes in 'casting bread on the waters', trusting in human decency and promise, belonging to one another, planting seed corn wherever possible not only in already privileged enclaves. It is convinced that growth can make more growth, that chances should be taken, that godliness – charity – should come before cleanliness; and about caring for shorn lambs. At its best, it is communal, generous and fraternal. It belongs to that England of Blake, Cobbett, Wordsworth, Coleridge, Arnold, Lawrence, Forster, Orwell, Tawney and Titmuss.

*

This succession of Tory governments has nevertheless been shrewd, indeed one might say imaginative, in some of its decisions. British Gas and British Telecom provide, on the whole, better – more responsive – services now than when they were nationalised. Even more striking, council houses were offered for sale. Textbook Socialism said council houses should be solely available for those who could only rent, not buy. It was a form of purism. It ignored two major facts: first, that too many local housing authorities were restrictive in their regulations (no pigeon lofts) and incompetent in the services they should have provided (plumbing and all manner of general repairs). They made tenants angry and infringed their sense of personal freedom. Second, and though this is a truism it is still true: an Englishman's home really is his castle. Whether we approve of it or not, English families do not like living in tenement blocks. They want to have their own front doors, opening on to the street or on a bit of front garden, doors which they can open or close as they will, to keep out the world; even the neighbours. Then they will 'do the house up', 'do things to it', make it fit their traditional taste in creating a 'living room', or aim to meet new aspirations which come with ownership of your own home. We do wrong to laugh at the plasticated/leaded lights and the carriage-lamps. In this the Tory governments hit the right button.

They went wrong in not recognising the essential corollary to their own insight: that it was still necessary to provide cheap rented housing for those who simply could not afford to buy; and who will always be with us. For that, they should have released the money from the house-sales. For a time they gave some help to Housing Associations, but that has now been reduced. Not to do more was a typical failure of both the political and the humane imagination.

One might go on to recall that these governments also promised lower taxes, an enticing promise to the middle class. By the mid-Nineties that class was complaining bitterly that the promise had not been kept, particularly because of the rise in indirect rather than direct taxes. This was to be expected. The fact is that, as compared with 1979 and immediately earlier years, direct taxation has been greatly reduced, to some extent for the lower-middle class but particularly for the middle class and above.

The case in the mid-Nineties for increasing direct taxation at the higher level is overwhelming, if adequate public services are to be provided. Few governments will admit that; it is a vote-loser. So these governments continue to grumble about and seek to reduce the cost of public services, even the most unexceptionable; and they blame the 'scroungers'. Most taxpayers have no memory for benefits, only for losses. Once a certain level or shelf in taxation has been reached by the more comfortable classes, no matter how prejudicially, that is taken as the norm and any reduction as an unacceptable imposition.

Another promise was to 'set the people free', to reduce the presence of central government, do away with all those Socialist/Stalinist controls, abolish 'the nanny state' (yet another favoured dismissive phrase, a particularly vulgar one, in phrasing and in thought). It will become clear throughout the following chapters that that has proved to be the most hollow promise of all; the freedom produced, especially by relaxing necessary protective legislation, has been chiefly for the money-makers. It has also produced a huge number of new authorities, technically not part of the government but appointed by the government and given executive powers: the unaccountable, not publicly nominated, politically loaded Quangos (quasi-autonomous non-governmental organisations), with their paid members. Other freedoms – see the Criminal Justice Act of 1994 – have been progressively reduced; all of course in the name of freedom itself.

After the promises, the myths. Consideration of them, direct and indirect, will also run through the coming chapters. Here they will be briefly noted.

The first myth is that we are all becoming middle-class nowadays and that that will be a splendid thing. Wrong on both counts; we aren't, and it wouldn't be. The middle class, the heartland of Tory voters, has many virtues; and many vices. So have other classes. Thank God for diversity.

Myth number two is related to the first, but less vacuous and more cunning in intent. It is that the country can be transformed into a 'share-holding democracy'. So when privatised industries and services go on the market a loudly lauded provision (though carefully not made at the expense of corporate buyers) is made for 'the ordinary citizen'. The cunning lies in the assumption that people with stocks and shares will not want a recurrence of socialist nationalisations and so will tend to lean towards Conservatism. This is obviously related to assumptions about the effect of council-house buying, but less an appeal to respectable and deep-seated English attitudes (as to the importance of a home of your own), more an appeal to the urge to make a fast buck. It is too soon to say whether this is entirely a myth, but the powerful and growing resistance to the government in the mid-Nineties, more than a decade after the 'share-holding democracy' was initiated, suggests that the assumption may prove more a myth than a shrewd political move.

The third myth is the most mythical and the most destructive. It is that 'the market solves, decides and justifies all'. It does not; it destroys some things and distorts some others. One need not waste time agreeing, though with qualifications, that such a rubric might be true of soap powders, motor-cars, electrical 'white goods'. In other and very much more important matters it makes new separations, based on privilege and buying power, differences which increase social divisions.

We are moving rapidly from a genuinely *national* Health Service to a three-tier service: the original form of National Health, the fund-holding GP practices, and the private sector. It is blindness or humbug to defend these on the ground that they all increase the available medical provision. If there were a fully unified service that provision would not be reduced; it would be as before but shared according to proper criteria, by need. The two aberrant forms, the privately funded area most evidently, are devices for queue-jumping. It is all too typical of these governments that payments for private medical care are tax-deductible. It is also typical of the effects of these relentlessly 'justified' but quite unjustifiable changes that the Chairman of a Hospital Trust could, by the mid-Nineties, assert that the first duty of the medical staff is to 'their employer' rather than to their patients. Beveridge, Bevan and Titmuss must be revolving violently in their well-deserved Heaven. Even seasoned Tory-watchers were startled by this new evidence of the limitations of the Market Driven Mentality.

There are many other instances, especially those having to do with the condition of the general culture, less tangible than physical well-being but not less important. Has the market improved the condition of the popular press? Of the freedom of publishers and booksellers to give reasonable attention to promise in writers rather than to quick sales of known favourites? Has the market solved the problems associated with making the arts accessible to wider audiences? Isn't the market distorting educational provision? These are rhetorical but real questions, and their answers obvious.

There are two particularly indicative instances of market-led inadequacy, the Public Libraries and Broadcasting. Since this range of governments took over, the Public Library system has been under unfriendly pressure. That pressure cannot be – or cannot wholly be – attributed to failings by Local Government. Local councils have certainly been squeezed; in making cuts they often go for what they sense is the soft underbelly; especially when they also see that that area is not much in favour with central government. Broadcasting, as it is now being transformed by the 1990 Act, is the worst cultural example of the malign effect of the myth that 'the market solves all'.

So one could go on. Of more general social decisions, that to privatise the prison services is as uncivilised as, in a different way, the changes forced on the broadcasting system. If an elected government in a democracy believes, as it should, that there are some things it must itself be responsible for, then the proper running of all aspects of the control of crime in the community ranks very high in the list. But so things continue – prisons as profit-making bodies, the national forests sold to the highest bidder, health a more and more marketable commodity, broadcasting led by the advertisers.

It is quite difficult to see why, apart from their residual puritanical-sexual kink, these governments can have any objection to licensed profit-led brothels. Or why they do not tell the postal services to charge for delivery according to distance. In the light of market-rules, why should people in the Orkneys pay only 25p for a letter? It costs a lot more than that to provide for them. Why should such remote people have as good technical provision for receiving broadcasts as Londoners? It is very costly indeed to set up such a service (as the cable operators have already amply demonstrated). Those and other such changes may well come once someone success-fully argues that the market should not provide any inherently loss-making services.

The validity of the word 'service' itself is now being destroyed. A society committed in some important and humane matters to the idea of public service – 'The Service Giving Society' – is rapidly yielding to 'The Opportunist Society', 'The Entrepreneurs' Society', 'The Get Rich Quick Society', 'The Stuff You, Jack Society' – the society whose governers 'know the price of everything and the value of nothing'.

PART TWO

Aspects of the Dominant Mood

For all knowledge and wonder (which is the seed of knowledge) is an impression of pleasure in itself.
Francis Bacon, *The Advancement of Learning*, 1605

Disinterested intellectual curiosity is the life-blood of real civilisation.
G. M. Trevelyan, *English Social History*, 1942

CHAPTER TWO

Distortions of Education

A free government cannot tolerate without extreme danger the want of education in the mass of the people.

Sir James Kay-Shuttleworth, *Thoughts and Suggestions on Certain Social Problems*. 'Popular Education in England',
1860

The whole use that the government . . . makes of the mighty engines of literacy in the education of the working classes amounts to little more, even when most successful, than the giving them the power to read newspapers.

Matthew Arnold, *Culture and Anarchy*, 1869

Upon the education of the people of this country the fate of this country depends.

Benjamin Disraeli, House of Commons, 1874

The ratio of literacy to illiteracy is constant but nowadays the illiterates can read and write.

Alberto Moravia, 1979

Such solemn assertions as these, spanning just short of four centuries, are likely to make many uneasy, as though in the presence of insistent preachers. A line of dates, chosen almost at random, can produce a similar effect: the founding of university extra-mural education in the mid-nineteenth century, followed in a few decades by the Workers' Educational Association; the 1870 Elementary Education Act; the assertion in the final decade of the nineteenth century that Britain, the first nation to be able to make the claim, was a substantially literate country; the 1944 Education Act, the Open University of 1969 . . . and today the *Sun*.

i THE CLIMATE

An apparent contradiction has been fuelling official attitudes towards education throughout the last two decades. On the one hand is the overwhelming insistence on the primary importance of vocationalism in education at all levels. That at first glance might seem a classless impulse, allowing talent to move through and up the ranks of society, if its aim, a successful economy, is to be achieved.

Going along with vocationalism is the acceptance, indeed the encouragement, of ingrained and now newly acquired privilege, through the public schools, the new 'independent' schools, the grant-maintained schools, the Assisted Places scheme, the City Technology Colleges – with tax benefits for some of these. All are as much agents of an old and a newer divisiveness as they are contributions to that current narrow sense of the vocational nature of education.

The apparent paradox is supported by the prevailing relativism. Vocationalism is or seems value-free to those who wish to avoid a definition of education which raises troubling questions about social justice, about the needs of a democracy and, an even worse threat, about education as a good in itself, whatever its practical benefits. Similarly, when ingrown and increasing privilege is being considered, relativism makes it easier to put such a question to one side, as probably born of envy, driven by a sour wish to make everyone alike, judging by fixed 'moralistic' categories.

*

Vocationalism is one way of avoiding difficult choices of value, of looking seriously at the injustice which runs through the educational system. It provides a functional area for anyone ill at ease with every other kind of educational purpose. Its jargon reinforces the sense of disinfection, from 'market-oriented' through 'cost-effective' to all the rest.

The almost single-minded stress on vocational education by the recent succession of Tory governments is therefore not simply a recognition that we must be better trained at all levels if we are to survive prosperously in an increasingly competitive world. Deeper down, it indicates mistrust of the free-ranging, speculative – not 'function-oriented' – mind and imagination.

A Cabinet Minister can enjoy a standing ovation at a party conference by mocking the to him obscure subjects for research in anthropology. 'We've taken the money from the people who write about ancient Egyptian scripts and the pre-nuptial habits of the Upper Volta valley.' That's as easy as tickling a dog's stomach. Such a man might just begin to listen if you talked about 'possible eventual applications for industry'. But that would be to concede his limited view. The right rebuttal is that such study is to be valued for its own sake, one sign of mankind's blessed obsession with seeking more and more truth. Also that, in a university, knowledge and teaching must be intertwined: teaching irrigated by the sense that the teacher is at a frontier, bringing back the news, questioning it with students.

'Don't teach my boy poetry. He's going to be a grocer' (or a grocer's daughter) is back with us after a century and a half. The suspicion of Workers' Education survives; or, more accurately, has resurfaced. That was a wonderful tradition: workers studying by choice in the evenings, only rarely for vocational purposes but for 'the glory of the Creator and the relief of man's estate', paying very little if anything to do so, warmly supported by the universities, the local educational authorities and the voluntary bodies, all often working together. A modern Education Minister is likely to view all that with suspicion. Surely it is a device to radicalise people, to create dissidents, put reds under many a bed.

Ingrained and new privilege, old and new string-pulling; all flourish. Ian McIntyre's biography of Lord Reith (*The Expense of Glory*, 1993) contains a good example of the style and language of this venerable British custom. It dates from just after the last war but has lost little of its relevance.

Reith's son was, in the emollient phrase, not academically gifted. Reith was very anxious that he should go to Oxford. He could not have gained a place on his own record. Reith then 'traded heavily' (what a sombre phrase) with J.C. Masterman, Provost of Worcester College. Reith noted: 'He will take C.S. to oblige me. He has turned down about a thousand fellows but said his conscience was quite clear because of what I had done for the country,' Reith had certainly done a great deal. Above all, he was the main founder of the idea of public service broadcasting. He founded it not from a wide, judicious and democratic base of thought and imagination. He was narrow-minded, excessively puritanical, a snob, in some important ways subservient to government, shamefully happy to 'trade' on his own public reputation. The oddity is that, like a few such people, Reith built better than he knew in creating his own public achievement, the BBC.

There is little doubt that such an approach would still be successful with many colleges today. One route nowadays, for a very wealthy parent whose offspring may have difficulty in gaining entrance, is to pay for a new college building. 'Don't deny my boy entry. I'm 'a multi-millionaire grocer.' Less obviously 'tied' donations include the fairly recent Murdoch and Kellogg moneys, both given to Oxford.

Once again and inevitably, one has to recognise the tough, as if organic, relationships of the English education system with social class. At this point many people, especially those who have benefited from these relationships, will react with irritation or even horror. Most of them will be sincere. To recognise the power of such an assertion is like being invited to climb out of your own skin.

This unacknowledged and unrecognised sense of class-distinction is not only distinctive but divisive. To claim that such a state of affairs is no bad thing is to confuse divisiveness with difference. Difference is variety and to be welcomed. Divisiveness points to those separations in society that are barriers over which different groups look at each other warily, looking down and up, feeling superior or subordinate. Divisiveness is therefore inhumane, uncharitable, illiberal. Of all the elements which go towards sustaining this much-divided society, education is the most powerful. Many other elements express that divisiveness; the system of education is, after the home, the main agent for inculcating it. Not altogether consciously, of course, whether in the home or the school; more like the ambient air.

The sequence: prep school–public school–Oxbridge–the major professions (and their Inns of Court, Clubs, Guilds, officers' messes, professional bodies) marks the most evident correlations and defining lines. No matter how much their spokesmen and apologists call on God to witness their democratic, their almost levelling spirit, the facts are against them. More honest more 'robust' – in the language of the time – is the Oxford don who, answering criticisms such as these, said that his college, much like the public schools he knew, was a kind of comprehensive educational institution and all the better for that. He took boys from, mainly, a few schools which he knew well and knew as giving a solid foundation to their pupils, educationally and socially, whatever each one's intellectual gifts. He could take over from that point and carry on giving a good intellectual and social education to those he admitted, who would not all be selected high-flyers. He understood their schools and they understood him. The process was simple and in his view fair. He saw no point in spending day after day each year trying to assess candidates from those multitudinous, local-authority-maintained comprehensive schools of which he knew nothing. He could use his time better. He was, he said, creating a Comprehensive College, in what he would like to think of as a Comprehensive University.

The relationship of 'vocationalism' with ingrained privilege is strong, long-standing and complex. Some grandees, especially from major public schools, will tend to brush aside vocationalism in education and educators. It was curious but characteristic to hear a Secretary of State for Education questioning members of a university's School of Education on the justification for Teacher Training. 'My teachers at Harrow had no such post-graduate diplomas and were splendid at their jobs.'

Yet vocationalism, in a socially much more powerful sense than is usually heard about, has traditionally been a feature of the preparation given, directly or indirectly (but mainly indirectly, as a matter of style as much as of skill), in the more important public schools and the older universities: training for the learned professions, for the Church, the senior Civil Service, the law, the commissioned members of the armed forces, medicine and so on (and now, broadcasting and parts of the press, and of the higher reaches of the new communications professions). It seems doubtful if the Secretary of State mentioned above had considered the relationships between the two types and meanings of 'vocationalism', the traditional and the new.

To sum up: vocationalism in its newer form provides a piece of firm dry land for many of today's politicians, barren though that land may be intellectually and imaginatively. But that is the source of its attraction. In societies which are both technologically advanced and politically reactionary the pressure to see all their drives (not 'purposes') as self-sufficient is even greater and more persuasive than in most other kinds of society. Vocationalism has more voices and more of a large common voice, a total conviction over a narrow span; and a kind of retreat.

As in so much else in the baggage of convictions the recent Tory governments trade in, the conviction that market forces will solve all problems dominates. It informs the belief that this is what a democracy is about, and (they do not shun the epithets) that a commercial, capitalist democracy is itself the most perfectly achieved or, in an admittedly imperfect world, most workable and promising form of society.

That myth, that mistaken but rigidly adhered to belief, is just that

– a myth, meaning here a profound error – because it confuses quantity with quality, collective satisfactions with individual values, the ordinary person (and we are all ordinary in some parts of our beings) with our extraordinary capacity sometimes to pull ourselves up by our own boot straps, occasionally to do better than we know, to reach towards the better even though that may be against our material advantage and instincts; not to count, not to assess, everything on a functional scale, but to try to understand hardly measurable and hardly tangible but more important things, in the round.

That is why one can fairly say that in some of the cardinal areas of our experience this succession of Tory governments has shown itself impercipient. The best Conservative traditions were more civilised. It is hard to imagine, of modern Conservatives, Edward Boyle being willing to serve in such a government as, say, Secretary of State for Education, or Minister with responsibility for Broadcasting matters, or for the Arts or even 'Heritage'. If he did accept he would, sooner rather than later, have to resign as an act of principle.

A society of thriving earthworms may indeed be thriving, in earthworms' terms; it will be inadequate in human terms. In Britain it will fail to see that one of its first responsibilities is to redress the historic injustices done over a very wide front to the great body of its people; starting with education.

ii SCHOOLS

Television, in those opening-of-shutters moments discussed at more length in Chapter 5, can give startling insights into social worlds-of-their-own. A small item: it can confirm that at bottom the continued existence of the prep schools and the public schools is rooted in the sense of class, the assumption of class-divisions, hierarchies.

The best evidence often comes from the least sophisticated people. The makers of one of the many television programmes putting the case for and against this important part of the system found a woman who spoke more truth than she knew. Her son was at a third-line public school in rural Sussex. The interviewer pointed out that the school, though not as expensive as the recognised major public schools, still cost a lot in relation to the family's income, was small and unlikely to attract first-rate teachers, or afford small group teaching in at least the sixth form, or exceptionally well-equipped labs and studios. Its results in public examinations were poor.

The mother did not hesitate. In an insecurely genteel voice, she brushed aside all such considerations as suitable only for tradesmen, and embarked on a well-rehearsed formula about the much more important qualifications such a school could provide: 'good bearing', the 'right sort' of friends, a 'respectable profession', 'proper principles'. There was an ill-focused yearning there which made you feel even sadder that such a reaching out to 'better things' could only express itself in so culturally hidebound and inadequate a set of principles. One wondered for what sort of professions her boy was being equipped. It was not difficult to think of a few, and the thought was chilling.

Such a woman was an ideal target for the dozens of advertisements for private schools in rural counties which appear in the local newspapers early each summer. They offer all these qualities and objects: 'parental involvement – caring – friendly – excellence in sport – realising full potential – successful preparation for entrance to senior schools – a lively, caring community – developing leadership – emphasis on manners, conduct, leadership – stimulating, friendly ethos – well-motivated staff – stretching – high standard of pastoral care – disciplined and caring – all-round character building to uphold values and standards – a very positive attitude to life – full and rounded education – leadership training – shooting-range and assault course – Christian tradition and environment – a broad academic and sporting curriculum – family atmosphere, firm and kindly discipline – semi-military discipline – self-discipline – upholding traditional values – purposeful – innovation with tradition – structured and disciplined – heart and soul and mind can grow.' Flaubert noted sardonically that nineteenth-century French boarding-schools promised 'wholesome and abundant' food; so do the English ones of today.

Revealing, imprisoned gestures, threnodies. Never so many hurrah and buzz words, a psalm of PR and uplifted Newboltian longings. Such, such were the joys.

It is all there, in microcosm: the religious feeling or that of religiosity, the clinging to established forms and 'traditions' such as the Church of England (and the Monarchy, though that hardly needs to be mentioned); the adherence to secondary rather than primary virtues. Few truly difficult calls such as to independence of spirit or a sharp, critical, fresh mind. Instead, good manners, loyalty, patriotism, fortitude, a healthy mind in a healthy body – qualities which could be applied to Fascism as easily as to British patriotism, rather than to the search for truth, the support of human rights or charity towards your neighbour whoever he or she may be. Prominent among all else in the prep schools, as their name indicates, is the half-promise: 'vocational' preparation – for the public schools.

There is a photograph of Hitler in the final, desperate stages of the war, walking down a line of lads in their early teens, the last fodder to be thrown into the disentegrating line. The boys' faces have a slightly transfigured, self-sacrificial look. Hitler is smiling and patting one of those faces stiff with the uplifting willingness to 'die for the fatherland'. 'Leadership ... character building ... military discipline ... traditional values ... purposeful'. Such adjectives from those local newspaper adverts come to mind. One could long for an ad which promised 'membership of the awkward squad ... eccentricity ... recalcitrance ... keeping well out of line ... making your own mind up ... taking nothing at second hand'.

Some public schools provide an excellent education. Given that they charge a great deal and so can provide generous pupil–teacher ratios, given their ability still to attract some excellent teachers, given the splendid facilities some have, it would be odd if schools such as these, whatever their social atmospheres, could not provide a first-rate education intellectually, and sometimes imaginatively.

Many, perhaps even most, public schools are well-intentioned towards their pupils in more than narrowly educational terms; that is in principle a worthy aim for schools and schoolmasters. Most of their staff believe in what they are doing, without a trace of cynicism. They believe they know the world their pupils will go into, and they are on the whole right in this. They respect that world, think its values proper for English gentlefolk. They do not think of reinforcing a 'hegemony'; such words would be alien to most and unattractive to almost all of them. They believe they are presenting a world as it is and, God willing, shall remain. Mr Chips was purblind but a decent old codger, and he soldiered on, a firm repository of those secondary and nationalistic values.

Naturally there are rebels, vocal or silent, a few permitted eccentrics among both staff and pupils. It would be difficult to convince most of the others that that picture, that world, is ludicrously inadequate to the world as it actually is, is at least a century out of date (no matter if their science labs would not disgrace first-year university courses). Almost insensibly they are still teaching their pupils to think of themselves as special by birth and opportunity, inheritors of influence and access, high on the British hog; they are giving above all a class-bound background to the education they so firmly value.

Here is a snapshot: of a dramatic performance of an Orwell short story by a visiting fringe theatre group at Eton. Older pupils, presumably members of the élite society Pop, enter noisily and ostentatiously at the last minute, climbing over the seats, gorgeously and expensively togged out – notably with that totemic sign, the fancy waistcoat – for Saturday night's recreations. All that in itself might seem no more than a curious social phenomenon, perhaps to be amusingly compared with the rituals of Saturday night lager-drinkers in pubs off the M25.

What did matter, what was at least as unpleasant as some group habits of the lager-drinkers, was the air all these youths had of having inherited their earth. Their coded casualness, their expensive dictated hair-styles, their manner of walking, their ways of holding their mouths and lips, their swooping convoluted vowels, all were part of their unspoken but firm assumptions. It was peer-group stuff, of course; but it would survive and be recognised over time across large public rooms, board-room tables and at suitable dinner-parties. Do at least some of their teachers assess all this and ask themselves: do I do right to sit at ease with, to help along, these boys' passages through the school so that they emerge with so secure a set of character-and-class signs, signs which suggest and support so mistaken, so unattractive, so snobbish a range of assumptions? An old-style elementary school run with devotion, a 1902 Act city grammar school similarly dedicated, had more attractive aims.

The public schools perpetuate an ill-based and uncivil divisiveness. Would it be regarded as 'undemocratic' to call for them all to be closed? Certainly that would be the charge, and there would be something in it. What about redefining their functions? There are many children who need, because of different sorts of family circumstances, to attend a boarding-school. It has become a habit for children from poor public schools to be brought home at sixteen and sent to the nearest sixth-form college. Some public schools, though not the poor ones, might well become sixth-form colleges, or might simply like grammar schools open their doors to local children on merit. The old Direct Grant system had a lot to be said for it.

In early 1995, it was announced that some public schools were disposed to make a small number of places available to state pupils who excelled at games and met other academic criteria. It was hoped that this would foster the spirit of fair play and sportsmanship. Will they never escape from their own traps?

Most proposals for reforms are premature. There is no widespread feeling that something must be done here, any more than there is for managing without the Monarchy, though that proposition is gaining ground. In such circumstances in a free society we must be left so far as ever possible to make our own mistakes on our own and our children's behalf; even though those errors may cumulatively have bad effects on society as a whole. What we should not so easily accept, any more than we should accept that private health schemes should enjoy those tax advantages, are financial concessions to private schools. They should not be registered as charities; charities should be devoted to helping others, not ourselves, and least of all the better-off among us. More (though there is no likelihood of persuading the Charity Commissioners to accept this argument): since registered charities cannot engage in political activities, these schools should not be admitted to the list. More deeply than explicitly political parties or pressure-groups, they are politically purposive.

The Labour Party proposes to remove the tax concessions enjoyed by private schools. That may well lose them votes. Some parents, for worthy or unworthy reasons, will continue to pay and will deeply resent that. Others will switch to state schools, and will make more demands on them, especially as to staff–student ratios and facilities. No bad thing.

The Assisted Places scheme could just be defended on the grounds that it offers a grammar school education to some who might otherwise not have it but seem qualified. The objections are heavier. It weakens the sixth-form academic strength of some of the most successful comprehensive schools. It does not objectively select the most eligible pupils; it is skewed away from bright working-class children towards those with alert parents of the lower-middle class and middle class who can make a persuasive case for financial help. Many of those parents are also and increasingly using all sorts of methods, some of them corrupt, to get their children at eleven into the best maintained schools within reasonable distance. The Assisted Places scheme is another example of the Tory governments' manoeuvres to woo voters by giving them a vested interest in maintaining them in power. In 1994 the scheme cost almost £100 million. There are better uses for that money.

*

There is yet another new form of contrived privilege, buttressed by that common and undisputed call to vocationalism, in this instance to vocationalism in its most aggressively separatist pre-university form: the City Technology Colleges. They were necessarily very expensive to set up; but they would, it was said, also call on that other shibboleth of the times: generous commercial sponsorship. Foundation money was poured into them by the government as a way of encouraging that outside sponsorship. What actually happened is rather different and has not been readily revealed by the government or by most of the press.

The story is concisely told by Francis Beckett in *The Spread of Sponsorship* (1993), edited by Roy Shaw. BP's educational adviser, for instance, said:

> Companies with a strong tradition of local community support and partnership have tended not to support CTC's. The problem is that companies want to make friends in the communities where they operate. They do not support high profile initiatives which are seen by many people in those communities as divisive. . . .
>
> There was a feeling that CTC's were going to focus a lot of resources on a few children. We want UK plc [here, he adopts the jargon of the government itself] to invest in the future of all its children. . . .
>
> We are also unhappy about the confusion of an educational agenda with a political agenda. The country needs to find means of educating more people to a higher level. . . .

Splendidly put; and not by a wild Leftie.

Smaller companies more directly committed to the Conservative cause were less discriminating. The security systems company ADT offered £1 million to Wandsworth Council towards the establishing of a CTC. The chairman of ADT wrote to the leader of Wandsworth Council: 'From a political point of view the higher the profile that can be given to the creation of the CTC concept in Wandsworth the better, and no doubt this will be of much help to your local Conservative candidates for the May 1990 elections.' Among other CTC sponsors approved by the Conservative government was British American Tobacco.

Avon County Council's deputy director of Education put his finger on the central case against the CTCs. They are taking money which is desperately needed elsewhere. For example, £10 million was raised (80 per cent of it eventually put in by the government) for a stumbling CTC in Bristol, to house 900 children. Avon had £4.5 million for capital expenditure on schools for the county's 150,000 other pupils put together. The whole enterprise was ill-conceived in educational, social and financial terms; characteristically. To save face, a much-modified plan was eventually put forward.

*

Industrial and commercial sponsorships spread further, wider, deeper; into the schools. Again, Francis Beckett has documented the process. This was another tie with vocationalism and the 'enterprise culture', another instance of a merely apparent 'disinterestedness'. Some head teachers and classroom teachers dislike and distrust the flood of sponsored material. Many accept it reluctantly because their own resources have been cut. Others, particularly schools which have opted out, see no problem in accepting any kind of sponsorship, no matter what self-serving demands the sponsors make. A high school in Essex insisted that school uniforms be bought from only one local supplier; that that supplier was making a substantial donation to school funds was not mentioned. Such people are particularly fond of words such as 'logo', 'image' and 'corporate identity'. Heads who go that far should be questioned as to their sense of vocation or, only slightly less intimidatingly uplifting, professionalism. Or common sense. Still, if an appeal were then made by a rebuked head teacher to the Department of Education and Science, the Department's response would in these days be predictable.

There are many such cases. One firm offered £150 to schools which would install their drinks-vending machines. The most striking offer was Tesco's (it is too complicated to go into at length here; the fuller story is in Francis Beckett). Briefly: Tesco's offered one voucher for every £25 spent in their shops (with some interesting exclusions). To win a top-of-the-range computer a school had to collect vouchers to the value of £100,000. Tesco's standard profit margin is 7.1 per cent = £7,100 on £100,000.

*

Comprehensive schools have been consistently and unfairly condemned by much of the press. Successive Conservative governments have shared that feeling. In fact, the record of the comprehensives is mixed; but, given the odds against which many of them have to work, the achievements for outweigh the failures. The best are very good indeed, as good as many among that other form of national comprehensive, the public schools.

The comprehensives' biggest single difficulty is that, as compared with public schools, they are usually area-based; and areas differ widely. Some areas simply do not provide enough pupils of a varied range of backgrounds to prevent the school from settling into an unacademic or even anti-academic culture of its own. Most readers will know of left-wing friends who, against all their instincts ('I didn't feel I had the right to put my child, who has intellectual interests, at a disadvantage for the sake of my own political beliefs'), have removed their children from a comprehensive school. One can sympathise.

The best comprehensive schools are likely to have a large and *mixed* catchment area and to be themselves very large. With intelligent and devoted direction and proper resources they can provide for many kinds of talent; they can reduce the likelihood of a dominant anti-intellectual school culture emerging; they can produce a solid post-sixteen academic group. They work well.

The most disadvantaged schools are likely to be in working-class areas and to have few pupils who develop intellectual or academic interests. The dominant culture is a thousand educational miles away from that of the selective local grammar schools which many of them replaced. Their teachers have a tough time no matter how devoted they may be. Some sensibly send their brighter pupils at sixteen to the nearest sixth-form college; others manage somehow. It is easy and probably self-deceptive to say, as regards the most difficult of such instances, that the democratic mixing provided by the school makes up for its academic limitations. The sixth-form colleges are one partial solution here. Those, with the academic sixth forms some more fortunate comprehensives can support, the establishment of more state grammar schools with wide catchment areas, and the greater opening of some public schools to day pupils without charge, should provide enough diversity until better ideas arrive.

Major problems still face those who welcomed and still approve of the comprehensive idea. But the successes in some schools could be learned from elsewhere, even in the most difficult areas; so long as the teachers are given the right sustained support. The principle demands no less, the humane principle of an education which is not socially divisive and yet still honours the development of intellectual and imaginative ability.

*

The outstanding failure of English education, for all its successive takings of thought in the last two centuries especially, has been its inability to cope with the inadequate education – in far more than vocational terms, though it has not been much of a success there either, except at the very top of the academic tree – of the great body of its people. There have been many substantial and usually well-meant initiatives through all the decades, but no one of them has solved this overarching problem. It has been more tortuous and more complex than even the best-endowed and least culturally captive proconsuls could bring themselves to believe.

(One wonders, incidentally, why Scottish and Welsh working-class parents have traditionally had a greater respect for education than the English. Has that to do with a stronger influence from church or chapel, especially in rural areas? Is education regarded as the best way out and in, out from the smaller culture to the larger, where there are more opportunities? Or the best way for those who stay in Scotland or Wales to confront the larger English culture?)

In an aggressively confident commercial society such as today's even the most intelligent, free and determined politician or official who says that education is failing the majority is rowing against the tide. It suits this kind of society to have the majority of people kept at a low level of literacy, so low that they will not argue.

So people are invited to believe that their condition of sub-literacy is as much as any reasonable chap could expect; indeed, it should be happily accepted. This is a self-sustaining world which the normal language of educational advance can scarcely break into. As to the majority of people, the decades since the 1870 Elementary Education Act have been, overall, an educational failure. We are still an under-, an ill-educated people. Health has improved, housing has improved, diet has improved (though all these with qualifications); fewer people are technically quite illiterate. But in the wider educational sense too many are still only literate enough to be handed over to the per-suaders, not yet literate enough to be able and willing to blow the gaff on them.

G. M. Trevelyan's has been for some time an unfashionable name to quote in social-historical circles. David Cannadine's biography should do much to redress that injustice. Those who, as students just after the last war, found Trevelyan's *English Social History* (1942) good food for the mind will be glad of this turn-around. When some of them became university extra-mural tutors they used to remind themselves, together with quotations from Tawney, Temple,

Mansbridge and Toynbee, of Trevelyan's sombre and economical utterances on the legacy as he then saw it of universal education: 'It has produced a vast population able to read but unable to distinguish what is worth reading.' That was a proper touchstone. But for many people today such a statement would be wholly unacceptable, élitist, bourgeois.

It should hardly need saying, but perhaps does since tempers are frayed in current talk about education, that many – perhaps most – teachers work devotedly for small pay and without counting the hours. Many, again perhaps most, have entered the profession out of idealism; some lose that idealism after years. But, as happens with people who have been once in love, the afterglow remains with many of them, no matter how desert-like the present situation. There are few professions where the promise of continual challenge outweighs low salary levels. There are very few professions, other than the Christian ministry and teaching, where ideals come before levels of salary, under-provision, and even before the expectation of new challenges after the first few years. Such ideals can make people in those professions work unregardedly and without major injections of excitement week after week, month after month, year after year.

All that is an affidavit of goodwill in advance of criticisms of some fashions in educational work. Too many teachers, too many teachers of teachers, have been seduced by fashionable ideas and their jargon. Two main impulses are pushing in this direction. One is a fixed philosophy of some on the far Left which, with a squeezing and chopping of the evidence, can be made to offer answers to most educational problems. More important and more pervasive is, yet again, relativism, and that can make it very hard for other teachers to find a bearing.

Here is a typical example, chosen from many found in a shelf-ful of books written by educational experts for the benefit of classroom teachers. One such book, on education and social class, reports that a headmaster suggested his pupils might donate part of their weekly pocket-money to good causes, especially in the Third World, and might also take up voluntary work on behalf of needy members of their own community. The author of the book continues: 'It is possible to read this passage [by the headmaster] as giving some substance to the view that schools attempt to foist dubious middle-class values on the poor.' Let us adopt the cautious phrasing and say: 'It is possible to read this passage as an expression of the headmaster's belief that, whatever your social class and whatever your opportuni-

ties in life, it is good to help the poor, the sick and the old.' Why did
the educational expert write in that way? Was he really so unclear
and uncertain about these fairly simple aspects of ethics?

It is more likely that he was trying to forestall a typical, contemporary, 'anti-bourgeois' reaction from some of his readers. From, for
example, those well-meaning teachers who will not allow the word
'weak' (as in 'this pupil's French is weak') to appear in any report
and require instead an evasive phrase. Or the teachers who refuse to
praise good work but will praise sporting ability; and so discourage
clever children and strengthen anti-intellectual peer-group cruelties
in the class. Or the educational expert who suggested that all children
should at all ages be given a similar education even if that would
mean that no intellectual challenges were given to clever children.
This opposition, fairly popular in some quarters, is false; doing the
best for all children whilst recognising their differing needs is a
compatible and better position.

Even more nervous was a distinguished writer on modern educational theory as he grappled with the matter of value-judgments in
the sea of assumed relativism: 'It is at least possible that some kinds
of knowledge are superior in some meaningful way to other kinds of
knowledge.' Well, yes, even though you put it like that.

At a meeting on 'Education Today' you will hear this thin stuff,
from a teacher of literature: 'The National Curriculum has been
forced on teachers by a reactionary Tory government which wants
us all to think alike. It is a form of state censorship since it tells
teachers what to do and takes away our freedom of action. It substitutes the traditional bourgeois canon for texts much nearer the
children's life experience, about which any good teacher knows far
more than the so-called ['so-called' always signals low-level argu-
ment] experts.' Incidentally, the National Curriculum was first floated
by a Labour Prime Minister, James Callaghan; there is much to be
said in its favour.

The committee which proposed a national curriculum in literature
thought all children should be introduced to some of the masterpieces
of English literature. They believed there were such writings, that
their value could not be culturally or historically explained away,
that they are among the greatest achievements of this nation and that,
properly presented, they can interest and excite children. The search
for the best that has been thought and said is worthwhile, though
we may all become muddled as we try to define it. That is inevitable,
but does not make the effort useless. There is nothing élitist or canon-

trapped in all that, nothing to be dismissed by a bundle of jargon. Such confused thinking is as if to say: 'There's no such thing as junk food. If you like it, it's OK. What those people call the best diet is a bourgeois heresy.' At the end of that line lies prescriptive writing, the end of writing as a difficult personal exploration, at which some people – though it has become a heresy to say so – are more gifted than others.

iii FURTHER EDUCATION: THE CINDERELLA

In the large and diverse range of Further Education institutions – Colleges of Further Education, Technical Colleges, Colleges of Art and Design, Sixth-Form Colleges, etc., etc. – there is, as there has been for many years, a similarly large and diverse range of hard-working teachers. Social changes since the war have greatly broadened the subjects offered and the kinds of students reached: there are programmes in literacy, programmes for ethnic minorities, for the special problems women face in a still male-dominated society, for the unemployed and for people with any of a great number of disadvantages, natural or adventitious. In scope the prospectus of a large Further Education College rivals that of some universities. The levels differ, of course, but response to known and, more important, suspected and potential needs is greater here than in any other part of the educational system.

Yet Further Education Colleges remain the most unsung, unprotected and unfashionable educational area. Few large donations for splendid new buildings or new initiatives come from admiring industrialists. Concentrated attention these colleges have certainly had in the last twenty years, from some angles more than the schools and universities. They have been a prime target for the promotion of the extremes of 'vocationalism'.

Some of them, feeling undefended, have accepted this twisted attention, if ruefully. Others have seen great opportunities for what they would probably call 'status enhancement'; more funds, splendid new professional titles. Meanwhile, most of the lecturers have gone on doing their jobs, often against increasingly unacademic pressures. Some Principals and Deputy Principals have given themselves more and more fancy titles – becoming 'Executive Directors' and the like – bigger and bigger suites of offices and company cars. Public Relations and Corporate Affairs Directors have joined the Finance Directors and Chief Secretaries; they all talk of 'Management Skills' and 'Action Plans'; some produce a 'Mission Statement' or 'Mission Report' in place of an Annual Report; the lecturers still have, or share, a desk in a crowded staff-room.

The government's Green Paper of 1987 set precisely the tone and purpose, with its repetitive chatter of 'market-oriented courses' and 'demand-led provisions'; and its demotion of 'recreational interests'. None of that old-fashioned nonsense about the wondering student asking speculative questions. Many of the students do seek straightforward remedial education and have the right to ask for it. But before the new constraints, the best Further Education Colleges (such as Kingsway College in London under Fred Flower's direction) saw it as their duty to offer more, to offer some uncovenanted, impartial, openings. Today a lecturer in English is likely to feel shunted sideways and to say: 'I would dearly like to introduce them to Orwell and Graham Greene but the whole atmosphere is against it. So I stick to the syllabus, knowing that public results (numbers of GCSE successes and the like) will be the only things that count, when they appear on the computer in the Admin Block.' Where is the education we have lost in assessment?

Still, some will break out. One lecturer, taking an ethnically mixed class of late-teenagers trying to acquire GCSEs, felt unhappy about the enclosed peer-group world they lived in, their small grasp of the public world, of that world's limitations and also of the openings it offered to those who knew how to take advantage of them.

Many of the students carried around huge ghetto-blasters and those became the lecturer's way in. He photocopied from *Which* the pages of comparative assessment of those monsters and asked the students to read. This was difficult since most were unused to charts, graphs, tables of comparative statistics, technical or even multi-syllable words in print. More important, they were not used, in looking at any of the fashionable purchases they made, to the very idea of comparative judgments of quality across a number of technical characteristics. They had chosen their stereos on the basis of a mixture of talk among friends, the hectic ads and the screaming high-street shop windows.

Suddenly one of them stood up and called out: 'Bloody hell, I've been conned.' A moment of revelation, a putting-up of new muscle in the intelligence. How would many modern Executive Directors allow for that kind of teaching in the application of 'Performance Indicators' to their lecturers? Not less than 10, surely, on a scale of 1 to 10? But the achievement would hardly be likely to be taken into account at all. Much easier to get the computer to count the GCSE results without allowing for inspired teaching, or recognising the point from which most students had started and so being able to measure their individual successes on the journey. More important still: how could they take into account the fact that good teachers have their best influence by intuition, brilliant insights, patience with each individual – so that their impact become immeasurable. Would Cabinet Ministers like to be subject to that kind of 'Performance Measurement'; or would they dream up important 'imponderables'?

The apogee of this excessive emphasis on the vocational measurement of everything educational has been reached in the government's support, through the Department of Employment, of some of the National Vocational Qualifications (NVQs). These qualifications are established by Training Councils; of which one, the Arts and Entertainment Training Council, is only untypical of the rest in that its area of application – which includes Creative Writing – is even more irrelevant than most other TCs for NVQs. These councils do not set examinations; they draw up 'frameworks of nationally recognised qualifications' across a wide field of activities (the Arts and their like are bedded uneasily with Entertainment). These frameworks are then expected to be used, in particular and no doubt with a 'steer' from the government, by the Further Education Colleges.

The language of these bodies' promotional material is so characteristic of that quasi-professional technologese which runs riot today that it merits fuller attention in Chapter 6. But here is a genuine sample to be going on with:

> Performance Criteria [for the artist]: Techniques are effectively exploited, manipulated and combined as investigative tools in order to analyse experiences. The effects of combining and juxtaposing a particular range of techniques are investigated and clearly noted.

That should help a budding writer a great deal. As might:

> CREATIVE WRITING (stages): Summary of occupational areas; establish and maintain artistic understanding; establish a personal style; establish and maintain financial viability; promote self as artist and entertainer; establish and maintain concept; develop characterisation; contribute to the creation of convincing sequences in the context of the artistic medium.

Poor aspirants, who are expected to take that nonsense seriously; poor lecturers, some of whose Executive Directors, blinded by pseudo-technical jargon and anxious for the funds which might be released if they welcomed all this, may expect their staffs to take it seriously and work with it; poor writers of such dry mealie-mealie, who probably do take it all seriously.

Yes, the compilers do take it all extremely seriously. At a one-day 'presentation', in 1993, to some writers and others in the literary world who might be expected to be interested and helpful, the presenters went so far as to suggest that the National Vocational Qualifications for writers might become so prestigious that publishers would agree only to accept a manuscript for consideration if the author had an NVQ in Creative Writing. It was also suggested that the Society of Authors might be willing to require that any applicant for membership should already hold the NVQ. At this point the few 'creative' writers among those present made their excuses and left.

iv HIGHER EDUCATION: THE UNIVERSITIES

There is some tendency latterly to substitute the captain of industry in place of the priest, as the head of seminars of the higher learning ... administrative ability and skill in advertising the enterprise count for rather more than they once did.

Thorstein Veblen, *The Theory of the Leisure Class*, 1899

That time of remarkable expansion in higher education, beginning in the the early 1960s, had some odd and not altogether expected results. What complicated psycho-social movements led to building styles which echoed each other right across the world, or to similar decisions about the number of acres a university needed, or that they should be placed outside the cities? The answers to some of those questions can be guessed; others are cloudier. But so it was. Virtually all developed nations decided to expand and in similar ways; it was a global movement which seemed almost instinctive: interconnections, influences, filterings-down and across.

In Britain the Robbins Report on Higher Education at the start of the Sixties was one of those lucky reports which chimed with the mood or emerging mood of the time (as the Albemarle Report on the Youth Services had done a couple of years before). The Pilkington Report on Broadcasting of 1962 marched to a different drum – it was rejected by the Conservative government because it had a higher view of the nature and possibilities of broadcasting than the commercialist Cabinet and their supporters.

The Robbins Report proved to have a Baconian-cum-Newmanian idea of the University, drawing on a strong sense that university entrance numbers in Britain were too small and socially too narrow. The report gave an intelligent and humane justification for the expansion which was already in the air: generous funding of university entrants; the provision of accommodation (though not for all), the continuance of small group teaching; the belief that tutors should be *in loco parentis* (that has officially gone with the changed age of majority, but in most universities students are still assigned to an 'adviser' and that role is usually taken seriously); the low failure rate as compared with those of most developed countries (though, as Eric James pointed out, entry figures at that time were still so low and entry demands so high that a high drop-out rate would have been chiefly a sign of failure on the part of the institution); and the idea that, though it is costly in the time of those who do not shirk it, academics should run their own institutions, not hand them over to professional administrators. The two main roles of a university were reasserted: teaching in the atmosphere of research and vice versa. The third role to which some hold – that of turning a disciplined eye on society itself – has never been accepted by most university people, let alone by politicians.

Expansion in itself raised the most clamant objections: that more would mean worse. There were easy rejoinders to that argument, especially as to entrance to Oxford and Cambridge in the years up to the last war: the Oxbridge system up to then did not make strenuous efforts to select, nationally, only the most earnest and talented. Children from the right schools, with the right contacts, could be fairly confident of a place; meanwhile Jude continued to wait outside. True, some of those admitted wasted their time in all generations; and some of those went on to spectacular achievements: Auden got a third-class degree. But you can't build a defence of talentless wastrels on a handful of Audens.

The more sober rejoinder is that Britain has wasted talent over many generations. If you can happily believe that for all those centuries a process had been successfully and hence justifiably in train by which there sank to the bottom, to form the permanent uneducated base in society, all those from apparently untalented families who were *ipso facto* untalented themselves, and that this winnowing ensured that all, except the odd scamps, socially above that level were talented or at least capable of making proper use of university

41

education, then you will sleep easy, secure in the enclosed hammock of your preconceptions.

There is waste in universities today, of course; that comes with early adult life and peer-group pressures. But before the war only the very gifted working-class children got to university and then usually to their local places. Expansion has confirmed that there was far more talent in the country than we had guessed or were willing, out of class-and-culture meanness, to recognise.

A middle-class intellectual, a writer, a graduate of Oxford, a Londoner, accepted an invitation in the mid-Sixties to join for a few weeks the staff of an expanding provincial university. Back in London he wrote to 'cry *peccavi*'. The experience, he said, had convinced him 'of the absolute necessity of providing education for boys and girls coming along to university level – one feels a human categorical imperative'.

How did the universities themselves deal with this opportunity to grow considerably and quickly? With good heart almost all of them but, socially and intellectually, as if sleepwalking; they missed important chances. Too many of the new institutions became 'Baedeker universities' in cathedral, or graciously countrified, cities, such as York, Canterbury and Norwich. So strong was the elegant-nostalgia pull that the new foundation within the boundaries of the city of Coventry was called Warwick University. Still, that allowed Coventry Polytechnic, years later, to become Coventry University.

With the Baedeker spirit went also the broad-acres-out-of-town spirit: two hundred acres and a few cows, about three or four miles out. If a university should have three constituencies (though, as with their possible roles, not all would accept the third) – the international, the national and the local – only the first two were given much attention. Some places did better than others, some did a fair amount to suggest to the natives that this was 'their' university. By contrast, Finnish universities make their libraries open to local, non-student, residents. No English new universities established themselves in the middle of the city and gave main attention to local students studying part-time. London University's Birkbeck College has had no successor. One justification for going outside was that city land was too costly, but that was not the whole reason (and the Polytechnics managed). The sense of local responsibility was weak as compared with, say, that in America or Canada.

So there was one main chance missed. The second was the failure, except in one or two places such as Sussex and Kent, to 'redraw the map of learning'. In general, expansion was linear. You used to have 150 students studying English and fifteen academic staff. In a few years you had 450 students and forty-five staff. In so far as there was academic change it did not, in the more entrenched departments, extend to reconsidering the syllabus. It did affect the attitude of staff towards their subjects. Professional areas narrowed. With fifteen staff most would cover, say, half a century. Now staff, especially newly recruited young staff, would be likely to say that their field was 1720–40 and be a little reluctant to give introductory lectures to the first year. The specialist bacon was sliced finer and finer. Latterly, the great expansion in student numbers without a comparable increase in staffing has worked against that reluctance.

At about this time a Labour government created the Polytechnics, under local authority control and financing, and monitored academically by the Council for National Academic Awards (CNAA) to be different from but in no way second-best to the universities. Some chance. The Polys widened the range of subjects, were especially strong in the technologies, were more hospitable to new teaching initiatives, methods of assessment, course patterns and new kinds of students than most universities were. The CNAA was a severe monitor of standards; some fashionable but dicey new subjects slipped though the net, though.

The general provision for the Polys – for example the supply of accommodation – was below that of the universities. In university 'hostels', it was argued, 'Nothing but the best would do'. Expensive curtains had a social purpose: they introduced residents to good taste and to the truth that good taste, though expensive, was also economical; it lasted longer. The Local Education Authorities were more used to lower, College of Education, standards in provision.

Much more important was the blunt and unappealing fact that from the start the Polys in general were regarded as the second division. Some of the former Colleges of Advanced Technology escaped this labelling; they were few and harder to discount; they quickly became new universities in the Sixties transformations.

Some people will resist this description of the reception of the Polys. More will resent the suggestion that on the whole Poly academic staff were not as well qualified as those of universities. But it is self-evident. People will seek to work at the highest centre when they see it, and a long-established university department with a good international record is obviously more attractive than a new institution. You may found a score or so of Polys over a very few years, but you would be mistaken to think that you could staff them all to the academic level of the well set-up universities. Some fine academics chose to go to the Polys because of the wider opportunities, the greater readiness to create new fields; some such staff were and are just as good as most university staff members but preferred the atmosphere of the new kinds of institution; some found their techno-logical-vocational field better served in the Polys than in some univer-sities. But all in all it would be mistaken to argue that the large staff these new institutions needed emerged over less than a decade as, in general and almost at once, a match for the staff and departments built up over many decades in the established universities; or those being built up, with an embarrassment of choice among highly quali-fied candidates, by the new universities.

These things are obvious, and to deny them takes the eye off the real unfairness of many people's attitudes to the Polys, which sprang from the basic and traditional British judgment by class. It was enshrined early, in the divisive but inaccurate phrase 'the public sector' for the non-UGC-funded institutions (though all were pub-licly funded at bottom). If some God, or mad scientist, had allowed the Polys to staff themselves with clones of the best university staff they would still have been regarded by many people as slightly inferior. There's a divinity doth hedge a university. No wonder some Polys tartly said they had no wish to be simulacra of the universities; or that others went into 'academic drift', trying to be as like the 'real' universities as possible. In such contortions the British are incorrigible. Years later many universities (usually after watching the Polys) began to take on board local Colleges of Education and Insti-tutes of Higher Education, and offer them their degrees. Anyone who has examined for both forms of degree will know how easily internal university staff slip into less demanding standards for the outside institutions than they would accept from their own final degree students.

*

Towards the end of the Sixties the expanded and the new universities, plus the Polys and the Colleges of Art, blew up here as elsewhere; though, compared with France and the United States, our explosions were in most places quite mild. Even those who had some sympathy with the revolting students can see now that little came out of all that *Sturm und Drang*. Edgar Faure may have still been able in 1969 to look out of his study window on to the traffic of the Bois de Boulogne and speak warmly of the success of his hasty, *événements*-inspired *loi d'orientation* for the universities, but it was plain by the middle of the next decade that his satisfaction was misplaced. By the beginning of the Eighties Pierre Salmon of the University of Dijon wrote an epitaph: 'The French universities acquired autonomy under unpropitious circumstances, and practically nothing has helped them to become fit for it . . . the reform of '68 is a pseudo reform.' The Italian universities, said Daalder and Shils (in *Universities, Politicians and Bureaucrats*, 1988) were damaged and German universities 'unofficially divided into two kinds, the steady and the politically raddled'. They concluded with even more depressive finality: 'Experiments with university "democracy" do not seem to have made European universities more adaptive than they were under exclusive Professorial rule.'

Towards the end of the Seventies even the Labour government was asking hard questions about the cost of this expanded higher education and about whether the best use was being made of the new funds. Just before the Conservatives took over, Shirley Williams, as Secretary of State for Education, put thirteen points, thirteen questions, to the universities. It is a sign of the changed climate between then and the present day that those questions now seem markedly sensible and polite; an even greater sign of the change in climate can be found in the rather grandly independent brush-off the universities gave her.

*

From the moment the first Conservative government took over, and increasingly thereafter, the climate became chillier for the universities. More power to the centre; that is, more direct intervention by the Department of Education and Science (DES); narrow vocational purposes together with suspicion of 'pure' science, recurrent demands for greater accountability, 'performance indicators', economic justifications plus several kinds of weakening of university autonomy, the loss of tenure for staff who were increasingly overworked as STEs (student–teacher equivalents) worsened, progressive decline in salary levels; so the roll went on. Worst of all, the atmosphere created by the government's general attitude to the universities was suspicious, like that of shopkeepers wary with toffs who might con them.

In the early Eighties the government had two years of consultations with the universities. Out of that came in 1985 a Green Paper about which the Chairman of the Committee of Vice-Chancellors and Principals (CVCP) said:

> a deeply disappointing document. Clearly the Government has learned little or nothing from the consultations . . . The real income of the universities is to fall during this decade by at least 20% and cuts in student numbers and further economies will follow so that we shall reach the year 2000 producing fewer [university] graduates than we do now [we shall see that the Government later produced a piece of legerdemain which confounded that conviction – by changing the Polytechnics into universities they at a stroke greatly increased the numbers of university students] . . . the Green Paper . . . will undermine the chance of achieving such admirable aims as raising research standards and ensuring an adequate supply of scientists and engineers. The Government must think again.

One short paragraph from the Green Paper reveals its quality:

> 6.15 Meanwhile, however, there are outstanding questions about the answerability of the universities when there are complaints from students, staff or the public. At present complaints, whether of academic inadequacy or neglect, financial extravagance, unfair treatment in examinations, or political bias in teaching, cannot effectively be pursued beyond the Vice-Chancellor, or in some cases the Visitor. But universities, though dependent on public funds, are privileged institutions with a very significant degree of self-government. It is important that they should take complaints seriously and be seen to do so. The Government is concerned about the present apparent lack of accountability and is discussing with the CVCP what might be done.

Just five sentences, the central three making what seem simple statements of fact, the first and last hinting rather than stating a concern ('outstanding questions . . . apparent lack').

Sentence one gives no indication of what the 'outstanding questions' are. Perhaps we shall be told more later? Sentence two says where, given the self-governing power of universities, complaints go. Those are facts and of a kind the universities have tended to be proud of and cherish, though they are here made to sound inherently inadequate.

The boot really goes in with sentence three. Apart from its first word, sentence three is in apposition to sentence two since it too acknowledges the universities' powers of self-regulation. So it might have been expected to begin: 'This is because . . . the universities have a significant degree . . .'. Instead, it begins: 'But . . .' and hence goes on to imply but not to state that there may be something *in itself* amiss, an undesirable 'privilege', in the very concept of self-government by institutions dependent on public funds.

Sentence four is a statement of a principle so blindingly obvious that merely to assert it in this way is to suggest that the principle is being neglected.

This tiny web of innuendo having been spun, sentence five feels bold enough to say that the government's 'concern' must be discussed with the CVCP. But it still can't bring itself to come out straight; the CVCP is to be talked to about an 'apparent' lack of accountability.

> Willing to wound, and yet afraid to strike,
> Just hint a fault and hesitate dislike;

The half-hidden message of the paragraph is a double one: that accounting is indeed not being exercised responsibly; and that the powers of universities in this respect are bad in themselves. This was the next move of the sustained Thatcherite attack on the 'arms-length' principle as applied to public bodies.

Even before the Green Paper most people in charge of institutions of higher education funded directly by the DES had come to know that the Secretary of State was likely to intervene personally if a complaint were made about their institutions. They had begun to feel that the onus was on them to prove not their innocence but that they were not guilty. In particular there emanated from the DES a suspicion that any charge of left-wing bias was likely to be well-founded. Word got round among students and staff: if in trouble write direct to the DES and allege a left-wing plot. If not left-wing, was the assumption from the Department, are you hiding something, being cavalier?

Para. 6.15 can now be rephrased, so that it actually says what it seems to imply:

1 We have evidence that the universities' accountability is not being responsibly exercised.
2 In discussing changes with the CVCP we have in mind reducing the universities' self-government by setting up external arbiters on complaints.

That's plainer, briefer and more honest.

Clearly, it was becoming more and more difficult for a Vice-

Chancellor to be an educational statesman thinking about best purposes, among the acknowledged company of the great and good. However high their intentions they had to think more and more about keeping on the right side of the DES and of wooing more and more money from the industrialists outside. The job become deeply unattractive to many who would have taken it on twenty years before. Inevitably, some new Vice-Chancellors were business men, Executive Directors, consummate fund-raisers ... and chosen for those talents. Oxbridge maintained or increased its tendency to look for fund-raisers as its college heads.

Then the government ensured that its predictions of growth in student numbers were not only met but greatly surpassed. They rose by 70 per cent in ten years, well surpassing all projections. Very soon the number of universities or university-type institutions had trebled. University sector colleges with power to award their own degrees appeared; and so on. There is a certain justice of principle in this, but it carried no concomitant increase in funds. The assumed inferiority of the Polys now became harder to sustain. Only a little; many people can smell a former Poly from a mile off, and downgrade it. The behaviour of the Public Relations departments of some former Polys reinforces that prejudice; they sound like promoters of the latest glossy saloon car.

Still, to recall what was said above; the established universities in general are academically stronger than most Polys. The universities would have been doing a bad job over many decades if they weren't. The challenge and opportunity for the former Polys, and for the original universities, lies just here: that some former Polys are equal to or better than some universities in some subjects; and some are doing first-rate work in subjects not known or hardly known in the original universities. If, therefore, the new nomenclature justifies itself and ceases to be subject to a merely conventional and class-defined pecking-order, then one should be able to look forward to the day when undergraduates and, even more, graduates, say; 'I am applying for a place at X [whether an original university or a former Poly will in such an instance have become irrelevant] because the department of this or that, or the Professor of that subject, is one of the very best in the country.' Then more choices between institutions will be made on academic rather than on social grounds.

So the élite system has largely gone; the numbers of those in higher education are huge as compared with twenty years ago; so are costs. It is time to introduce a better loan system than the present one.

Coda, in case there is any doubt as to what is being said about Oxbridge. Oxford and Cambridge are world-class academic institutions, can usually attract superb staff, and we should be proud of them. The case against them rests chiefly on the social bias in their undergraduate admissions systems; they have widened the search to some degree but with an emphasis on middle-class areas where maintained schools tend to be academically better than elsewhere. Many will deny this and so make it harder for those systems to become more just. What is to be done, especially if Oxbridge will not put its own houses in order? As usual, Michael Young has floated an interesting idea: make Oxford and Cambridge into entirely postgraduate universities; make them in some ways like the French Grandes Écoles. The traditionalists will call on democratic freedom, on God, so as to stamp such an idea into the ground. In that case, they should, again, think about fairer and more efficient undergraduate entry methods. One up-to-date figure indicates the problem. Private schools have 7 per cent of the country's pupils, and 50 per cent of Oxbridge entrants come from that 7 per cent. Are private schools seven times as good as the rest? Even though some public schools offer privileged teaching, will anyone seriously contend that that disparity represents a just distribution of ability across the country or a just method of finding talent?

Further changes are proposed or in train. Oxford seems about to abolish its entrance examination. It is felt to favour applicants from those schools who know best how to prepare for it. It also gave some really clever children from state schools the opportunity to show their abilities. The new system must be sufficiently sophisticated, not over-conditioned culturally, to make up for that loss.

V ADULT EDUCATION TODAY

Some experience of popular lecturing had convinced me that the necessity of making things plain to uninstructed people was one of the very best means of clearing up the obscure corners in one's own mind.

T. H. Huxley, *Evidence on Man's Place in Nature*, 1863

The government's own priorities are for education which will help adults improve their qualifications.

Kenneth Clarke, Conservative Secretary of State for Education
in the 1980s

Her Majesty's Inspector, talking casually after listening to a university's annual lecture on Adult Education in 1984, was having no nostalgic nonsense about the Great Days. 'All that heroic stuff about marvellous three-year tutorial classes, wonderful worker-students with their superb written work, takes a lot of believing.' Then one remembered that her special area for inspection was in vocational and technical courses. That fitted; she had the Thatcherite total conviction. Some heads of university Adult and Continuing Education departments have taken the same path, with no apparent hesitation.

That particular HMI would no doubt have said much the same about the subjects particularly prized from the end of the nineteenth century onwards, subjects which Archbishop Temple and R. H. Tawney held to be part of the backbone of an educated democracy: politics, civics, industrial relations, social history; plus civilising subjects studied for their own sake – philosophy, literature, music.

One good new emphasis in this field is the stress on Continuing Education, end-on education, the idea that education should be regarded as, if we wish, a lifetime interest available life long. Not simply vocational education, education with a prize-tag at each stage, but also education undertaken for its own sake. The old style was rather sternly proud of its intellectual purity, so has suffered most in recent years. To some degree it has long suffered. Even just after the last war there were extra-mural tutors who believed they best carried on the Great Tradition by sticking to 'hard' subjects and suspecting the 'soft' such as literature. In this the Trade Unions tended to side with them. Philosophy? Trade Union History and Law, certainly. The French Trade Unions, having won paid educational leave for their members, made no such division or restriction.

Adult Education brings adults together in a very wide range of classes and related activities, not for gain or advancement but from an individual and shared wish to develop their understanding, their creativity and their grasp of personal and social problems.

In the early Fifties Florence Horsbrugh, an unusually rigid Tory Minister of Education (she would have been more at home today), tried to cut adult education's funds. Churchill was asked by the TUC to intervene. Not a populist or a socialist or a leveller but certainly one kind of democrat (as in supporting the Army Bureau of Current Affairs), Churchill responded in a style unthinkable from a Prime Minister today:

There is perhaps no branch of our vast educational system which should more attract within its particular sphere the aid and encouragement of the State than adult education. How many must there be in Britain, after the disturbance of two destructive wars, who thirst in later life to learn about the humanities, the history of their country, the philosophies of the human race, and the arts and letters which sustain and are borne forward by the ever-conquering English language?

This ranks in my opinion far above science and technical instruction which are well sustained and not without their reward in our present system. The mental and moral outlook of free men studying the past with free minds in order to discern the future, demands the highest measures which our hard-pressed finances can sustain. I have no doubt myself that a man or woman earnestly seeking in grown-up life to be guided to wide and suggestive knowledge in its largest and most uplifted sphere will make the best of all pupils in this age of clutter and buzz, of gape and gloat. The appetite of adults to be shown the foundations and processes of thought will never be denied by a British administration cherishing the continuity of our island life.

Rolling rhetoric but with its heart in the right place. It is heart-breaking – not much too strong a word – to think that the final assertion has been proved mistaken, has been specifically denied by a succession of governments incapable of rising to the rhetoric or of revealing that kind of good heart.

Horsbrugh backed down. But we are today back to Horsbrugh; with vocationally justifying knobs on. Some time ago a group called on the responsible Junior Minister to urge that the Adult Literacy Unit have its tenure extended and its funds increased. There was, said the Minister, 'going to be difficulty in persuading the hard men at the Treasury to help those who had not made the effort to become literate at school'. No doubt a good public school, such as the Treasury mandarins attended, would have looked after them better. Who are these grey, faceless men who are always invoked at such times? The Minister added that the Treasury would not be greatly affected by high-minded arguments that a society as rich and sophisticated as this should be ashamed to have more than two million functionally illiterate citizens. He was echoed later by an extremely high-ranking civil servant from another department. More money for the police, yes, with this kind of government; but education and the arts simply aren't 'sexy'. Fashionable crude jargon sounds even worse in those high-ceilinged Whitehall rooms. The Junior Minister discussing the Adult Literacy Unit – clearly not an ill-intentioned man – suggested that the enterprise might fare better if it sounded more vocational, related to training and skill. It became ALBSU, the Adult Literacy and Basic Skills Unit; with rather more money. The government could understand the case for 'functional' but not for 'critical' literacy.

Given these Tory governments' obsession with vocationalism and certification combined with their fear that free intellectual enquiry foments revolutionary feelings, the old style of adult education has suffered badly. The Open University sits, somewhat uneasily, in between these attitudes. When it was proposed, under a Labour government, the central impulse was Tawneyesque. A Tory government nearly killed it at the mouth of the womb. Successive Tory governments have not been particularly favourable towards it. The unspoken compromise reached is typical: you do more clearly vocational work and we will not lean on you so heavily.

The White Paper 'Education and Training for the Twenty-First Century' (1991) had to push on strongly this act of near-demolition of adult education. It did so in crude and shifty language. It proposed shoving all non-vocational adult and further education into a bag now marked 'leisure' (rather than 'recreational') interests and then – since leisure (and recreation) are surely our own affairs, like fretwork and flower-arranging – suggested they should be paid for by the individual not from public funds (except in 'disadvantaged areas' where they might have 'a valuable social function'). So down that drain went classes in philosophy, the plays of Shakespeare and, of course, democratic politics, as subjects of study – and everything else between those and the obviously marketable.

However, figures from the Further Education Colleges showed that the demand for non-vocational courses was still strong. There had been objections to the Green and White Papers, slighter than those to Horsbrugh but strong enough to affect the language of the 1992 Act itself. Though not much. Schedule 2 of the Act, on courses in Further Education, has nine sub-sections, all of them vocational or practical. The gross 'recreational' paragraph of the White Paper has been modified into the more evasive gobbledegook of: 'In sub-section (3)(b) above 'organised leisure-time occupation' means leisure-time occupation in such organised cultural, training and recreative activities as are suited to their requirements for any persons over compulsory school age who are able and willing to profit by facilities provided for that purpose.' We know lawyers have to have their say. But do they have to reduce, to this chewed-cardboard prose, documents from the Department of Education; in the land of

Chaucer, Shakespeare, Milton, Marvell, Pope, Wordsworth, Carlyle, the Brontës, Samuel Butler?

The cold-shouldering of old-style adult education does not come only from this range of Tory governments. There are some on the hard Left who find it unpalatable. One of the dedicated race of immediately post-war university extra-mural tutors was for long troubled in his mind about whether he should convert to Roman Catholicism. Students from his classes in philosophy all said later that he was so purist in his teaching that they had no idea what his religious convictions, if any, might be. Perhaps he was too severe with himself; he might have used his own explicit personal questioning, fairly put, as a help to others to find their own positions. But it was a heroic teaching achievement.

Years later a much younger man, writing a thesis on teaching within adult education, approached the older tutor with a series of questions which showed clearly that the enquirer assumed that a teacher – especially a Roman Catholic – would proselytize; and that one would also be fighting off the Department of Education – who were in turn assumed to lean on tutors to ensure no deviation from established opinion.

Students have to be helped to find their own way, to shape their own tools. They have to learn to sit down before the material and attend to it as objectively as possible. Tutors will not be objective; they can't be. But they will try; and along the way will learn a lot about the limits and perhaps the fruits of their efforts at 'objectivity'. This is a different process from one which pre-emptively distorts or abuses a subject so as to fit the tutor's preconceptions. In a sense, therefore, adult education is quietist, time out – a time, a space, for reflection, the better to find our way, to arrive at things by our own paths, in our own time. It is, again, a form of respect.

*

The need and claim for better education for the great majority should not need repeating or defending. It is manifest, both for those who know they need it and for the much greater number who do not know. Those who do seek more education in their adult life are commonly dismissed as a small and declining minority. Yet, as Chapter 13 argues, many still slip through the nets, are handicapped in several ways, do not wake to their needs until they have left school.

If more provision for adults is made, people will come for it. A large and varied body of mature students can form an intricate tracery of healthy muscles and nerves running though the body politic. We have a national habit of arguing against a plainly good thing until the last minute, and then, once the case has sunk in, of doing a volte-face and going further, faster, than we or anyone else would have predicted. This should be such a moment.

Final word: in late 1994 adult education institutions reported that the vocational pressures, and especially the higher fees for cultural and recreative courses, were having their effect. The demand for those courses was falling.

CHAPTER THREE

The Arts: Intellectual, Artistic and Academic Relativism

Lavatorial graffiti are not to be distinguished in any qualitative way from the drawings of Rembrandt.

Oxford don, 1993

No leisure activity is intrinsically superior to any other.
A conclusion of a recent Arts Council/Library Association conference

It is not that these cultural forms [classical music, drama, painting] are 'above people's heads' but that it is a bourgeois culture and ... only immediately meaningful to that group. The great artistic deception of the twentieth century has been to insist to all people that this was their culture. The Arts Council of Great Britain was established on this premise.
Su Braden, *Artists and People*, 1978

Culture does not (cannot) transcend the material forces and relations of production.
Anthony Easthope, *Literary into Cultural Studies*, 1991

i THE PECULIAR DEBATE; COMMUNITARIAN ART

Who is the Tolstoy of the Zulus? The Proust of the Papuans? I'd be glad to read them.

Saul Bellow

Today all forms of art provide the arena for fierce relativistic assertions. 'It's only your opinion' is one of the simplest and most lax cries; above that, the tone becomes more confident, historically thin but but-ing no buts, as the passages quoted at the head of this chapter illustrate. All these clashing slogans are concerned to admit no distinctions of worth; they assert that though life is short art is not difficult nor long to learn, and its powers are given to all. Populism, consumerism, mercantilism can all, in their own selective ways, cohabit with this view of the arts. The authors quoted above would be displeased to think their non-discriminatory views make it easier for consumerism and its allies to appropriate those parts of the arts which suit their external purposes; but so it is.

Naturally, politics figure a great deal in these discussions and almost entirely the politics of the Left. The Right don't mind; they know they know what the arts are and who they are for. For all those who do engage with The Arts – that unattractive capital-letters package becomes inescapable if you read much in these debates – for all such debaters there are now stick-on labels to match.

The Arts Council

In the middle of these battles is the Arts Council, to which almost no one will give any credit. It has many weaknesses, but only ignorance or perversity would allow the Council itself or its officers to be called lazy or difficult to deal with. Some things the Council clearly was required to do and did do. One simple but useful example concerns an aspect of 'accessibility'.

The Council was the main agent in setting up a network of good professional theatres right across the country and trying to make them more than the preserve of 'the bourgeoisie'. Compared with most pre-war repertory companies they are admirable, in principle and practice (though by the mid-Nineties cuts in the grants have made some go temporarily dark).

The Council realised that without its support certain very expensive forms of performing arts would either collapse or become unavailable to all but the wealthy – opera, ballet, orchestral music, serious drama. One may say they should die if they cannot be sustained by box-office receipts but if you think such a collapse would be a pity then a public body has to help. The Council's weakness was in not making the case for them firmly enough, and, as important, in not sufficiently tying that support to a required widening of the audiences. Covent Garden's bums on the best seats are well-upholstered bums; the large subsidy per seat ensures those bums sit comfortably.

The Council could not easily handle literature and fell into some traps there, to the anger of the literary bursary seekers. There *are* ways in which the Council could help literature, but the most useful are likely to concern readers – through inventive help to libraries, bookshops and some publishing initiatives – rather than direct help to writers (there are occasions when that can be justified). But at bottom literature is a cottage industry; one writer, one pen, one pad.

The Arts Council's main problem over the last twenty years has been the rise of that aggravated, general rather than 'genre-specific' debate about The Arts; and the Council's inability to face it adequately. Of recent Secretaries-General only Roy Shaw saw the size of the problems, but he was virtually a lone voice. Most Council members and staff found themselves caught in that acerbic, foolish push-and-shove and did not know which way to turn. One hugely devoted member of staff was embarrassed when asked to consider that there might be differences of quality in human creativeness. 'Well,' he at last said, 'some people like Mahler and some like driving powerful motorbikes. We shouldn't judge between them.' Mercifully, he did not add: 'It's as simple as that,' or 'That's all there is to it.'

Many of the Council's staff and most Council members were therefore pushovers for the insistences of the 'grass roots . . . coalface . . . communitarian . . . provincial . . . folk' promoters. Some of the initiatives to which money was handed in these conditions were worthwhile; others were ludicrous and gave aid to the Conservative opposition. To say so was made to seem like denying basic nourishment to an orphan child. The poet Roy Fuller was a Council member at the peak of this period and took it all very crustily, which was a pity for he was needed. He resigned and took the occasion to land some well-deserved blows: 'The bestowal of money for the arts inevitably attracts the idle, the dotty, the minimally talented, the self-promoters.'

*

The Arts Council, it is clear, was caught ill-equipped to meet the heated and confused arguments about the arts in late-twentieth-century Britain, the debate about 'standards'.

Why are the arguments so angry? Why are so many people so violently disinclined to admit any differences in the value of different works of art; or between human choices as to activities? This is the most revealing of our multiple cultural hang-ups. It involves many people who – the conclusion is inescapable – almost entirely reject 'great' works of art in any form (people who will dismiss George Eliot as 'merely a reflection of nineteenth-century bourgeois values' and clearly have not read her work). Such people as these are well-versed in one or the other art but unwilling any longer to make value-judgments between them. By extension, they are uneasy about talk of art's possible relations to 'meaning'. They avoid any vertical judgments, in favour of the endlessly horizontal. By the Nineties a senior official with Radio 3 could announce: 'There is no art; only culture.' A spiritual mate adds: 'Each man is his own culture.'

They therefore invent a new range of sub-genres, designed to fence off their arts from any comparative judgments. They speak of 'popular poetry', of 'the literary novel', of 'workers' literature', of 'oral literature' (but not, in this part of the field so far, of 'adult fiction', itself a smarmy conflation of 'soft porn' and 'hard-core porn'), as though these designations carry within themselves their own self-enclosed terms of judgment.

The suggestion that there is a difference of quality between *North and South* and *The Ragged Trousered Philanthropists* or *Brother to the Ox*, valuable though Tressell's and Kitchen's books are, will produce letters accusing you of a narrow, highbrow vision, socially motivated snobbishness and an out-of-date clinging to a received order you do not have the guts to question.

At the extreme such people will allow no comparative judgments at all, even within a mini-genre. If you ask them how, since there is not enough public money to go round, they would choose what to support and what not, they become angry or at the best stiffly humourless. Or they subject the Arts Council or Local Government officers to a harangue.

Relevant here is the story of the London taxi-driver for whom supporters had asked an Arts Council grant so that his memoirs might be published. They proved that, though the man had spent many years driving round the city and no doubt had had many interesting experiences and met many interesting passengers, he had no capacity to separate the routine from the special. 'I well remember the day I had Mr (as he then was) Roy Thomson in my cab. I recognised him from his photo in the papers. He did not speak during the whole journey.' 'Many changes have taken place in the cabbie's life since I began, but on the whole the job is much the same.' His sponsors did him no favour by handing in his text; they could have done better by asking him questions, with a tape-recorder running; until, perhaps, he fired into imaginative life. The Council gave this advice but no grant, and were duly abused as snobs trampling on humble, emerging shoots.

On the other hand, a middle-aged Jamaican woman who worked as a cleaner in a London college set down her memories of childhood in a village a few miles outside Kingston. She had a sharp eye for ironic detail – on the habits of a drunken farmer, on the complicated wrongs and rights of wives' lives, on tortured village relationships. She had a gift, a feeling for the resonances of that world. She could *write*.

In America, ideology tends to go further. At a recent large conference on Cultural Studies in the Midwest the paper of a particularly distinguished scholar from England was interrupted by a group of women graduate students who mounted the platform and demanded access to the microphone. They objected, they said, to any more 'so-called experts' being allowed to speak from the rostrum when they had not been invited to do so. They demanded equal rights on the ground that their opinions were, as a matter of principle and fact, as good as anyone else's; to have only 'established specialists' giving papers was 'unacceptable academic élitism'.

Here enters the more cunning 'good of its kind' argument. It might just be admitted by some people that there may be differences in complexity and range (anything to avoid 'value') between *Paradise Lost* and a Bob Dylan lyric; but each is 'good of its kind' and so they should not be 'set against each other'. One might usefully develop and reinforce the judge-things-on-their-own-terms theme by comparing, say, *Paradise Lost* wih a typical early-seventeenth-century lyric. But a Dylan lyric? It seems as though any length will be gone to to avoid ever having to say: 'But this *is* a better work than that.'

To someone unacquainted with this range of arguments the foregoing may seem exaggerated. Do apparently intelligent people really argue in this way? Yes, and with no sense of incongruity. It has been going on a long time, merely acquiring new curlicues.

To anyone from a bookless home the suggestion that there should be such an approach to literature, a prior social filtering rather than a judgment of differing qualities, is offensive and ill-judged. The thought that such a creed is being offered to people who still live in a bookless culture, as a justification for being satisfied with the popular press, the shoddier television programmes and other such barbarisms, is yet another instance of the 'stay as sweet as you are' syndrome – all too often used by 'good democrats' who seem not to see that they are consigning other people to the worst aspects of consumer capitalism.

The most common pit into which upholders of the 'no distinctions' position fall is that of numerical populism. If no distinctions of quality can be made, why should it not be agreed that the one distinction which can be made, the one test, is that of popularity by numbers? So the charts rule. Some people, especially those in the popular music business, find no difficulty in this position. For them, popularity *is* the test of quality; if it sells, it's good. For others the fall can be unconscious. They are sufficiently intelligent and even intellectual not to wish to join the pop-promoters here. But where else is there to go? If you refuse comparative judgments based on a work's perceptiveness, power of language, attempted and to some degree achieved truth and honesty before experience, you have to accept the definitive power of numbers; you are in a world entirely relativist except for head-counting.

'This view implicitly rejects the notion that there is a hierarchy of tastes and preferences'. That statement therefore rejects the 'notion' that there might be, let alone should be, any such hierarchy in the arts. It goes on: 'It [this view] explicitly rejects the idea that the creative artist, the performing artist, or the informed aesthete can perform these services or have any special status in the community when it comes to the allocation of resources to the arts.' That this is muddled and modish brass-tackery is obvious. That it is to be found in a discussion document issued by the Arts Council – number 4 in a large group proposed by the Arts Minister and designed to plot a course for public support for the arts – is even today surprising. Had the Council itself no role in judging the quality of the papers it was co-ordinating? Or would any intervention by the Council have been automatically damned as a form of censorship? Yes, it would. Having asked for the papers the Council did right to issue them. But it should, if only after all the papers had been issued, have made its own position on them clear.

Here is more from the same group with an unconvincing 'hard economic gloss' to it. 'The individual should be free to buy whatever goods and services he wants [true]. He should not be *forced or persuaded* [italics added] to pay more or less than the competitive market-price for such goods or services' (bang goes much of the advertising industry).

True again, but are they talking about public support for the arts – to which such an assertion is beside the point – or about the mass persuaders for soap powders, cars and the rest? Perhaps, being free marketeers, they would find it difficult to be so directly critical of those engines of persuasions, which have no more to do with the arts than sugar has with poetry. After 'goods and services' the sentence ends; 'which implies no direct subsidies to producers of them'.

The deceptive slide is revealed. Does the writer know just what he is doing? Perhaps he is so committed to his 'the market solves all matters of choice' ideology that he simply cannot see what a quagmire he has walked into. What he says is entirely accurate for and relevant to the market-place for consumer goods. As to help with provision for the arts from the public purse, this assertion (it is not an argued case) is irrelevant since it ignores questions about distorted access, unequal education, and differences in financial standing. It ignores also the fact that some of the more important arts are too expensive to mount for them to be fully paid for by individuals, and are not likely to be covered by corporate sponsors, even if that were desirable. You cannot sensibly talk about this kind of provision as if it were on the same level as the competitive provision of soap and sugar. 'The Threepenny Opera' is a metaphor not a price-tag. So would be an unsubsidised 'All seats 50p' *Aida*.

Here is another firm statement from the same group of Arts Council discussion papers: 'Wedgwood and Elgar are not better than Tupperware and Bob Marley – they just belong to different clubs.' The slippery word here is 'clubs'. Tupperware parties form a sort of lower-middle-class, *ad hoc* set of sponsored, profit-seeking get-togethers. In whatever ways admirers of Elgar's music come together it would be nonsense to talk about the capacity to be affected *individually* by Elgar's music as though it necessarily implied cosy membership of a group of the Tupperware sort. Can one compare such a club of Elgar's admirers, if it does exist, to a group persuaded by a saleswoman to meet in one of the group's sitting rooms so that they may be urged to buy plastic kitchen equipment?

It is odd that the voices which speak in the above ways, as well as being assertively grinding in rejecting differences of level, are yet as absolutist as hell-fire Calvinistic preachers pushing in your face their inescapable and virtually self-evident rules, values: 'the only rule is that there is no golden rule' – and don't forget it, on pain of being cast out from the one true church if you do.

Communitarian art

Linked to the rejection of the 'bourgeois canon' is the meant-to-be-damaging assertion that that canon – especially literature – is individualistic; whereas the best art is more often than not communitarian, the outcome of a shared and egalitarian activity. This is greatly hoped for since it seems warmer; the individual artist has always been rather off-putting to the English. Hence the Labour Party, when it produces its pamphlets on the arts, stresses communal fun-and-games, what is described as the need for a 'Come to the Fair' atmosphere in approaches to the arts (sounds like misapplied Bahktin on carnival). Go home, *Macbeth*, Dostoevsky, *Bleak House*, *Tess*.

Writing about the Giotto frescoes in the Scrovegni chapel just outside Padua, one author suggests that the credit for these master-pieces (at least he recognises that quality) should be shared between the artist, his assistants and the man who held the ladder.

The asserters do not really mean 'communal'; that would have to imply shared values, shared beliefs, shared convictions about life, faith, the good and true and beautiful. This might be true of the Giotto frescoes, but usually the examples given reveal not a con-sidered belief in the collective spirit but merely the rejection of differ-ence, the assertion of a levelling spirit which admits no distinctions either in sustained effort or in ability; rule by numbers.

Ability, the gift; and effort, craft; the two foundations of art. 'The life so short, the craft so long to learn.' Here is the most important clue to the aggression of communitarian writers: the idea of differ-ences in individual gifts and of the solitary search for goals. 'The Federation of Writers and Community Publishers challenges the assumption that only individuals with rare talent are capable of producing art of good quality.' Apart from being slightly bet-hedging that is a good example of the mode, especially in its out-and-out form. Here, for comparison, is solitary Goethe:

> I had toward the poetic art a quite peculiar relation which was only practical after I had cherished in my mind for a long time a subject which possessed me, a model which inspired me, a predecessor who attracted me, until at length, after I had molded it in silence for years, something resulted which might be regarded as a creation of my own; and finally, all at once, and almost instinctively, as if it had become ripe, I set it down on paper.

The inescapable individuality of some art for some people – among them many of the best – implies neither an anti-social individuality nor a moral solipsism.

Some arts are essentially communitarian, though on the whole these are lesser forms, at least in the Western world and especially in Europe. It is an error to claim today that because drama and music need people other than the creating artists themselves to 'put on', 'express', a particular work of art, then those arts are communitarian. They are not. They are individual creations which require others to embody them in their particular ways; with greater or lesser talent and to greater or lesser effect.

Nevertheless it has become regarded as, yet again, élitism to assert that most of our arts begin in solitary creative activity. That is taken as an insult to everyone outside; they are regarded as having the right not only to look over the artists' shoulders and make suggestions, or to pick up the brush and have a go (both acceptable), but to assert that the practice of art is only 'correct' when it is communal, instantly available and comprehensible.

The urge to 'communitise' – if that is the right word – all art, the irritated refusal to recognise individuality and difference, could hardly go further. This is one of the main fallacies of those who talk about 'democratising' the arts, without realising how distortingly irrelevant such phrasing is (assuming the author can give a meaning to it). The real, the actual, the manifest walls – social, cultural, imaginative, intellectual, spiritual – do not fall from a misdirected puff such as that.

Being charitable, one might say that the communitarian confusion may arise out of a well-meant democratic instinct; but it has muddled itself into that pervasive condition of populism. So once again and rather wearily, it has to be said that though we are no doubt all equal in the sight of God and perhaps of the Bench, and certainly in our capacities to make or mar our lives in our own ways, nevertheless we are not equal in all things. We are not born equal in beauty, though our faces may grow into beauty or ugliness of spirit; but that is to use different meanings of 'beautiful' and 'ugly'. Most gifts fall on the just and the unjust without advance moral book-keeping. Hence Auden on the death of Yeats (in a passage he later deleted):

> Time that with this strange excuse
> Pardons Kipling and his views,
> And will pardon Paul Claudel,
> Pardons him for writing well.

The reverse of the rejection of difference in individual gifts is the affirmation that all humans are gifted. The over-used text here, usually attributed to Eric Gill though it may be from an Indian sage such as Tagore or Coomaraswamy, is that 'The artist is not a special kind of man but every man is a special kind of artist.' It would be lovely to be able to believe that. Perhaps one can, looking very closely, say that almost everyone *may well* have hidden gifts, that the possibility should be honoured and the effort made to develop them (without at the same time admitting that all those gifts are of equal power and effectiveness). Some children, before peer-group culture swallows them, can show felicity in observation and expression. The case for giving everyone the chance to develop what talent they might possibly have is strong.

Raymond Williams gave a quite different but valuable leg-up to all such claims when he argued that working-class creativity could not easily express itself in 'bourgeois' art-forms but found expression in the creation of the Trade Unions, the Co-ops, the Friendly Societies, the Working Men's Clubs, the Labour Party.

But this would not at all do for the out-and-outers such as this writer: 'Many of the comments on life which people get out of Shakespeare could have been reached by very modest talents without his assistance.' Just didn't get round to it, presumably; not the workers nor the middle class nor the aristocracy. 'Comments on life . . . got out of Shakespeare' suggests a reduced, denatured reading; an unpleasant party game might require quick descriptions of the 'comments on life' to be got out of *Othello*, *Measure for Measure*, *Hamlet*. That author's metaphorical half-sister was a Mills and Boon contracted novelist who, speaking at one of those NVQ seminars, insisted that on a proper understanding of the word 'creative' her novels are 'as creative as Lawrence's *Women in Love*'.

As so often, Auden is a good guide through this sort of fog. Roughly, he says: ask your child what he (or she) wants to be. If he says a parson or a Prime Minister let him go in for the church or politics. If he says he doesn't know, but does like 'hanging around words', then give him a small allowance and let him try to learn to be a poet. He also says of a composer: 'Only your song is an absolute gift' – a nice conjunction of the idea of the gratuitousness of the possession of artistic ability and a pun on the American phrase for something which comes, and comes across, happily, supremely easily.

A good test of the gratuitousness of 'the gift', free of social and cultural conditioning, not to be explained in materialist terms, not to be explained away at all, is to be found in the entirely unexpected and often surrealist touches of which most considerable writers are capable. They can be found in Trollope; they abound in Dickens.

The pompous Collector in *Nicholas Nickleby* learns that his wife has left him for a half-pay Captain and his grief goes straight to the roots of his sense of himself: 'I shall never be able to knock a double-knock again.' Plucked out of the air; perfect. Mrs Gamp describes her husband's laying-out in hospital, ending: 'and they put his wooden leg under his left arm'. It is that 'left' which does the trick; entirely unnecessary but, again, upliftingly precise. Mr Pumblechook is robbed, mugged, tied to the bedpost, ' . . . and they stuffed his mouth full of flowering annuals to prevent his crying out', reports Joe. It is the mad, unnecessary precision and determined comprehensiveness of 'his *left* arm' and of the '*flowering annuals*' (not 'bunches of flowers' or 'seed packets') which mark the inspired writer, taking off. There is no 'need', no 'need' at all, for the exactness of 'flowering annuals', Mrs Gamp's remark about one of her patients is another free-floating surreal image, "is 'owls was organs'. So is Mrs Todger's comment on the tribulations of keeping a lodging house for single gentlemen who are greatly demanding about their food: 'The gravy alone is enough.' Or there is Sloppy in *Our Mutual Friend*: "E do the police in different voices.'

One could go on like this for ever. Would that one had such a gift. Or the gift which caused George Eliot to make Celia say to the rather preachy Dorothea, in *Middlemarch*, that people were watching not listening. Or the way by which, in chapter 50 of *Martin Chuzzlewit*, Tom Pinch comes out of his almost overwhelmingly kindly shell and tells his sister that life is not art, is real, and can be unkind; at that moment he becomes what Forster called a 'round' character; there is no need to describe the switch as 'early post-modernism'. Such art can hardly be said to 'reflect and reinforce the bourgeois ideology'; it inhabits another world.

ii READING

I have led a life of business so long that I have lost my taste for reading, and now – what shall I do?
  Horace Walpole, cit. in Mrs Thrale's *Thraliana*, 1776–1809

Yes, books! Cicero and Ovid have told us that to literature only they can look for consolation in their banishment. But then they speak of a remedy for sorrow, not of a source of joy. No young man should dare to neglect literature.
  Anthony Trollope, *The Duke's Children*, 1880 (a nice echo of
                                                    Dr Johnson on consolation)

People assume the printed word is reality. But speech is reality – the printed word is sub-normal. The printed word will diminish in importance . . . audio-visual must happen more and more.

An executive in a Communications Technology enterprise

But you must understand a printed page as you understand people talking to you. That is a stupendous feat of sheer learning. Much the most difficult I have ever achieved.

George Bernard Shaw

Since most children learn to read without apparent effort, Shaw must have been using the word in a sophisticated sense, to indicate the highly developed act of interpretation which language and literature at their best require.

It is not accidental that we use the word 'reading' as a metaphor for 'understand', 'get my drift', 'see right into'; as in 'Do you read me?' down a telephone line, or 'I am trying to read the meaning of this act – gesture – even this picture or piece of music or film or photograph.'

Such a truth needs stressing today, when even highly educated people are often willing to wave goodbye to reading – for others at least – on the grounds that we are now living within the post-Gutenberg visual revolution. Some people pass their lives without once reading a work of creative literature all the way through. It was always so. Today, though, very many know how to cope with an advanced computer; and some of those, as is clear from one of the quotations above, believe thay have bypassed one unnecessary activity.

Music is commonly called the Queen of the Arts and one need not quarrel with that – but could be tempted to call literature the King. Of all the arts, literature has the most explicit and direct hold on conscious as well as implicit knowledge – on ideas and beliefs and values stated or implied. It can be and is subject to exegesis, often contradictory, but it needs no prior translation into words; it *is* words. It is also much more than all this, but there is where it begins.

Libraries under the harrow

The Public Library is a magnificent mid-nineteenth-century innovation now under attack from several sides; notably from the ideological-political, from that old error – populism mistaken for democracy, from relativism and low mercantilism. As may easily be shown: 'The public library service was set up to facilitate social control of the literate proletariat by the newly-emerged capitalist class' (from a letter to the present author). Behind that late-twentieth-century jargon there is some truth. Even Edith and Tom Kelly, the historians of the system, noted that to some extent and for some people the libraries were seen as as much a social as an educational reform – 'to head off drunkenness' (*Books for the People*, 1977). But no social reform is quite so simple; we have no right to pick the aspect which – as one might say – suits our book. When he presented to Parliament the Bill which became the Libraries Act of 1850, William Ewart argued that it was meant particularly to help the working classes, was 'for the cultivation of their minds, and the refinement of their tastes in science and art'. That point of view was as important in its time and as honestly meant as that of the control-theory.

A favourable review of W. J. West's well-documented book *The Strange Rise of Semi-Literate England* (1991) on the decline of the Public Libraries brings forth this sort of rejoinder, from a librarian: 'It is not in selecting what bourgeois intellectuals assume to be "good" for other people that professional skills need to be exercised, but in providing the widest range of information possible within the financial restrictions imposed by central government.' That sudden drop into blaming the government at the end of a passage which reveals the real fault, populist relativism, is a typical cop-out in these discussions. Less wordy defenders merely say they will not 'clutter' their shelves with the 'classics'. Half a dozen of each Jack Higgins title and a dozen of each Barbara Cartland need the space. If you want the newest important book on changing British culture, they will order it from inter-library loans, at your expense and after a delay. The staff in the branches virtually always remain friendly and helpful.

Those librarians more inclined towards linguistic PR produce: 'What is needed is a lean, muscular, light-turnover stock presented in attractive and imaginative ways.' The more insecure take refuge in Informatics, germ-free in 'value' terms. They seem happier with cassettes, CDs, VDUs, modems and the rest than with books. You half expect them to wear white technocrat's coats, with large round badges on the lapels announcing: 'Hi! I'm Sid. Can I assist you?' It would be churlish to deny Informatics seekers or middle-aged recreational readers their shelf-space. But, especially when 'central government is imposing financial restrictions', bright children reaching for the 'classics' and today's self-improving readers should not be made to accept an unfair slice of the cuts. In addition, libraries could do more than many are doing (there are good exceptions) to bring in more people from the less-endowed parts of society.

In the early Nineties the Arts Council and the Library Association collaborated in trying to encourage more reading. The oddity of some of their proposals underlined today's situation. The Council 'launched a Library Fund for the promotion of literature in libraries' – rather like having a fund to promote spiritual issues in churches. Much the same was proposed for librarians themselves: 'The Arts Council is also examining possibilities for training programmes for librarians in imaginative literature.' As so often, the giveaway is in the adjective. That 'imaginative' effectively puts to the sidelines any thought that that difficult form 'imaginative literature' might be at the heart of a library's purposes. To what are the Schools of Librarianship introducing their students if not, among much else, to the importance of imaginative literature? Above all, their introductions appear to be to two things: to Informatics, the most fashionable new area; and to muddled political history – which prompts young librarians to meet any talk of classic 'imaginative writing' as 'bourgeois élitism . . . paternalism'. A defensive pamphlet of 1993 recalls that 'The Public Libraries Act of 1964 includes no specific provision for the support of literature.' Nor, presumably, does it have a sentence running: 'Literature is a Good Thing.' Peggy Heeks notes neutrally and probably accurately that 'A majority of librarians feel no special commitment to literature' (*The Heeks Report: Public Libraries and the Acts*, 1989). It would be difficult to find a neater example of the damage which the current climate of opinion is inflicting on the life of the mind.

Above all, no users must be strained. Several branch libraries exhibit a stand of CDs with the caption 'Easy Listening'; just like Woolworths. 'Hard Listening but Worth It' would have been more to the point. In the early days of Mrs Thatcher's succession of governments a joke was going round Whitehall. A head-in-the-clouds Rip Van Winkle of an idealist approached the Department of Education with a bright idea. Why not open a warm room in each city and town, fill it with books, provide tables and chairs, and also let the books be taken out on loan, and without payment? The Secretary of State was appalled: 'But such an Executive Agency would have to be cost-effective. So how on earth could we make it a free service, and why should we anyway?'

The joke was fulfilled in real life. By 1994 a Commission set up by the Department of National Heritage was considering the contracting-out of libraries to the private sector. One hundred and forty years on and straight into reverse gear.

Ideologies of the arts

Very politically conscious people might be thought likely to be as absolutist in their approach to the arts as they are to much else. That would seem to be the attitude of those who speak of 'the present corporate state, benign-type fascism' in public provision for the arts. That manages to have things both ways, the speaker's own sureness of conviction and a recognition that matters don't always *look* so 'fascist'. Or they claim 'to challenge the concept of a canon on the grounds that it is the instrument of a dominant ideology'.

They tend to be absolutist too in their belief in the determining nature which 'the culture imposes on the artist and his art'. Following Marx, they say: 'A dominant class employs an ideal formula, to give its ideas the form of universality and to represent them as the only rational and universally valid ones.' At this point modern writers almost invariably invoke Gramsci and 'hegemony'. It is no disrespect to the power and penetration of Gramsci's writing to suggest that other people (e.g. Henry Adams) have for many years, whatever word they may have used to describe the process, recognised the force and ramifications of those pressures from society.

Writers are certainly conditioned by their age but, if they have reasonable ability, not determined by it: the young television arts interviewer who suggested that almost all of Kipling's writing was limited because 'contextualised' by his age had misread Kipling because she used, without listening closely to the texts, her ready-made semantic/theoretic tool-kit. An even more constricted cultural-materialistic critic, writing on Shakespeare, managed at last to squeeze out: 'It is rarely possible to argue that a play of his has an unequivocally "pro-Establishment" meaning.' That's a relief, then. Schiller was altogether subtler: 'The artist is the child of his time, but woe to him if he is also its disciple or even its favourite.' Shelley was neat and adequate, in saying that artists are both creations of and creators of their age.

At a lower level some critics deploy that old tag 'relevant' as a demand on literature and a major constitutent of worth. This is a form of the socially purposive or social-ambulance work approach:

Gissing and Tressell and Fred Kitchen are placed high in the pantheon. They are Snowdons or perhaps even Ben Nevises of our literature; but not Everests.

This kind of thinking embodies the dream of communitarianism which was met earlier. Its exponents mistrust individualism because it is a 'characteristic of capitalism: 'The most perfect examples of written ideology are the "classic" novels of the nineteenth century, the literary expression of capitalist individualism.' The individualism, the solitariness, of writing has to be disowned. As we saw, it then follows, and this is even more important, that the idea of an individual 'gift' must also be disowned. Edward Thompson had more right than most to make this point, generally and also with particular reference to the arts:

> I can't assume... that intellectual violence and élitism are only to be found on the Right... There are some on the 'Left' who flirt with conceits of violence and aggression in a way which suggests a disorder of the imagination, a mere bravura of opinions... Within the vocabularly of this kind of 'Left' are many 'dainty terms for fratricide'... If the message of the Left is to be *bang! bang!* then I wish they would get themselves poets to imagine this, to join feeling and attach form to the bangs... Somewhere (if poets did their work) another cluster of values would be defining themselves. These might be a little quieter, less invigilatory and dominative, less strident and more compassionate than those recently to be noted on the Left.
>
> E. P. Thompson, *Stand*, Vol. 20/2

The arts as commodities

More and more the arts, whatever the ideological battles about them or the virtuous assertions of support for them made by the main political parties, become aspects of consumerism, of the advertising and PR world. Those who pay any attention to the arts become, simply, 'consumers of the arts'; that is the standard formulation. The field is not very important compared with, say, the selling of motorcars or beauty aids but it is being developed. It is a small service/refreshment area on the motorway of modern social life, providing specialised commodities for a fair-sized line of slightly up-market, slightly mink-lined consumers. It belongs in that area of *soi-disant* 'democratic life' where de Tocqueville detected above all 'a virtuous materialism'; where art is devoured because it has itself been presented as an item for consumption and display, like hand-tooled leather accessories, or the most customer-friendly of Filofaxes.

The production of books (82,000 titles in Britain in 1993) is as good an example as any. The book trade has over the last decade or so been increasingly concentrated into a few large corporations. The old names are often kept, as good selling-points, but the accountants rule more and more. To them as to their bosses in the City or in the United States, books are not different from cleverly packaged 'luxury accessories', and the overwhelming question is: 'What is the profit margin?' So they and the booksellers go increasingly for the best-seller. It may be in the lists for only a few weeks, but in that time a lot of copies will be 'shifted'. In this world, recommendation by enthusiastic word of mouth progressively gives way to commercial promotion. Remy de Gourmont (1858–1915) spotted the trend early: 'The more a work is admired [read 'hyped'], the more beautiful it grows for the multitude.' Hence that line of books written to recipe by MPs, hack journalists and, above all, a lengthening line of writers for the crime, sex, violence, romantic and historico-romantic, politi-cal, commercial and general scandal markets.

In this world, inevitably, style does duty for substance; the 'hum and buzz of implication' which a good novel contains fades and the sense of life itself is thinned out. Such books belong to the world of fast food where taste is chemically intensified but the palate desen-sitised.

In England this process is assisted by our ambivalence towards things artistic. We mistrust them, we associate them with fancy people who are no better than they should be, people who we think should instead do an honest day's work. Yet they tease and mildly haunt us and we would like to be in some way associated with them. Hence the 'corporate' seats at Covent Garden and the ever-growing number of literary prizes sponsored by industry and commerce. As Kipling knew and made fun of in 'The Conundrum of the Workshops', one fundamental English axiom is 'It's clever/pretty, but is it art?'

In these circumstances, how do books of the kind to which the present one belongs still manage to come off the presses? And how long will this continue? They survive partly because there are still editors devoted to the cause of literature and of serious discursive writing; and those people, though now often within the great machines of big corporations, fight and sometimes triumph over or genuinely convince the accountants. They survive because there are still people who will break away and found their own houses; like new shoots under the great and greedy jungle trees. They may continue to survive, though probably more and more in corners. Meanwhile, in this harsh and market-driven world, some writers have good cause to salute and thank them.

What does 'reading' mean?

Thus they fall to denying what they cannot comprehend ... they like to discern the object which engages their attention with extreme clearness ... their disposition of mind soon leads them to condemn forms which they regard as useless and inconvenient veils placed between them and the truth.

Alexis de Tocqueville, *Democracy in America*, (1835–40)

The question 'what does reading mean?' will itself be rejected as irrelevant and élitist by almost all who stand on the line of 'rejectors' of the literary canon described above. Some people may have 'read' *Emma* in the sense of turning over its pages as though using it from outside (perhaps guided by 'theory') or – much less likely – in the sense of responding to it inwardly, patiently, cumulatively. The simpler among them, it seems plain, have not even 'read', in anything other than the sense of going through on the surface, any major works. The level of debate is as bad as that. With some 'readers' we are now at the point where they will admit to liking *Viz* but will brush aside *Women in Love, Scarlet and Black* and *Four Quartets*. The more aggressive are unmoved by the ending of *King Lear*; it is simply so many words in so many places and shapes, a text, not related to feeling or judgment on the nature of our common experiences. Its meanings, if meanings it has, are no more than whatever different readers or watchers feel able to make of them. For some, this is a natural not an ideological condition, a fact from birth which they accept. By others it is used to reinforce an ideology, low- or high-level, political or literary-theoretical.

In this world the landscape of art is a flat and featureless plain; there are not and apparently cannot be heights or depths. This can be a tonic approach, especially in clearing away untethered guff. Presumably such people do not have in their heads what Matthew Arnold called 'touchstones', those passages which come into the mind without warning or intention: on the point of sleep, when halted at traffic lights or when moved by some depressing or cheering experience:

The rainbow comes and goes,
And lovely is the rose,
The moon doth with delight
Look round her when the heavens are bare;
Waters on a starry night
Are beautiful and fair;
The sunshine is a glorious birth;
But yet I know, where'er I go,
That there hath passed away a glory from the earth.

About the shark, phlegmatical one
Pale sot of the Maldive sea
The sleek little pilot fish,
Azure and slim,
How alert in attendance be.

I was adored once too.

That best portion of a good man's life,
His little, nameless, unremembered acts
Of kindness and of love.

We are such stuff
As dreams are made on, and our little life
Is sounded with a sleep

– and so on through a whole internal anthology.

It is just possible to reduce all such passages, their haunting language and evocative rhythms, to typical elements of English – or Western – culture, as rhythms and language both the poets and their readers are conditioned to be moved by. In that sense they can be made to belong to at least the fringes of cultural-materialist theory as applied to literature.

So there is a hierarchy or canon. But not one which should be narrowly determined – socially, culturally, temporally. That is where the work really starts; there is no North-West Passage to the imaginative life. The work has to be done, though, or we fall into the hands of the ideologues. Only a truncated false-moralism would think words such as 'patronage' and 'paternal' entirely derisory. They can indicate the wish to pass on to others something you believe of value. They have their dignity. They can come from a world which recognises differences and believes the privileged should try to pass on those understandings. If they sound portentous today, that is today's loss.

Two observations, one from the eighteenth century, the other modern, are apt here. The modern one is by Iris Murdoch: 'Innumerable forms of evaluation haunt our simplest decisions.' Clearly said, unfashionable but true once one has thought about it for only a minute or so. There is no escape from judgment, though not necessarily conscious judgment. For most of the time and most occasions judgment will be unconscious; but it will be there, a choice will have been made. Will it 'haunt'? Yes, for some people. But the contemporary climate is against haunting, and so most people appear not to be haunted, consciously or unconsciously; yet the judgments will have been reached. It is tempting to suspect then a lack of self-consciousness and sometimes a lack of humility; but that might be harsh. More likely is a disability in seeing, especially a disinclination to see mountains and chasms in place of that endless but perhaps complex flatness; no mental or spiritual agoraphobia sets in.

Some who insist on these attitudes are, as those Arts Council Discussion papers amply bear out, imaginatively undernourished. But the attitudes are widespread and some of their forms are subtle. Human wisdom and human intelligence are not necessarily correlated; an extremely complex mind can arrive at, hold on to and elaborate a point of view which is at bottom, stripped of its complications, as silly as one held by the simple-minded – and vice versa.

The eighteenth-century observation is from Voltaire and pricklier than Iris Murdoch's; hard at first to understand, hard to swallow once understood, rather frightening because severe, and unpalatable to current opinion: 'The best is the enemy of the good.' That is unacceptable today because it takes for granted and takes seriously the belief in hierarchies. Voltaire is not willing to waste time on trivia; he concerns himself with matters of significance. He recognises the 'good' and ignores anything below it. He also recognises the 'best', which is better than the 'good'; and says that though the word 'good' may indeed indicate something 'good' we must not resile from judgment and fail to recognise and honour what is better than the 'good' – that is, to respect the 'best'. Recognition, acknowledgment of the 'best', puts even the 'good' into its proper subordinate place. It would have been interesting to hear Voltaire take on current arguments about things which are 'good of their kind', not to be set against anything else, not to be judged.

Voltaire's observation would have seemed natural to F. R. Leavis.

Another relevant phrase for him would have been 'The trivial is the enemy of the good'; for he said again and again that life is too short for time to be spent on anything but the best. That is why Leavis is in some circles excoriated today. The Puritan! The Elitist! What does he know of the pleasures, even the merits, of 'the popular arts'? How dare he assert that no properly educated person should be ignorant of 'The Great Tradition in English Literature'; or would think it worthwhile to read 'light fiction' whilst knowing nothing of Hardy?

Few have Leavis's rigour and intellectual earnestness. But some know with a corner of their minds that he is saying something vital. 'We needs must love the highest when we see it' sounds splendid but is simply not true. One can see the highest, recognise it, resent it, and turn back to a less-demanding world. In 'In Praise of Limestone' Auden too recognised the attractions of the snuggling life, of being like everybody else, of implicitly agreeing to issue no challenges so long as no one challenges us, and invites us to turn our eyes to the uplands of the mind:

> If it form the one landscape that we, the inconstant ones,
> Are consistently homesick for, this is chiefly
> Because it dissolves in water.

iii LITERARY ESSENCES

The special attraction of literature is that it is compromised; muddy, absorbed with detail, with what Blake called 'minutely organised particulars'. Its medium – language itself – is so used and abused each day that one wonders whether it can ever be rescued for better use. It can be rescued, in the hands of those obsessed with it; a drab given a Pygmalian transformation.

Literature is irredeemably of the earth and so bound up all the time with possible meanings, hints of meanings, with the weighed, creative and creaturely life; bacon and eggs, fish and chips, snot, farts, sleep, love, boredom. The relationships analysed in a novel of some texture, or the proto- or crypto-statements which can emerge from a powerful poem, may be extracted and talked about (though always by an act of midwifery, and not all the midwives will agree or be much better than Mrs Gamp). This is more difficult, though not entirely impossible, with music, painting or sculpture. That word 'texture' is often used but rarely defined; here, it means that sense of intellectual and moral fibre, of 'body' as in a fine cloth, which a

75

complex prose style can give as it seeks to grapple more precisely with the complexity of relationship and choices.

From there one moves to its consequent elements, large and small, premeditated and unexpected. Such as the germs which can initiate a story or poem or, probably more likely, act as the catalyst for all the disordered elements which have been lying uneasily at the back of the head, like a rabble waiting to be called to order. Arnold Bennett sees a fussy old woman being slighted in a Paris restaurant and from that comes the first inspiration for *The Old Wives' Tale*; and that led eventually to the wonderfully poignant and charitable deathbed scene in Manchester, where the 'fussy old woman' sees after many years the man who had led her astray.

Conrad hears a police inspector at a London party make a dismissive remark about an anarchist who blew himself up, and so is set on to write *The Secret Agent*, as he records in the Preface:

> *There must have been, however, some sort of atmosphere in the whole incident because all of a sudden I felt myself stimulated. And then ensued in my mind what a student of chemistry would best understand from the analogy of the addition of the tiniest little drop of the right kind, precipitating the process of crystallization in a test tube containing some colourless solution.*

As to the origin of *Nostromo*, Conrad spoke of being inspired by 'a vagrant anecdote', with no details in it, but one to which he subsequently gave detail and redeemed from squalor (low-level greed) into a sort of drab heroism. Henry James wrote well about how such a germ not only orders the disordered but can contain within itself the elements of enormously complex evidence.

Everyone can have such witnesses, even if they never make creative use of them. Here, a London taxi-driver is reporting, in the early Nineties, being stopped by a policeman and accused of making a rude sign at him. The driver denied this and the policeman finally released him with 'All right, then; but it would have been a different matter if you had *insulted the uniform*.' There is a whole world of popular mis-belief behind that, in which the police uniform belongs to the same numinous and dominating company as the monarchy and the church. It offers a glimpse into the world the taxi-driver, perhaps many taxi-drivers, do seem to inhabit – this one was sufficiently shaken by the incident to tell several of his subsequent passengers – in which a policeman can charge you for this form of 'insulting the flag'. Perhaps he also believes that it is an indictable offence to stick a stamp – 'The Queen's Head' – upside down on an envelope.

A television crew was making, in the Seventies, a film about Tunisian marriage customs. It entailed half an hour's filming after midnight on the last working day. The crew were booked to fly home in the early afternoon of the following day. The producer asked the crew if they were willing to do a half-hour shoot on that morning, to add what would have been a good final touch. He had to ask the crew's agreement because under union rules they were not required to start work until the afternoon if they had worked past the previous midnight; they could agree not to invoke that rule. All but one of the crew of five, four of them aged between thirty and forty, agreed. The fifth, the assistant sound-man, a taciturn youth of about twenty, refused, invoking the rule. The others caved in and the final touch was not made to the film.

There are two disturbing elements in such an encounter. Not the union rule; that was reasonable and could reasonably be waived. But the sight of four mature men simply yielding to the intransigence of one young man was unpleasant. Perhaps even worse was the thought that that young man had no care at all for the producer's (and what should have been his) professional integrity: no argument that the film was an interesting exploration of Tunisian culture, but was missing one tiny element, had the slightest meaning for him. He entirely lacked any professional sense. This, though small, was a chilling incident because so self-enclosed, self-regarding, implacable. Perhaps he eventually became, technically, a fully trained sound-man; he promised no more. Giotto would certainly not have asked him to hold the ladder.

Then, a scene in the bar at Surbiton station in the early Eighties. A man of about twenty-five is talking in a low but urgent voice to a slightly older man. The first face is foxy, the other weak. Quite soon the content of the talk becomes clear. The older man is a bar steward on InterCity. The young man is trying to persuade him to buy some very cheap hamburgers. That trick is an old one. The bent steward intersperses between his sales of British Rail hamburgers the cheap and nasty ones – not too often or the trick will be detected – but charging the customers well over a pound for hamburgers which have cost 20p is tempting. Small, low-level corruption; but the scene was memorable: Iago in the outer suburbs; the face of evil and the face of suggestibility.

Finally, and as contrast, a picture whose implications are so obvious that it has no suggestiveness, leads nowhere, simply leaves you thinking: 'That life can be so reduced to the basics!' – A young chambermaid in a New Delhi hotel offers to have sex with one of the guests for a pound. On being refused she offers to strip naked for 25p.

About forty years ago, a young critic remarked to Graham Greene that dreams occurred very often in his novels. 'Yes,' Greene answered, 'I find that I seem to need a good dream or two in almost all of them.'

So one could go on; such things are aspects of that larger element, that degree of surprise at being partly led by forces below the level of recognition at the time. This most evidently occurs when a character may be said to have taken over from the author. In a celebrated passage D. H. Lawrence talked about the novelist trying to pin down his characters with a nail and of some characters' capacity to get up and walk away with the nail. E. M. Forster was also famously interested – it begins to seem as though many modern writers are – in the way characters can take over and assert their personalities against what their authors thought they were or should be. Something escapes, takes off and away on its own, is unplanned and fortuitous. Conrad again, in a letter to Cunninghame Graham; 'You must remember that I don't start with an abstract notion. I start with definite images.'

There may be no magic here. As one begins to put down what one thinks is known, hidden reserves of memory are tapped, elements forgotten or overlaid or concealed by self-censorship. The process of writing about such things in the controlled way one is happy to accept is not allowed to have its way; one is ineluctably led on and outwards by those hidden reserves and finds that the initial confidence, if confidence there was, is ill-founded.

One comes to value more highly than the controlled parts these elements over which there is no conscious or full control; perhaps because they are 'gratuitous', given. It would be incorrect to say that the hand 'flies over the paper' at such times; it certainly moves faster and feels more liberated and confident. The result can also seem more 'true', though one hardly knows what that means – perhaps it is a revelation that at bottom there is self-mistrust and never-ending acts of manoeuvring self-censorship. There is a little relief therefore, like that of a minor Dostoevskyan character who has been found out and, no matter how gently and understandably, been made to face the fact of his guilt; or at least to face what he really believes, beyond all the self-justifications.

A peculiar and unique engagement with language and a peculiar and unique engagement with experience; a responsible, unimposed, skilled and crafty, but free and perhaps perverse act of creating; these are among the writer's necessary tools; gifts. Such a preliminary attempt at a definition does not necessarily imply an overt moral purpose. Nor does it in any way give second place to the need for literature to give pleasure; the definition of pleasure has not, though, to rest in the trivial. Nor does it remove from creative writing the importance of poise – poise which can hide or appear to hide a mischievous or immoral or morally disavowing sense. Sterne or, in a very different way, Proust are not to be marked down, whatever their apparent stances before life (not that they are likely to be set aside today, both having been appropriated as fathers of post-modernism); at the end both of them are subject to similar considerations as those brought to Meredith. The web, the texture, the fabric is iridescent and all its sheens can be revealing as well as enjoyable. Lawrence rightly called the novel 'the one bright book of life', and the word 'bright' has many meanings there.

A game of knowledge

To set up as a critic is to set up as a judge of values. For the arts are inevitably and, quite apart from any intention of the artist, an appraisal of existence. Matthew Arnold, when he said that poetry is a criticism of life, was saying something so important that it is constantly overlooked. The artist is concerned with the record and perpetuation of the experiences which seem to him most worth having.

I. A. Richards

Richards is in one sense right, but would not have denied that from another angle literature – art – is gratuitous, free, unnecessary, a kind of play quite different from the 'group play and fun' often promoted today – from communal finger-painting of each other's faces to many higher-level childishnesses; all in the name of 'The Arts'. Whatever the current fashion, no one *has* to practise an art, nor other people to approve of one's efforts, or be willing to pay the artist for exercising them.

There are several kinds of proposed justifications for literature and each satisfies some people. No one else has to believe them. Nor do any of them in themselves, except to the determinably ideological, justify making artists into pensioners whether of the State or of any other body or person. It is better to say, until forced to say otherwise, that 'Art makes nothing happen' (Auden, of course). In this context that word 'gratuitous', liberated from its restricted modern use, comes into its own again; and wealthy patrons at least can still give away as much as they want to whomever they want.

In some countries the belief that art is necessary because socially valuable has become so publicly accepted that the authorities have agreed that artists should be kept by the State. The Netherlands, for example, ruled that artists recognised by their peers should have at least some of their work each year bought by the State. Stuff piled up in cellars. The recession of the late-Eighties has, it is said, reined in that munificence.

Art is free, gratuitous, unnecessary and unavoidable, if you are driven that way; as unavoidable as breathing and equally personal in its inception. You owe it to no one, owe no one anything; nor do they owe you anything. When you have finished writing one book you may be given a small respite, or you may engineer one by immersing yourself in the temporary, the immediate, the relatively trivial; almost anything will serve as excuse for not starting another. But the tiny pain will not altogether go away; and then at some moment it becomes a foetus growing all the time and not to be denied. This feeling of not being entirely in control of something to which you may eventually be required to give birth is different from the sensation given by meeting an external commission, no matter how prestigious any particular commission may seem, or how well you come to think you have fulfilled it. This is yours, has to be yours.

Some people, though often in a vague and easy way, simply assume that this personal and individual process is common, even normal, in the writing of poetry. Almost as many will assume it for fiction, but fewer again for drama since that is regarded as sooner or later a collective or corporate act. This unspoken grading of creativity by genre reaches its lowest level in attitudes towards autobiography and all kinds of discursive writing. But there is no real difference of kind. Those last two forms can be as little under fully conscious control as poetry and fiction, can require not only close observation but also controlled impressionism, the need to find a natural order or organic shape, and the willingness to be led by memories, insights, images you had not till then known you had.

Another modern fallacy about 'The Arts' is best looked at when standards are being discussed. Here one need only say that to write interestingly one has to have something to say, and that that in turn will only be released if you have worked hard on how to say it, and also if you have some degree of 'gift' for moving within your peculiar medium, language. Strange that such simple truths should be so often and so widely rejected nowadays.

Patterns

Life is very nice, but it has no shape. The object of art is actually to give it some and to do it by every artifice possible – truer than the truth.
Jean Anouilh, The Rehearsal 1950

Art is the imposing of a pattern on experience, and our aesthetic enjoyment is recognition of the pattern.
A. N. Whitehead, (10 June 1943) Dialogues, 1954

Art that has not found its natural order, unnatural though that order may sometimes seem, is often but not always a sort of renegade art. Some artists push out the boundaries of their particular disciplines by creating new conceptions of order; as, in this century Joyce, Eliot, Beckett, Pinter. But somehow, somewhere, order, shape, coherence there will be, even in the denial of coherence; like an invisible net holding together what would otherwise be fragments, meaningless bits; or odd flashes of imaginative lightning.

Arriving at a shape, even on the run, is a form of control, or suggests control. It inevitably orders, weighs; and so can begin to suggest more than an internal or aesthetic coherence alone. It can suggest a harmony, even though harmony may seem an odd word to describe, say, the endings of *King Lear* or *Othello*. Harmony may not mean 'happy' it may just as well mean 'Call no man happy'. Perhaps better to say that an achieved harmony is always reaching out to at least hint at a meaning; a meaning which, yet again, the writer may not know he is reaching after until the work is done; or until a reader points it out; and which he may not like once it becomes or is made clear.

It can seem as though this tense and fragile, this just 'held' order can be a sort of comfort, close to what Dr Johnson and Trollope's Duke of Omnium meant when they spoke of literature as 'consolation' (see the quotation at the head of section ii). It has seemed to suggest order out of disorder and chaos, even whilst recognising the reality of chaos, its inescapability and continuance. So it can become a shelter from the horror of disordered, unordered reality. In this light one can begin to understand what Nietzsche may have meant when he said: 'We have art that we may not perish from the truth.'

Knowledge

The argument is moving steadily away from the idea of art as 'play'; one has begun to talk, no matter how tentatively, of art as at least hinting at coherence and meaning. This is where the elements of an apparent conflict can be brought together, and possibly resolved. In a typically clever aphorism, Auden described literature as 'a game of knowledge'. To anyone teased by the apparent separation of those two elements – 'gratuitousness' and 'meaning' – which it nevertheless seems essential to hold together, Auden's four words can be a small revelation; they click together the most difficult elements in that part of the jigsaw. Art is play, but serious play. Art is about knowledge, but the knowledge can only be apprehended through the play. The artist and the individuals who come to his work might be as it were abstracted, committing a higher form of doodling, playing around, not apparently going anywhere; or, conversely, totally preoccupied with one little bit of a tapestry whose whole shape and pattern they cannot yet see, which is probably not yet seeable because still inchoate, still emerging.

Another of Auden's apophthegms makes the same point as the one above but is jollier and more American. A work of literature is 'a contraption with a guy inside it'. That too brings together the idea of the craftiness of art, of art presenting itself first as an act of deliberate skill; and also of art as a created object which has someone inside it, a personality engaged with more than craft, with experience and meaning.

iv ACADEMIC RESPONSES: MEANING AND MODERN THEORY

At least be sure that you go to the author to get at his meaning, not to find yours.

John Ruskin, *Sesame and Lilies*, 1865

Never trust the artist. Trust the tale.
D. H. Lawrence, *Studies in Classic American Literature*, 1923

How can we ever come to an understanding if I put in the words I utter the sense and value of things as I see them, while you who listen to me must inevitably translate them according to the conception of things each one of you has within himself.

Luigi Pirandello

There is no such thing as intrinsic merit.

Stanley Fish

Professor Fish is a clever man and incorrigibly jokey, especially when he is making an interesting and useful point by exaggeration. His followers tend to take his extrapolations as truisms, as in this extract:

Even if 'classics' of Eurocentric literature were not oppressive in content, granting them a 'privileged' place in the literary canon would violate the central precept of such modern literary theories as deconstructionism and reader-response criticism that no work is inherently more valuable than any other (an entirely circular argument – 'classics' which don't fit prior theory may be discarded.)

[Deconstructionism] is the philosophy that makes the reader more important than the author, placing the interpretation higher than the text. That word text *is central; in the old days, a flesh-and-blood author created a work; nowadays, a critic studies a stand-alone text. Deconstructionism is a way of analyzing literature [and popular culture, the mass media, etc.] by denying the traditional meanings of words, breaking their links with real things and insisting that they have significance only in relation to other words or signs. Author's intent, agreed upon meanings of words, historic or cultural settings – all go by the board.*

William Safire

The attempt to distinguish between good, bad and indifferent work in specific practices is, when made in full seriousness and without the presumption of privileged classes and habits, an indispensable element of the central process of conscious human production.

Raymond Williams

Ruskin's courteous reminder of the initial duty of a reader is not denied by Lawrence's warning. Both are valid; the attempt to read as the author intended and the recognition that the work may, probably will, have meanings hidden from the author in the writing. Pirandello's character is asking for at least the Ruskinian initial courtesy. Safire's satire is aimed at the furthest fringes of modern 'literary' theory. Williams's remark should be a caution to those who see and use him as an unqualified 'cultural-materialist' critic.

It had best be said straight away, and with no wish to straddle the fence in an 'on the one hand, on the other . . . much to be said on both sides' placatory posture, that modern literary theories can illuminate works of literature at all levels; it will not do to react against them as forms of intellectual wilfulness by people who appear unable to read a poem or novel or play, 'straight'. Some but not the most subtle critics certainly give an impression of people who have little imaginative responsiveness to language and who could apply their complicated intellects just as well to computer programming as to literature, and probably more relevantly. Applications of modern theory to 'popular culture, the mass media, etc.' can be more obviously made and have been eagerly applied.

Literary Studies within universities has always been an insecure discipline. At the turn of the century various kinds of linguistics were added as roughage. Other stiffeners (morals before art, Marxism) have followed; deconstructionism and its siblings are the latest.

'Cultural materialism' can lead astray, as Raymond Williams points out above, but is inherently less Laocoön-like than the attitudes Safire is satirising. Its most common limiting factor is insensitivity to tone. George Eliot's plangent observations on the ensuing life of Dorothea, in the final paragraph of *Middlemarch*, provides a good instance:

> Her finely-touched spirit had still its fine issues, though they were not widely visible. Her full nature . . . spent itself in channels which had no great name on the earth. But the effect of her being on those around her was incalculably diffusive: for the growing good of the world is partly dependent on unhistoric acts; and that things are not so ill with you and me as they might have been, is half owing to the number who lived faithfully a hidden life, and rest in unvisited tombs.

An academic cultural materialist claimed that this passage expressed George Eliot's sense of how women were thwarted by the political restrictions of mid-nineteenth-century England. He did not say whether he meant that George Eliot was consciously expressing regret at those inhibitions or that the regret, thwartedness, showed itself without her being aware of it. The second seems unlikely, with George Eliot. The preceding paragraph does remark on how a 'young and noble impulse' – *always*, is implied, though she does not have to say that – has to struggle against the conditions of 'an imperfect social state'. It is possible, if reductive, to interpret that as a direct comment on the position of women in early Victorian England; but not so with the great final paragraph. There, George Eliot meant much more. That critic has lost the search for 'a significant past' so as to interpret what parts of the past he wants for his own purposes. 'Cultural materialism' can reveal by how much writers can be conditioned by their societies. But it can also overestimate conditioning; and its limitations are best revealed in the capacity of some major writers to break out into a free, often surrealist, image-driven world which cannot by any means be explained in socio-materialist terms.

More important is the difference in tone between the penultimate and the final paragraph of *Middlemarch*. The penultimate paragraph is typical of George Eliot's controlled tone for intellectual discourse. Her final paragraph sings; its song belongs to the world of Gray's 'Elegy' and of 'Who sweeps a room as for Thy laws/Makes that and the action fine.' It is a poem in praise of the un-self-seeking, quiet life devoted to others, and has behind it the full weight of George Eliot's enormous respect for such lives, in whatever country or generation or social conditions they are lived. To override tone to that degree so as to make an ideological point is deeply mistaken.

*

From the more detachedly theoretic critics one is likely to hear that any reading of a book and so any assertion of its value in comparison with that of any other work is a self-induced error; all books are invented and reinvented and variously invented by their readers, usually to satisfy whatever may need to be satisfied in those readers' imaginations; such matters cannot be discussed in universal or external or comparative or evaluative terms. Here, though at a different intellectual level, these self-referring critics themselves become part of that relativist disposition whose different expressions run throughout this book. If discussion about books comes down to what each different reader makes of each different book, then the literary-intellectual world also has become entirely relativistic; the high-powered literary analyst, detached from meaning, is in the same self-referring room as the most raucous populist for 'The Arts'.

However, A. A. Berger has noted that:

Some critics now argue that there are 'preferred readings' and that it is not quite 'everyone for himself or herself' when it comes to interpreting and understanding texts. This preferred reading is not necessarily what the creators of the text had in mind, I should point out. (Authors, critics argue, don't understand what they are doing and how they did it; if they did, they could write a short essay at the end of each work and we wouldn't need all the literary critics and media analysts we have.)

So a good point – 'never trust the teller, trust the tale' – is distorted to support the negation of any intentional meaning, and to reinforce the authority of those assumed to be qualified to define 'preferred readings'; unless that's meant to be done by a show of hands; or perhaps it harks back to the importance of the common opinion of intelligent lay-readers.

Endless different readings of any text of subtlety are always possible. Many, not all, are useful; no one reading is exhaustive, and we must each be prepared to defend those we arrive at and to modify them if necessary. Some current theorists live in a different world from that invoked by the celebrated Leavisian formulation; that, after a mutual, sustained and close attention to a text, one might hope to arrive at a point where it is possible to say. 'This is so, is it not?' Anyone present has the right to answer: 'Yes,' or 'Well, actually, no.' But the very fact of being willing to sit down before the text and undergo such a process and to ask the 'This is so?' question implies the possibility of a shared significant past and the meaningfulness of the search for 'true judgment' outside ourselves, which can also be shared.

Berger continues:

Some critics describe the controversy over semiotics and reconstruction in terms of two competing theories – 'God's Truth' and 'Hocus-Pocus'. The 'God's Truth' notion is that semioticians and those doing culture studies find what is hidden in texts and thus reveal what is there. The 'Hocus-Pocus' notion is that semioticians and others create ingenious structures which they 'read into' texts and this criticism is, essentially, 'Hocus-Pocus' or, in other words, a sham.

Hence all statements such as these become irrelevant, self-deceptions, meaningless; that 'great' works of literature supremely embody the meanings within cultures; that they perceptively and honestly explore and recreate the natures of societies and the experiences of human beings within them; that 'great' writing bears its meanings by creating orders within itself and so helps to reveal the orders of values within societies whether by mirroring them or by resisting them and proposing, usually obliquely, new orders; and so the expressive arts, and especially literature, are guides of a unique kind to the value-bearing nature of societies. And so on, through all such old-hat but burr-like claims.

And so on also through the memory of all those moments in literature which have seemed most strongly to speak about the terms of human life; Dostoevsky's Grushenka remembering her one supreme act of human pity, in dreaming of giving a damned soul her one onion; his Aloysha waking in the chill, unloving atmosphere of the police station and saying: 'I've had a good dream, gentlemen'; and his Ivan Karamazov giving back to God his entrance ticket to life because he cannot accept a God who will allow children to suffer horribly and meaninglessly. Or Jane Austen's Emma on Box Hill having to face the realisation of her own insensitivity; Melville's Queeqweg looking down into the whale nursery; George Eliot's Mrs Bulstrode facing her husband after his corruption has been revealed; Lawrence's Will and Anna Brangwen lost in rapturous love in the honeymoon cottage. Or Cordelia responding with 'No cause, no cause' to Lear's request for her forgiveness; Lear refusing to believe that Cordelia is dead; Hardy's Tess baptising her baby in the cottage bedroom; the distraught father of the dead Bazarov in Turgenev's *Fathers and Sons* raising his hands in fury to heaven:

> 'I declare that I protest, that I protest, that I protest!' . . . Upon that, old Arina Vlasievna, suffused in tears, laid her arms around his neck, and the two sank forward upon the floor. Said Anfisushka later, when relating the story in the servants' quarters: 'There they knelt together – side by side, their heads drooping like those of two sheep at midday.'

That is only one quick cull of prose memories, 'touchstones'; poetry is even more fecund.

Works of literature, even those traditionally thought most tower-ing, can in a certain sense be 'taken apart', and in many different ways. But the process bears no relation to taking apart an engine, no matter how complicated. It is of a different order; so much so that the very metaphor of 'taking apart' cannot, if it is used of an engine, be also used of a complex work of literature. The image of the dissecting table rather than of the engine-shed is nearer the nature of the process. It is a living body which is on the table, one endlessly pored over but never actually cut, except perhaps by surgeons who have the exceptional power to put back the living tissue so that the body is whole again; or, better, the body sits up and jumps off the table after the operation.

Two useful and articulate guides to this large and confused debate are Bernard Bergonzi's *Exploring English: Criticism, Theory, Culture* (1990) and Valentine Cunningham's *In the Reading Gaol* (1994). Laurence Lerner provides a good epilogue in *Reconstructing Literature* (1983). He is discussing the relationship between Lydgate and Rosamund Vincy in *Middlemarch*, and quotes this 'wonderful passage':

> Our passions do not live apart in locked chambers, but, dressed in their small wardrobe of notions, bring their provisions to a common table and mess together, feeding out of the common store according to their appetite.

Rosamund, in fact, was entirely occupied, not exactly with Tertius as he was in himself, but with his relation to her; and it was excusable in a girl who was accustomed to hear that all young men might, could, would be, or actually were in love with her, to believe at once that Lydgate could be no exception. Lerner comments:

> She is totally unaware of anything about the man except his conformity to the image. . . . There is a difficult art of realism of which George Eliot is one of our great masters. The critic who believes that literature has not signified because it consists solely of the play of signifiers may be as obtuse as Rosamund, who did not believe that Lydgate has any existence outside the image she had fitted him to.

Literature exists before anyone approaches it; it is not given life by its readers, though they can find and respond to the life within it, and help others to respond to it also.

V LITERARY INFLUENCES

The central function of imaginative literature is to make you realise that other people act on moral convictions different from your own.

William Empson

As with so much in these parts, nothing is provable about the influences and effects of literature; or of the arts as a whole. But much has been written, though nowhere near as much as on television's effects; and with differing degrees of conviction, especially according to period and culture.

It is easy to identify three main groups. First those, mostly from the last century, who were sure that art does have effects and that those effects can be generally for the good (that even very gifted art may have bad results is rarely broached – Beardsley and a few around his time are typical exceptions; and art addressed to 'the lower orders' tends to be sniffed at for subversive tendencies of many kinds).

Second are those, mainly in this century, who believe that art has no effects; or that if it does, they are random and unmeasurable; or even that the very question is idiotic. They alternate between scorn and a nervousness towards those who still think, hope, try to show that to talk about effects is not misguided nonsense. The third group do not have the Victorian assurance but wish they could say that art does have effects and that they are predominantly for good; but these people are few.

Among those who had few doubts are some of the weightiest of the weighty pre-Victorians and Victorians, who could speak thrillingly on the theme. So Byron, slightly surprising, in *Childe Harold's Pilgrimage*, III, 6.

> 'Tis to create, and in creating live
> A being more intense that we endow
> With form our fancy, gaining as we give
> The life we image . . .

That's an exceptionally packed prescription: an act of creation which makes one's own life lived more intensely; by gathering fancies together through finding a form, a shape, an order. Thus, as we create that artistic life and find that order, we begin ourselves to incorporate both in our own lives.

In his *Autobiography*, Charles Darwin was lucid on what he had lost by neglecting literature, especially poetry, in his intense pursuit of science: 'The atrophy of that part of the brain alone, on which the higher faculties depend' – this because his mind had become 'a machine for grinding general laws out of large collections of facts . . .'; but no poetry, no music. So he invokes a direct connection between the reading of literature – but good literature, of course, literature which makes a just demand on the attention of an intelligent and serious person – and the health of the higher faculties; which one may infer are the imagination, the sympathetic consciousness, a wide responsiveness of thought and feeling towards the world, experience, other people, ones' own vagaries. The most impressive aspect of that statement is its magisterial humility before itself. You have to be a very big human being, especially after a life of such monumental achievements as Darwin's, to show such modesty.

No less impressive was John Stuart Mill in his *Autobiography* (1873):

> What made Wordsworth's poems a medicine for my state of mind was that they expressed, not mere outward beauty, but states of feeling, and of thought coloured by feeling, under the excitement of beauty. They seemed to be the very culture of the feelings, which I was in quest of.

That too is a remarkable statement: poems as medicine for the mind, as healing. And there is the confidence of the language before the progress of the mind itself, the assured precision of movement between 'beauty' (about whose definition there is no doubt) and the 'states of feeling' induced by beauty, and so (the next stage) of thought then coloured by those feelings which have been first excited by beauty. There is a complex pocket-aesthetics here. To a reader who knows, say, *The Prelude*, it is also an exact and enlightening network of observations on Wordsworth's poetry and on how, as Mill believed, fine poetry works on us; its relation to, in that striking phrase, 'the culture of the feelings'.

Matthew Arnold made it his special business to explore – more accurately, to assert – the relations between culture, and especially literature, and the intellectual and imaginative life. At this point one of his many well-known assertions will serve: '[The business of culture/literature] it to turn a stream of fresh and free thought upon our stock notions and habits.'

Who would write like that today, who would dare? Even those who try to make a searching case in favour of the arts and their possible influences sound muted before these earlier organ voices. Others, as we have seen, sound like amplified electric guitars; or like accountants or marketing men settling for the hard-nosed position and talking about the financial resources the arts can extract from natives and tourists, thus reducing the arts to glossy consumption. The searching case goes by default; there is always a smart and totally confident arts journalist, such as the one who tossed off the fancy that 'the idea that the arts can have a recognisable spiritual value is now decidedly quaint'.

Still, some modern or modernish writers, less cavalier than the arts journalist but roughly on his side because they doubt the value of most talk about influences, can be tonic and challenging because uninflated, ungrand, unrhetorical. They ask for more and better evidence, if not absolute proof, that influences of that sort can be found in literature, outside what particular people may choose to father on particular works; they see nothing of general, transferable validity. Again, a form of relativism, but a more respectable one than usual.

Somewhere between the Eminent Victorians and the Modern Scepticals stands the philosopher and mathematician A. N. Whitehead: 'The canons of art are merely the expression in specialised form of the requirements for depth of experience' (*Dialogues*). The most interesting word there is 'merely', and one wonders why it has been inserted. The whole sense of the sentence suggests that the 'merely' is not meant to be reductive; there is nothing reductive about something – 'the canons of art' – which expresses what 'depth of experience' requires. Perhaps Whitehead is saying: 'Art is important – that is obvious – but please don't set it up as superior to philosophy; both seek to express the nature of "depth of experience" and each has its canons; the "canons of art" are only one specialised form for expressing the attempt to understand those depths.' If this is so, modern differences from the grand utterances of the Victorians become even clearer, but in a writer such as Whitehead less extreme. Whitehead's voice is almost tart and certainly clipped, a very Oxbridge voice but a voice which echoes those monumental Victorians in the sense that it is still willing to use such phrases as 'depths of experience', recognises that there are such depths and that they have to be swum within.

I. A. Richards also had one of the Oxbridge voices of his time and great firmness of expression (but we need to remember that both he and Whitehead wrote in the first half of the twentieth century, when it was much easier to express assurance of belief and when the vocabulary of belief was still just to hand. As in the passage from Richards quoted earlier in this chapter: 'an appraisal of existence . . . the record and perpetuation of the experiences which seem to him most worth having'. Not the sonority of the Victorians; rather the confidence of a somewhat didactic lecturer; but nearer to Victorian utterance than to the language, tone, conviction readily available at the end of this century.

All of those quoted above regarded art as one of the most important forms of insight into the nature of the experiences we all live through (but which few of us much think about, being preoccupied with enjoying life or with just going on going on). Browning is the most direct of all when he speaks of art as 'The one way possible/ Of speaking truths, to mouths like mine at least' (*The Ring and the Book*). That final qualification rings oddly. A natural end would have come at 'speaking truths'. Why did Browning feel the need to add those last six words? They sound slightly nervous, as though he is saying: 'You may not agree, you may think me odd in believing this, but so it is.' Such words recall that common modern, face-saving phrasing (which will be seen in action in Chapter 12), following some usually tentative statement of conviction: 'Well, that's only my opinion.' But that's hardly Browning's style. Of course, the clause makes a nicely rounded poetic close; it is still puzzling because not worth the rounded effect.

*

Something has already been said about 'deafness' to words and literature, but it is obviously relevant again, when one speaks about effects. The effects of literature are intensely difficult to assess, even on those who are responsive; perhaps unassessable, even though some readers may feel that some effects 'stand to reason', to the 'truth' of the imagination. Matthew Arnold, with no more than the qualifier 'tend', could be sure of this:

> Good poetry does undoubtedly tend to form the soul and character; it tends to beget a love of beauty and of truth in alliance together; it suggests . . . high and noble principles of action, and it inspires the emotions so helpful in making principles operative. Hence, its extreme importance to all of us.

Phew! Would that we could accept that with an alacrity equal to his conviction.

One cannot say that to respond fully to George Herbert or Byron is somehow thereafter and by a kind of osmosis to be a more sensitive person. Everyone knows dreadful people who are more informed about and apparently responsive to literature (or music) than they themselves are. At this point Hitler's admiration for Wagner's music is usually invoked. Yet no one knows what he took from Wagner, in what ways Wagner moved him. Perhaps he extracted from Wagner, through the mill of his own distorted mind, reinforcements for those distortions. It is easy to think of passages in Wagner which could have moved Hitler but would hardly have contributed to his greater humane sympathy.

Or here is a scene from the mid-Seventies. Mme Furtseva, the iron Minister of Culture for the Soviet Union, was attending a United Nations conference of European Ministers of Culture in Helsinki. The Leningrad Symphony Orchestra had been flown over to give a concert of which the highlight was one of Tchaikovsky's later symphonies. It was played with a charismatic inwardness one did not remember hearing from Western orchestras. At the end Mme Furtseva leaned back, presumably to say something about the brilliant performance. Her eyes were brimming with tears. This was the woman who, in Beria's day, had seen or connived at more than one man being shot dead, in the dank cellars of the Lubyanka, with a bullet to the back of the neck.

So one makes fumbling steps towards shoring up fragments of an understanding of the arts' relations with our inner characters. Beginning with the thought that if you have been lucky enough to have access to great literature it is difficult to imagine what your consciousness would have been like without that experience. This does not mean that you go around quoting T. S. Eliot.

It means – perhaps as a protection one should say 'can mean' – that your mind is informed by the knowledge that things wider and deeper than you have guessed, as well as reflections of your own mundanity, exist in the world and that you have been made privy to them. They have 'taken you out of yourself', 'sought you out', allowed you to 'see the world differently', if only at intervals; taken you out of your temporal, routine, boring self; and this seems humbling and enlarging and is certainly gratifying because a kind of relief. You have been offered a fuller sense of the possibilities – the depths, heights, complexities, ambiguities, disorders, strivings for order – within human life. The passage from Empson quoted at the head of this section is relevant here. You have been offered an analogical or symbolic exploration, in itself absorbing and beautiful but also seeming to point beyond itself, one which challenges your tendency always to narrow life to the predictable, repeatable and contingent. It thereafter seems hard to imagine what your mental landscape, your intellectual and imaginative sub-soil, would have been like without those new hand-holds and muscles. You wish many others could have that access.

To which some will respond: 'How can they feel starved if they don't know what they are missing? They seem perfectly content.

Don't be a cultural do-gooder, paternalistic if not even patronising.'
Back to square one, then, in the mental perspective of this horizontal
world. 'Fraternity' might be a better word than 'patronising', to
indicate the sense of doing all in our power to help open the way
to that world for others.

Another observation, obliquely related to that above. Compare the
'correct' view of the nature of the Russian character and temper as
they are presented in orthodox Soviet literature with that gained
from other Russian literature, from Turgenev to Solzhenitsyn. The
one is composed of ideologically sound cardboard cut-outs, the other
presents portraits in the round, paintings in oils, which both illuminates the nature of that hugely imaginative race, and also makes one
of the most enduring contributions to the understanding of human
experience through literature, from anywhere and any time.

All the above are guesses, and none suggests that the reading of
good literature has a direct influence on action. More sure is the fact
that a direct result would be unlikely and even undesirable. If we
were so simply changed, life itself would be greatly simpler. We
would have been subject not to a willing or willed change but to a
form of mind-control, which could be reproduced endlessly from our
childhoods onwards. That would be absurd. It is natural to think
that some children are brutalised through being brought up by brutal
parents. Even that, no matter how brutal the experience, is not
automatic; some children take a different lesson. So do some children
brought up in an atmosphere of loving care and thoughtfulness
towards others. How much more tentative must be the assumptions
about the influence of great works of literature, works which are not
so direct, nor so day-to-day, as relations with others, and which have
to be in some subtle sense translated into action; if the reader is so
disposed.

That 'if the reader is so disposed' holds the key. Each reader must
decide, and the decision may be conscious or submerged, to be
influenced in conduct by the illuminations art can bring. If it were
otherwise, more an automatic process, there would be no free-will.
However intense, subtle, sophisticated, morally alert the response to
literature, we are still, and should insist on being, free to take note
but no more, to be influenced thereafter or not, to define our own
fates. Much the same must be true of the artists themselves. Auden
used to say he had known three great artists who were dreadful
human beings. Great artists may be able to produce sublime music
or poetry, or descriptions of character and relationships which move

beyond all else in one's indirect experience; but they may be in their private lives appalling.

To put more fully something suggested earlier: why should it be assumed, as is common, that the influence of great art must be redemptive? Frank Kermode remarks: 'We are in love with the idea of fulfilment, and our interpretations show it.' Precisely. We are also aware of, can be in love with, the void, the emptiness; as through, in modern writers, Kafka and Beckett. Why should any reader not decide that the Devil or Edmund or Iago shall be the chosen men, those who act villainously and refuse to be reconstructed? 'Now God stand up for bastards'; 'Simply the thing I am shall make me be'. Those are proud and impressive statements, from a moral universe much profounder than that of low-level villainy.

The best one can do, the most one can say, is not that art certainly does influence us, whether for good or ill; but that it may, according to its own internal power and inclination, *stand available* to influence us if we so will.

'To stand available' is not a great thing to say and is, yet again, not provable; but it does both recognise the value of great art and preserve our own free-will. Even more; as a result of reading such books one may be more aware of having in some ways fallen short in human sympathy and so in virtue. It is good to have had such opportunities, to have been offered such insights with immediacy and texture into the nature of humanity and humane connections, the weight and fragility and tensile strength of life; to have glanced into our own whale-nursery.

CHAPTER FOUR

Angles on Mass and Popular Culture

Only two things the people anxiously desire, bread and circus games.
Juvenal, *Satires*, X, *c.* AD 100

Why, look you now, how unworthy a thing you make of me! You would play upon me; you would seem to know my stops; you would pluck out the heart of my mystery . . .
William Shakespeare, Hamlet to Rosencrantz and Guildenstern

None can love freedom heartily but good men. The rest love not freedom but licence.
John Milton, *The Tenure of Kings and Magistrates*, 1649

The public . . . lives in a perpetual turmoil of acquisition and consumption . . . All pleasures, even the theatre, are only supposed to distract . . .
Goethe writing to Schiller

Be interesting and weak like us, and we will love you as we love ourselves.
W. H. Auden, 'For the Time Being', 1944

I have to ask you to write very simply, given that our readers are cretins.
Features editor of a popular 'middlebrow' paper, inviting a review, 1994

Juvenal and Goethe express, unqualified, a common, a very old and a current disillusion. Auden does it through the mouth of Herod, the sophisticated but distraught ruler – but it was also his own view. The young yuppie tones of the features editor told his kind of selective truth. Milton is magisterially concise. To some degree all the others are selective, even Hamlet. But Hamlet's truth, though less often stated, is at least as reliable as the others'. After a long immersion in the muddy lake of mass culture we all tend to overemphasise its effects. Hamlet was a prince ticking off people beneath him; yet that kind of shrugging away can be found in people who otherwise might seem unquestioning consumers of mass culture. That's just a reminder before we dive in.

Mass culture as we know it is, in spite of de Tocqueville, Goethe, Arnold and the rest, substantially a product of the twentieth century. It is the foreseeable result of advanced communications technology, the general low level of literacy, available time and 'disposable income' for a great body of people in the more highly developed societies, and of the processes of capitalism – which bring all these together for profit – and, with them, persuasion. The whole ramifying operation is lubricated by persuaders, in public relations and advertising. They aim to create a world in which all are apparently amiably equal so long as they have something to spend, an all-embracing world by which and within which the money in the pocket is sucked out for the executives and shareholders.

Hence the label 'consumerism', which has by now been used so often and so loosely as to lose much of its force. It is in fact no less apposite today than when it was first minted; better than 'fetishisation of commodities'. If it did not exist one would have to invent it or a synonym. It points to an overwhelmingly self-justifying world. Technological advance is self-justifying; the profit motive is self-justifying to its operators. Give the people what the people want – so long as they can pay. Never mind the damage to less attractive but essential needs of this society, or of other societies which have neither the technology nor the money.

i CHARACTERISTICS OF MASS CULTURE

It is easy to list the main characteristics of mass culture. To begin with and at its most effective: talent and energy. You can't easily parody or plagiarise it, any more than best-selling romantic novels can be easily produced; you have to have a certain gift. Ian Fleming describing seduction in his James Bond novels has an eye and ear for the indirect approach. Do not describe the act head-on; describe its effect on the KGB agents filming it – the sweat running down their paper collars as they are aroused. Fleming was talented; others are not so gifted, but have an exploitative knack, simply to prejudge the tastes of their audience; the audience defines the object.

This produces the consistent, boneless, apparent good nature of much mass culture: its impulse is to be seductive at all times and costs. There has to be constant flattery, which can soon become a disguised or even unconscious low opinion of the audience to whom it is addressed. Above all, it must be valueless, must not take sides ¿ except in the simplest cops-and-robbers style; or when rejecting something which undermines populism.

Second, and almost as central: mass art has to exhibit intellectual, imaginative and moral horizontality; it thrives in a relativist world in which it would be fatal to admit differences.

Mass culture is partial, in two senses: it addresses itself to parts of our personalities only; and it expresses extremely partial attitudes, which it assumes will reflect our own prejudices. Defenders of mass culture, especially in the tabloid press, say: 'We must know just how to speak to people, to know what they are really like underneath or our product wouldn't sell in its millions. We don't misrepresent or misinterpret them. We mirror them and their outlooks.' Much of the time, perhaps. Their misreadings, though, can be considerable. After the long television interview with Prince Charles in mid-1994 most of the tabloids, confidently reading the runes, thumpingly predicted that their readers would on that evidence have decided he was not fit to be King. Perhaps they overestimated their readers' prudery, or underestimated their charity and tolerance. They were wrong.

Tabloid newspapers certainly appeal most of the time; they do to some extent 'mirror'. That is why Cecil King two or three decades ago was able to make his famous remark about the stupidity of his readers. Still, his *Daily Mirror* had little in common with the present effusion of that name, and not to the later one's credit. (H. L. Mencken's similar *obiter dicta* opines that no one ever lost money by underestimating the taste of the American public.) Cecil King has been described as a 'shy, lofty, self-embarrassing Wykehamist, honed in Christ Church, Oxford'. At least he had the frankness of his partial and partisan convictions. Most of us are *hommes moyens sensuels* and in that part of our beings are not at our most discriminating. If like Cecil King – himself rather patrician and a considerable supporter of a National Youth Orchestra – you take that part of our beings as a round picture of our personalities then you will produce your newspaper accordingly and receive an according echo back. But you have presented a distorted picture of the people for whom you claim to speak, neglecting some aspects of their personalities and extending others; these actions, taken together, result in a caricature.

To think the *Sun* represents the common norms of English working-class life is like assuming that low-budget, urban-violence American films represent life in the towns of the Midwest.

So mass culture selects and concentrates. It cannot be catholic except in the sense that relativism encourages a false catholicity; not the catholicity of a wide, responsive and discriminating mind, but that of a mind which has no edges. Partiality and spread; the contradiction is only apparent; partiality leads and decides how far and to what the spread shall go. In doing that it manipulates symbols and icons, which begin to look like shared values.

Mass culture has a very short breath, it has to be successive, to move on always and restlessly. It can rarely stay with any subject, even if that subject is, on a more careful view, very important and in need of longer attention. Hence the addiction to jerky, short-breath trivia; 'word-bites' to match television's 'sound-bites': instant gratifications. Television advertisements must assume a very short attention span. Air time is costly so the message must be punched home quickly. It would be interesting to examine how far this relentless process feeds into and affects general programming.

Mass culture has to be predatory, like a small voracious creature whose belly has little capacity but can and must all the time and rapidly digest small items and as rapidly void them; or the world of a mouse on an endlessly revolving wheel. 'Not our kind of thing'; 'Dead. Yesterday's news.' (Even outsiders know that nothing is as dead as yesterday's news, especially in the tabloids. From those one doesn't put pages aside, for a careful later reading of a particular article. That would be like setting aside on Saturday a half-opened packet of salt-and-vinegar-flavoured crisps for your Sunday dinner.)

All the time this process seems, to those caught up in it, a set of objective decisions – 'judgments' – made according to the lights of an objective profession. Really it is a culturally and commercially enforced set of inhibitions or eggings-on.

Another only apparent paradox: short, short-term and instant breath can live with progressivism or, better, futurism. As so often, de Tocqueville in *Democracy in America* (1835–40) spotted it early: 'Democratic nations care but little for what has been [little historic sense or sense of tradition, except as manufactured nostalgia], but they are haunted by visions of what will be [futurism].' The futurism has no 'bottom' to it, very little sense of emerging improvement except in so far as that concerns objects and new consumer opportunities; it produces a world at once open and closed. Progressivism gives way to a bloodless futurism (see Chapter 15).

Mass culture is or always seeks to be communitarian, 'homey', bland, puritanical and at the same time sexually voyeuristic; it provides warm straw to huddle in. In most of the developed world it dislikes abstract things and especially 'issues' in themselves; it moves instantly to personalisation. When a major public figure is disgraced, especially on a sexual matter, little attention is given to the public implications of such a scandal, much to the intimate details of the sexual fall. So common is this approach that we take it for granted. It is not universal. A successful editor of an English tabloid was, some years ago, sent to establish a similar paper in an Anglophone African state. He came back soon, having failed. True to type, he personalised politics – which puzzled his African readers, who wanted him to talk about political issues not warts on noses. It was a Western European novelist, André Malraux, who described fiction as 'one of the happier consequences of the fall of man'. It was an Italian newspaper editor who asserted: 'The public does not want to know what Napoleon III said to William of Prussia. It wants to know whether he wore beige or red trousers and whether he smoked a cigar.'

So: wide-open, partly catholic, untethered. Yet mass culture is closely focused; but not on to anything that can be weighed or fitted into a structure of differing meanings and values. It focuses rather on what can be seen, measured ('assessed' would be an inappropriate word), market-researched; it focuses on existing taste. Yet there its role is a double one: it must first measure and then reflect existing taste or it will not capture audiences; so much is simple and obvious. That is the flattering side. It must also go further; it must in very restricted senses try to widen – no, that is the wrong word, as 'change' would also be – to extend existing taste in directions acceptable to the reader and also to the newspaper and its need to search for and hold readers; it must extend from the known base, ever so gradually and yet quickly enough to suggest novelty, newness. It must persuade its audiences that their existing tastes can be excitingly extended in these ways, and that all the people in the know are doing just that. A move has to be made equivalent to that of going from fish and chips towards hamburgers, from Tizer to Coke, from stout to Babycham; and to what will follow all those.

Thus the mirroring of existing taste and the extension from it on firmly defined lines are both part of another function; reinforcement.

Already narrow horizons are held tighter; within those narrow horizons images become bolder and more stubborn. This is a poor diet for a society which likes to claim it is healthily democratic but which many people find more alien year after year; less genuinely (rather than sentimentally) human; a society many of whose members, often without knowing it, feel themselves increasingly in the grip of massive, non-democratic, exterior forces which have their own self-sufficient agenda.

Processing demands something to process. So mass culture is parasitic. When some new form of popular art, however small (say, skiffle in the 1950s), comes up from outside the system, with its own particular and attractive elements, and when that new form does become very popular, then it is only a matter of time before the machines of mass culture take it over, create a simulacrum of it, one with increasingly machine-made elements, and flood the market. The original survives somewhere, tries to adapt itself, or is absorbed. Others will be along and will be also taken over. Today's equivalent of Tin Pan Alley (Denmark Street off Charing Cross Road) keeps its musical ear very close to the ground; and money very often talks.

Mass culture processes experience so that the customers don't catch troublesome fish-bones in their mental throats; things like that put people off. The products of mass culture must at first glance seem like the real thing. The colour is there and perhaps even something of the smell – that can be chemically introduced. Yet there is something altogether too bland, worked-over, made to slide down easily without snagging, about it – even in the permitted deviations and 'shocking' instances. It is the equivalent of, in food, processed cheese and tinned mushy peas (fish-shop flavour). Customer-content has to be manufactured on the widest scale and so must be shallow, like a flooded water-meadow.

Is all this at bottom hiding a dislike for the readers, the customers, the 'punters'? Sometimes. Sometimes openly and cynically. But matters can be less cut-and-dried. Some media people believe their own propaganda, their own exculpations and justifications; some really do believe they represent and speak for 'the common man'. Yet overall, a sort of near-hatred lies not far below the surface. It would otherwise be hard for the more aggressive door-steppers of the popular press to live with themselves. They do have in a certain sense to despise their audience; as you may learn from listening to conversations in their favourite bars. They deal, after all, in commodities produced for the mass market, and the business is cut-throat; since the competition is fierce – especially now from cable and satellite – you can't afford sentiment. So: become more and more 'sexy' (in the current wide sense), less and less substantial or subversive. These people are the lubricants to this kind of synthetic society; not out to tell truth but to keep these particular wheels turning by selling convenient images. It was admirable of the BBC for so long to refuse to have a PR office; by now that decision seems to belong to a very old-fashioned age.

The effort must always be to make everything touched part of the great conveyor belt, to make everything consumable, part of the world of 'disposables'; 'collectibles' are in the same world but another sector. Coming together the whole process forms what Blake called 'mind-forged manacles'; and heavy plastic manacles can be almost as hard to escape from as steel.

Yet, processed mass culture never quite succeeds in its object. Does it, then, lead to cynicism or, worse, to indifferentism in the customers? Sometimes but not always. 'People are not as daft ... etc.' The discrimination which makes them, though they may 'take' the *Sun*, look to the BBC for opinions on current affairs is only one heartening sign of that.

ii ELEMENTS OF POPULAR CULTURE

The existence of good bad literature – the fact that one can be amused or excited or even moved by a book that one's intellect simply refuses to take seriously – is a reminder that art is not the same thing as cerebration.
George Orwell (Richard Llewellyn's *How Green Was My Valley*, 1939, is a good example of Orwell's point)

The preceding few pages were enjoyable, at least for the writer. It's always pleasant to lay about you, especially with paradoxes and contrast: mass culture is machine-tooled, popular culture can be spontaneous; mass culture is processed, popular culture is live; mass culture is evasive, popular culture is honest; mass culture is conventional, popular culture is challenging; mass culture is falsely resolving, popular culture is exploratory; mass culture is stereotyped, popular culture is representative; mass culture is exploitative, popular culture is straight. That's neat, quite helpful, but far too hard at the edges, unqualified. Mass culture isn't quite that bad sometimes, and popular culture is only that good in parts and at times.

Look and listen more carefully, especially at mass culture, and qualifications set in. Good starting points for our better education are to be found in C. S. Lewis, T. S. Eliot, though by him in a broad-brushed way (the hints are suggestive), and of course Orwell. All three were writing thirty and more years ago, but few later writers have been so fruitful for the reader. All implicitly counsel more modesty. They counsel first, and especially Lewis, that to examine the question 'But what do people *do* with mass culture?' can lead to a rebuke to any feeling of intellectual superiority one may have enjoyed. They, particularly Orwell, counsel first sitting down patiently before the thing itself. Eliot too, for all his patrician manner, counsels openness to material of every kind, right across the culture.

C. S. Lewis's *An Experiment in Criticism* (1961) is unlike almost all his other books, and not immediately palatable to those who have learned much from Dr Leavis about modern culture (it is in part a broadside against Dr and Mrs Leavis). Lewis is remembered among scholars, intellectuals and the religious for other writings, and his Narnia stories are much read by children. His autobiographical *Surprised by Joy* inspired the play and film *Shadowlands*.

An Experiment in Criticism contains threaded insights of unusual value. Like most such insights they seem simple and self-evident, the kind of thing that anyone might have said if they had got round to it. They didn't, though, and only recognise them as true and import-ant when someone such as Lewis says: 'Look at it this way.' So one of his most suggestive perceptions was that readers may bring worthy impulses to trashy literature, good responses to poor fiction and poetry; that readers are not empty vessels into which anything can be poured, not people whose whole being is mirrored in the conven-tional sentimentalities of the time.

Trollope on Marie Melmotte in *The Way We Live Now* hit the point: 'The books she read, poor though they generally were, left something bright on her imagination.' R. P. Blackmur, a rather more sophisticated reader, made a related point, that we can learn some-thing from second- and third-rate work – so long as we supply our own irony towards it. You salt it yourself.

So far this does not seem a surprising idea. It has for years pene-trated and altered even the simpler early work on the effects of television. It is saying that people 'accept' mass art not as ciphers but as individuals already deeply imbrued within their culture, what-ever that culture may be; this protects them from a naked radiation of ideas and attitudes from the mass media.

Lewis went explicitly further: he said that readers (listeners, viewers, he would probably have said now) use, adapt, make their own, elements of mass art which they can cause to speak to them. Worthy impulses brought from mass culture do not alter that culture in itself; they have been raided so as to reinforce and validate existing attitudes. So what may strike a sophisticated reader as 'sentimental twaddle' about the importance of married fidelity – decked out in melodramatic situations and resolutions – may be filtered by less sophisticated readers so as to be a warm vindication that this is the way such things should rightly be. 'It is inaccurate to say that the majority "enjoy bad pictures". They enjoy the ideas suggested by bad pictures.' What has been written may be a mere representation of a feeling many, perhaps most, have. That does not necessarily make the feeling false. On the other hand, the writing may be doing no more than cosset the feeling; and that is a very difficult distinction. Once these ideas have begun to be looked at in this way they become more complex than they at first seem; one can go on teasing out their implications.

Lewis himself takes the insights further: 'The ideally bad book is one of which a good reading is impossible.' There are, he is saying, some works from which nothing of worth can be extracted, which are too dead to allow any live impulses to be inspired by them. He is not saying that all books are equally valuable. He puts on one and the same side (but values differently) objects of mass culture of which a good reading is impossible and others which can elicit a worthwhile reading. Elsewhere there are 'better books', books which could reasonably be called good art, not bad art capable of transmutations; they are different things altogether.

Lewis is not saying that there 'are no canonical texts'; or that 'all books have equal emblematic value'. He is saying: look carefully at much you are disposed simply to reject; you may find more in it than you had at first suspected; some people do: 'the *prima facie* case that anything which has ever been truly read [that word "truly" is a little worrying – he means, presumably, one which has been read openly not with a peg in the nose] and obstinately loved by any reader has some virtue in it, is overwhelming.' He is there accepting neither an adman's nor a contemporary literary relativist's approach to mass culture.

Approaches such as these can be applied to a wide range of mass art. To 'In Memoriam' verses in the newspapers, or to the most widely sold Christmas cards – ruddy-faced, *Pickwick Papers*-style coachmen driving past half-timbered inns in the snow; robins and holly and Christmas pudding; Jane Austen-ish fireside scenes. They appeal to existing sentimentalities and have done so for a long time; they are bought as a routine though often with a feeling that they are still saying something to us, something about a more liveable past.

Most people will not tell you what they draw from such things, from the books, the magazines, the cards, the verses; they have not had to articulate these elicited impulses. Given the right attitude, even an 'outsider' can go a long way towards understanding, or guessing he understands, what those impulses are. This is where Orwell is one of the best early guides: he shows in action the prime importance of sitting down before what it is the outsider is trying to 'read' (in more than one sense), putting aside any irritable reaching after fact and reason, listening to it – until it comes up to you, until you have at last the feeling 'Ah, now I see just what it is, see into complexities I had not suspected.' The novel has, in another phrase of C. S. Lewis, been 'reading us'. Undogmatic sensitivity and respect for the medium. Orwell's essay 'The Art of Donald McGill' is the test case here. It was in its time (it appeared in 1941) a revelation and should still be to younger people. Anyone entering into this kind of study, even a quite young post-graduate student, who does not see the revolutionary force of the Orwell essay in its day and the fundamental importance of its approach even today has much to learn.

Those saucy comic postcards used to appear on the rack outside newsagent's shops, especially at the seaside. They still do in some places, though now rather self-consciously and as reprints. Originals are collectors' items. We could do with an essay today on the main types of card sent home from the Costa Brava and Majorca.

At first glance the McGill cards seem trite and repetitive: here are the rather henpecked little middle-aged husbands, the nagging wives, the huge-bottomed mothers-in-law, the 'flappers' with neat bottoms and pert breasts, being covertly ogled when 'the missus' isn't looking. Here are all the old staples in smut, up to the legitimated limits: especially about those breasts and, rather more cautiously, about what's under the man's swimming costume, an all too quickly erect prick. It plays with – no more than that – what used to be the exciting and furtive idea of sex before marriage, of commercial-traveller Don Juans who know a willing one when they see her, or will have a go anyway.

There's the sometimes fairly witty wordplay: 'I've been struggling for years to get a fur coat. How did you get yours?' 'I left off struggling.' (The phrasing is of its time: predatory males expecting to have to overcome resistance, girls protecting their treasure.)

Orwell took all that in his stride and neither glamorised nor patronised it. He saw below the conventional images and jokes to what they were bedded in. He listed the conventions: the firm place of marriage even though husbands might strain against the ropes; the constant and accepted irritations of married life; the release for men through booze and the fools they then make of themselves; the stock paraphernalia – chamber pots, lamp-posts for drunks to lean against and dogs to pee on, bowler hats which blow off embarrassingly, even more embarrassingly Scotsmen's kilts and the wind, the sexual appetites of honeymoon couples (there is a complementary range of dirty jokes about that, of which the best known is the one ending: 'The sculptors of Rome with their tools in their hands'). Behind it all is the implication of 'a stable society in which marriage is indissoluble and family loyalty taken for granted'.

So Orwell is able to end:

> In the past the mood of the comic post card could enter into the central stream of literature, and jokes barely different from McGill's could casually be uttered between the murders in Shakespeare's tragedies. That is no longer possible, and a whole category of humour, integral to our literature till 1800 or thereabouts, has dwindled down to these ill-drawn post cards . . . The corner of the human heart that they speak for might easily manifest itself in worse forms.

Orwell's importance is just here: that before he wrote that essay, and 'Raffles and Miss Blandish', it was normal to dismiss all plainly unintellectual and unselfconscious material as undifferentiated, to be lumped together and put aside as what working-class people read. Orwell's strength is that he looked openly, honestly, with sympathy but not sentimentally, at material of that kind; he did not indulge in *nostalgie de la boue*, cultural slumming (the other face of culture-vulturing), the pretence of being an Hon. Member of a metaphorical working men's club; nor did he snigger or express superiority or dismay. He was firm and often puritanical, but charitable; he looked and listened without preconceptions. He 'read' the postcards beyond and below a surface reading or looking. Without that there is the risk of an unbridgeable distancing, or a custard of unlegitimated total acceptance.

This is an extremely difficult feat of both the intellect and the imagination. Without it readers may not 'know' those postcards; they may be gliding across the surface, perhaps making clever remarks culled from prior knowledge of a theory, perhaps keeping a moral distance, perhaps rejecting the relevance of any moral comment. What will then not happen is what did happen to Orwell: the meanings of the postcards will not begin to rise before the reader, to offer themselves as if to say: 'Look, this is what we are like, what we are, inwardly. This is our real being. You have begun to feel through to what we are underneath.'

If that stage is reached one will have earned the right to an ending as straightforwardly humane, as magisterial-without-seeming-magisterial, as that of Orwell. It is worth a few years of that sitting down before even 'mass art' to get there.

Nowadays the second attitude described above – not establishing a sympathetic but controlled distance, but jumping straight into the pool of mass culture with a glad cry (just one of the chaps) – is more common. A study of a very popular television soap opera which is most of the time contrived, uninventive, and so finally patronising, may be approached in so anxious a way – prompted by the fear of seeming élitist – that such analytic tools as the student may have are blunted from the start. There is then little possibility of cutting through the routine material to the point where real questions can be asked about such programmes and their undoubted attractions, to where the viewers are being neither dismissed nor patronised.

*

In the gallery of twentieth-century 'condition of England' writing, T. S. Eliot might seem an outsider, an intruder. He tends to be dismissed today; a classicist, a monarchist, a high churchman. Even *Notes Towards the Definition of Culture* (1948) is assumed to have little if anything to teach contemporary students of this society. It is in fact one of the best challenges we can meet if we belong to those who would describe themselves as democratic, liberal or left-wing, agnostic, perhaps republican, liberated in all the right ways. Eliot should be taken on; he may not convince but he will shake; he will discourage the making of straw figures of those with whom we disagree. He will ask for a rethinking of words such as 'tradition . . . continuity . . . responsibility . . . belonging . . . roots'. It then becomes more difficult simply to dismiss his attempt at describing the nature of British or English culture.

Raymond Williams declared that 'culture is ordinary', and his neat phrase has understandably been quoted countless times. Many who quote it seem not to know that the idea was Eliot's before Williams'; and probably someone else's years before that. Eliot's approach is not the same as Williams', but there are similarities. Williams meant that culture was not high art and whatever the bourgeoisie defined it as. It embraced ordinary life and all its forms and social areas: Trade Unions, Burial Societies, Co-ops, Working Men's Clubs, chapel hymn singing. Eliot's list was not so aware of class and political distinctions but was catholic and unbourgeois:

> ... how much is here embraced by the term 'culture'. It includes all the characteristic activities and interests of a people: Derby Day, Henley Regatta, Cowes, the 12th. August, a cup final, the dog races, the pin table, the dart board, Wensleydale cheese, boiled cabbage cut into sections, beetroot in vinegar, nineteenth-century Gothic churches and the music of Elgar. The reader can make his own list.

Eliot and Williams, very different writers on culture, were therefore saying much the same thing: that they belonged to or started nearer the anthropologist's than the Matthew Arnold concept of 'culture'. It is not surprising that Orwell had a similar list (knobbly knees, ill-fitting false teeth, etc.).

*

C. S. Lewis's lead can be adapted to song, to trying to distinguish between the mass and the popular. 'Each listener can make his own list', so long as he is qualified; which this writer isn't, being musically illiterate. But here is a first stab, through the words of songs. Country and Western songs – especially Patsy Cline's – might be as good a place as any to start, if you wished to think about the power of mass culture to be pushed beyond itself; sometimes and in the right circumstances.

Take the scene in a Torquay pub on a Saturday night in the mid-Eighties; Country and Western night. Loss in love, plangent chords, all those haunting, melancholy swoops. 'Why did you leave me, Charlene?' is being belted out; not a new tune, even then. The three or four couples on the floor are all expert dancers, in their forties, who have obviously been patronising such sessions for several decades.

It is all a remarkable exhibition of devotion and skill. This is what they enjoy above all, it seems, even if their jobs are not in themselves boring. Hard to tell what those jobs are, especially since the dancers are wearing some Country and Western trimmings. Not labourers, one would guess from their faces, nor professionals; somewhere in between.

One couple, probably husband and wife moving into their late forties, seem the most skilled even in that skilful group; they stay on the floor after all others have sat down, and the song is replayed for their benefit. Their timing, their complex synchronised movements, their exact responsiveness to the music and to each other, their total charmed absorption, would have made it worth going to Torquay just to watch them. The music ends and they begin to walk off the floor, still wrapt. But there is something odd; he is still closely guiding her, bending towards her, as if the song had not ended, would never end. Suddenly one realises that she is blind. That realisation, that moment, is intensely moving – like the epiphany in *Ulysses* when Joyce uses the language of a trite romantic novelette to describe Gertie McDowell sitting on the beach; and at the very end reveals a sentiment so gentle that it has great power: Gertie is lame. Joyce's pastiche there (it is not parody) has no trace of cleverness or superiority; he is catching us up in that quality of mass art which can now and again release within us just what C. S. Lewis had observed – emotions more genuine and moving than we would have predicted. Similarly, that moment in Torquay captured all in one the hold of enthusiasms and skills, the power of popular song ('Strange how potent cheap music is'); and, behind that, fidelities, lasting marriage, care and love.

*

What may have been sent into the world as merely a mass product can, then, prove to be more than that, to have a tune, a turn, a snatch of text, which listeners take to and return to. One could then begin to think of it as popular art, at least in part. Conversely, some machine-made songs can be plugged so hard that they become short-term market successes; but that soon fades; they do not qualify. The ones of which something remains are those Noël Coward called 'potent'. It would have wrecked his line to say: 'Strange how potent some cheap music is', but would have been more accurate. Little is written about this in Britain; the analysis of mass/popular music is almost entirely confined to specialist music or cultural studies journals; and even those tend to suffer from the fear of making sharp distinctions. Unless those kinds of distinction are attempted, the interesting mixture – 'mass-moving-into-popular' – will not be properly analysed.

It is not entirely useless, even through the words alone, to make suggestive first distinctions within mass art in songs. Inevitably, some people would quarrel with them; but they would take you somewhere. Here, first, are songs dead in words or music or probably mechanical, Tin Pan Alley products, machine-made mass songs, songs which may sometimes stick like ticks in the memory but do not, cannot, draw on any of those worthwhile responses which C. S. Lewis pointed to. They are locked into indefensible, often silly, emotions: jingoism, false bucolics, palliness pretending to be the feeling of community, insincere regrets. These titles, from the Twenties to the present, are put down just as they came to mind:

'Who do you think you're kidding, Mr Hitler?' (which could have come out of Orwell's mass art factory in *1984*)
'I like a nice cup of tea in the morning'
'Amy, Wonderful Amy'
'There'll always be an England'
'How much is that doggy in the window?'
'How much do I love you?'
'Keep right on to the end of the road'
'You'll never walk Alone'
'Stand by your man'

Most of those are English, pure Denmark Street, and that is no accident, simply proof that America does these things better than we do. She has her duds, naturally. Think of the music and words of 'How About You?' as compared with 'Miss Otis Regrets'.

Those are all category C, dead ringers. Category B are the central C. S. Lewis types, trite but potent songs to which it is easy to attach feelings of true sentiment:

'Danny Boy'
'My Way'
'The best things in life are free'

'Every time we say goodbye'
'When you've got a little springtime in your heart'
'I'll see you again'
'The way you look tonight'
'As Time Goes By'
'Yours'
'My Blue Heaven'
'The Very Thought of You'
'La Paloma'
'I get along without you very well'
'Que sera, sera'
'Goodnight, Sweetheart'

The joker in this pack would be 'Don't cry for me, Argentina'. Its ostensible subject, Eva Perón, is not really, could not possibly be, a serious/sentimental subject at all. The theme is too publicly melodramatic to attract personal feelings of loss. It is a haunting tune, no more; and floats free. It could be about anyone and any incident. It is disembodied, easy and haunting art; whatever 'meanings' it has are detached from reality, interchangeable. Any age, any culture, can adopt but not adapt it; not in the C. S. Lewis sense. It is as multipurpose as the tune of most national anthems; or Coca-Cola's 'It's the real thing' and 'I'd like to teach the world to sing'. Rock-bottom here is the theme tune of the Australian television soap opera *Neighbours*. No: that should be in category C.

Category A contains popular songs, examples of popular art, songs with some life in them beyond what may be adventitiously drawn from them by the hearers. They stand on their own; not provable here, though, since there is no music. Many of them, in this loose trawl, prove to be sparky, perky, funny. It may well be harder for a song of sentiment to enter this category:

'Anything you can do I can do better'
'Let's face the music and dance'
'Nice work if you can get it'
'A Fine Romance'
'Anything Goes'
'These Foolish Things'
'Jeepers Creepers'
'Jambalaya'
'Rum and Coca-Cola'

'This Ole House'
'Diamonds are a girl's best friend'
'Wake up little Susie'
'Lulu's back in town'
'Yo' feets too big'
'It had to be you'
'Ain't Misbehavin' '
'Don't get around much anymore'

There are some songs of sentiment in this group but they usually avoid sentimentality:

'Blueberry Hill'
'But I Do' (as sung by Clarence 'Frogman' Henry. Others who put their mark on this kind of song include Brenda Lee, Fats Waller, Nat King Cole and again, Patsy Cline)
'Button up your overcoat'
'Smoke gets in your eyes' (the straightest of all)
'You're the cream in my coffee'
'Eleanor Rigby'
'Hey Jude' (and some others from the Beatles)

All this deserves a massive amount of working over and through; without patronage, without making claims which are themselves expressions of reverse cultural snobbery.

Among contemporary writers on such subjects it is rare to find a well-qualified approach to mass and popular art. The days of 'Trite and conventional material for trite and conventional minds' have gone except in obscure corners. The stance is all the other way, sometimes to an over-easy acceptance and identification.

One of the best English writers in this general area is, with Dick Hebdige, Paul Willis. Willis wrote one of those Arts Council discussion documents quoted before, one of the better ones. He works empathetically, withholding exterior judgment until it is forced upon him. Then he can say: 'Much of popular culture is manipulative and formalistic, weighing down daily life with banality.' The only worrying element in that sentence is the phrase 'weighing down'. Is it really being suggested that mass culture has so powerful and direct an effect on the texture of daily life in the home and workplace as to, so to speak, almost smother it? But Willis goes on: 'Yet some of its materials can be bent to, and extend, the rhythm of daily life.' 'Bent to' is a strange phrase, but the general point is related to one running through this chapter, and chapters 8 and 12: about the way the elements of mass culture can be *used* by people so as to sit well with their existing assumptions.

Paul Willis is fair-minded and optimistic. He goes on: 'Out of this daily symbolic and cultural productivity more democratic arts practices might grow, if given the chance.' Well, maybe; but, as they say, 'chance would be a fine thing'. It is hard to see why 'more democratic arts practices' should emerge. Why shouldn't the grip of the mass-production system become even tighter? It has grown to its present size and influence precisely because it has learned how to speak to demotic, even apparently democratic, impulses, wishes, desires. And what can 'given the chance' mean? State intervention? Citizens' intervention? And why should either of those involve and concern more than a handful of people? Communitarian hopes so easily sound like cheering each other up, in the dark. Until such hopes are made more likely some of us will be left saying: 'Let us increase critical ability for as many as can be persuaded to listen, more obstinate and awkward resistances, more Calibans.'

To recapitulate: mass art has its eye on the audience, as large an audience as possible, and conceived as one or to be melded into one. It is therefore inherently formulaic, like a warm and relaxing or, conversely, artificially exciting bath; which can be endlessly repeated. Popular culture will have some elements of its own, something put in without thought of the possible audience. Mass culture does not surprise or make its hearers think: 'Well, I never saw things that way.' Partiality plus reinforcement work against that. Mass culture doesn't want to rock the boat, though it likes artificial rockings, as in a fairground – which is where it metaphorically is. It needs a value-free world. The Film of the Book is usually both thinner and bolder than the book itself. The Book of the Film of the Book continues that process. Art to Mass Art in two simple stages; with all the awkward bones filleted out.

Popular culture has some elements which occur for the love of it or the heck of it. It can therefore speak to at least some people out there; perhaps a lot of people but not a mass, because they have not been at that point approached as a mass. The artist has been tickled; so may the audience be. No boundaries are ever or all the time watertight.

CHAPTER FIVE

The Betrayal of Broadcasting

Those who aim to give the public what the public wants begin by under-estimating the public taste; they end by debauching it.
> T. S. Eliot, in evidence to the Pilkington Committee on the
> future of broadcasting, 1962 (an echo of Reith in the
> Twenties)

If we gave the public exactly what it wanted, it would be a perfectly appalling service.
> Norman Collins in the early days of commercial television
> (less smooth than today's commercial top-brass)

Don't be an old Reithian fart.
> BBC producers to a colleague who had suggested that a
> programme had too much unnecessary violence, 1980s

i THE PUBLIC SERVICE AND PROFESSIONALISM

It is much against the current conventional wisdom to say that one of the best of British domestic achievements in the twentieth century was the invention of the concept of public service broadcasting; but so it was. From its beginning in the Twenties that medium was established by different nations in one of two opposed forms or as a mixture of both. Structure is ideology. In most states broadcasting was either an instrument of state policy or the servant of commercial advertising. Most new nations took the first course, often with dreadful results. The United States is the prime example of the second. There were soon and increasingly, among other developed nations, mixed forms: some financed partly by advertising and partly by a form of licence fee, some in receipt of a government subsidy. The last did not always mean that such systems were the creatures of government, but they were usually under some pressure, overt or more likely covert, to keep their noses clean.

Whatever the formal or constitutional position, finance – more accurately, the system of financing – is always the keystone. The managers of an unqualified state-financed system know where their bread is made and buttered. A system entirely financed by advertising may not be wholly at the advertisers' whim but cannot avoid intrusions from them, especially at peak viewing times.

Even the United States recognised from the start that in this field the market is not always right, does not always if left alone deliver good broadcasting in any broad and representative sense; it distorts. The Federal Communications Commission was set up to try, as well as having technical responsibilities, to ensure that the advertisers do not have too much their own way. Its success was predictably mixed. In the Sixties one Chairman of the FCC described American television as 'a vast waste land'. Much of American broadcasting is puerile and repetitive. Many good things which broadcasting could do on behalf of its citizens it hardly touches, because they do not attract advertising. A great deal is left all the time by the wayside, in programmes not done and people not served. But America is a big country in more senses than one and has some built-in antibodies against its own worst excesses.

American broadcasting can also lead the world, especially in covering great public events responsibly, from wars to the exposure of political corruption. Even the comedy shows and the ubiquitous soap operas range, such is the force of talent whatever the system, from the abysmal to the brilliant.

State-controlled systems in sophisticated countries – such as Hungary and Czechoslovakia before 1989 – do not allow broadcast dissidence. Broadcasting, especially television, is very easy to control centrally. But imagination will out. Some of those Iron Curtain countries found ways of producing creative work which escaped the eyes of the censors: in innocent-seeming children's programmes and animation, cartoons; some of them were cleverly subversive but not in a way the commissars always noticed.

The British system is not and never has been a perfect model. From the start too many elements in British culture limited it in too many ways. But its strengths were considerable. It had been decided from the beginning that broadcasting was too important to be left in the hands of the government of the day or to be put under pressure from advertisers. The merit of that decision has not been sufficiently recognised in Britain itself; many other nations saw its merits and either tried to adapt it to their own situation or remained looking longingly at it.

Two decisions had then to flow from the first: if not government, who would be responsible for the overseeing and development of broadcasting; and, if not from the government, whence would the money come? Two characteristically British solutions were found. Let the Corporation, as it was soon called, be supervised by a Quango, established not under Act of Parliament but by Royal Charter. That should do something to distance broadcasting from direct governmental involvement, at least formally. To respond to that by saying that nevertheless there have been, especially in the last one and a half decades, many attempts at government interference, is to rediscover original sin. The more remarkable fact is that such interferences counted for so little for so long that the BBC was able to build up such a strong sense of professional independence – strong enough for it to be regarded during the last war, in other parts of the world and even in Germany, as an objective not a government voice.

This independence showed itself notably in action when Sir Anthony Eden, then Prime Minister, tried to make the BBC into the voice of the government during the Suez crisis of 1956. A later and even nastier attack on the Corporation came during the Falklands War, when a large group of Tory MPs bayed for its blood since it was not sufficiently jingoistic for their taste.

It is worthwhile at this point commenting on the BBC World Service, since that is directly financed by government, through the Foreign and Commonwealth Office. Inevitably, its budgets are frequently challenged by the FCO, and cuts proposed and sometimes made. One does not hear of interventions of substance; one does hear, at times of crisis, that the government is not happy about some of the World Service's reporting of those crises; but the distancing has generally held.

Does that mean, then, that we could have a domestic broadcasting system directly financed by government, that would have worked? It is possible but not altogether likely. There would be checks and balances, of course; yet when one considers the risks of government interference during crises, the World Service and the domestic BBC are not comparable. The World Service's crises of that kind are infrequent and do not always impinge directly on Parliament and its elected members or on the daily friction between government and opposition. The domestic services must day by day and hour after hour report the contentious flow of political life. The temptation to interfere with funding so as to bring the broadcasters into line would be stronger if that financing came from government and Parliament. Even now, some MPs of all parties do not recognise the distinctions in play as to both funding and formal constitution, and demand that BBC funds be cut and broadcasters' behaviour corralled on one ground or another.

The second characteristically British device is the licence fee. That is odder than it at first looks: let the BBC be funded, it says, by money paid by each citizen or family, not for the right to receive broadcasts but to operate a broadcast receiver. Rather like a dog licence. This apparently weird distinction is in fact very clever. If the licence fee were payment for receiving the BBC's programmes then there would have been a strong argument for the whole of the proceeds to pass to the BBC. But a licence to operate a receiver is a governmental charge and the proceeds due to them; the fee is not hypothecated (assigned in advance to a particular purpose). The government gives to the Corporation, after much discussion, what it thinks is about right.

Is the amount so decided related to the size of the licence fee income? Not exactly or even directly, says the Treasury. So you could in theory give the BBC more than the full proceeds from the licence fee? In theory, perhaps; in fact, no, is the smoothly smiling answer. Thus in different years different amounts from the licence fee have fed the general revenue.

Commercial broadcasters might, in the light of this tortuous argument, have grounds for saying they too should be given government funds since the receivers for operating which the licence fee is paid are also used to receive their programmes. To which the Treasury would no doubt again smilingly reply, though in their own form of language: 'Pull the other one. You are profit-making bodies and we will continue to milk your profits for as much as we can, to add to the General Fund.'

So the BBC is in fact funded by the government, and the MPs who demand a reduction in the Corporation's funding are not up the wrong creek after all? Correct. So we are back to asking: 'Why not fund directly, without all this flim-flam?' 'That wouldn't quite do,' says the ever-smiling Treasury official, adding another argument for the licence fee to the one above: 'The licence fee suggests a *Platonic* distinction but one none the less effective for all that.' The misconception that the licence fee is a payment to the BBC for making programmes does at least suggest a free and direct relationship between the broadcasters and their listeners and viewers, without government intervention.

The proponents of wholesale commercial broadcasting like to assert that the licence fee is generally and deeply resented. If you produce loaded and simplistic market-research questions you will have answers which suit your book. If you ask questions with some texture to them about likely profit and loss, about range and quality of programmes, in a wholly commercial system, you will have very different answers. Even if you ask simply: 'Do you resent paying the licence fee?' you will find that most people do not. They recognise a bargain when they see one (especially now in comparison with the cost of BSkyB and cable services). They feel the BBC plays a special and valuable role in the national broadcasting pattern.

*

By this time any foreign readers may be reeling. Do the British really play such arcane games with themselves? Yes, as in the invention of the Quangos with the Royal Charter (they include the British Council and the Arts Council); as in the creation of *Her Majesty's* Inspectors of Schools and *Her Majesty's* commissions to officers of the armed services. Somehow, much of the time and more or less, they work as intended; or have done.

Two inventions, then – the charter and the licence – to reduce the risk of governmental or other interference. Against some totally immovable hostile opinion, this oddity has worked well. Anyone who declares that the BBC is an instrument of state is as misguided as those who call commercial television 'Independent' (that word was a cheeky invention by the original Independent Television Authority). The dual formal arrangement had created a system which most of the time respected the diversity of tastes and the rights of all those tastes to be provided for.

From the start the BBC was accused of being 'too Oxbridge' (it was, but in this mirrored a national myopia in the corridors of power), 'patronising' (on the whole it wasn't, but its plummy accents sometimes made it sound as though it was), and 'paternalistic' (true, if 'paternalistic' can mean suggesting that some things are more worthwhile than others). In this light, exploitation is certainly worse than 'paternalism'. The formal structure, the system of financing, offered the freedom to grow so that, as a consequence of range and scale, a true broadcasting professionalism could emerge, one with its eyes on both the possibilities of the medium and the potentialities of the available audiences.

Lord Reith wobbled badly during the General Strike of 1926; he was by nature Establishment-minded, ready to consult government. Still, he created a creature more given to freedom than he realised or had probably intended. There was government interference to prevent Churchill from warning about the Hitler peril in the Thirties. But on the whole, with a high-point at the time of Suez, the BBC has been willing to stand up to government. They probe Cabinet Ministers quite irreverently, as they should. Some of their 'pugnacious' interviewers on radio and TV now sound like jejune and cocksure undergraduates, but that is a small price to pay; and even the cockiest may learn to do less promoting of their own personalities and to give more attention to clarifying the issues.

From these foundations and from the extraordinarily simple but tenacious directive – 'inform, educate and entertain' (first enunciated, oddly enough, by an American, David Sarnoff, some months before the BBC was set up; he went on to say that broadcasting 'should be distinctly regarded as a public service') – from that simple directive the BBC was able to evolve a code in which the business of broadcasting was good broadcasting only. All this came to be known as the idea of Public Service broadcasting; no idea in the social life of this century has been more misunderstood, more deliberately maligned, or more worthwhile.

The national Broadcasting Research Unit, which had a productive half-dozen years of life in the 1980s (when governmental pressures on the BBC and the commercial broadcasters' finances caused both to withdraw their sponsoring of this independent body), asked a score of broadcasters, reviewers, critics and well-informed outsiders what they regarded as the central principles of the Public Service idea. The answers came together remarkably quickly and focused firmly on eight points:

1 Geographic universality: Programmes should be available to the whole population, whether urbanised or isolated, and whatever the cost (like postal charges).
2 Universality of appeal: Programmes should over a reasonable span of time cater for the widest possible range of interests and tastes.
3 Minorities should receive particular attention, especially disadvantaged minorities. But we are all members of some large overlapping minorities at some times as well as of some majorities. (That

definition crisply puts aside the tendency to assume that 'minority' means flat-earthers or some other inconsiderable and probably crack-headed fringe group.)

4 National Identity: Broadcasters should recognise a special relationship with the sense of national identity and community. (That is the trickiest principle and needs attention below.)

5 No vested interests: Broadcasting should be distanced from all vested interests and in particular from the government of the day.

6 Universality of payment: One of the main instruments of broadcasting should be directly funded by the corpus of users.

7 Eyes on the ball: Broadcasting should be structured so as to encourage competition in good programming rather than competition for numbers.

8 Liberate, not restrict: The public guidelines for broadcasting should be designed to liberate rather than restrict the programme-makers. (Another suggestive, enabling, point: legislation should create breathing space within which broadcasters can experiment, take chances, make mistakes, take listeners and viewers by surprise. Without that, no *South Bank Show* and the like, or arts or education or other 'unprofitable' subjects.)

One senior broadcaster carried the brochure in his briefcase; a reminder, by the mid-Eighties, of purer days.

To turn for a short time to point 4. The BBC has been accused – though in this the commercial companies are not far behind; they just don't manage in so top-drawer a way – of having an inadequate, a culturally hidebound sense of what 'the national spirit' is. This is not to challenge the BBC's role as 'the national instrument of broadcasting'. It is to say that the Corporation in particular is too toe-curlingly deferential towards some of the more traditional areas of national life: the Royal Family ('Today is the birthday of—— We wish his Royal Highness a *Happy* Day'; cue the National Anthem); the Queen's speech on Christmas Day; the tail-wagging tones at any major Royal ceremony; and the Established Church – that is still greatly over-provided for, though by now as out-of-date as the drapes over supermarket booze until 12 noon each Sunday.

The Boat Race as a national event is an oddity born of the early Oxbridge days in broadcasting and of London fixation. The Remembrance Day ceremony at the Cenotaph is different; so are the Cup Final and the test matches. A Commoner's State funeral – Churchill's – was a genuine national event of its time but probably a one-off.

None of these things breaks the surface of a serious definition of national character. Orwell's suggestion, with modifications, that the English are in some ways 'a family' is more penetrating but hard to fill out.

Manifestly, this island people has a long history, some elements of which may be said to be shared. Out of that have come a number of attitudes, good and bad, many of which are also shared: exclusiveness with tolerance, charity and neighbourliness with brutality and exploitation, a taste for linguistic and melodramatic cock-eyedness. All this in spite of the clear and continuing divisiveness.

Other shared attitudes can 'Bring the nation together'. Not the over-hyped, personality-ridden 'Children in Need' appeals, but the quieter response from all parts of society to current affairs programmes showing, say, suffering in Africa. Still, that quality is not uniquely British; nations most of whose citizens are above the level of poverty can afford, and exercise, big hearts towards others in need.

The most interesting aspect of broadcasting's power to show this nation to itself, to tap common inherited characteristics, is less noticed. Comedy tickles the peculiar national funny-bone in its two main aspects: surrealist language and surrealist situations. *Alice in Wonderland* is ineradicably English. Mad situations show most evidently on television, but radio can suggest them to the inner eye.

Related to these is the habit – the reverse of the strong tendency to deference – of taking the mickey out of 'those above us', 'the powers that be'. The best early instance is in the satire shows of the Sixties. The original attitude towards them of the BBC upper hierarchy of executives was typical of entrenched assumptions. It was thought that satire, particularly political satire, might be caviare to the general – in the land where that kind of thing had run from Chaucer to Nelly Wallace and after. The satire shows were transmitted quite late, also according to the received wisdom that most 'ordinary' people, come what may, went to bed around 10.40 p.m. Those programmes were quickly very successful and with all classes of society. That cross-class achievement is remarkable in itself; no newspaper could hope to achieve it. It is inevitably intermittent and does not indicate general consensus, consistency or coherence.

Through such occasions one is more in touch with 'the national spirit' than through the conventionally respected great public occasions. The English are most characteristic of their collective selves when being irreverent, vulgar, nutty rather than when brought together in deference or respect for occasions invented by their betters. The importance of holy hush is, in its links with the common character, less than that of raucousness.

*

Important programming implications and, more importantly, opportunities for both radio and television flow from the idea of public service broadcasting. They are the harder to follow because, though broadcasting is above all a social art, it is also a kind of conveyor-belt industry; not operating a uniform-sausage conveyor belt but a sequence of interlocking belts running at different speeds according to differing technologies and delivering a variety of constantly changing goods twenty-four hours a day. Yet it must all the time transcend the industrialised system to which it is bound.

The heart of broadcasting has therefore to be, once again, the emergence of a professionalism which is vocational (in the sense, this time, of 'inspired by a sense of vocation' rather than simply technical), which is always trying for other than routine reasons to break out of its most pressing constraints. This tension is a major reason why broadcasting professionalism, even more than that of other vocations, is always at risk of becoming ingrown, an inturned self-protective mystery; and why it is always trying to export that ingrown-ness to its audience as a form of narcissism.

There has to be a triple act of balance, of commitment: to the fascination of the medium in itself; to the integrity of the subjects chosen, an integrity which operates best when it pays attention to those subjects rather than to possible audiences; and a disinterested commitment to those audiences – which is not the same as a nervous looking over the shoulder as at a strange herd, or a belief that you can assess public opinion by having a word with the man from whom you buy your fags each morning before disappearing into the broadcasting maw. These are all forms of impartial professionalism.

From then on the public service idea provides, demands, exceptional opportunities and all are forms of freedom. It allows for the right to make mistakes, to lose money, to take a long breath, to experiment. Such a commitment does not guarantee success all the time. It has its costly flops; and it has produced some of British broadcasting's best achievements. The obvious example is the plays of Dennis Potter. He began as a BBC blue-chip trainee, one of those selected after a succession of interviews as what the Civil Service calls 'fast-track' candidates, likely to go high. He soon proved to be not at all an organisation man. This was in the Sixties. In today's straitened circumstances he would probably have been given a polite goodbye. Instead, the Corporation put him under contract for an initial couple of years so that he would be free to write the plays he had in him. The rest is an important paragraph in television history. There are many other less striking instances, of success as of failure. That kind of gamble is essential to public service broadcasting if it is to fulfil its nature; bread is cast on the waters, in subjects chosen and in hopes from the audiences.

Gambling concerns also the right approach to audiences. We are virtually all, from whatever part of society we come, caught within our bit of the culture – or, better, cultures. Broadcasting, so much freer than the printed word, is able to say: 'The world is wider than we think; listen and look.' So far as audiences are concerned, this is the heart of the public service notion. Other forms of broadcasting, other impulses behind other structures, are implicitly committed to the formulation: 'We know you like this. Here's more of it'; or, at the limit: 'We know you like this sort of thing. Here it is, hotter and stronger or with a new twist to it, you poor nits.' So invent an imitation or buy one in from the competition. That spirit spreads everywhere, even into 'objective' newscasting: to the subjects chosen, the length each item is given, the ordering of items, the language used. 'Objective' broadcast news can range between the tabloids and the broadsheets but is nowadays heading towards the tabloids. The differences are critical. It is unjustifiable that the fact that a footballer, Eric Cantona, had drop-kicked a spectator should have had headline coverage for days on both the BBC and the independent channels. That truly is playing to the terraces.

To gamble on the potential interests of listeners and viewers, to try to take them by surprise, is not to patronise but to treat fairly, to recognise the limitations of all, of both audiences and programme-makers. But how to decide between the vast numbers of possible subjects which may be offered? There is no easy and complete answer, though there are sensible general guidelines. In the 1960s Huw Wheldon used to say he would find it impossible to lay down rules on why a particular programme should be risked because it was likely to be successful in the right ways. It is very much easier to guess that a programme might attract large audiences. He would not decide, Wheldon went on, that a programme of which he was shown a pilot and which seemed likely to be an instant hit, would on that ground alone be approved for a series. If he found its subject interesting and worthwhile, if the presentation lived up to the demands of the subject, if it had those kinds of intelligence and honesty so far as he could judge – and it was his responsibility as Controller of BBC Television to judge – then he would probably agree to what was still bound to be a gamble. Such remarks show professionalism in action.

He also liked to give his own particular rules of thumb, his working insights; they too showed professionalism in play. Speaking of *Dad's Army*, he said something like this. The expectation, this being Britain, would be that the really posh character would be the officer, and the lower-middle-class one the NCO. That expectation was turned upside down; the lower-middle-class bank manager was the commanding officer of the Home Ground company, and the public-school product (his chief cashier) the NCO. That made all the difference, took the programme's very basis out of stereotyping and introduced all sorts of unexpected social and cultural reverberations. It was one important reason for the programme's success. Other, more obvious rules of thumb include listening to your peers in broadcasting and to lots of people outside that circle – but that is not as simple as it sounds; you have to try to judge the judgment of the people you are questioning, inside or outside the work circle. You are many miles away from adding up numbers; that is always an evasion.

Behind all such working-practices there lies respect for the audience, and for its judgment if courteously approached and closely listened to, often for the ideas behind the words. Research underwrites that rule. People can, in short, reveal greater maturity of judgment than commercial broadcasting dare give them credit for.

At its best British broadcasting, with the BBC – and to some extent Granada until the 1990s, and Channel 4 – in the van has consistently and deliberately sought growing points, new frontiers. So much so that the editor of a broadsheet newspaper said, some years ago. 'The initiative has now passed to the BBC. I know that most of our readers watch the BBC's in-depth discussion programmes even after they've looked at my newspaper, because they know that in these things the BBC has learned to talk to them in a more effective way than we have.' Michael Grade of Channel 4 went further: 'The BBC exists to keep us all honest.'

*

At its worst the BBC, as well as its competitors, has committed all the main intellectual and artistic errors. It has used stereotyping of characters, situations and ideas. It has often failed, out of fear of being thought 'do-gooding', to fulfil the public service mandate, not realising that here as elsewhere if you do not try to do well you will end doing ill. The Corporation has made formulaic work since it seems more likely than fresh work to have at least moderate success; programmes that are carbon copies of their safe predecessors.

All such work is a form of professional death. We may learn from someone else's success, try to understand why a programme works so well, decide whether that success has been bought at too much cost to integrity (which has nothing to do with height of brow), and yet see how such inventiveness as is there may push towards new and good ideas.

Any programme which avoids such considerations and settles for having its eyes always and only on audience reaction as the measure of success is practising a form of overt or hidden censorship towards those audiences, seeing them as nothing more than 'bodies delivered'. We can and should all be offered programmes out of a mood of respect for both what is being offered and for those to whom it is being offered. If those attitudes have been replaced by cynicism then trivialisation soon follows; and trivialisation, as Tawney pointed out, is worse for the soul than wickedness.

The Pilkington Report appeared over thirty years ago, but its main conclusions on this are as true as ever. It dared speak of 'trivialis-ation'; the more intellectual journalists either passed by in embarrass-ment at such earnestness or fell about laughing. What was said then is still apposite because it is about gimmickry, the point at which the packages become more important than the products:

> Triviality is not necessarily related to the subject matter of a programme; it can appear in drama, current affairs programmes, religious programmes or sports programmes just as easily as in light comedy or variety shows. One programme may be gay [meaning cheerful] and frivolous and yet not be trivial. Another programme may seek prestige because it deals with intellectual or artistic affairs – and yet be trivial in its grasp or treatment; it may, for example, rely for its appeal on technical tricks or the status of its compère, rather than on the worth of the subject matter, and the depth of its treatment. Triviality resides in the way the subject matter is approached and the manner in which it is presented . . . A trivial approach can consist in a failure to respect the potentialites of the subject matter, no matter what it be, or in a too ready reliance on well-tried themes, or

in a habit of conformity to established patterns, or in a reluctance to be imaginatively adventurous . . .

Compare *EastEnders* with *Neighbours*. Think of *Through the Keyhole*.

The Broadcasting Research Unit's later booklet *Quality in Television* (1989) is even sharper and speaks of programmes which 'however perfect in performance are essentially meretricious'. This is straight talking about some things which are offered on television every day; that intelligent people are not willing to recognise this is surprising, but prevalent. Good judgment does not change according to increasing commercial pressures, least of all over only a few decades; life is not as relativist as that.

ii RADIO

I can't do my job as a broadcaster if a composer doesn't do his and sound nice.

Senior spokesman for Classic FM

In spite of the great and increasing competition from commercial radio stations, the BBC still manages to provide a remarkable and on the whole admirable range of services. Radio 1 is obliged to confront the pop commercial stations head-on and on much their terms; after all, in the mid-Nineties it lost 4 million listeners. Not altogether on their terms, though; to emulate the worst of commercial pop radio would be too much even for a beleaguered BBC. As E. E. Cummings said: 'There is some shit I will not eat.' Many commercial stations, as any walk past a building site will confirm, put out a diet of the cheaper kind of pop music and one so unrelieved that you have to conclude that the market researchers have told them that the 16–25 cohort, especially among manual labourers, is irredeemably stupid and offers the most lucrative market for some kinds of advertisements.

Radio 2 (originally called The Light Programme) tries and to a largely unrecognised extent succeeds in leavening that pap. In particular it transmits a two-hour art and culture programme in the evening. These two stations have to exist, and especially Radio 1, if the Corporation is not to be pushed into a corner. In this sort of debate as in so much else, Parliament rarely shows itself capable of intelligent social thought – except for no more than a handful of members.

Labour has until recently tended to be unthinkingly populist; most Tories practise their special mixture of contempt and complaisance.

'Generic' radio came in over a quarter of a century ago and, in spite of highly articulate rationalisations, was really a direct response to the challenge of commercial radio. 'Generic' is an escapist word, adopted to avoid saying: 'Channels will be divided according to our judgment of listeners' *existing* tastes' – i.e. less surprising or stretching. Mixed main national channels and well-resourced regional channels gave way to channels focused on specific kinds of listener, by age, by class, by educational level. This was an early form of that computerised 'imaging' of individuals which by now some insurance companies have highly developed. Fit our precise categories as to age, profession, salary, and we will provide a trimmed premium for your house or your car or you. Deviate in any way from those categories and we do not wish to know you; the computer will reject you.

It could be argued that the establishment of Radio 3 (then called The Third Programme) just after the war was an early instance of generic dividing; the intended audience was very precisely identifiable. True, but the aims were different; they were based on an admittedly narrow social judgement, not on an estimate of profitable target-audiences or, at that date, of the need to match competition. They included some well-meant but mistaken onwards-and-upwards assumptions but did not also feel the need to give leg-ups to aspirants.

Radio 4 (the old Home Service) has at least kept something of its predecessor's pleasantly mixed character. 'The bulletin board of the middle classes' is one of its favoured nicknames, and there is some truth in that. It could also be called 'the bulletin board of the small town fête', or of the British addiction to wayward and amateur or intelligently concerned interests which are sometimes class-bound but also sometimes cross-class. Listen to *Woman's Hour* for a week, in its current feminist mode, to take that point.

Radio 5 Live seeks to reach wider and therefore somewhat lower. Where it fails – and in its first months it had many failures – the reasons were, as usual, misguided cultural judgments drawn from the conventional bag. It was, for example, foolish enough to give considerable air time to a clairvoyant pronouncing on the chances of survival of the marriage between Michael Jackson and the daughter of Elvis Presley. If they took that seriously they are in the wrong job. If they did not, they were disdaining their audiences. If they tried to defend it as a joke item, that would be a cop-out because it would deny the way the item was presented. But Radio 5 Live's successes so far – especially its demotic handling of current affairs and sport – suggest it may eventually be a worthy partner to Radio 4.

Radio 4

Whatever other nicknames Radio 4 may have, it can also be defined as having its centre somewhere between the middle classes and the lower-middle classes, the slightly genteel and the cosily suburban. It goes wider than the above class-identified description suggests, much wider, and offers many more varied things; it tries to stretch-and-surprise. It gives so much attention to disabilities of different kinds that you sometimes wonder, listening over the washing-up in the evening, whether it is at those times almost entirely committed to the 'visually impaired', 'the physically challenged' and other kinds of handicap. A mistaken impression; but Radio 4 does cater admirably for a very large range of minorities, and not only 'disadvantaged' minorities. No other station, probably no other station in Europe (leaving aside any subscription channel which may cater specifically and at a price for one or more minorities) gives so much of its time to providing services and to following up by post and telephone those programmes for relatively small groups and sub-divisions within them: legal, medical, educational, artistic, athletic, ethnic. No *broadcast* programme financed directly by advertising would dare do that; they are more likely to be underfunded, with their eyes always on cash.

Because it aims at the more alert people within its central social parameters (those boundaries are, of course, loose, not watertight; they leak) Radio 4's tones are rarely those of the nursery-school teacher or the comfort-giving dentist. No 'How now, brown cow?' or 'This isn't going to hurt a bit.' Its programmes on important current issues are generally well-informed, well-presented, accessible without being either specialist or ingratiating as if addressing a near-idiot.

It does have other tonal limitations, especially nowadays. It reveals an excessive belief in the value of the semi-intellectual chat-show. Its programmers are much too hooked on the 'phone-in'. If you invite people to telephone their views you cannot reasonably be downright rude to them if those views are bizarre. That does happen on some programmes from commercial stations; that sort of show-off brutalism does them no credit. Yet those who phone in are in no sense representative; they are people who *would* phone in, and many of them are prejudiced, fixated, opinionated. A phone-in is not needed to establish that fact about this or any other society. Such programmes easily become a verbal Roman circus that allows listeners the luxury of feeling superior to the callers. The broadcasters need to think harder about how best to tap public opinion. At the other end of that spectrum are programmes such as *The Moral Maze*. That has been carefully thought out in advance. From it – though this may be an unintended bonus – you at least learn that possessors of well-informed opinions can also be unwilling to think again, and may enjoy 'hearing themselves speak' as much as attending to the argument. Radio discussion of all kinds does tend to the condition of that Roman circus.

Quality goes up and down. At the time of writing, drama and short stories are in an odd state. Afternoon drama seems more often than is reasonable to be aimed at hospital patients who do not wish to be greatly disturbed or challenged, able to take a few frissons but on the whole expecting things always to turn out right in the end. Much the same can be said about the short stories: this stuff is too often the Mills and Boon of the air-waves.

Comedy on Radio 4 is in the oddest condition of all. It is probably inherently the most difficult form to handle. The record has been very good indeed in some periods so perhaps, since these things tend to go in waves, today's may be an unavoidable trough. All too often now comedy sounds as though designed for a student review. Strange – on Radio 4. Then a repeat of *ITMA* or *Round the Horne* is transmitted and – discounting age and nostalgia – we realise what is missing and how difficult it is to arrive at the best.

Radio 4 is very English – Welsh, Scottish and Northern Irish in parts, but at its core English. It has the typically long English nostalgic memory, and of that the flagship is *The Archers*. Not 'the enormous condescension of posterity' but the sentimental attachment to ancestry in all its forms, especially the bucolic. Radio 4 is English in its virtues and its limitations – nervous about the arts, sensible and shrewd rather than intellectual, so tolerant as to verge on the endlessly and relativistically wide-open, caring for the handicapped of all kinds, respectful of the gentler pastimes, anxious to be honest even if honesty sometimes angers listeners, too deferential towards some of those who write or phone in, on the whole not chauvinistic. Its journalism, as should go without saying, is wider, deeper and so more responsible than that of all but two or three newspapers. That's not a bad check-list.

Radio 3

Even from its start just after the war the Third Programme – later Radio 3 – seemed a curious invention; but by no means as curious as it seems almost half a century later. To some living in the provinces, far from a good Public Library or concert hall, the Third Programme and its spiritual partner *The Listener* were lifelines of the mind. Such people were not always 'highbrow', were not in fashionable professions; but they enjoyed having available in their homes classical music, intelligent talks, classic and experimental drama, even clever comedy at times. The Third Programme immediately attracted some of the brightest writers, artists, intellectuals and adventurous broadcasters in the country: Laurence Gilliam, Henry Reed, Louis MacNeice, Dylan Thomas, Terence Tiller, W. R. Rogers, Rayner Heppenstall. It produced some unique and memorable programmes.

It could never have been called a 'democratic' initiative and did not mean to be – not if 'democratic' means appealing to a very wide range of tastes, and feeling guilty if you do not. It was deliberately, explicitly, unashamedly 'highbrow', because its founders believed that there was such a thing as high art, that it was one of the greatest achievements of the human spirit (not only of Western civilisation), and that a national broadcasting system which did not recognise and cater for such things was not fulfilling its brief. In such a perspective head-counting and an intense concentration on the level of average taste and knowledge would be debased democracy. There was a kind of eccentric intellectual heroism in using scarce resources in wave lengths and money to establish a channel so alien to what its founders would have probably called 'lowbrow' and 'middlebrow' tastes.

Yet that enclosed minority and its world could not survive long once broadcasting become more competitive, with one branch commercial. Nor at bottom did it deserve to, for its reading of culture and of cultural needs was far too narrow. It turned up its collective nose at even the most serious attempts at the dreaded 'popularisation'. It sought, it claimed, to create something like 'the conversation in the better kind of Senior Common Room' (that 'better' is a most refined touch), like 'dons talking to dons'. To those who had not had such are advantages, this sounded like 'keep off our private lawn', an offputting drawing back of Oxbridge or Bloomsbury skirts, cliquish.

George Barnes, the Director of the Spoken Word, pronounced loftily that there would be few 'hearing-aids' for listeners to the Third Programme.

Even on the best-justified of élitist arguments the Third Programme was hugely expensive in relation to the numbers it reached. Even by the mid-Fifties it was being listened to by on average about a quarter of a million people each evening. If more programmes had been more accessible millions more could have been attracted. Douglas Cleverdon, one of its founders, said that it gradually became 'more and more metropolitan and clever – élitist in the worst sense, and self-indulgent in relation to audience demand'.

It is hard to disagree with that judgment. The organisers of the Third Programme assigned the Judes and the Leonard Basts to the twilight world of explicitly 'educational broadcasting', and towards that they were very superior. They were culturally too buttoned-up, unable to imagine a genuine middle-ground, elevated fiddlers while Rome burned, conniving at their own destruction, ripe for the picking as the skies darkened.

Many of their voices perfectly echoed that world: high from the roof of the mouth, exactly fitted to the cocktail party or Combination Room circuit, but offputting even to the most earnest of intelligent laymen and women. Audience research showed that the same thoughtful talk delivered in that kind of voice on the Third Programme put off many more people than it did when delivered on the Home Service in a less snobby voice.

Times changed for two reasons, one a secular movement in ideas about culture-and-society, the other the advent of direct competition. The secular movement was the emergence of that relativism in attitudes to art as to other things, which runs throughout this book. The collapse of the old certainties was easier and quicker than any could have predicted, though not in all parts complete. But by the beginning of the Nineties, a Radio 3 spokesmen discarded 'art' in favour of a carpet-bag culture. Into that capacious receptacle anything might be stuffed, from Beethoven to Boy George.

*

At roughly the same time the commercial station Classic FM was born. From the beginning Classic FM knew that there was such a thing as 'art', at any rate musical 'art': it all came down to market research on the unfulfilled taste for 'the classics'. That research was very effectively carried out.

Classic FM's marketing was extremely successful; it quickly built up what seemed the most friendly of 'images'. It believed in interactions; it refused to be too metropolitan in manner; it encouraged its listeners to attend a surprisingly large range of musical events, large and small, going on across the country. It invented special offers and promotions; it brand-marked events constantly; it aimed to be your totally wrap-around, homely but not lowbrow station.

It was a triumph of a kind of marketing, yet a triumph on a limited and predictable base: an undemanding middle-range anthology, a repetitive nosegay. With few exceptions, it dared not move too far from its listeners' existing tastes or test their patience too long. It has attracted good presenters (more than one from the BBC), but somewhere at the backs of their heads these presenters assume, no doubt without knowing it, that most of their listeners are bird-brained romantics. It is always a good exercise when thinking of broadcasting to ask of a presenter's voice and tones: 'What kind of assumed listener does this voice suggest?' The voices of some Classic FM presenters suggest the assumption that most listeners are bored housewives trapped at the kitchen sink in mid-afternoon. They are glutinously wooing voices as of an insecure brush-salesman on the doorstep and anxious to get in. Better the Senior Common Room than this placket-stroking stuff. One presenter clearly knows little about classical music. He has also that most insular of conversational give-aways: he pronounces the names of foreign composers in an over-articulated and over-stressed voice, as though to imply, chummily: 'Don't they have funny names, these frogs and krauts?'

But, then, Classic FM is a commercial station and the music weaves in and out of the ads. Odd to recognise in these the voices of famous actors and actresses – and presenters and other 'media personalities' – delivering the stuff with every effort at conviction. They bring to mind that old question of 'sincerity in broadcasting' and the common belief that insincerity reveals itself over the air. Radio and television are not insincerity-detectors; for a professional or a 'natural broadcaster' sincerity is easy to affect and to convince with.

The success of Classic FM has pushed Radio 3 into 'democratising' itself – with, at the time of writing, mixed results. Sometimes the old lady seems no longer to be drawing back her elegant skirts but to be lifting them for the customers. Other changes are intelligent efforts to meet a wider public in an artistically defensible way. It was chilling to hear a senior BBC radio executive saying that Classic FM could teach Radio 3 a good deal. Well, something, yes; but the phrasing suggested that all Classic FM could 'teach' was *good* habits.

By contrast, the BBC – and not only through the Third Programme, now Radio 3 – has transformed the musical life of this country. This is no longer the land without music. Classic FM is selectively parasitic on that achievement.

*

It is clear that BBC Radio is in a sensitive condition; not surprisingly, in view of the pressures. It does many silly things in the name of popular broadcasting; and almost all these errors are the result of faulty cultural judgments. The language of presenters and newsreaders has become increasingly sloppy in the effort to be up-to-date. They live uncritically in a world of intrusive prepositions: they never 'free' something but always 'free it up'; they never 'meet' anyone but always 'meet up with' them. They 'firm up', 'lose out', 'miss out', They jump from cliché-link to cliché-link: no process ever 'stops'; they all 'grind to a halt'. They do not say 'daily' but 'on a daily basis'. This is semantic illiteracy.

BBC Radio persists with ludicrously overblown programme titles such as *Brain of Britain* (as on television with *Mastermind*) both merely programmes testing the memory for heaps of disconnected facts. Language, and therefore thought, confusion, once again. The lunchtime news programme, when apparently considering whether a vicar who had lost his 'belief' should remain in his living, asked an orchestral musician if he had to 'believe in' a composition before being happy to play it, and a barrister if he had to 'believe in' an accused's innocence before being willing to represent him or her. Did no one in that news room know the three different meanings of the phrase 'believe in' which were being tossed about there? It is hard to 'believe' that BBC Radio would have committed such solecisms thirty years ago.

iii TELEVISION

Television produces some remarkably good programmes across the whole range of existing tastes, at all levels, and sometimes against heavy odds. It also produces tripe. Since many people watch tripe those viewers can hardly be expected to admit that description (though some do – tripe can have its fascination though only, for those who recognise it, by an act of distancing).

Television is by its nature an undiscriminating world, so the prevailing relativism suits it well. Television is demotic, but inexorably pushes towards the populist; a sort of fast food of the relaxed attention; detached from anything one has to *do* about one's active daily life. It comes to us all in our own homes, in our millions. It melds those millions into huge, successive groups, but groups whose compositions are always changing: into the tens of millions for police dramas or sport, or into smaller but still large overlapping minorities of several millions for gardening, cooking, travel. It is less divisive by voices than radio is and so less class-separated. Viewers soon learn its visual language, which is related to but not the same as the cinematic. It insinuates itself so well that it becomes part of the pattern, shape, texture of our everyday lives – over supper, through the weekend, at other recognised times. It marks and defines our lives, becomes as much a part of them as the routine household sights, smells, habits.

Television suggests significance; it is heavy with implied meaning. It is the natural home of thereness, thisness, nowness. It has immediacy and fluidity, and at the same time heightens and stamps identity on what it touches. Great public occasions seem more real through it, and so do ordinary occasions; it heightens and seems to validate that ordinariness. Some events seem real only if they are on television. The old-fashioned phrase 'It's true. I saw it in the papers' has been supplanted by 'I know. I saw it on the telly.'

Style supplants content. It is not entirely true to say that 'the medium is the message', but many people working in television implicitly take that as given and the implication may be absorbed by many viewers.

In front of television we are all spectators of the drama of life, just sufficiently distanced to be predominantly voyeurs – without responsibility; the privilege of the helot through the ages. At the same time we are within that which we watch, but disconnectedly.

Television is self-validating and striving always to be self-sufficient. It therefore pushes towards the creation of 'personalities' – which are in relative terms as evanescent as last season's starlings. That inturned characteristic leads, again inevitably, to narcissism, to television making programmes about its own people, quiz-show panels manned by families of television addicts or by 'television personalities'. This is rock-bottom non-thinking – or audience-despising thinking.

*

Given the great difficulties of the BBC in facing competitors chiefly interested in reaching mass audiences, the Corporation does better than might have been expected in still fulfilling the public service brief on television. But the pressure is so great that in some areas the pass is sold.

An early Nineties example is in the handling of Ken Russell's television adaptation of *Lady Chatterley's Lover*. Knowing Ken Russell's wilfulness one was bound to wonder what he would make of the transposition. In fact, he treated the book with great respect, as though its basic seriousness had taken him by surprise. Only once or twice did he commit typical Russell gratuitous swirls. One might even have argued that he was too respectful to the plot and the language; both sometimes seemed archaic, but they were faithful to Lawrence. The film did not, above all, exploit the sexual passages. It was an adaptation taken straight and seriously.

A Radio 4 arts programme could not forbear asking a guest reviewer loaded questions, less about the film than about the book; loaded because they invoked a predictable interest in little other than its sexual scenes and sexual language. A discussion followed, chaired by a regular presenter – whose knowledge of the book was inadequate. Both radio and television expect too much of their regular presenters; they cannot find the time to acquire enough knowledge and grasp of the multifarious topics, so they are pushed into superficial off-the-top-of-the-head questioning.

Worse was to come. Trailers on television for the four-part film were deliberately and deceptively sexy; background music added to that effect. A great irony: that we might have expected some perversities from Russell, but he was self-controlled, apparently out of respect as much as from BBC pressures. We might have expected in the trailers a suitable, informed approach from the BBC; but they committed vulgarities hardly thinkable from someone who knew the book. Clearly, the Presentation Unit didn't, and seemed not to have consulted the programme's producer. A letter to the BBC elicited the expected response. 'Sorry; but the film did have large and appreciative audiences.' That is beside the point; the first need is to do right by

Lawrence's book, the second to play fair by the audience, not to treat them as children, with phoney come-ons.

The confusion at the BBC now runs deep. They do not always reveal a 'robust' hold on the interpretation of public service broadcasting, on television or radio. Senior executives are afraid to seem holier than thou in relation to competitors in either medium. Remember the senior executive saying that Classic FM has a lot to teach Radio 3 about making listeners feel welcome. Ingratiatingly, patronisingly welcome? Or welcome as one sensible human being to another? Was the difference not recognised?

'Moments' on television

Little remarked on but one of television's best gifts is its ability to produce moments of revelation not always planned by the producer. So: the moon landing does not qualify but the shooting of Lee Harvey Oswald does. Most 'moments' are less tied to great public occasions than either of those. They get under the carapace, reveal character, relationships, attitudes of which the participants are usually unaware. A window has opened, a great and unexpectedly focused light has shone. Cinema and video can to some extent show such moments, but not with such immediacy. On television we see such things as if at the moment they are happening, as if at a private viewing; and often they are happening just then, live. This is true actuality.

A very early example. Ernest Bevin, then Foreign Secretary, was arriving with his wife in a large limousine for some great occasion. The car stopped and he stepped out, apparently entirely forgetful of his wife. An aide rushed to help her. That moment seemed to be saying something important, but what was it? That Bevin was so preoccupied with matters of state that he forgot everything else, even his wife? That he habitually did not have her in mind? It teased, and held your attention more than anything else on that evening's news.

Duncan Sandys, then Commonwealth Secretary, came down the steps of an aircraft after a mission to Africa. A journalist asked him a question at the foot of the steps. Sandys responded with a harsh and arrogant dismissal. Was he excessively tired? Disappointed with his mission? Surely on most public occasions he would have been practised at exercising at least a veneer of politeness? Was he an unredeemable snob, habitually rude to his 'inferiors'?

At the funeral of General de Gaulle the limousines of heads of state were arriving at the great door of Notre-Dame. President Nixon arrived. His bodyguards were a little slow in reaching his car door. He was forgetful for a moment and did not wait until they were in position. After two steps he realised he was unprotected, ducked and scurried back to the car. Few pictures could have so emphasised the hidden fear in which an American President must always live when in public.

In the montage of shots introducing a 'Food and Drink' programme there is one which explodes all others, which tend to be amiable bait. This is a shot of a young man carrying a large side of meat over his shoulder, for throwing into a van. His face is suddenly contorted with a vile rage as he realises he is on camera – it is an awful, a hellish, a caught-out face. Then you suddenly see why: the side of beef is stamped in purple 'Condemned'. We have been witnesses to a crime.

In all but one of those instances the main subject is silent – that is more often than not the mark of a television 'moment' – and many such moments are unique to television, because live. They are all richly revelatory.

Once you have picked up the point, instances appear on most days: the young professional wife and mother talking about *au pairs* and unwittingly revealing a harsh, callous uncharitableness whilst assuming that she is being intelligent and measured, expressing what all right-thinking women know. Young men drinking beer in a working men's club, in the Midlands; saying, as if stating a truism, that they made up to young women chiefly so they could fuck them; admitting to having fathered children and recognising no commitment but leaving the mothers to 'get on with it' as best they could. They could almost always persuade the women to do without a condom. If a baby came along, well: 'That's their fucking look out, in't it?' A culture selfish to its roots, captured in two or three minutes.

Then: a man running several old people's homes for profit, cornered beside his big Mercedes by a brave young woman journalist, a model of low-level corruption as he evaded every question. And a youth, plainly only near-literate, but articulate enough to say he saw nothing wrong in organising dog-fights to the death. 'They're only animals.' A Leeds policeman unconcernedly revealing ugly racist attitudes, South African whites agreeing that 'Kaffirs' are little better than beasts while revealing themselves as barely civilised in speech and attitudes. Edward Thompson's brimming eyes as he remembered his brother, executed in the Balkans during the war. Dennis Potter's last television broadcast.

All these are extraordinary demonstrations of the 'thisness' of television, its power to transmit the 'thisness' of life. One remembers the ugly incidents more easily than the honourable – gin is more immediately powerful than spring water – but charitable moments, moments of touching sentiment, appear also; and not only in the expected and more dramatic places, whether tragic or celebratory. The way a mother's face lights up when, after some delay, she finally recognises her child coming out of the school gates; or the easy, habitual way she tucks her arms into her husband's as they move off after meeting at the station. How much of all this, somehow and somewhere, gets through to us? Perhaps more than we are aware of; that may be one of the more important effects of television. But we do not rightly know.

iv BROADCASTING AND THE ARTS

There are three good reasons why the arts should appear on radio and television: that a sizeable minority appreciate them; that the arts have to be kept up, even if only a minority at present appreciates them and that in this under-educated society every means should be sought to spread their practice and appreciation.

Yet, for a variety of reasons – the difficulties in successfully presenting the arts on either broadcasting medium, and the never-ending barrage of populism – broadcasters tend to be less than brave in their defence of the arts' claim to much general broadcasting time; or they bend to the wind and seek ever more exciting-seeming ways of presenting them. Unsurprisingly, the Arts Council gave to a 1992 conference on 'The Arts and Broadcasting' the title 'The Odd Couple'; fair, in a way; but the coupling is not necessarily as odd as it has sometimes seemed.

For obvious reasons Radio 3's substantial contributions to broadcast arts can be simply nodded at again here and left. So may Channel 4's, though that needs a look later on. The central channels are most relevant here.

Radio 4 pays attention to the arts in more than one way. *Start the Week* looks at books, some of them weighty, from time to time; and at drama and the other arts. Radio 2 has a shot too, in one programme rather late at night, and wrapped up in more general talkative material. The long-serving flagship of the arts on radio is Radio 4's *Kaleidoscope*.

Over the last dozen years, *Kaleidoscope* has shown a tendency to

decline into smart populism. Never highbrow in the Third Programme or even Radio 3 sense, it was at the start a quite serious
programme designed for the intelligent and well-informed lay listener
and amateur devotee of the arts. It mixed very good popular education with entertainment. It can still do such things. But over the
years it has slid towards a desperate trendiness. Many of its regular
presenters exhibit an urgent, knowing brightness, a desperation not
to be caught with their modish shirt-tails hanging out. Above all,
Kaleidoscope does not want to seem highbrow, to put off anyone by
appearing to make distinctions, by saying that any single thing is
worse than any other. The problem arises where something is both
fashionable and popular – a form of that easy glitter or allowed
sentiment or pseudo-artiness or imitation intellectuality which pre-
occupies for a time a would-be intellectual crowd; until they move
on to the next example of the form. Unable to *judge* or to dismiss,
such programmes fall back on *celebration*, as someone well observed
a few years ago.

For example, in 1993 Channel 4 began to transmit, with many
preliminary fanfares, Armistead Maupin's *Tales of San Francisco*, a
dramatisation of newspaper short stories; anecdotes which, we were
breathily told, American TV had found too frank in their handling
of sex, heterosexual, homosexual and lesbian. Certainly, the written
version was more astringent than the TV series shown in Britain.
Kaleidoscope had an advance item on the series, the printed material
and the television adaptation. With few small exceptions the discussion was wholly and uncritically favourable. You began to feel
that the regular presenter would have to break the psychological
mould and say: 'Hang on a bit. Can it really be as good as that?'

When the series reached the screens we saw a semi-liberated soap
opera, manipulating all the usual clichés about San Francisco life in
the Sixties, all the dreary icons of the uncommitted pursuit of a false
freedom; laced with the sentence of death from cancer for one but
assuaged by late love from a tough landlady – with a heart of gold.
This was what we had been urged to receive with rapture. And all
around lie works of more power and honesty, for which we no longer
have adequate words, since we have devalued the good words by
showering them on anything and everything.

All this is an old argument in Britain and well predates universal
suffrage and universal literacy. Here is Walter Bagehot, in 1864:

We live in the realm of the *half* educated. The number of readers grows daily, but the quality of readers does not improve rapidly. The middle-class is scattered, headless; it is well-meaning but aimless; wishing to be wise, but ignorant how to be wise. The aristocracy of England never was a literary aristocracy, never even in the days of its full power – of its unquestioned predominance did it guide – did it even seriously try to guide – the taste of England. Without guidance young men, and tired men, are thrown amongst a mass of books; they have to choose which they like; many of them would much like to improve their culture, to chasten their taste, if they knew how. But left to themselves they take, not pure art, but showy art; not that which permanently relieves the eye and makes it happy whenever it looks, and as long as it looks, but *glaring* art which captures and arrests the eye for a moment, but which in the end fatigues it. But before the wholesome remedy of nature – the fatigue – arrives the hasty reader has passed on to some new excitement, which in its turn stimulates for an instant, and then is passed by forever. These conditions are not favourable to the due appreciation of pure art – of that art which must be known before it is admired – which must have fastened irrevocably on the brain before you appreciate it, which you must love ere it will seem worthy of your love. ('Wordsworth, Tennyson and Browning or Pure, Ornate and Grotesque Art in English Poetry')

The same counters in the argument go round and round over the decades. There are differences over time as the passage from Bagehot quoted above recalls, differences in the way it is approached and expressed. If heard on radio book programmes today such a passage would sound like the Bible in Ancient Greek. Contemporaries of Bagehot were hardly likely to invoke cultural and class relativism so as to argue that Jane Austen and George Eliot had no value outside their bourgeois origins, settings, conditions and readerships, that their works were not judgeable outside that self-sustaining bourgeois culture. Occasionally on the radio today, more often on Radio 3 than on Kaleidoscope, one hears peculiarly assertive and grinding voices, male and female, proclaiming that position as self-evident.

In the light of today's climate one wonders and admires the fact that the same Corporation produced, from not long after its start in the Twenties, fine drama specifically written for radio, for the unseen voice, intelligent and inventive documentaries in prose and verse, criticism worthy of unedited printing in well-nourished journals; and that radio retained for years, apart from those already named, people such as Alfred Bradley, Charles Parker, Stephen Potter, Phillip Don-nellan. Radio also provided nursery slopes for dramatists who later wrote for TV and the theatre: Harold Pinter, David Howarth, Giles Cooper, Tom Stoppard, Peter Nichols, Alan Ayckbourn.

*

Across television but most of all in the commercial sector the arts are in decline. Arts executives have been sacked on the sound commercial principle that if you don't positively have to do that kind of stuff as a condition of your franchise, why should you bother? If the franchise lacks muscle, is conveniently worded in that area, then do a few such things if needs must; on the cheap, and push them to the margins of viewing time.

That is only one of many restrictive elements of the 1990 Broadcasting Act, the result of structural and financing change, and entirely to be expected. Much more interesting are television's natural difficulties in presenting the arts, poetry above all. Most poetry programmes resort to visual gimmickry; even the best cannot escape the most difficult truth of all, that poetry is to be seen or heard but always to be registered on the inner ear; visuals distract, introduce something alien. Programmes on the visual arts, though, might seem to lend themselves to television treatment, and to some extent they do. But the world of visual arts is in so much of an intellectual mess, so torn with aggressive charge and counter-charge, that that was certain to spill over on to television treatments, sometimes with comically dire results.

*

A little has already been said about fiction on television. Given the difficulties, the best adaptations can be, in their own different and limited terms, justified. But they inhibit the imagination by imposing one visual interpretation on each book and elbowing out others. Above all, they cannot express in other than a limited way the authorial voice (*Middlemarch* had one of the best shots at this, but only in the last few minutes, when George Eliot herself reaches a superb pack of the authorial voice). They can reasonably well handle close-up, and even interior monologue; which is why some of Henry James's novels translate better than most to the small, domestic screen. Even at the best, especially since even a 13-part series of one hour to each instalment must distort the balance and thin out the mixture of narrative, dialogue and reflection, success with good fiction is relative. Perhaps second-rate novels adapt more easily, give television a better chance of creating something of its own from simpler materials.

Television's greatest artistic success is in drama specially written for it, from police dramas to comedy series. Dennis Potter saw this early, saw that the medium had fluidities denied the theatrical stage and loved to extend them. He cherished too the thought that only a small proportion of those who saw his plays on television had seen much if any live theatre, and hence little fine acting. Neither for Potter nor for Alan Plater or Alan Bleasdale or Alan Bennett was television drama a second best. It was, in the subjects it was open to, wider than those usual on the West End stage, in its technical possibilities and in its available audiences precisely what they wanted.

No look at the arts on television should omit the work of Denis Mitchell. After radio documentary in Manchester, he became the father of television documentary as a work of the disciplined imagination, and in that has had no true successors. Years with the BBC were followed by years with Granada when that commercial company was run by people who believed in the medium as much as in the profits it might produce and who cast their nets widely. Their patronage of Denis Mitchell was somewhat similar to that of the BBC for Dennis Potter. *Morning in the Streets* indicated at once that an unusual poetic intelligence, working through vision and sound, was at work. To make *Strangeways* Mitchell spent a lot of time in that prison, just looking and listening; he was as unobtrusive and attentive a listener as a priest at a terrible confession. Once out of Strangeways and beginning to set up the film he said: 'Light and noise. That's what it is. Naked bulbs high up and switched on all the time. The sound of iron doors grating on the floor and clanging (and overall the slopping-out smell). You've got it there.'

Musically well-informed people tend to disparage the transmission of symphonies, concertos, sonatas on television. Their point is not difficult to understand so far as it concerns the inevitable awareness of the cameras at work; and television sound reproduction is not usually as fine as that from a good stereo outfit or hi-fi radio. Yet to transmit music on television does not require the sort of surgery needed to adopt a long and complex novel; the composition can go out whole, as composed. For the less musically proficient the carefully scripted movement of cameras across the sections of the orchestra can be illuminating – even though that word will not be liked by the knowledgeable. To hear Elgar played by Jacqueline du Pré and at the same time see her movements and expression in close-up was an enrichment it would be wrong to disparage. The music was flowing from her memory through every fibre of her being and so into her arms and hands, and to her cello. The situation is different with opera; to watch grand opera on even the largest domestic screen is to be aware all the time that it has been squeezed. But the experience is better than seeing no opera at all, particularly for those, the majority, who cannot attend an opera house: the televised *La Traviata* in 1994 was an outstanding instance of that.

*

Looked at as a whole, television sometimes seems like those new refuse trucks, with a big revolving mouth at the back which is fed all the time. Television is similar in its revolving appetites; similar also in that it seeks to reduce all that goes into it to a uniform mulch; but it fails much of the time; some things are designed to work against the machine's powerful impulses. Some modern theorists find this natural disposition entirely acceptable since they believe that art should be transient and disposable; so television is the technological image and supreme exponent of that 'truth' – no, not 'truth', 'assertion'.

Of all the escapes on television from the difficulty of treating the arts in and for themselves, the most common (as with news) is 'personalisation'. Don't try to 'express' poetry on the screen; show the poet walking over his nearby hills, deep in thought; ask the novelist, face to face, how she manages to combine writing with looking after the children; show the composer preoccupiedly bent over the piano. Talk about the daily details of their lives, how far they have come, where they think they are going. Let the camera linger on this desk, this window, these mean streets; anything but attention to the work itself.

*

An interesting byway emerges here. Has broadcasting, especially because of its disposition to move towards shared and undemanding tastes, damaged our most individual imaginative capacity, that for solitary reading? Yes and no. Before broadcasting appeared most people read little if anything, and many read only disposable rubbish (except where that was C. S. Lewis's or Orwell's 'good bad literature'). Broadcasting offers a far wider and clearer range of windows on the world than most people had access to before.

Not everyone takes advantage of these offerings; many, perhaps most, settle for a narrow, repetitive and easily accommodated range of programmes. Yet here again qualifications set in. As in the range of soap operas. Some are no more than regular repetitive fodder; some are at times probing, honest, critical, witty, about the lives they present – to a degree and at a level rarely reached by the popular novels they have superseded.

Has television reduced reading among the sort of people who are used to reading regularly? Sometimes, yes. Partly because it can be such a fascinating medium, partly because much of intelligence and imagination is at work there – in current affairs, drama, documentaries, comedy, sport, science, natural history and so on. Time has to be found somewhere, so to some extent reading is reduced. This underlines yet again the exceptionally good qualities of much British broadcasting as that has developed within the public service mandate. Many British academics will discuss television programmes without thinking they are slumming and without having a professional interest in the medium. Academics in America, unless they do have a professional interest (say, as students of Contemporary Cultural Studies), will assume that except for a very narrow range of programmes radio and television have nothing to say to them, are no more than an aspect of the market, and one more often than not of that market at its shoddiest.

The differences between different media of communication can be usefully compared by what we have ourselves to put into them. On such a scale, reading would rank highest as the medium to which we have to bring most. Radio would be second and television third. So much being said, one can also add that television, selectively approached rather than used as audio-visual wallpaper, can offer a lot.

V THE 1990 BROADCASTING ACT AND AFTER

If you decide to have a system of people's television, then people's television you must expect it to be. It will reflect their likes and dislikes, their tastes and aversions, what they can comprehend and what is beyond them. Every person of common sense knows that people of superior mental constitution are bound to find much of television intellectually beneath them. If such innately fortunate people cannot realise this gently, and considerately and with good manners, if in their hearts they despise popular pleasures and interests, then of course they will be angrily dissatisfied with television. But it is not really television with which they are dissatisfied. It is with people.

Sir Robert Fraser, first Director-General of ITA, the commercial Television Authority, that network's watchdog, Speech to a conference in the late 1950s

(Clearly Sir Robert was worth a fortune to the commercial companies as its apologist. Students of the English language and of the mass media might be interested to analyse the linguistic shifts and slides there: it is easy to reach a dozen instances.)

When one no longer knows what to do in order to astonish and survive one offers only pudenda to the public gaze.

Paul Valéry

Now three trying to fight against the flood:

The BBC governors have embraced the free market and set the BBC on a course of terminal decline. . . . The high ground policy smells alarmingly like programming by prescription – the enemy of all good works in my experience.

Michael Grade, the 1992 MacTaggart Lecture

Here was a medium of great power, of potentially wondrous delights, that could help to emancipate us from many of the stifling tyrannies of class and status and gutter-press ignorance.

Dennis Potter, the 1993 MacTaggart Lecture

The problem is that the 1990 Broadcasting Act effectively told ITV companies that being a business was more important than being a broad-caster.

Greg Dyke, the 1994 MacTaggart Lecture

Other times, other voices. Now a few more from the Nineties, about 'commercial reality'. The language is as worth watching as the assertions:

TV will exploit the lifting of regulatory protection of certain types of programme; none will be preserved in peak-time just because they are 'worthy'; this is a warning to current affairs producers to keep their subject matter populist.

A strict control of projects is being imposed for no other reason than that their [the schedulers'] brief is to reach the widest audience for the least amount of expenditure.

It means a closer relationship with advertisers ... the beginning of ITV marketing itself properly.

It is madness for programme directors to say they don't want to listen to advertisers.

The days of the Golden Men, the Platonic Guardians, are over.

The above five quotations are all from senior commercial television executives 'facing up to' the new Act. They are even more blunt and 'realistic' when not going into print. They define TV, but not in public, as entertainment designed to deliver viewers to the advertisers; they are sending TV downhill fast in pursuit of that purpose.

As was easily to be predicted, the new Broadcasting Act is destroying the foundations of the public service idea and substituting for it the rule (not the principle) of 'Get Rich Quick through the broadcasting advertising market'. The Tory government (always more narrowly and misguidedly ideological than the Left whom they routinely accuse of that failing) introduced the Act in the name of freedom. They also wanted more of the not politically intransigent broadcasters which the market encourages. The Treasury – like the hard men of the City, the high-interest-led sharks – saw the new commercial broadcasting companies as its milch-cows.

Of course the new commercial bosses had put their hands on their hearts and sworn they would abide by the best and widest definition of broadcasting. They didn't. They are profiteers who will, so far as their watchdog permits, milk the system and then move on to motorway catering or new executive golf-courses.

The Act which is permitting them to line their pockets is (with the damage done to education by narrow vocationalism) among the worst disservices to the quality of life in Britain of the many committed by this sequence of Tory governments. They created what is becoming a broadcasting desert and called it a splendid free city.

Politicians are not usually intellectuals, but they need intellectuals and hate to be without what looks like intellectual backing. The shifty language of the political and commercial lobbies need no longer surprise; the justifications of outside 'authorities' do and should. Among those Arts Council discussion documents described elsewhere is one on 'Mass Culture, the Mass Media and Broadcasting'. It says: 'The Committee on Financing the B.B.C. (1986) [popularly known as the Peacock Committee] had the temerity to question the "principles of public service broadcasting" which prominent broadcasters themselves had drawn up [as we saw earlier, this is an error; the phrase "inform, educate and entertain" which is the basic plank of the public service idea, came from America].' The broadcasters over the years interpreted the implications of those principles, rightly seeing that they were the best defence against commercial exploitation and the best incentive to the full development of good broadcasting. That erroneous sentence in the Council discussion paper adds that the broadcasters did this 'without reference to consumer choice'. Shifty words and shifty ideas again.

The implication, which the author of the discussion document hesitates actually to assert, is that 'prominent broadcasters' cavalierly drew up principles for broadcasting, not with disinterested intentions, but so far as possible to suit their starchy book. In this writer's world nobody does anything out of a wish to get an activity right, but only to serve their turn; usually for gain. The sentence ends with that most popular of Tory populist rallying-cries, 'consumer choice' – which means what we choose to give you so as to get most advertising revenue out of you. Anyone who ignores the 'democratic wishes of the consumer' (that last is another word straight out of the market and unpleasantly downgrading when applied to listeners and viewers), is an élitist. The main and most interesting question about broadcasting in the early years was that no one could know what people's wishes from the medium would or could be; here was a whole population before a new form of domestic communication. It was right to cast the net as widely as possible. The net was not, even so, as wide as it might have been, given the BBC's highly educated but culturally narrow senior personnel and the driven puritanism of Reith; it was still a lot wider than market-driven programming would have produced. So: cast wide, even towards subjects of which most of us have no knowledge, try to produce the best of each kind and see how it all fares.

A prior decision as to what is 'consumer choice' would be no more than a best guess at the existing tastes of the majority; stuff minorities, it implies, unless they are well-lined and can attract advertising aimed at their kind; even so, provide those off-peak. These are obvious results of handing broadcasting to the advertisers and their parasites. They would still surprise very many people since the PR buzz against allowing most people to hear such facts is as powerful as the erstwhile Soviet Union's jamming of the BBC World Service. So it will be, so it will inevitably be. Unless corralled by legislation the commercial contractors will do according to their nature. Their early morning hymn is the same as that of the makers of 'beauty aids' or cheap carpets: 'My first duty is to my shareholders.' That recurrent phrase – particularly repellent when it refers to a monopoly, privatised, public service – is presumed to solve and absolve all.

One can imagine a bizarre conjunction. Suppose several new acts of social legislation came together, and that as a result of pressure from both the commercial and the anti-censorship lobbies all legislation to control aspects of broadcasting was lifted. Transmit whatever you want. Suppose also that a referendum were held on a return to capital punishment. It might well succeed, since 75 per cent of the population favour the return of capital punishment. Suppose that change also included, 'as a deterrent', a return to public executions. That might well have a smaller majority than the main clause but might pass. The conjunctions are not inconceivable. It can be safely predicted that from the date those changes were on the statute book commercial television would transmit public executions; on the best democratic grounds, of course. The BBC would soon feel forced to join in. Those programmes would have the highest viewing figures in any week during which they were shown. So be it, some out-and-out libertarians might say. Others would be left pondering on what those events would tell us about the nature of democracy itself, about its essential checks and balances, about the difference between the democratic dream and the reality, and about the responsibilities which flow from such sobering thoughts.

'The bottom line', as the current cod-phrase is, is simple and clear – as is often the case when the dust-throwing of special interests and special pleading has to stop: in a reasonably organised democracy the sole business of broadcasting will be good broadcasting, in its fullest possible definition. Any other purpose – such as pleasing the government or the advertisers – makes the broadcasters squint. Apply other aims to them and you put their proper professional work under improper pressure. This test – that a false aim introduced into a true profession ruins that profession – can be applied elsewhere; to medicine, to scholarship, to education, to the Public Libraries, to the running of prisons. We didn't really need a demonstration of this fact; if we had, the former regimes of Eastern Europe offered it.

But even if the post-1990 decline goes on, there will still be the BBC, won't there? That depends. Suppose the BBC remains a protected enclave, still funded by the licence fee (a tenuous hope in these circumstances), won't it still be, for other broadcasters prepared to listen, the benchmark of the idea of public service? If the BBC were driven into what would be called a narrow, perhaps even a minority, corner then the pressure to reduce the licence fee would intensify; as always on 'democratic' grounds. The BBC itself as an institution would fight hard to prevent that happening. All large bodies (small ones too, but the tendency increases with size) fight at all costs to save themselves. To do that they will redefine their founding purposes so that black becomes white; and staffing adjusts accordingly. Survival is all. Semantic shifts are always to hand to prove that no shifts have taken place.

The pattern of television is clearly becoming worse: in the programme subjects, in their order and timing and length, and in the quality of the attention given. Five years ago, to take one further example from news management, the 10 p.m. news would not have run an item stoking the most ignorant prejudices by asking: 'Do you want your tax-money spent on fancy native dances [that is, should the Commonwealth Institute continue to receive the meagre funds it is allotted?]' Or the Crafts Council? Or the Countryside Commission? The names alone are sufficient to provoke illiterate cries. This is low-level rabble-rousing, rock-bottom crowd-flattering.

It was clear years ago to all but the ideologically or financially interested that, unless the right precautions were taken, more channels would not mean more choice. Even on one commercial channel (leaving Channel 4 to one side, as rather different) choice can narrow unless the regulations and the regulatory body are tougher than at present. Former Ministers involved in preparing the Act will insist against the evidence that the checks are even now working well. Get them in a corner, off camera, and ask: 'What if they find they are not making as much profit as they think they should be due? What about the regulations then?' The former Cabinet Minister replies. 'Oh, that might be a different matter.'

Everything comes down to head-counting, from estimates as basic as those of a fairground seller of cheap crockery to assessments of what would prise most money from the pockets of the better-off and supposedly more intelligent. It is all, at bottom, a form of trick; to feed the ads. Looking at the greater insistence and skill of the ads themselves one sighs: 'What a pity so much money and talent is diverted from making programmes to making glossier ads'; and immediately that sounds like a Sunday School hope. Since all is relative no such judgments can be made; you may exploit to the limit at present permitted by the Act – which you'll hope to alter even more in your favour before long. The pushing never stops.

Of course the advertisers, we were told, would have no real say in programme choice and content. The commercial TV bosses believe otherwise. More surprisingly, a few years ago it was revealed that a Channel 4 commissioning editor had invited potential advertisers to see the pilot of a proposed soap opera and comment. This was brought to the attention of Michael Grade, Managing Director of Channel 4. He agreed that the procedure was improper and said he had immediately ordered it to be stopped.

It was also said that sponsorship would be rigorously controlled, but it is spreading fast up to and beyond those limits. 'Companies will be looking', it is admitted, 'for opportunities to link up with independent producers to develop proposals to make programmes, *provided* [their italics] that there's also a link-up with the broadcaster to ensure that the programme gets on air' – in short, they'll be looking for co-production opportunities. An outside research worker approaches from another angle:

> As sponsorship money becomes a larger element of channel revenue and of independent producers' survival, the greater will be the temptation to create programmes consistent with potential sponsors' values; wholesome, decent, family and, above all, uncontroversial. (Cit. in *The Spread of Sponsorship*, ed. Shaw, 1993)

In case there is still any doubt about the spread of sponsorship, here is yet one more quotation, from the Nineties:

> Sponsorship still has a long way to go before it attains the kind of impact on the viewer of which it is capable. A more sophisticated marriage between programme and product and increased creativity are the keys to sponsorship coming of age. (Source as above)

An especially interesting statement that, semantically: 'sophisticated marriage . . . creativity . . . coming of age'. Smooth as synthetic cream. The satellite channels will hasten this whole process. Perversely but not surprisingly, some people will continue against the evidence to imply that the licence fee is onerous – these are often the satellite companies who aim to remove major popular events to their separately charged areas.

There are still a few semi-protected areas in commercial television, enabling rather than denying areas, areas saying 'thou shalt' not 'thou shalt not'; not only 'thou shalt not be explicitly pornographic but thou shalt pay attention to, among other non-mass-audience grabbers, the arts and education'. There are still some people sheltering under that protection and doing good work. Not for long.

Channel 4

The most curious 'sport' in all this is Channel 4. So far as it works structurally, Channel 4 is the son of Pilkington. The Pilkington Report recommended that the squint be removed from the eyes of commercial television by separating the programme-making function from the advertising-revenue function. The Independent Television Authority would take in all advertising revenue and commission programmes from the producing companies; with its eyes only on the widest range of good broadcasting. That was more or less the basis of Channel 4's founding in 1981. True to form, this sequence of governments has now put those two functions together; it will become progressively harder for Channel 4 to fulfil its brief, rather than to 'maximise' advertising revenue, even though it does not have to answer to profit-seeking shareholders.

Channel 4 was set up to promote a piping-off of certain minority tastes; on audience size alone it could not be justified; it is expensive, one might even say undemocratic (as could have been said about the Third Programme). But it took the threat of direct competition for ads away from Channel 3. It would have been easy to devise a range of more democratic uses for the channel. It is not preponderantly an intellectual or artistic or educational channel. But it can be welcomed because it is, at least, not mass-advertising driven; it looks at a range of minority activities and tastes, some very intelligent, some oddball, some plain silly.

Its hour-long news, from 7 to 8 p.m., rightly valued though not a crowd puller, is said to be already feeling strain. The channel has chosen good films and subsidised good low-budget British enterprises at a time when the home film industry is in poor shape. It has made some good artistic gambles and looked for visually interesting activities which the other channels have not felt able, on grounds of viewing numbers, to transmit. Its main weakness is, as always, relativism; it has no compass for judgment, so some of its commissioning editors slither and slide in and out of the latest fashion. On Saturdays, late, it goes in for 'adult' (oh, that word!) comedy, cabaret, chat-shows. They can be as adult as a boy writing rude words on the school's lavatory walls. Or a girl. One woman performer brought the invited house down with: 'My husband's so egotistical that when we are bonking, and he comes, he shouts out his own name'. That was better than most of her jokes; but the very slightly delayed-action laughter was evoked more because she had dared to say 'bonk' and, even more, 'come'.

Naturally, the box of excuses is always ready, with language to match. Asked why Channel 4 felt the need – many other subjects being available – to devote a succession of late Saturday nights to a series about erotica across the world, the editor responsible evaded the question but said the series would be 'forthright and honest'. Well, then, in forthright language: 'Balls!' These people are destroying the language before one's eyes.

Two other main and interconnected questions remain, both of them of concern to recent governments, even though these are governments which believe 'in letting everything hang out'. Of course, they do not take that slogan to the limit; it is merely a 'set the market free' tic. They Worry-with-Whitehouse about likely bad effects from broadcasting; and so they are quick-fingered in trying to censor sex, violence or what does not suit their politics or voting figures. Both this 'effects debate' and the 'censorship debate' – though 'debate' is too favourable a label – will be looked at in Chapter 11, within a wider context.

vi CONCLUSION

The laws of the free market for material goods are not the same as for cultural goods. The latter are largely hand-made, carry risks, have surprising and unpredictable effects. Who would have forecast that Antiques Roadshow *would attract twice as many viewers as a football match?*

The television fiction of the Eighties has touched on 'truths' in an imaginative and recognisable way. It is no accident that Bread *is a popular comedy; no accident that* A Very Peculiar Practice *became something of a cult success, that* Edge of Darkness *excited the 'green' imagination, that – earlier –* Boys from the Blackstuff *told more about the underside of Britain than a raft of factual programmes would have done.*

Quality in Television, Broadcasting Research Unit, 1989

Reith's days are long over, and the contribution of that anguished man to British broadcasting is generally undervalued. So is that of Sir William Haley, who came after Reith as Director-General. Haley's idea of the BBC's duty to encourage people to move up a pyramid of taste is, if it is ever remembered, only the subject for a dismissal; but it has its dignity and worth. Another of Haley's ideas is magnificent: that broadcasting should aim to put itself out of business because it should show us that the world is wider and more interesting than we had ever imagined – so that we desert radio and the box, or at least give them less attention. That is already true of some people; for others it is becoming less and less likely. Certainly the idea would be another Chinese puzzle to the monoglot army of commercialists. More understandable and even more regarded as risible was the Labour Minister Ellen Wilkinson's remark that she looked forward to seeing the emergence of a 'Third Programme nation'. Not quite apt for the early Third Programme; but she meant an intelligent and discriminating nation. This sounds astonishing nowadays since it is entirely against the tide. It's better than looking forward to a 'game-show nation', though. At least none of these earnest remarks demeans the people it is speaking about. To repeat: in setting up broadcasting, we did get something in our domestic decisions better than most such decisions. One shameful act of this sequence of governments is their undermining of that achievement.

It is worth coming back at this point to Pilkington's bold – as it proved – use of the word 'moral' in discussing broadcasting. The Report said, to a background response of tinny laughter, that broadcasters 'are in a constant and living engagement with the moral condition of society'. Bravo to the self-evident, to a sentence which means that the texture, the quality of the life, of a society – its habits and ways of life as expressions of assumptions and values – will be reflected and to some extent affected by broadcasting. So, to repeat yet another splendid phrase, broadcasting presents a society to itself and would have failed in its duty if it did not 'reflect the quarrels of society with itself', if it were not, as it should also be, an arena for those quarrels. Broadcasting must aim to break the mould, the crust of convention which all societies, like frenetic ants, always try to put over free questioning. It must not be afraid of challenging and of sometimes putting off its listeners and viewers.

Broadcasting must not therefore patronise or underestimate the possibilities of its audiences, no matter how many disappointments it has on the way. Broadcasters should stand up for the common man's right to be respected, to recognise the highest when he sees it, and so to deserve being offered nothing but the best in all kinds of programme, to be capable of more than the superficial. The real patronage is to level down. Since the popular press has dived for the deepest ditch where lie the lowest common denominators, there is all the more reason for the freer network to aim higher.

Good tests are often simple. For those who justify the deterioration in British broadcasting whilst perhaps not greatly watching it themselves, a simple question is apposite: would you be happy to think that when your own children grow up they would spend forty hours a week as couch-potatoes watching television?

*

Near the end of its life two members of the Broadcasting Research Unit drew up a draft 'Broadcasting Charter – Duties and Rights for Listeners, Viewers, Programme-makers and Legislators'. It arrived too late to be published. The 'Duties' of listeners and viewers were deliberately put before 'Rights' and included the obvious, such as not interfering with others people's listening; and less understood duties such as respecting other people's tastes and looking at the range of overall provision before complaining that something to our particular taste is not always available.

'Rights' cover much the same ground as the principles of public service broadcasting given earlier; but 'rights' in this later publication elaborate on them and are often sharper:

> We have the right to be approached as adults . . . the right to resist the present dual tendency by which we are more and more seen as market-fodder and at the same time are more and more subject to external, narrow, moralising controls . . . we claim the right not to be got at politically, commercially, piously. We want to be trusted, not over-protected . . . Most of us can recognise prejudice when we see it . . . We do not need a Broadcasting Standards Council; existing laws and systems of supervision are enough . . .

The 'Duties' of the programme-makers point out first that their duties are greater than those of print journalists, who write for self-selected audiences; they include the obligation 'to treat each subject at the *right* pitch of comprehension', to respect the listener and viewer, the subject and the medium; 'to play fair in editing contributions', and to be honestly not 'corruptly' creative. Those particular Duties and Rights take up six closely typed pages.

The Duties and Rights of the Legislators are briefer; not to legislate too tightly, to finance in the way which best helps broadcasting itself, not to be pushed around by the narrower kind of moralists, to put the emphasis firmly on liberating not restricting legislation, and to encourage the broadcasters to reflect that 'quarrel of society with itself'.

BRU's *Quality in Television* ended more crisply. The necessary conditions for quality, its producer-respondents said, were editorial freedom, especially from the obligation to maximise audiences, time, high craft, well-nourished intelligence, risk-taking, peer-group admiration and a sense of mission (professionalism). Quality is driven down by ratings-chasing and fear of failure and so leads to copying existing audience-pleasers, to shortage of time and so formulaic programme-making, peer-group admiration for high ratings and no sense of mission – 'only there for the money'.

Broadcasters can exploit ignorance, apathy and cruelty; more and more do. To describe objections to all this as 'do-goodery' is to take refuge in misguided slogans so as to avoid embarrassing interrogations. No programme is ever justified by the answer: 'But they enjoyed it.' So does a cat playing with a dying sparrow. The tendency to meet such charges with a ribald dismissal is yet another instance of moral bankruptcy of the rotten 'give the punters what they want' spirit.

One has to return in the end to 'professionalism', which arises from respect for the medium, its themes, its listeners and viewers. It emerges from the mutual respect and support of one's peers, the sense of working honestly towards a common end, a constant to'ing and fro'ing of skilled judgments. We are back with the need for a clear eye, not a squint. 'Virtue [Alasdair MacIntyre is deliberately using an old-fashioned noun so as to indicate professionalism's inescapable moral roots] defines our relationship to those other people with whom we share the kind of purposes and standards which inform practices. . . . Without the professional virtues, practices could not resist the corrupting power of institutions' (*After Virtue*, 1981).

In the light of all the irrelevant pressures under which broadcasters work today it is remarkable how much good work is still produced. Mention of those fine, sometimes splendid, programmes recalls the main point. Excellent programmes there are, as good as there ever were. Appalling programmes there are also, worse even than before.

There is a chasm between the two and their audiences, a chasm wider than ever before – another instance of the divisions which suit the commercial-persuading world since they keep the top-status group happily fenced off and allow the rape of the rest to continue and strengthen.

CHAPTER SIX

Misuses of Language

The last thing a political party gives up is its vocabulary.
  Alexis Tocqueville, *Democracy in America*, 1835–40

*Unity of speech is essential to the unity of a people. Community of
language is a stronger bond than identity of religion or government.*
  G. P. Marsh, cit. Rod Mengham, *The Descent of Language*,
1993

My language is the universal whore I have to make into a virgin.
  Karl Kraus, *Die Fackel*

Advertising has annihilated the power of the most powerful adjectives.
  Paul Valéry

The universal nausea of advertisements.

  Charles Baudelaire

Kraus gives a reminder of the beauty and fragility of language in all
its aspects. Since it is an essential part of how one tries to make sense
of experience and of oneself it is always under threat – used to solve
or evade or manageably redefine problems. Language is always being
corrupted, though in different ways at different times; contemporary
corruptions come more than anything from the wide-openness of
this world. The whole process is made more difficult by the fact that
the particular languages we each inherit act themselves as controls
on consciousness; they prompt required attitudes and inhibit those
less acceptable to the culture; and it all then seems like 'common
sense' and 'plain talking'; always and everywhere. This is not to
disagree with Pinker (*The Language Instinct*, 1994) when he argues
that sloppy language needn't lead to sloppy thought; the point is
different.

The Way We Live Now

i LINGUISTIC TICS

Tell me what language you use and I'll tell you what kind of man you are.

after Ruskin

Corruptions today come most obviously from the public relations and advertising people, in whatever field they operate, from clothing to politics to religion. PR probably does more harm than the ads because it more often tries to insinuate itself by a direct, *ad hominem* approach; advertising more often moves obliquely, through its descriptions of the objects or services it is promoting.

An example of PR language at its typically ingratiating found in a newspaper:

> [X] does very well indeed. He says this attitude is what the English revolution is all about. He talks about how people have changed. How they face things squarely. Wants life to be straightforward, not full of unwritten rules. He says it shows in everything they do. The way they dress, talk, write, think, even drink. He talks about what people drink nowadays. He says it's vodka. Cossack vodka because it's a clean drink. Cossack vodka because it's straightforward and makes no pretence.

This unctuous vodka ad sounds like a thin echo of some elements in Hemingway: short, down-to-earth sentences, avoidance of abstractions, few polysyllabic words. But Hemingway does not nudge and sidle:

> I was always embarrassed by the words. There were many words that you could not stand to hear and finally only the names of places had dignity. Abstract words were obscene beside the concrete names of villages. (*A Farewell to Arms*)

Hemingway says 'I' but keeps his distance by the force of his moral position before his subject, which is itself the debasement of language. In the world of the persuaders, words used by Hemingway such as 'dignity' and 'concrete' (meaning true to what it says) are used merely as persuasive counters. Their most favoured word is 'image', which means what surface they hope engagingly to present to their audience, whatever the reality underneath

A famous passage from Ezra Pound comes in here. He is talking of literature, but what he says is just as apt for language:

Has literature [language] a function in the state, in the aggregate of humans . . .?

It has to do with the clarity and vigour of 'any and every' thought and opinion. It has to do with maintaining the very cleanliness of the tools, the health of the very matter of thought itself. Save the rare and limited instances of invention in the plastic arts, or in mathematics, the individual cannot think and communicate his thought, the governor and legislator cannot act effectively or frame his laws, without words, and the solidity and validity of these words is in the care of the damned and despised *litterati*. When their work goes rotten – by that I do not mean when they express indecorous thoughts – but when their very medium, the very essence of their work, the application of word to thing goes rotten, i.e. becomes slushy and inexact, or excessive or bloated, the whole machinery of social and individual thought and order goes to pot. ('How to Read', 1931; repr. in *Literary Essays of Ezra Pound*, ed. T. S. Eliot, 1954)

Words still have their charm; and their dread. The charm is shown in the successive but always short-term use of pleasing words, phrases and images which give a new twist to tired ordinary language; another person's borrowed flowers, the tribute which linguistic laziness pays to the idea that language should be fresh. Hence the popularity of phrases about language itself; as in 'sound-bites', which are the semantic equivalent of 'Chicken nuggets'. Or the taking over of sonorous words such as 'culture' and 'literacy': 'the culture of television', 'computer literacy'; or, for that matter, 'computer culture or 'television literacy'. There are also 'gay culture'; and 'ethnic culture', which is a tautology. Odder still is the demand for 'a culture of rights', which presumably means that we should demand a Bill of Rights. Any group, if not a 'community', is an 'Establishment': as in, perhaps, 'the rabbit-fancying Establishment'; no doubt one exists.

Colour of a kind insists on creeping in. Every six months or so a quite striking image pops up: 'the flavour of the month', 'brownie points' (in Britain that sounds as innocuous as the Girl Guides; in America it has a grosser meaning), 'cutting edge', 'give me a bell', 'shelf-life', 'dead in the water', 'grass-roots', 'at the coalface', 'an accident waiting to happen', 'a level playing-field', 'till the fat lady sings', 'sending the wrong signals', 'the bottom line', 'on the back burner', 'punters', 'a tad', 'kick-start', 'window of opportunity', 'moving the chairs on the *Titanic*', 'more than you can shake a stick at', 'opens up a whole new can of worms', 'past its sell-by date', 'like a rat out of a trap', 'cusp', 'eat your heart out, Mr X', 'a feeding-frenzy', 'No more Mr Nice Guy'. And a particularly cheap dismissal: 'anal retentive'.

The origins of some are obvious; others are verbal hula-hoops or skate-boards with little or no social or psychological reverberations. Equally obviously, some are 'boo' and some 'hurrah' words. Some favourites seem like hangovers from a more male chauvinistic era or small blasts against feminism: 'rugged', 'sinewy', 'sturdy', 'vigorous', 'wiry' and 'robust'. The then Foreign Secretary, Douglas Hurd, twisting and turning out of the Pergau Dam embarrassments, announced that he 'took a fairly robust view of where the interests of this country lie' ('no prizes' for substituting a more appropriate word for 'robust'). The same man, clearly discriminating and very well-mannered, seems attracted to beefy words as if to prove his political 'street-cred'. He will say in the middle of an elegant speech, that he takes a 'hard-nosed' view of a matter. The sign of gear-changing in style is the slight pause before the out-of-character word is uttered; it then sounds as though a dowager is swallowing a humbug. Mr Hurd would, one feels sure, draw the line at labelling critics of prisons policy, as his colleague the Home Secretary did, 'do-gooders'; too low-level. Perhaps equally unlikely would be Mr Hurd's use of one of his Cabinet's favoured horrors: 'the feel-good factor'; but one never knows.

It might be interesting to float a racy invention and see how long it took to be picked up and how long its 'shelf-life' was. Almost all such images flourish and fade. But they are needed, a half-teaspoon of yeast in the dough of modern oral communicating; and now and again one will continue to hang around and be duly entered in the *Oxford English Dictionary*.

ii DODGING REALITY AND JUDGMENT

All words like peace and love,
All sane affirmative speech,
Had been soiled, profaned, debased
To a horrid mechanical screech ...
W. H. Auden, dedication to *Nones*, 1951

When one considers one's relation to the language one was born into, and the way in which that language – in which one has vital relations with other human beings – exists then the fundamental recognition can least be escaped, but challenges thought insistently. Where language is concerned, 'life' is human life.

F. R. Leavis, 'English as a Discipline of Thought', *The Way Ahead*, 1975

Trickier and more interesting is that range of words which suggest a wish, probably unconscious, to evade reality; and judgment. Such words and phrases range from cotton-wool to clear plastic to blunt instruments. Most obviously they attempt to place life, through language, in a germ-free, technocratic world, hard, unassailable, non-impressionistic, would-be objective, 'non-judgmental'. (As was seen earlier, 'judgmental' is itself an escape from saying 'judgment'. Judgment stands awkwardly before you; 'judgmental' is clearly a fusspot's attitude.)

Some forms are well recognised for what they unpleasantly are, such as the early 'liquidate'; 'take out' is more recent. The coiners in the Pentagon's PR office slipped up with the bizarrely insensitive 'friendly fire'.

Less colourful adaptations are more revealing. Advertisements for highly paid executive jobs, usually put in the newspapers by specialist recruitment agencies, are rich in this kind of escapist jargon. They don't talk about the people or the staff whom the executives will have to guide, encourage and – the staff may hope – treat properly. They say, as though they are talking about computers or fax machines, that you will 'control adequate human resources'. That formulation is some distance from the reality of the lives of your individual members of staff, from their fears and difficulties and needs for reassurance. It is easier to declare a part of your 'human resources' surplus to requirements than to sack a man or woman. Recently, a peer, announcing losses for the company he is chairman of, said there would have to be some 'head-count reductions'. Words used like this despoil all they touch: family bonds, good bread, the innocence of children, joy and sorrow.

More and more this language sounds as though it has fallen off the back of a computer: virement, tranche (and no doubt 'viring a tranche'), revise downwards, trialled, strategies, function analysis, spectrum of views, structured, targeted, flow-charts, matrix management, a higher profile, continuing dialogue, focal, pivotal, interactive, flexible, mainstreaming, sensitised. Many of these words and phrases have justifiable professional uses. They are more often used loosely and inaccurately, as modish signs.

*

In a world in which the expression of moral values is feared, those who have explicit, personal as distinct from group-ideological beliefs confine avowal of them to church, home or friends of a similar persuasion. There is no longer a valid public currency in that bank; its notes and coins are historic curiosities, like nineteenth-century Albanian State Railway bonds.

Look again at the expensive advertisements put out by professional recruiting agencies 'trawling' for a 'high-powered' executive. They ask for people with 'strong motivation' as though they are asking for a very special virtue. But if strong motivation is a virtue it belongs to that second-class kind: successful crooks must have it; every tyrant has it. They mean they are looking for a ruthless pusher. Or they ask, even more sententiously, for someone 'with a strong *commitment* to the success of the enterprise', which translates into the hectic pursuit of increased sales. The Devil may not always have the best tunes; he certainly has the most good words nicked from God; they then become weasel words.

It follows that there is also a disinclination to use words which may seem based on thought with tentacular roots into our reflective personality. So a phrase such as 'I hold to the belief that . . .' gives way to 'My concept is . . .', as though a concept springs out of the head like a thin, sterilised steel aerial. Or there is 'My perception is . . .', which leaves the implication that one perception is at least as good as any other. The attempt to escape from being caught making judgments goes on, through a succession of substitutes for thought, But there can be no effective escape. Though we cannot possibly say: 'Here I stand. I can do no other,' the need to express conviction survives.

Listen to conversations which reach an area where judgment does seem called for. There will be, first, a disinclination to pass or hear anyone else pass judgment: 'Well, that's only your point of view/ opinion'; 'Aren't you being a bit élitist/bourgeois/judgmental?'; 'But isn't that a *value*-judgment?'; 'It's not my place to pass judgment'.

But judgments can't be altogether evaded, so at a certain point someone usually says: 'I *actually* think . . .' or 'I *definitely* think . . .'. The revealing words are the stressed 'actually' and 'definitely'. The word being avoided is 'believe', for that's hardly sayable. To say only 'I think' would not be strong enough at that moment. The stressed 'actually' and 'definitely' transform 'I think' into a subcutaneous 'I believe'.

iii LANGUAGE AND IDEOLOGY

It was intended that when Newspeak had been adopted once and for all and Oldspeak forgotten, a heretical thought... should be literally unthinkable, at least so far as thought is dependent on words.

George Orwell, *1984*

Most active and disabling of all, in the effort for clear speech, is language used as ideology. This can be relativist if that suits the speaker's or writer's turn; it can also be entirely unrelativist, sure of the absolute rightness of what is being said. Their own bank still cashes their own cheques. There are, once more and commonly, 'boo' and 'hurrah' words and compounds ('bourgeois cultural imperialism'). There is also, even in the more ideologically active, a tendency to evade; or perhaps the distortion is from simple confusion – as in the old 'Nuclear-free zone', which means 'anti-nuclear Local Council' and which inevitably called out the rejoinder: 'I hope they've told the Soviet Union, then.'

The more humane euphemisms are worth more attention. Some are obvious sugar-coatings, some come strangely from people whose language for individuals and people with whom they disagree can be entirely unmollified, some reek of PR, some are slimy ('care in the community'), some are simply well-meant. 'Senior citizens' for 'old people' is saccharine, meant to confer dignity on old age pensioners. They are, to use the language of some African tribes, the 'elders', the wise elders. That hardly fits the treatment of OAPs in Britain today, by governments or individuals. The phrase is a bogus attribution, dreamed up by a public relations executive, cheap and insincere flattery.

'Positive discrimination' is a sly phrase whose accurate meaning is 'loading the dice in favour of people whom we have decided need a leg-up, on grounds irrelevant to the actual choice we now have to make'. It is certainly possible to make a case for the practice. But it should not be hidden under odourless abstractions; unless you are also willing to accept 'negative discrimination'.

Then there are the blanket terms, some so obviously well-intentioned as to be just acceptable, others not; it is the degree of blanketing in the way they are commonly used which makes the difference. 'Disadvantaged' can have a moderately precise use but is spread so widely, from the genuinely disadvantaged to any kind of criminal, as often to be no more than a thin cellophane covering. 'Unwaged' began as an attempt to avoid calling anyone, starkly, 'unemployed'; it is now brought into service as a small, disguising portmanteau for 'unemployed . . . students . . . OAPs' ('concessions for the unwaged' at an event means 'admitted for less'). That's just passable though a get-out. 'One-parent families' is, like 'disadvantaged', a very large blanket, and again well-meant. There are women – and most 'one-parent' families have a woman parent – who reject the cover and say, straight: 'Me – I'm a deserted wife/partner.'

The more explicitly ideological habits in language are more toughly pushed; listen only to the way 'empowerment' is now used. 'You're being provocative' is an old one and translates as: 'You've hit on one of my weaknesses.' One of the most common is in the use of 'ethnic'. 'Ethnic' means belonging to a particular ethnic group, so we are all ethnics of one sort or another. Today the word is used to refer to people who belong to ethnic groups other than our own. The British – English, Scottish, Welsh – are not ethnics; they are what they are; anybody outside is ethnic. So what is meant to be a recognition and acceptance of other people's differences – 'Ethnic dances in the chapel hall tonight' will not mean Glossop clog-dancers but, probably, dancers from a part of Asia – becomes another form, unconsciously, of British insularity.

Some authors, discussing violence in the home, will insist on describing it as 'gender-specific'. They mean that more – probably many more – men are violent towards their wives or partners than the other way round. No explanation that 'gender-specific' means unique to one sex – like a vagina or a penis – will persuade them to drop the phrase. Strange how even unreverberating abstractions can for some people pick up powerful emotional reverberations.

'Grass-roots' suggests the honest, the down-to-earth, the non-metropolitan, the spontaneous, the unaffectedly provincial or working-class. A variant is 'at the coalface', which suggests that teachers, producers, actors are always more 'insightful' than anyone in charge and, worse, operating from a desk, 'desk-bound'.

'Community' has even stronger resonances. Perhaps because the sense of 'community' is under such attack nowadays, the word has become magic, a talisman. It suggests connections now lost; 'No man is an island'. So there are 'the Asian community', 'the ethnic communities', 'the radical community', 'the progressive community' and – a beauty, since it carries two approbations in one – 'the gay community'. A moment's thought should indicate that homosexuals and Asians and radicals can dislike each other just as much as can people in any other group, even those whose members have a single and often fortuitous common characteristic. 'Community' is a potent word on one side of the fence; how often have you seen references to 'the right-wing community', 'the skinhead community' – or to 'grass-roots fascists'? 'Community' too often takes a word for the deed. For print and broadcasting journalists in particular it is a nervous twitch. Even more; they can scarcely ever use the single word; all communities are, by definition, 'close-knit communities'; the phrase is by now an empty shell.

There is a good sense in which one might, very carefully, refer to 'our common culture'. One could also speak of 'the cultures of Britain'; or of Scotland and Wales. But these are different from the casual and habitual references to Britain as 'a multi-cultural society' (newsreaders begin: 'In today's multi-cultural Britain . . .'). There have been large immigrations of people from different cultures in the last twenty or thirty years. These people should be accepted fully. But the phrase 'We are now a multi-cultural society and so we should . . .' is often aggressively and loosely used, as though the speaker thinks Britain is by now a patchwork of several roughly equal ethnic and religious groups. This is simply not so; the claim is often employed out of ignorance or as a form of linguistic bullying. In 1994 a study at Manchester University showed that blacks and Asians together (the groups these users of the phrase are pointing at, not – say – Jews or the Irish) comprised 5.6 per cent of people living in Britain. There were of course higher percentages in some cities, and differences in birth-rates. The 1992 Census had arrived at the overall figure of 5.5 per cent. Such figures make the phrase 'a multi-cultural society', as it is commonly used, excessive. It would fall foul of any Trades Descriptions Act. To any white racist in Britain the exaggeration gives ammunition; it damages a fair cause. The case should be based not on a phantom equality in numbers but on human justice.

During a coffee-break at a conference on cultural differences, a member remarked that Jews were exceptionally clever, inventive, intellectual, artistic. She may have been mistaken, but it was a fair comment, a proper intellectual question. She was roundly criticised for 'racism'. If she had said that Asian shopkeepers tend to work harder than English ones she would have been equally attacked. This thoughtless obstructionism is a minor but growing restriction on free enquiry. Perhaps that woman should also have been charged with 'Semitism' as opposed to 'anti-Semitism'. At this point the mind seizes up. Peter Ustinov guyed exactly this kind of inhibition by carefully avoiding any race-identifying noun: 'I believe that human beings have made a contribution to the human condition out of all proportion to their numbers.'

Such distortings of the language have more downs than ups. The downs indicate fears, evasions, corruptions in thought and so in the general culture. The ups are when language sympathetically, gently, is adapted to unpleasant circumstances.

iv HOSPITAL KINDLY GENTILITY

But still the heart doth need a language . . .
Samuel Taylor Coleridge, *The Piccolomini*

Hospital language is a good example, the old-fashioned Marshall and Snelgrove kindly gentility of the wards. 'How are the waterworks today, Mrs Smith?' Or 'Has the tummy settled down?' '*The* tummy', '*the* waterworks', not '*your* tummy' or '*your* waterworks'. Such locutions reduce the embarrassment, especially for people whose local attitudes make them easily embarrassed about 'intimate bodily functions'. 'Waterworks' and similar euphemisms mollify the harsh reality: that you are now forced to rely on others to carry out such jobs.

The language seeks to create a temporary and very friendly community, against the odds. Christian names are obligatory. Phatic phrases rule: 'There you go, Jack' or 'Here you go, John' as they hand you a bedpan; 'Cheers, Jim' as they pass your bed; 'Brilliant' or 'Brill' for anything which pleases them. A temporary cocoon, a wrap-around world. Such humane and kindly uses are worth more regard, wherever they are found. As so often, tone is the key.

*

We often refuse to accept an idea merely because the tone of voice in which it has been expressed is unsympathetic to us. Friedrich Nietzsche

Other than in specialist studies, relatively little has been written about the great varieties of tone in English speech and writing. 'Who do you think you're talking to?' is a direct response to tone as much as to substance. More direct is 'Don't use that tone of voice with me.' 'Tone' can suggest an unconsciously reached-for audience, or a consciously conceived but not necessarily known ideal audience. It may be a crude class-indicator running through a range of attitudes, from superiority to subservience; or it may reveal a talking to oneself – inturned, musing. Writers especially, but not only writers, have many tones; and some are put on like different kinds of clothing, again especially by writers as part of their trade. We all like to feel, though, that we can by acquaintance begin to recognise a writer's and a speaker's 'true' tone, characteristic intonations, arrests and flows; but that is a more difficult exercise than is usually recognised.

Tones are integrally linked with facial expressions; tones of voice and looks. 'I didn't like the look he gave me' is simple. This can graduate to 'Then he gave me a meaning look' or 'His looks spoke daggers'. *Punch* once caught the connection exactly: 'Don't look at me, Sir, with – ah – in that tone of voice.'

V EMBARRASSED BY THE WORDS

Much further back a more extended visit was promised to the Arts and Entertainment Council's seminar of the early 1990s and its rioting language. Like most institutions today, the Council loves acronyms. One could easily imagine a conversation between the cognoscenti: 'Of course, I told M/ORG that BIISNA couldn't be proactive in that way. There's no window of opportunity for them there, only for D/STR and his AS/COM outfit.' It recalls the old story about commercial travellers exchanging dirty jokes in the train. Since they all knew the jokes word for word one of them had only to say 'Number 33' to set the others sniggering.

In modern outfits the love of technologese acronyms is counter-pointed with an addiction to shortened, pally first names: 'Rod will now introduce the new customised formula for UG/4/C. Debby is holding up the pie chart.' Rick, Libby, Gerry, Cathy, Maggie, Jacqui, Chris are standing by in the wings, 'to provide expert servicing support'. The conjunction of mechanistic acronyms and chummily shortened first name produces a similar air of unreality to that felt during a feature film when the mechanical man steps forward and speaks – like Boris Karloff, in an all too humanised and so undeceiv-ing, friendly but metallic purr: 'Folks. I'm a real pal.'

The language of the AETC seminar and of its publications was entirely predictable. Among the drizzle of those 'in' words and phrases listed earlier, one met: 'significant modifiers . . . modular competencies [which] underpinned knowledge and understanding [two human words have crept in there] ... key functions ... range statements and concepts ... time-based ... live art-works' – a blizzard of thin-chrome language handled with an uncritical, almost a pure, certainly an innocent, but unfortunately a linguistically ignorant, passion.

One might imagine that someone called Sid would say, just to clear the air: 'We need to know more about how writing works and what publishers expect today'. Very practical and down-to-earth. Instead he would step forward and say: 'Some further clarification of the writing functions is required, and a more comprehensive overview of the professional standards already developed for publishing and journalism by other industry-led bodies in the sector.'

It might have been better if this 'team' had distinguished between writing as a business, written specifically for gain, and directed at known 'outlets' and 'target-audiences'; and writing regarded as an area of free creativity. The distinction is not and cannot be absolute. In this century Graham Greene wrote to live, but divided his novels into 'entertainments' and the others, the more committed. D. H. Lawrence to some extent and James Joyce almost entirely lived on private patronage so that their work could be more freely done, not haunted by the shadow of a known market and editors who might think only in terms of that market.

Of the many institutions which promise to teach you how to write successfully for the market, some can be useful in a limited way and for the right – somewhat gifted – people; some are rip-offs. The University of East Anglia's MA course in creative writing belongs to a different area. It can select people who already seem both gifted and dedicated, and put them with their peers under the supervision of talented, dedicated and successful writers. If some of its students did not go on to successful creative careers – as some do – that would be surprising.

The organisers at the seminar described above seem not to have conceived that there is any impulse to write which is not directed strictly at 'the market'. If everything is measurable and assessable, as they seem to think, then surely publishers would be glad to have a first filter in the form of the tests of Qualifications they are drawing up? Has the Thatcheresque mania to measure everything, even the least tangible of human efforts, gone this far? With some people, apparently so.

People such as that – market-centred, linguistically deaf – recall the advertising world's gross misuse of the word 'creative'. It is a sign of the highest kind of 'creativity', indeed of 'creative genius', to show a picture of an apparently pregnant man so as to encourage contraception; or of a huge crowd in a field, grouped so as to produce British Airways' colours and singing a matey song. If this is 'creative genius' then even a moderately successful novelist or poet or dramatist exhibits it again and again in every work. The money's different; being so excessively paid, the admen don't need the good titles as well.

It is clear that public funds can be released for almost any educational notion so long as it can be labelled 'vocational'. And almost anything can be so labelled, at a pinch. Such as 'Rules for Personality Enhancement as a Vocational Tool' (though this is invented, the course may exist already). 'Rules towards Ensuring Eternal Life' are probably some way off but may just creep under the 'vocational' net since they might increase the 'work-force'. Rules for arriving at greater goodness would probably be ruled out as of no wider social use and, to the organisers' infinite sadness, unmeasurable. Nevertheless, people continue to rise from the depths, like carp with the secret gold ring in their mouths, only too willing to translate its arcane message into accessible segments; for pay.

The Department of Employment may not contain many literary critics, linguistic experts or creative writers. Yet surely there are some people there who can recognise balderdash when they see it and say: 'To subsidise people who write like this about writing would be like paying a tone-deaf person to advise on music, or a blind man on painting or one with no sense of smell on perfume creation, or one with no taste buds as a trainer of chefs.'

Direct relativism is also at work in major outlying linguistic areas. It shows itself in the hammering about 'rights' – rights can be conceived as wide-open, catholic, ours and ours alone. They then belong in the realm of the endlessly unqualified and unconditional; or seem to. But to see 'rights' as inextricably founded in 'duties' does not reduce the importance of 'rights'; it anchors them and removes them from the free-floating relativist air. We can have rights because we recognise duties, whether that is to do with simple matters such as driving discipline or the most important and all-embracing of all: 'Human Rights'. Human Rights cannot be promoted except by those who have recognised the duty and the difficulty of that promotion. But we hear almost nothing of 'duties' today, only more and more about 'rights'.

'The medium is the message'? No: the message is carried by the medium and is more important than the medium. This confusion is so deep-seated that someone criticised for plainly bad work will, in the effort not to accept or face those criticisms, almost invariably say: 'I'm afraid that what we have here is "a failure in communication".' Not at all. Your work is not up to the mark. To understand is not necessarily to forgive; it might compound the sins and the dislike. To put all criticism down to a technological block in the communicative works is to remove all unacceptable judgments, to live in that world where there can be no judgments, only greater or lesser degrees of openness in channels – whatever ignored intrinsic 'messages' those channels may actually be carrying.

This galloping convinced non-conviction has moved from the words to the accents in which they are spoken. A modern author declares: 'Accents are intrinsically neither beautiful nor ugly.' One accent is usually no less interesting than another, certainly. But can no judgments of aural quality be offered between, say, the Liverpool accent and that of Edinburgh? Or between most big-city accents and the softer West Country accents? Sense can be slovenly, we should all be able to recognise; sound can be slovenly also, as in the habitual use of the glottal stop. Does each fall on the ear as euphoniously as the next? Or does it indicate a failure in thought? Are we simply making false and irrelevant judgments if we say not only: 'I do find that accent unattractive to listen to' or 'That one falls nicely on the ear'; or 'That's a lazy accent'? Apparently so, according to this author: 'Our positive or negative reaction [to accents] is merely [watch that 'merely' – like 'so-called', it almost always gives adventitious stress so as to cross insecure patches] the result (or cause) of our positive or negative attitude to the people using them.' Speak for yourself, squire. Class attitudes do spill over into almost everything British, but that dog is not quite as shaggy as all that. We can recognise and make aesthetic judgments on sounds, judgments free of class feeling; just as we can on a solo violin player's performance.

*

It will be pleasant to escape, at last, into fresh air. An old, very gentle, Church of England pious lady of the Lancashire working class appeared one day before her relatives in great embarrassment. She had, she said, used for years a phrase picked up from her father:

'Them fornicating Methodists'. 'And today,' she added, 'I've found out what "fornicating" means!'

By now she would have been encouraged to say: 'The Methodists are entirely disadvantaged, not religiously literate nor sufficiently positively discriminatory, not a truly multi-cultural community even though accessible to senior citizens, not relevantly open to or in touch with the significant grass-roots or even the crucial coal faces; and not, actually, a viable community or culture at all.'

> *. . . decent means poor. I should die if I heard my family called decent.*
> Thomas Love Peacock *Crotchet Castle*, 1831

Coda: To write about language is not only to examine contemporary misuses; it also reveals your own difficulties and limitations. You have to be 'judgmental'; but what is the language for judgment, for good and bad, approval and disapproval? You make do with, almost make to fit your own needs, words such as 'tricky', 'glib', 'smart Alec', 'conman', 'cheap and nasty', 'tawdry', 'shallow', 'processed'. And their opposites, starting with 'decent', 'disinterested', 'objective', 'fair', 'respectable' and 'respectful', 'honest'.

Who are you speaking to? Can you say 'we' as though there were a group of 'intelligent lay readers' outside, listening? No, reply lots of people today. All are divided, by status and profession. Don't invent a cosy group to cheer yourself up.

And have you spotted your own recurrent images, which tell so much about you: 'climbing', 'hanging from the chandelier', always being slightly outside but trying to give out little points of light, touching, trying to make inward contact with things, experiences, people. After all . . .

CHAPTER SEVEN

Ways of Looking: Compass Bearings in a Wide-Open Society?

To tell about a drunken muzhik's beating his wife is incomparably harder than to compose a whole tract about 'the woman question'.
Ivan Turgenev

Cultural Studies is a discipline that is morally cretinous because it is the bastard child of the media it claims to expose.
Keith Tester, *Media, Culture and Morality*, 1994

That is an over-harsh judgment; Angela McRobbie, below, is more to the point.

i THE NEED FOR A DISCIPLINE

We have gone so far down the road of the popular (where there is no art/ non-art, no good/bad) that we are in danger of choosing our own canon for analysis and being able to justify this only on the grounds that it has mass appeal. Worse still, we now run the risk of entering into a meaning-lessly pluralist paradigm for studying the popular, where everything goes, where only in the popular does there lie the possibility of resistance, and where unpopular questions like the value to young people of reading literary classics rather than teen magazines are simply no longer asked.
Angela McRobbie, *Post-Modernism and Popular Culture*, 1994

This chapter might seem, since it is about a fairly new academic subject – Contemporary Cultural Studies – too parochial to figure here. We saw in Chapter 3 how relativism has invaded one traditional academic discipline, Literary Studies. The invasion into Cultural Studies began with the founding of the subject itself; which is often markedly non-traditional, and concerns itself with the phenomena of modern life at all levels, and especially with mass culture and popular culture in all their forms. It is therefore in the thick of the relativist society and is itself affected by that relativism, sometimes disablingly. It then becomes a more intellectual form of the 'Peculiar Debate' discussed in Chapter 3.

Contemporary Cultural Studies is now an extremely popular field all over the international academic world. In 1995 Media Studies, a branch of Cultural Studies, was the subject most sought by all applicants to Higher Education courses in the U.K. Some of the results are brilliant, exciting – and challenging, especially to more traditional humanistic disciplines. Just as much in Cultural Studies is a form of easy-riding on other people's original work, an over-reliant adoption of others' theories and a fascinated, lax use of technical language; which by that laxness becomes jargon: '[The word] "paradigm" also neatly signals the dependence of understanding on discourse while including the idea of knowledge, and so, crucially, an epistemology involving a subject/object relation.'

Another justification for the plain and unacademic title of this chapter is that the approach is much narrower than the term 'Cultural Studies' implies today and one doesn't want to put in the shop window more than is found to be on offer once you enter the shop. This approach does not underestimate the value of theory and the proper uses of its language, but does not itself propose a theory. Indeed, it places theory after observation – 'in the destructive element immerse'. It invites us, first, to attend to what Scholes calls the 'text' but would be better described here as the object, the material, the thing in itself.

A theory should not be confused with a discipline. A theory is an intellectual framework meant to clarify, make sense of, illuminate objects, events, phenomena, attitudes which otherwise seem inchoate. A discipline is a particular trained approach to that material itself, a set of tools with which you bend to the material.

Cultural Studies uses many theories but is not a discipline; it is a field or area of study and can draw fruitfully from several disciplines: the social sciences, history, psychology, anthropology, literary study and others. Each discipline can make its case for pre-eminence; the case made here is for literary study as a way into Cultural Studies. One thing is sure: the student should have an initial discipline outside Cultural Studies, an academic and intellectual training, and a severe one. Without that, all may be a jackdaw's hopping from one fascinating item to another, a bringing together of glittering, unordered and unassessed heaps; a ragbag of butterfly interests, of opinions shallowly rooted; the relativist outlook, applied directly to the study of the relativist society.

The reluctance to make judgments is particularly rife in Cultural Studies. Some will accept no judgments of value between works long recognised as of sustained and continuing merit and the latest ephemera in the popular magazines, between a 'classic' symphony and the latest pop song. To devote an essay to a comparison between Conrad's *Heart of Darkness* and Burroughs' *Tarzan of the Apes* without raising the question of level is largely futile, playing around in the shallows.

There is indeed a sense in which they *are* all 'equal'. They should all be entertained with an open mind, but it is against good sense and intelligent observation to keep the mind endlessly and gapingly open; it has to close on something solid or will be both in the beginning and the end purposeless, a yawning chasm, as Chesterton remarked. This condition leads some writers to slither between sociological points, literary-critical observations, political remarks . . . all the time switching descriptive criteria on the way, as conveniences, but never making an actual judgment.

The rules of thumb proposed later could sensibly be applied to starting work in almost any field; in Cultural Studies they, and others like them, are essential; they are preliminary 'ways of looking'. None of them should be surprising. In fact, of some it could be said: 'Oh, that's obvious.' So it is, once said. Obvious or not, they are often not recognised or followed.

ii WHERE DID IT ALL BEGIN?

These growing pains, as we must hope they are, are illustrated in the continuing argument about where Cultural Studies began, from which discipline or general field of interest. One contemporary practitioner refers to 'The *seminal* [his italics] drive and spirit of broaching new subject areas – with a clear view of politicising them – that initially propelled the discipline has been sapped'. That may be so if there were several contemporaneous starts (perhaps there were, though it is arguable that Birmingham was the first). It is not true of some starts and some individuals' impulses. The sentence sounds like the taking of a particular part for a larger and more diverse whole – with the aim of allowing the author to go on to argue that direction has been generally lost, because of the loss of what especially interests him, a politicising thrust. Problems there are, confusions about direction; but they do not lie where that writer thinks. It could be argued

that one of the current problems is still that of over-ready politic-
isation.

Another modern student asserts that the main object of attention
in Contemporary Cultural Studies was from the start 'the mass media
and popular culture'. That is partly true. One aim, though not the
only aim, was to study those things. There is, though, nothing to
discourage the study of the nature of 'cultivated taste' today; but
that does not seem as attractive and needs even more preparatory
slog.

The prior purpose, though, for some of the originators was not to
look at particular things but to develop particular approaches. In
what *ways* were such things, and many other elements of modern
culture, to be studied? That is a difference of kind, putting the horse
back where it should be: seeking to understand modern society better,
especially by beginning with the use of one or more disciplines such
as . . . and . . . and . . .; and applying them to the mass media, popular
culture, etc., etc., etc.

A third writer may be nearer the mark when he says that over the
last three decades 'the movement in these studies has been from
literature to society'. One good strain in Cultural Studies *at any time*
will certainly be 'from literature to society'; that is, from the use of
literary-critical methods to many other aspects of popular culture.
Much early work was of this kind. Yet gradually, and this may be
what the above writer meant, the starts began to be more and more
in sociological theory, with no particular literary foundation or connection; and often with little historic sense. A typical early subject
might be an analysis of the provincial press, or cartoons or television
soap operas; and they demand literary-critical skills. A more modern
subject might be the place of women in factory life or of motor-cycle
gangs as alternative societies. That can be a sound and related move
from language to gesture. Nothing at all in society is alien to such
an approach, from the Beatles to beer-mats. This can be a proper
perspective but it does not define or determine subsequent
approaches.

One could argue that good literary-type analysis, especially close
linguistic analysis, would be helpful in looking at the motor-cyclists
also. But as the movement from 'literature' to 'society' has developed,
so the sense of the importance of the literary/linguistic contribution
has dwindled. More directly political approaches have increased.
The announcement 'This study has been undertaken from a cultural
materialistic perspective' is likely to appear in the Introduction to a

doctoral thesis. Even more, theories of many kinds – French, Italian, British – have been used and adapted, sometimes very helpfully, sometimes as a matter of fashion; and have taken precedence.

It cannot reasonably be argued that the business of looking at society within this area now generally called Cultural Studies, especially since its boundaries are so ill-defined (and likely to remain substantially so), must start from only one intellectual discipline. But it should be noted for the record that much in the range of work which began in England in the early Sixties did claim to start there. It can also be firmly said that for the study of popular or mass culture a grounding in the study of literature at the highest levels provides a unique approach. To assume that popular culture can be explored with crude tools because it is, in advance but unspokenly, assumed to be crude, uncomplex, easily 'read', is a serious mistake.

To put the case provocatively: no one who is not able to read *Persuasion* closely, to speak analytically and imaginatively about it, can be trusted to 'read' television soap operas. Happily, post-graduate students originally trained in a discipline other than literary criticism often show quite soon that their intelligence is transferable; they learn to 'read' in the literary critic's sense, and to respect their new-found abilities.

Unfortunately, some exponents of Contemporary Cultural Studies, though these are not likely to be among the most impressive, reject the offer. They have little knowledge of literature, or of writing and language generally, at their most demanding and so most revealing. They will even argue that such knowledge is irrelevant to their studies.

Instead, they juggle with new theoretic language; that is both a kind of game and a warm indication that they have joined a club, an in-group, a mystery, a modish clique. Theoretic language used exactly can clarify and increase understanding but that needs practice. It is not enough to talk about works being 'iconic . . . heuristic . . . paradigmatic' or to sprinkle the text with 'hegemony . . . homology . . . reifications'; and there are, just for a change, long-standing synonyms for 'foregrounding' and 'prioritising', not to mention 'problematising'.

It is easy to see why some academics regard Cultural Studies as a soft option. Some members of Departments of English Literature, who might in the early literary-criticism-influenced days have been expected to welcome such a respectful and admiring newcomer to their field, were even less welcoming than others. They retained their own historic uncertainties as against the firmer claims of more classical subjects, and felt obliged to look at the intruder as if it were some disreputable thing the resident cat had brought into the house. Like the French professor who screamed at an investigatory body asking similar questions: 'I must protect *mes cours, mes cours,*' they felt themselves to be defending both the first and last bastions. An English professor of English was less unrestrained: 'All very interesting but don't see how to fit it in. The syllabus is already crammed.' That syllabus having apparently descended, fully formed, from heaven; no cultural conditioning there.

To this moderately common reaction was added, in English Departments which at last introduced an undergraduate paper in Cultural Studies or a post-graduate element, the realisation that many of the best and brightest students selected those options. It was inevitable that they would be accused of going for the flashy choice; it would have been truer to recognise that many of those students were inspired by an idealistic impulse: the conviction that the university should have a fuller understanding than was usually offered of the society outside its walls. Ironic but not an accident was the fact that some of the founders of Cultural Studies had themselves begun their careers as university extra-mural lecturers. These students thought it important to analyse societies such as this, to be aware of the necessary 'conversations of society with itself'.

iii THEORY? NATURALLY

Before a fuller look is taken at the nature of literary criticism's contributions to cultural studies a few provisos should be made. First: one does not wish to undervalue the importance of theory and the need for theoretic languages. But Lucien Goldmann pointed out that some theories go beyond themselves and become 'formalistic systems that tend to eliminate in a radical way all interest in history and the problem of meaning' ('The Human Sciences and Philosophy', 1969).

Those who headily play tricks with the languages also soon go beyond themselves. Three typical examples, all from the proceedings of an American Cultural Studies Conference (*Cultural Studies*, ed. Grossberg, Nelson and Treichler, 1992):

> Certainly its premises [those of audience research] problematize the optimistic attribution of agency to consumers ...

The often paradoxical dynamics of contemporary culture as it is technologically articulated with the changing spatialities of social production . . .

At the point at which the hierarchy and the subordinations of the sentence
are replaced by the definitive discontinuity of the text, at that point,
the subject of discourse spatializes and moves beyond the sententious . . .
Writing aloud is the hybrid he proposes in language lined with flesh, the
metonymic art of the articulation of the body not as pure presence of
Voice, but as a kind of affective writing, after the sumptuousness or
suffering of the signifier.

One can wrest a simpler form even from that last love song with
language; after, among much else, sorting out the redefinitions given
to certain keywords other than any of their normal dictionary
meanings.

We can learn from both the main structures of theories and from
their particular words and summary phrases. The same thing can
offer different meanings to different readers, listeners or viewers:
'Polysemic' is a handy brief way of saying that, but doesn't in itself
say anything new about such diverse meanings. In Media Studies
there are, among many others, 'uses and gratifications', 'agenda setting', and its relative 'structures of reality'. Those last two, applied
to the examination of television news, prise open more meanings
than news people are happy with. They reveal the four main elements
in the putting together of that 'news' – technical and temporal constraints, the mystique of 'TV values', the professional concept of
'news values' and the way the cultural atmosphere at any one time
and place defines all except the first, the technical and temporal
limitations (not enough gear, not enough time); though, further back,
those also are culturally conditioned; what the professional defines
as 'news out there', apparently as much a fact of life and nature as
the air from which it is plucked, is then revealed in all its subjectivity;
a complicated construction from which it is difficult to escape.
'Biased' is the wrong word for this process. It is, rather, artificially
selected, shaped, given its highlights, by preconceived beliefs as to
what the news is. So BBC Radio 4 is able to sign off, with concrete
confidence: 'And that's the world at one-forty.'

Good theory brings together, like a magnet in iron filings, an
enormous number of previously unorganised thoughts. But we have
to earn the right to use it. It must not be made into a charm, or a
prop; or a waffle-iron to be banged on top of the material, so that
the vile body is cut to the shape which fits the preconceived, pre-

shaped theory. For example, if you go to Jamaica to make a film about its remarkable Literacy programme and are convinced before you start that that programme is chiefly a device by American capitalists to provide themselves with more effective workers on their plantations, you may well miss, even though then listening on the ground, the long and prior importance of Methodism to the idea of self-improvement. This recalls that initial claim by a PhD candidate referred to earlier – that the material was approached through the prism of 'cultural materialism'. The result in that particular instance was that the research worker under-read and mis-read his magnificent tapes of oral evidence which he had elicited from amateur writers. Properly read they would have revealed that the material conditions of most of his witnesses were less important than their driven private impulses. A similar post-graduate student, considering the influence of home and early school, hesitated to say that they were the two major influences on young children. Perhaps that seemed too obvious. So he wrote something like this: 'As Foucault has animadverted, the two dominant causal factors in progressive acculturation are on the one hand the enforcing domestic milieu and on the other the power of the hegemonic structures of state-determined education.'

A good motto: From perception to concept. Better, from your perceptions to your concepts or those of others, so long as you use them properly. Some students play complex thematic/abstract games which rarely hit the real – the 'phenomenological' – ground. They don't move sufficiently carefully from what 'represents' (within) to what it discloses (outside).

iv ELEMENTS OF CULTURAL READING

Cultural analysis is always about words . . . until we stop treating the areas of culture as a footnote to literature, or worse, the 'superstructure' that sits upon an economic 'base', we will never arrive at a sociology of culture worth much.

I. L. Horowitz, *The Democratic Imagination*, 1994

The phrase 'cultural reading' is not happy; 'reading' should come first; but 'reading for cultural understanding' is impossible. Both forms sound like an offshoot of 'the sociology of literature' and that, though useful, is not cultural reading; nor, even more, would be 'literature and ideas'. Cultural reading has much in common with a normal critical reading by a literature student of any age. The aim is as always first to read for pleasure or, if there is little of that, out of intrinsic interest. Then to read for as full a group of meanings as possible, to listen to tone as directed at the reader and as an important element of the writer's unevadable personality, to try to reach the point at which you can say something about the values inherent in the work; and so through all the rest. It is also important, for a new student, to begin with the most demanding works.

It is useful to read (in more than one sense) the whole thing right through at least twice, in a condition of 'negative capability', suspended attentiveness, not straining for any kind of articulated response; reading but not skimming. An expressive, not instrumental or operational, reading; a search for what Weber called 'empathic understanding'; and all the time in the knowledge that such a work is a form of play, a fiction, a carnival of sorts, an 'imaginary garden' (though with real toads in it), a contraption. Even so, by the end of the second reading some reactions will have swum to the surface and should be noted: about themes, resolutions, tics, recurrent tunes, odd meanings, what seem key passages. Though, for clarity, the process is shown as successive below, it will be going on all the time, simultaneously.

So the following order is not critical. But it is generally useful to start with the texture of the prose itself: repetitions of words, images, phrases; ambiguities, blurs, freshness as compared with cliché, verbal gestures of all kinds; differences of speed, stress, pressure; omissions. (How do you guess at the latter? You stand back from the text and ask yourself what might have been in it, what seemed called for, and so ask also why it was omitted.)

As you move into the larger frame, possible relations with the reader and with the culture begin to surface, but shouldn't be pushed at this stage. So: structure – *this* rather than that, symbols, myths, archetypes; characters, relations and actions and, as always, what they might have been as compared with what seem to be assumptions stated or implicit.

Attitudes to the reader might now be looked for; they won't always show and may take the form of the writer apparently talking to himself, disinterested or doodling. Even if the author seems manifestly present, he may have an ironic mask. All this is part of 'tone', and tone, as was noted earlier, is not easy to read, especially since in English English it gets tangled with class accents; and class has much to do with the suggestion of shared assumptions, about how one expresses oneself and about how life goes. You are again paying attention to changes of pressure, nudges, tropes, stances which are essential to the persuasive character; all on the surface or subterranean.

Compare the openings of *Sons and Lovers* and *A Passage to India*. 'The Bottoms succeeded to Hell Row. Hell Row was a block of thatched, bulging cottages that stood by the brookside on Greenhill Lane'; Lawrence's prose is thumping, idiomatic, successive, vernacular, spoken out loud. Then: 'Except for the Marabar Caves – and they are twenty miles off – the city of Chandrapore presents nothing extraordinary. Edged rather than washed by the river Ganges, it trails . . .'; gentle, pianissimo, to be read, highly literate, grammatically elaborate.

By now we can begin directly to think of cultural meanings, the things taken for granted and those simply not approached. The best literary criticism has subtly attended to this for many decades, so any Cultural Studies student would be foolish not to give careful attention to the finest writers on, let's say as a start, Hardy. They may not agree with earlier critics about his relationships with his culture or about the importance of those to judgments on his writing; but they should come out of that battlefield well exercised.

To acquire an inwardness with any work we have both to be aware of our own culture and to step outside it. This might be one sense in which it would be right to accept the phrase 'value-free'; if that means the attempt to become as free as possible from the assumptions, not just the obvious prejudices, of our own time. It would then be necessary to add some such phrase as 'responsive to value', meaning the need to respond to the values within the work – as was said before, they are always there – to feel them on the pulses.

Those who have been given a conventional literary training and have not thought much about their culture in itself are likely to misread cultural meanings because their own aesthetic criteria seem dominant, more important, and so get in the way; or because they have been handed a set of cultural models and judgments which foreclose on understanding whilst keeping their enclosed literary world unruffled. See some of the readings of *The Waste Land*, in particular those which read that poem in a wholly Anglocentric way.

Still, and for some exponents of Cultural Studies this needs stressing, it is important for the cultural critic to be aware of the formal nature and requirements of a work so as not to wrest cultural meanings from elements which are primarily aesthetic; and that starts with the author's 'presence'. To say this is only to say again in a different way that 'cultural reading' has to begin with and indeed continue as a reading of the work in and for itself.

V SOME RULES OF THUMB

And what about our hands? With them we request, promise, summon, dismiss, menace . . . What of the head? We summon, dismiss, admit, reject, deny . . . And what of our eyebrows and our shoulders? None of their movements fails to talk a meaningful language . . .
Michel de Montaigne, *Complete Essays*, trans. M. A. Screech, 1991

We must work from the clearly observable, concrete phenomena, as concrete as social habits, rituals or gestures, but with even more subtlety, since they are richer, more complex, and in touch with more dimensions of our being than are most social 'facts'.
J. D. Douglas

In the last analysis, there is no substitute for a good idea, and both seem to be contained in what literary people call 'imagination'.
Bernard Berelson, *Content Analysis*, 1954

Try to be one of the people on whom nothing is lost.
Henry James

Here we push, more directly than before, at a theme which has run through the last few pages: the need to have as inward as possible a sense of the material we are studying (presuming that it is not a matter of graphs and numbers). Eventually, if we are lucky, we will begin to know our own particular strengths, which of our senses work best; and our hang-ups, blind spots, limits.

If we are luckier still, we may begin to find and recognise 'significant' detail. Not that it can be proved to be significant, any more than can most elements in this whole area. But we will come to think we know it when we see it. Conrad called it simply 'inspiration' – he could still use that word.

This is, again, a 'germ'. It is not enough to label the process a form of 'impressionism'. It is more a matter of intense concentration alternating with entire relaxation, a holding together of uncounted details and a winnowing, until Conrad's 'precipitation' occurs. Then, to change the metaphor, the new insight comes up and lays its head in your hand; and you are surprised by what you see. The find, the 'strike', can be large or small.

A small example. You may find yourself intrigued by the charity shops which proliferate in British towns. Their different roles are quite hard to 'read'. Then one day, in a predominantly middle-class town, yet another glance at the rack of discarded men's clothing holds your attention. You notice for the first time that much of that clothing, all freshly cleaned and pressed to go on display, is casual wear – sports jackets, blousons, fawn cavalry twill trousers, grey flannels, short leather coats, Barbour jackets – all of very good quality and all, you suddenly see, in styles adopted by elderly professional men. Then you have a vision of middle-class widows clearing out their husband's wardrobes as soon as they can bring themselves to do it and carrying it all down to Oxfam or one of its cousins. A little, whole world.

Or a larger perspective may suddenly open so that you can then say: 'Ah, this is how it works. This is the tap-root.' Or, yet again if you are lucky, a principle, a guiding insight ('theory' is at this point far too grand a word), emerges and you are able to say, gratefully: 'As a general rule this kind of thing moves in this way, and that tells us something important about it and all its kind.'

*

To say such things is to undervalue neither the place of theory nor the languages of theory – at the right times. Perhaps this needs stressing. There is no suggestion that 'brass tacks' are always better than finely tooled surgical instruments; nor is this a call on that 'commonsensical' outlook which can more often than not be a way of evading mental difficulties, the *ad hominem* cry which rallies the lazy. It is, though, a way of registering suspicion of those uses of theory which chiefly delight in belonging to a 'mystery', a badge of specialist arrival, a defensive hedge. 'As that great theorist, X, observed: "The agents of the hegemonic authorities who find themselves under attack react repressively".' 'Policemen don't shit roses.' The exaggeration there is only slight.

It is worth trying to strip down highly theoretic sentences to their simplest. Many can be reduced to 'plain common sense' and are none the worse for that. But their owners may feel like kings with no clothes and accuse the stripper of being simple-minded. Conversely, the weightiest may well resist stripping, since it would cause great loss.

One can move out from one's own close observations not only to essaying a bit of theory oneself or to seeing afresh the importance of others' relevant theories. Or perhaps that is the way, the order, in which the minds of those Berelson called 'literary people' work. Perhaps social-scientific people work differently. Thus Gunnar Myrdal says:

> The chaos of possible data for research does not organize itself into systematic knowledge by mere observation [the creative writer would jib at that 'mere']. Hypotheses are necessary. We must raise questions before we can expect answers from the facts [material], and the questions must be 'significant' [strange that he should use that word so loved by literary people; it subverts his argument since to sense significance is hardest of all]. The questions, furthermore, have to be complicated before they reach down to the facts [material]. Even apparently simple concepts presume elaborate theories. These theories – or systems of hypotheses – contain, of necessity, no matter how scrupulously the statements of them are presented, elements of *a priori* speculation. (*Value in Social Theory*)

This is fascinating stuff and not difficult to agree with in large part. The difference between Myrdal and a literary person is chiefly one of order and timing. Myrdal – and the firm force of his language embodies this – sees himself and his kind as active participants from the start; the literary person is as if passive or, as he might hope, negatively capable in front of the material. But, to sense 'significance', both have to wait on much the same mental movements.

Writing about the relation between material and hypothesis, Theodor Adorno says: 'I would put the greatest emphasis on audacity and originality in proposing a solution' (*On the Logic of the Social Sciences*, 1962). Fine, again; the literary person would cheer at that; at the right moment, once you have something on board.

There need be no attempt to undervalue the language of theory – but rather to respect it by not using it as a charm and as if plucked for the first time out of the air. Usually it isn't. Here is Henry Adams at the beginning of the century: 'All State Education is a sort of dynamo machine for polarising the popular mind; for turning and holding its lines of force in the direction supposed to be most effective for State purposes' (*The Education of Henry Adams*, 1918). Echoes of that post-graduate student, who attributed this insight to Foucault;

and of the one who seemed to think that 'cultural materialism' meant a group of ideas invented in the Sixties. Many before Adams had noted his assertion and he would not have denied that. Some students of Cultural Studies today would attribute it, if not to Foucault, then – this is more likely – to Gramsci. It is to do with the definition of 'hegemony'. Gramsci's explorations of hegemony are subtle and suggestive and, though the word is now losing ground as a charm, have been of much use to British students in Cultural Studies; and have been taken further by some, notably Stuart Hall.

The pity is that some writers give the the impression of picking up a word as a talisman, to indicate a group of concepts none of which has been thought of before. The world isn't quite as young as that; it may not always have put its thoughts into abstract structures (which can be helpful, a transferable currency, whereas literary images are slippery); but thoughts it has had, very subtle thoughts, often indelibly caught in those metaphors. Here is Hazlitt:

> Men do not become what by nature they are meant to become, but what society makes them. The generous feelings, and high propensities of the soul are, as it were, shrunk up, seared, violently wrenched, and amputated, to fit us for our intercourse with the world, something in the manner that beggars maim and mutilate their children, to make them fit for their future situation in life. (*The Life of Thomas Holcroft*, contd. Hazlitt, Colby, 1925)

Two other mild cautions. The first is to avoid that 'stay as sweet as you are' syndrome when studying groups of people who have in some senses 'fallen out of society', are little regarded and easily assumed to be entirely inarticulate, atomised, suffering from 'anomie', drifting. One of the best relatively early rejoinders to such assumptions is to be found in Labov's studies of New York street gangs: *Language in the Inner City*. That has justifiably had a great deal of influence in Britain and inspired some admirable studies – Paul Willis's eloquent book on English motor-cycle gangs, for instance.

Such studies can show, above all, that those groups are not inarticulate; they can have languages for their own purposes, and subtle inter-relationships with each other. So much is a clear gain. The temptation is then – once it has been noticed that these group-languages have usually 'placed' the outside public world by a set of dismissals, ironic put-downs – to make too large a claim for them. The points may be true enough, but not new. Dissidence, bloody-mindedness, sarky or bypassing, has a very long history. Start with Chaucer and come right up through Sam Weller to *Saturday Night and Sunday Morning*.

Some writers make much of the power of these groups to subvert the society which has tried to make them conform and, when that has failed, has put them out of sight. Here is an American of the 'keep on subverting' type:

> [In spite of the grip of 'hegemony', of the powerful main forces in society] the powerless, the people, are able to evade these structures and conduct a guerilla warfare of resistance in which they win tactical victories which subvert the strategies of the powerful.

In face of such airy statements one wishes neither to patronise ('his heart's in the right place') nor to poke crude deflating fun ('a fart is not a subversive statement'). But there is a defensive romanticism there. That these groups have subtler relationships with each other and a subtler language than most people have imagined may be a 'tactical victory' but is hardly a 'guerilla warfare'. These are not today's equivalents of Raymond Williams' nineteenth-century working men who, in the face of public oppression or indifference, put their collective creative energies into the Trade Union movement, the Friendly Societies, the Co-ops; or, for that matter, the Levellers before them.

Studies of this kind habitually ignore or underplay the fact that these groups are almost entirely enclosed from and are refusing even to attempt to cope with the public life of their societies. That rejection cannot reasonably be given some idealistic ideological foundation. It is a rejection, certainly, and in that rejection may be making some implicit criticisms of the 'hegemony', and those criticisms need to be understood. But such groups are doing nothing about it except to retreat. Groups such as these may be marginally less downtrodden than the disoriented individuals found among what is now called 'the underclass'. But can an open and critical democracy afford not to see that they too are trapped, that they are not, either as individuals or as a group, liberated into a more maturely understood place? Not to give this fact its due importance is to blunt the right instruments for change.

*

The second caution is about the need to avoid, especially in examining the role of the mass media, too great a reliance on the pleasures
of 'conspiracy theory'. It is comforting and slightly spooky to assume
that there is always a villain behind the arras, a wicked manipulator
for whom the end always justifies the means. There sometimes is
such a person or group. But to a remarkable extent the end can also
justify the means for those of convinced good intentions. This is one
of the more common and persuasive and dangerous of easy, moral
banana skins. 'The greatest treason' may well be 'to do the right
deed for the wrong reason'. But in either kind of instance there is
often less intent, less will, less conspiracy than some like to think.
The truth is usually more complicated and more interesting. It is best
to look at the possible complexities before deciding that there really
is a conspiracy here.

To recall a simple instance: the impulse behind the vulgarities of
the popular press. In this some see villainous proprietors deliberately
seeking to debauch 'the common man', 'ordinary people'. Their
newspapers certainly exploit and extend crass vulgarity; but it is
doubtful whether the proprietors have thought about what they are
doing with their money even as far as that simple point. They do see
their newspapers as a source of wealth and may have little respect
for their readers. They see nothing wrong in what they are doing: 'If
that is what people want, who am I to deny it to them? It's a free
country.' It would distort language to call such attitudes a conspiracy;
self-interested self-justification perhaps, but not something more
wickedly or cleverly planned.

The point becomes clearer when one looks at the editors of these
newspapers. Are they horrible men and women who cynically
manipulate people more simple than themselves? Not really. 'Horrible', yes; cynical in a certain sense also, but not in the sense of *from
outside* manipulating emotions, prejudices, alien to themselves. They
are doing according to their kind. They have, they must have, a nose,
a feel, for vulgarities, prejudices, sentimentalities, brutalities which,
they assume, most of their readers share ('or why would we have the
biggest sales of all?'); and then they exploit and probably extend and
reinforce those attitudes. From a new angle, we are back with 'the
structuring of reality'.

This is not only the reflective but also the reinforcing process.
One may talk about the dangers of *disguised* contempt in television
producers; that is because television producers have to be technologically sophisticated and to some extent imaginative, more so than

most of their viewers; they are at the controls in a technically very sophisticated system. Popular journalism is of its nature predatory, ruthless, remorselessly hectic; but for most of those who feed it its processes are not sophisticated; they are rock-bottom vulgar. The industry needs rock-bottom vulgarians right up to and including the occupiers of the editors' chairs. Today's editors of such papers, as you may see when they appear on television, are not subtle string-pullers. Confident, loud-mouthed, quick on their feet, certainly; and also archetypal holders of the attitudes they assume in their readers or assume their readers most want to see expressed.

If there is a conspiracy it starts higher; but to sniff out conspiracy even there rather than aggressive commercialism is to start work with your smelling apparatus disabled. We don't need in these cases to invoke the private line to Downing Street or the City. That is 'high-conspiracy theory' and will usually call forth the word 'hegemony'; attacks on the popular press are more likely to be examples of 'low-conspiracy theory'.

As to low conspiracy, we could do with but do not have many examinations of the kinds of people who accept such work. Theirs is not a treason of the clerks; they are not clerks. They are sharp, articulate in a certain way, and short on concern for others where that gets in the way of scoops. They are as likely as not to come from the sort of people to whom their papers are addressed, from the exploited not the exploiting; they are committing a treason of the ordinary people. All are and have to be tough, but some are toughly sentimental and some toughly cynical. All enjoy much in the daily battle and all like the money.

For such people, for all such people right across the spectrum of mass communications – aspects of broadcasting, of book publishing, of print journalism, of cinema film and video, of popular music – this is their psychological world; and they are confident within it, wrapped round by it so that hardly a dissident, a questioning thought can penetrate. They cannot, must not question, or that world would begin to fall apart. So the Corporate Affairs Director of a very large retail group, a group with hundreds of outlets for print and recorded sound and vision, says with unquestioning blandness: 'We are all in the business of supplying the majority.' That is exact and true to the situation as it is; no nonsense about developing knowledge, feeding the mind, catering for minorities. 'Business', 'Majorities'; these impulses hold it all. Of course this 'reinforces hegemony', is agenda setting, allows permitted deviations. Profit, principle, whim, deviance all have their places.

vi INSTANCES OF SURPRISE

To come back to happier moments, occasional though they may be. All of us may have, after a fair amount of study, insights which at the time seem our own: such as the realisation, when looking at working-class life and trying to assess the pace of change, that that pace is far slower than we and most other observers had imagined. This leads to the further realisation that working-class people are past masters at adapting the agents of change to their own purposes. More of both of those points in the next chapter.

We will probably discover, and sooner rather than later, that others have had these ideas before and taken them further. Still, it is good that we have had them; and other, more personal perceptions, such as the point at which we realise that an important continuous part of our effort is to learn to distinguish stereotypes from representative figures or events – a distinction not commonly made, and not easy to sustain.

Finally, there are the insights which you receive from others but which, you again realise with a slight shock, have been nagging away at the back of your mind and have now been given their focuses. You gratefully adopt them as among your own accepted truths though not your discoveries, because making such an intellectual discovery articulate is the equivalent of copyrighting a practical invention.

So: Conrad in *The Secret Agent* brings home unforgettably how thin is the fabric of civilised society over which we walk confidently each day; how much we take for granted that order will remain; and what a huge assumption that is. To nineteenth-century Poles that thought no doubt came more easily than it has to most British people for several centuries. Yet once it has penetrated your mind, how obvious and true it seems, even in Britain. What would it take to shatter the fabric? If the quite small number of police in each town or city were removed, how long would it be before violent crime of all kinds broke out? The 'established order' is to a large extent a walking on the water, a trick, a triumph of confidence – in, as Conrad never tired of remarking, the belief that a sufficient number of people can be trusted to steer straight and go on steering straight, thus keeping the social order from being more than a huge illusion. It is in the nature of such insights that, once they have become 'outsights', they seem obvious, to go without saying. To more thoughtful people, that is its own sort of deception. 'Simple truths' only become simple when someone, such as Conrad, utters them simply.

PART THREE

Grit on the Flywheel

What are the roots that clutch, what branches grow
Out of this stony rubbish?

T. S. Eliot, *The Waste Land*

CHAPTER EIGHT

Home Thoughts: Old-Style Checks and Balances

As has been said often enough, none of us are blank sheets on which politicians, journalists, broadcasters and a whole army of hucksters can write what suits their purposes. It is difficult, almost impossible, to find a single image to set against that obsolete empty slate; it would need to catch the equally obvious truth that human character, even the most apparently simple, is a complex network of attitudes – of tastes and desires certainly, but also of resistances and rejections. Change is often refused, almost unconsciously, by residual rejecting judgments.

This is true of all social classes but particularly revealing in working-class groups. A proviso, though: to argue this part of the case by describing the attitudes prevalent among pre-war working-class communities is not an act of sentimental nostalgia; it is an attempt to fill that wrongly presumed blank space with detail and background, stacking up on the blackboard all those elements which can provide resistance to the more hectic persuasions which seek to make us acquire different habits. If you do not make some such comparison there is no ground from which to judge likely effects. You need at least a little historical background for contrasts; say, over half a century at least.

*

Consider, therefore, the fact that working-class people now have access to, and have largely taken possession of, major consumer goods which would have been beyond their parents' wildest dreams. If those goods had in their time appeared on the market, that earlier generation would have assumed that they were intended only for people 'above us'.

Apart from the more obviously utilitarian 'white goods' (washing-machines, vacuum cleaners, fridges, microwave oven, freezers) which most working-class people in employment now have, there are the recreational objects, notably cars (still generally second- or third-hand), televisions, video recorders and satellite dishes. Even today, these cost more than many working-class families can lay out in one go, but many buy them on hire purchase.

In the early Sixties slightly battered cars began to appear on council estates and in the streets of older working-class districts. About that time the cry first went up that the working classes were becoming 'embourgeoisified'. The object had been translated into the attitude. Since some working-class people now had cars they must be moving into the lower-middle or middle class with all that implied in changed styles of life. Such as washing the car each Sunday morning, especially when it was pristine? No. Like going for a 'run' or a 'spin' in the country after Sunday dinner, to get a breath of fresh air? Not exactly. A trip out, perhaps, but probably to the nearest popular seaside resort, with all those family members still living at home and perhaps Grandma; and the dog; plus food and drink and a radio. Once at the sea-front the car might remain, windows wound down, the focal point of the visit; and some of the family didn't leave it, whatever the loss of fresh air.

In short, the working-class use of the car was in important ways different from that of the middle-class. A sociologist then made one of those intuitive leaps of the kind described earlier. For working-class people, the author recalled, the living-room is the centre of the home. Working-class people, he went on, have turned the car into a mobile living-room. By this single insight he not only damaged the concept of 'embourgeoisification' but also introduced some of us to a concept which can be given all sorts of fancy names: 'selective-adaptation/modification/translation/assimilation'; or to what, more simply but still polysyllabically, has been called 'transferred incorporation'. There has to be a hook, or the connection will not be made; the graft won't take. Working-class people recognise when a new object or service can, sometimes amended, cater to their traditional tastes; they will then pick it up and do the transforming. Such things do eventually alter working-class tastes, but the process, if it touches deep roots, starts with modification and is slower than we have been used to thinking. Washing-machines are a simple good and need no modification before assimilation. Others are more active involvements.

A related but slightly different response was brought out by the arrival of television. In the early years television sets were expensive and it was assumed that the first buyers would be middle-class; after all, most working-class people couldn't reasonably afford them. Again, hire purchase looked after that problem. Television even more than the motor-car spoke straight to traditional working-class tastes. It was seen as a giver of pleasure, a major new recreational aid; and it settled perfectly into the living-room. What could be better? Middle-class people took their careful time and many of them mistrusted the new machines.' 'Goggle boxes', 'Idiots' lanterns', they said.

A couple of decades later video recorders arrived and to some extent followed the pattern of television. The ways of using each of them could partly be defined and differentiated by social class. With video the differences were clearer, sharper, than with television. In general, middle-class people used video for time-shift purposes – recording a programme so that they could see it at a more convenient time. Working-class people saw the video as a form of home cinema – the living-room again – and soon Britain had one of the highest percentages of video-rental shops among all developed countries.

The buying of their own council houses by working-class people, promoted by the Conservative governments, was a considerable success. It most acutely focuses the argument about 'embourgeoisification'. Surely to buy your own home, no longer to have to rely on the local council to look after repairs and painting, is quintessentially a move into at least the lower reaches of the middle class? Didn't many who bought begin to add equally quintessential middle-class or more accurately lower-middle-class embellishments: bottle-glass windows, carriage-lamps, gnomes and often their pocket-handkerchief pools for fishing in? The act of becoming a house-buyer, especially on the terms offered, was extremely sensible. No doubt Tory governments thought it would tempt many buyers to become self-protective Tory voters. 'I have property; Tory governments made that possible; Labour was against it. Where is my bread buttered now?' No doubt some would follow that path; it is doubtful whether a majority made the connections.

As to the embellishments, we are again with a form of adoption, assimilation. Those items, from the ducks flying up the wall onwards and outwards, to the Regency-style doors and all the rest, convey more than anything else the cosiness, the slightly historic nostalgia, the whimsy which come together entirely successfully as lower-middle-class. But it is not the label that attracts, it's the objects. Most people adopt them not so as to aspire socially but to absorb, within what is otherwise their own kind of home, adornments they find attractive and believe will add to the established warmth of that home. Once again, they have taken over and taken in, not themselves moved out; or been taken in.

All such responses slow the process of change, provide brakes on the pressure to change, to accept the increasing openness. They are active; they are meeting change; but they are doing so by engaging in a process of 'making over', of transmutation on their own terms, not being bowled over. They have a very heavy frictional base.

A more obvious example of this skill (and of that of the entrepreneurs) is in the way hamburgers and pizzas have slid into place alongside fish and chips. 'Tastiness', that premier requirement in working-class food, is the clue. The new fast takeaway foods differ from the old chiefly in their wider class-spread; after all, they came from America. McDonald's is the linear descendant of fish and chips.

Conversely, there are rejections, refusals to adopt and adapt; as in the hardly conscious refusal of working-class young women to adopt the hair-styles of their middle-class peers. Their models are not derived from the English class-system but from the worlds of pop culture and Hollywood.

There are more submerged, less active but no less powerful resistances. Such as domesticity. In large parts of the country and in great swathes of some age-groups, sexual habits have changed further and faster than could have been imagined only thirty years ago. We all know the roster: the Pill (probably the most important agent of all), the increase in the divorce-rate, the increase in living together outside of or before marriage, the increase in one-parent families. Yet walk round a typical English provincial town, wander into its shops, eavesdrop on the conversations among both the staff and the customers – working-class, lower-middle-class, middle-class – and you will be impressed by the continuity of the sense of domesticity, domesticity within marriage or a stable partnership or on your own with children. It is a kind of domesticity which is inherently resistant to change, the disinclination of the family-minded to think of other horizons.

The success of certain types of museum – those devoted to re-creating a not too distant past, not the National Heritage past but that of one's grandparents, and probably industrial-urban – is part of the same pattern (one has to avoid saying 'movement' because this is precisely a disinclination to move, to be pushed along). 'Nostalgia', once again, is the common term of dismissal, but bobs out too loosely. You can hear in these places parents and grandparents talking to children about 'what it was like in those days'. To say there is at least a touch of nostalgia in their talk says little; of course there is. They are being reminded of a time when life was on a more human scale, was not so shapeless and contourless, loose in every direction. That in turn reminds a hearer that, though few go to church or chapel nowadays, many people still if rather apologetically use moral judgments drawn from their own or their parents' Christian backgrounds. Chapter 12 takes this further.

Such resistances go deep and can be very discriminating. In spite of all the pressures against, there is still a very large demand among working-class people and others for adult education, for its old-fashioned purposes and in old-fashioned words – 'self-improvement . . . so as to understand things better . . . to be a fuller person'.

All the above is about the settled, domestic life as a centre of adaptation and so of a certain kind of resistance. The leisure-styles of younger people sometimes seem to owe little to the persuaders. Booze, sex, punch-ups, Saturday night raves have always existed, though for centuries the Law has sought to control them. Are these kinds of 'resistance'? Some writers on working-class culture, in particular, think so. Angela McRobbie in the passage quoted at the start of Chapter 7, rightly doubts if 'resistance' is the correct word. Those styles are often little more than late-twentieth-century forms of Juvenal's circuses; and are in fact infiltrated and affected by modern consumerism. Outside domesticity, there may be more to learn from the continuance of pursuits such as fishing. Or from early-middle-aged working-class people who 'still know how to enjoy themselves' in the old more gregarious ways, in pubs and clubs; which harks back to the Torquay dancers described in Chapter 4, and all the other loose groups of aficionados of leisure.

So most people, it seems, and not just working-class people, have forces working against their too easily accepting, being rapidly influenced by, those massed and predominantly relativist forces turned towards them every day. They will change; but the resistances are stronger than is normally thought.

CHAPTER NINE

From Class to Status: Resistance by Transference

Two nations; between whom there is no intercourse and no sympathy; who are as ignorant of each other's habits, thoughts and feelings, as if they were dwellers in different zones, or inhabitants of different planets; who are formed by a different breeding, are fed by a different food, are ordered by different manners, and are not governed by the same laws.

Benjamin Disraeli, *Sybil*, 1845

The Conservative wishes to maintain the differences which separate the highly-placed from the lower brethren.

Anthony Trollope

i THE SURVIVAL OF CLASS?

Here we come upon a very different force, which slows down change, works against the easy acceptance of a more or less unsignposted world: a less attractive force than that described in Chapter 8, but one which is likely to see out the life of anybody at present in early middle age and later. This is the resistance put up by the sense of class in England to anything which appears to be at work in loosening if not dissolving it. One of the most commonly voiced misconceptions is that 'we are all classless nowadays'. It has been said for at least half a century, though with mounting irritation in those who assert it but have to accept the slow pace; and not only among wishful thinkers in the securer parts of the middle class. Looking at Western Europe as a whole, Hannah Arendt foresaw the disintegration of the class-bound society; but she may have been inspired by the contrast between the manners of the pre-war continental European bourgeoisie and that of the USA. In less thoughtful people the claim is another instance of mistaking changes in available objects for changes in attitudes, a simple form of taking the deed for the will (third-hand motor-cars = middle-class attitudes). It is to be blind to evidence all around of the enduring power of the English sense of class-divisions. Disraeli's celebrated passage quoted above is still relevant, but would have to be amended today and speak of three nations.

You may meet the sense of class every day and almost everywhere, and most of those who express it are unaware of what they are expressing; hence the irritation. It is to be met in railway stations, supermarkets, work-places, among those taxi-drivers who have not yet decided to call all their fares 'guv' or 'mate', and from policemen. Though policemen's behaviour is nowadays often modified from the traditional pattern of lessening deference as they move down the social ladder, it still often varies according to class. Towards well-dressed and well-spoken people they can practise, for example, not deference but a provocatively snide pseudo-deference: 'Did you really mean to leave your car there – *sir*?'

We are still branded on the tongue. We have some intonations, particularly unattractive, which say without putting it into words: 'Keep off, you horrible lower-class person'; and intonations which produce the same effect with a disengaged and totally confident drawl; and miserably subservient intonations which hop like neurotic fleas from 'sir' to 'sir' with every sentence; and, like those of the police, pseudo-subservient accents which also carry many 'sirs' but all as a form of contempt for people who talk posh. Educated, as distinct from merely posh accents, are another matter – if they are recognised; some people are deaf to them. Those who cannot instantly decipher your class from your clothes or bearing tend to assume that you are a kind of nondescript. Then, because they are at that point compassless, they are likely to respond in a cagily indifferent manner, until they have found a bearing. An educated accent can then make the needle swing violently, usually to the safer, more polite side of the scale.

The belief that those who carry the accents of privilege and power count for more than the rest of the population is still strong, at least among those who have those accents and those who are impressed by them, even if such people don't actually run many things any longer; though some still do. A recent Provost of Eton told the assembled pupils that they were being educated so as 'to exercise authority'.

The hallmarked events of the privileged are the annual peacock parades, especially if members of the Royal Family make an appearance, such as Ascot and Henley; then Glyndebourne, Covent Garden and a few other events more often sporting than artistic. The habitués are drawn from the major public schools, Oxbridge, the City and its prouder Guilds, the more exclusive London clubs; plus some *nouveaux-riches* and some temporary celebrities of the showbiz world, all eager to climb on those particular waggons.

That sense of separation, of dividedness and distinction, runs through every crevice of the lives of people born securely into the world of privileges, and not only through sports and other selected recreations. It defines also the nature of their often admirable participation in voluntary work for 'the less fortunate'; and, of course, through choice of marriage partner. (The occasional flip-over into marriage with, say, a bus-driver or a pop star and the adoption of his accent – so eagerly seized on by those who want to go on asserting that class-consciousness is dead – is just that: occasional, a blip. Its only sizeable recent manifestation was as far back as the Sixties.)

One phenomenon, a paradox not much remarked on, can be seen in the tabloid newspapers. On the one hand is their persistent claim to be the voice of the ordinary bloke (by now the phrase 'I speak for the common man' can have an old-fashioned respectful air which doesn't apply here). Tabloid journalists call a spade a spade or more likely a bloody shovel; they will be talked down to by no one; they are no longer horny-handed sons of toil but are still the salt of the earth or at any rate are of the earth, earthy, not effete seat-warmers in offices; they are the true democrats. But as has been shown, to be a democrat is much harder than to be a populist, and these papers are populist above all else.

So, oddly, they are intensely class-conscious, with this part of their professional personality as class-conscious as a crusty duke; but only within a narrow band and with transmutations. They do not on the whole like or pay much attention to the middle classes or lower, and even less to the middling-secure, except where remarkable instances of crime or sexual misdemeanour come into play. They are deeply interested in the Royal Family and the aristocracy. Towards them they have the attitudes of fawning dogs, Peeping Toms, Dr Slope, Uriah Heep and Pecksniff.

The transmutations occur in the treatment of the Royal Family. They are accepted by the tabloids, but not for what they are officially presented as being, in terms of the dignity of their national role and its responsibilities; that would be too Establishment-minded. That kind of presentation is left to those right-wing writers who, like latter-day pen-and-ink Knights of the Shires who have read Bagehot, sally out in defence whenever the institution of monarchy is challenged. Their particular difficulty today is that, all else being unusable, they have to fall back on defence-by-symbolism. For 'the great body of ordinary people', they claim, the monarchy is a magnificent and glittering symbol of the historic national spirit such as no dreary elected President could match. Which means that the defence has become a form of that old habit, disguised contempt for 'ordinary people'; they are assumed, like children making cardboard models of the opening of Parliament, to want pretty side-shows. If these plummy-voiced upholders of Royalty are among our modern 'gatekeepers of opinion' their gates haven't been oiled for generations. The popular press's mishandling of the monarchy is not worse than that.

The Royal Family used to be reduced to a picture-postcard version of petit-bourgeois life: chintz, gladioli, the dogs, the framed photos of the family. This is 'the Woganising of the Windsors'; or was until a few years ago. Now they have become, spectacularly, the stars of a real-life television soap opera almost on a par with the more indiscreet stars of Hollywood.

Going down a peg or two, the tabloid newspapers will concern themselves with MPs, the professions, the mercantile classes – and especially the *nouveaux-riches*; if they misbehave. In the 1950s the antics of Lady Docker, a former chorus-girl and wife of Sir Bernard Docker, a wealthy industrialist, preoccupied the popular press and its readers. Sir Bernard's business went downhill, the workers avidly read about Lady Docker's vulgar jaunts in her gold-plated Daimler, and eventually hundreds of them, unaware of the shaky foundations of their industry, had to be sacked; a classic pattern. The Dockers have their equivalents today, but these are usually more louche and backstairs, not so ostentatious.

The tabloids (whose owners and editors will happily accept knighthoods or better – well, they have after all rendered certain services towards a certain kind of national cohesion) and their readers are able to have things both ways. They hear what seems like rough democratic plain-speaking whilst enjoying the most mawkish and soft-pornographic of vicarious relations with the toffest of toffs and the nobbiest of nobs.

ii STATUS AND LIFE-STYLE

Yet change there is, and the mistaken blanket-belief that change has already come about blinds its adherents to its slowness and the resistances to it; and above all to the actual nature of the changes which are in fact in train. That argument can be taken a very long way but then seems to bite its own tail. Status, which seemed to have replaced class, has then changed back into a new form of class. The gates have closed again against openness, the relevant aspect here of relativism.

The argument in favour of an emerging secular change – to be called the move from class to status – starts from saying first that the old pattern was based on birth, education at all levels and the main professions. These last were substantially (there were always leaks) open only to the right people, people suitably educated, with the right accents, contacts, opinions for the time of year and overall assumptions (with what is in the USA more pointedly called 'mind-set'). Brains came in handy too and many had them. This powerful corralling virtually ensured place, privilege and continuity for your kind.

The next point in the class-to-status argument is that the import-ance of class-consciousness, as a separator of the wheat from the chaff in this society, is being slowly eroded in favour of the sense of status by competence, of professional status. In some instances a better phrase might be 'executive status', since 'executive' has become the strongest single word to indicate a line which divides a new upper group from those below. Yet already that distinction has been eroded and misused. It is almost mandatory, in advertisements for quite junior posts, to use the word. It goes with the company car, free enrolment in a private health-care scheme, perhaps even membership of American Express. 'Executive' as compared with 'Professional' has become slightly dog-eared and doggy, running down from powerful managerial posts to harassed and harrowed commission-only sales-men of double-glazing. Best to stick with 'Status'.

Status is based on ability or effectiveness (they are not the same) and more and more carries with it a pretentious name tag. 'Customer Relations Representative' regularly means someone who, asked why the firm follows a curious and unhelpful practice with clients, replies in a computerised letter written in erratic English, and as though pointing to the hump on the camel, that that is the firm's practice. Status increases with increasing skill at delivering the goods in a world which is very much harsher than is commonly known or often publicly admitted. That is the ugly, the naturally competitive and corner-cutting, nature of capitalism. It has been said many times in the last one and a half decades that competition benefits the buyer because it reduces prices. Even if that were always true, as it certainly is not, one is not told that the cost is increasing pressure, most of all on 'executives'; which can be nerve-racking on the more tender and brutalising on the less.

Visit the Stock Exchange and you have, first, the impression that little has altered. Many of the same indisputably public-school voices and manners are there; how can so few things have changed? You will be given two answers. Go down into the places where the tough dealing is done and you are as likely to find a cockney voice, and that a young woman's, as that of a public-school man. Those places must respond to the need for new, technologically competent talent. But the predominantly male public-school products elsewhere in the building? The old boy network is still operating to a fair extent? Yes, will be the answer, but nowadays we can't 'carry' such people if they prove to be incompetent, whatever their family connections. Nor can they be advised to go out and govern New South Wales. They go to look after the family acres in Yorkshire, to join the staff of a racecourse, to start a restaurant with friends or to train for hotel management.

England being what she is, there are no doubt a good number of places to which these people can be transferred; but few can be 'carried' in modern professions and those areas are narrowing. It has in this century been increasingly true that the universities are more open to talent when appointing staff. Before then, the difficulties working-class and middle-class people had in entering university at all meant that few reached the point at which they could be considered for posts there. This has progressively improved but bias exists, chiefly because the best public schools are better equipped to nurture talent. Still, even a broad Yorkshire accent will not count against you if your sponsors say you are one of the brightest mathematicians of your generation. Mrs Ramsay's reaction in *To the Lighthouse* to the young scientist she thought uncouth is a late moment of the old style. As in so many things, the last war was a watershed, for the universities at least; in some other places (for instance, parts of the City) such divisions still thrive.

More illuminating are the new professions, those which are being created almost daily as a result of the development of technology, especially communications technology. To say, as some do, that by the end of the century 90 per cent of people will work in communications sounds startling at first, even though we may know that productive work now requires fewer and fewer people. All depends on how you define 'communications'. Start by saying that the word really means 'pushing things around' – people, goods, money, information, ideas – and you can include computer skills, frontier research both scientific and technological, telecommunications of all kinds, banking, insurance, transport, travel agencies, retailing, teaching at all levels, broadcasting, the press, publishing, advertising, public relations, market research, the Stock Exchange. Ninety per cent now looks less surprising.

It becomes clear that two related forces are at work. First, if you cannot cope with the higher technologies you will fail and go, who-ever your father may be. Too much depends on success to allow the carrying of duds. If you can cope you will be rewarded far beyond the intrinsic importance of the work (probably an uncomprehended and irrelevant concept) or of your wider abilities. You will be paid several times more than an internationally distinguished professor who turns down the lure of the USA (though few such professors would want to swap with you). You will be peremptorily sacked if you begin to fail. That is one way in which birth is becoming less important than it has been historically.

Second – but this applies only to certain of the new communi-cations professions – the owners or top managers may positively want someone who is not upper-crust; they may want someone downright crude and vulgar. Rupert Murdoch may not have the leather-bound taste of earlier press barons but neither has he those of his readers. Neither he nor his predecessors need to share, but only to know how to get others to tap, their readers' tastes.

Less melodramatic examples of the way in which new professions, especially those in mass communications, recruit according to their need for specific talents, can be found in broadcasting. Compare the very early recruiting pattern of the BBC, the weight of Oxbridge, with later recruitments; the change is great and unmistakable.

With the right connections you may still just have a head-start in broadcasting, BBC or commercial. People tend to look after their own, either because they assume that a candidate from a known 'good family' will have a fine cultural, entrepreneurial and educational background, or from a sense of *noblesse oblige*, or from crude self-interest or from a mixture of all three. But, again, even if the 'right'

educational and family background is still particularly acceptable in
the old way in some places, or even if one of your parents is a senior
executive in commercial broadcasting or PR or advertising, you will
not last long if you cannot 'deliver', if your programmes are flops.

More and more the two systems merge as the pressure for numbers
affects both systems; and that process has to be buttressed by suitable
recruitment. Sit in a BBC canteen nowadays and you may hear a
man nearby whose conversation indicates shallowness, vulgarity, sex-
obsession. Perhaps he has a minor servicing job? 'No,' says your
host, 'he produces X [he names one of the more frenetic programmes
aimed at teenagers]. We bought him from the competition and very
effective he is.' All institutions and especially very large ones, adapt
to survive, and justify the changes of spots as they go along.

Do they have by nature a sense of the need for divisions, a sense
of those below and, just as strong in many people, of those above?
And why do those divisions so often fall into threes – first, second
and third class on the old railway system; upper, middle and lower
in assumptions about class; gold, silver and bronze in the award of
medals? Perhaps it has something to do with the vertical composition
of our bodies – head, trunk and legs; or with the Holy Trinity, though
that may be another instance rather than an originating cause.

As, therefore, the sense of class gradually gives way to the sense
of status-difference, so there emerges from one angle an old, from
another angle a new, dividing of society. It can be called 'compart-
mentalisation' so as to indicate its less richly historical nature than
the sense of class, an almost neutral sociological term without the
weight given to 'class' by echoes of heredity, land, traditional rank.
'Upper compartment' – not that the ferry-boat term is useable – is
taking over from 'upper class'.

So: three groups as before and as always. Opinions differ on
exactly how large each group is, and it would be a waste of time to
argue here about percentages. It is fairly clear that the first and third
groups are much smaller than the second one. Perhaps that middle
group might usefully be divided into two.

The working principle will be that the top group contains between
15 and 25 per cent of the population (and grows, steadily); it com-
prises some people who had fairly an easy ride there, but more
meritocrats who climbed there, lifted by their ability to serve the new
technological-communications-led society.

The middle group probably holds 60–70 per cent of the population. They are below the specialist and genuinely executive levels

but do not all belong to what used to be called 'working-class' (that expression is now out of popular favour but can still have its uses, as the preceding chapter showed). They include some of the old mid-middle class, lower-middle class (for instance, small shopkeepers) and, increasingly, the respectable working class (formerly craftsmen, foremen, NCO types, those in solid, uniformed jobs, qualified line-workers, the technically trained within limited levels, up to middle management).

Members of this group will usually be financially fairly comfortable, though often overstretched by the mortgage on the house and by fulfilling other basic expectations: a car, though not one changed before it is four years or more old and certainly not a large one; foreign holidays through a firmly known range of tour companies and, more and more, some day-school fees and even private medical subscriptions. Though apparently 'embourgeoisified' in some respects, many of them cannot be called middle-class nor, except occasionally, lower-middle- or respectable-working-class. They have done quite well out of the new society, though the threat of redundancy has hung heavily over some, especially in the last dozen years; as it does over some in the first group – but up there it hangs more over the executives than the technocrats. For the middle group we need a new title, emotionally neutral yet suitably evocative.

Finding titles for the third, bottom, group is a common pursuit. One social scientist suggests 'the service class', to indicate that this group contains people who do jobs which those in groups 1 and 2 increasingly do not care to do for themselves but can afford to pay others to do. That has a point, but the title could also fit those in the lower reaches of the middle group. 'Servant class', another proposal, is more frank and fits the upper areas of group 3. That group as a whole probably holds about 10–15 per cent of society.

Group 3's upper areas are not occupied by people now most commonly called 'the underclass'; the underclass are on the floor of group 3, of society. Many, perhaps most of them, find it increasingly hard to retain self-respect: they are likely to be out of work and not within sight of a job; they are probably surviving on social security, are untrained, and may not be able to cope with the increasing complexities of modern life. Though they are hardly worth wooing by the big advertisers, they are very often victims of the lower-level persuasive sharks (especially loan sharks) who prey on people in their precarious position. They may be old and have no other income than the state pension. They contain, increasingly, one-parent families. If they do have a home, they often live in the remnants of those pre-war working-class areas which have lost their heavy industries, from which most lucky enough to be in work have fled to new suburbs. Many other working-class people have gone to new council estates on the edges of the cities. In these areas a sustaining neighbourliness is now very difficult to nourish.

*

It is fairly easy to identify each group by its predominant tastes, by – in the jargon – its 'life-style'. Those in group 1 do not take the popular newspapers unless they need, for business-information purposes, to keep in touch with what seem to be changes in tabloid readers' tastes, or out of a habit of cultural skimming. Their newspaper buying runs from *The Times* and *Telegraph* to the *Guardian* and *Independent*. The *Independent* is a precise marker of one strand in this group, and its founding was a brilliant response to the changes described here. It hit an identifiable sub-group within group 1: people not entirely happy with the existing broadsheets and quite unlikely to buy the tabloids, people not particularly thrusting in the executive manner nor strongly ideological in their politics. Liberal Democrat rather than firmly Conservative or Labour, intelligent, slightly sobersides, the archetypal middle-people of that first group. The *Independent*'s difficulties in the early Nineties have complicated origins, including some editorial loss of touch. Much more important was the inevitable and growing pressure of competition, and that led to efforts to imitate some of those characteristics of the competition which the *Independent* had been founded specifically to avoid.

Across the ranks of group 1 are to be found many who turn to Channel 4 or at least to its 7 to 8 p.m. news, who patronise Eurocamps when the children are young and Swan Hellenic when the children are long gone; with Jules Verne in between. They shop at Sainsbury's, or Waitrose if there is a branch handy. They know about extra-virgin olive oil, pesto and speciality breads. Their cars are not usually Fords unless the firm supplies a Granada or, lower down in the group, a Mondeo – BMWs, rather, and Saabs, Land-Rovers, Range Rovers, Audis, Mercedes, possibly Peugeot or Volvo estates, Rovers as they climb back into reliability, top-of-the-range Renaults and Citroëns. For the more intellectual free spirits, motorised caravans. This group contains 'gold card' holders, Habitat and Waterstone's browsers, gourmet-cookery-book buyers, whole-food fans, hang-gliders, joggers, designer-labelled women and men, Laura Ashley and Christie's Contemporary Arts customers, patrons of private schools and private medical care. Much cultural top-dressing, for the man or woman who has everything . . . All of these revolve according to stages on the personal ladders and to group changes in taste.

A quick entry to the overall theme can be gained from a look at the monthly magazine section of a station bookstall; the patterns by groups are soon clear. The range is enormous, and runs from old-fashioned 'hobbies' to communications technology to cultural aspirations to sport, pets, cars and the Home. Golfing magazines deserve an entry of their own. They are numerous and include one which illustrates this general theme better than any other: *Executive Golf*. That's fine-tuning for you. Presumably executives don't have their own rules for golf; they do attract different and more top-of-the-market ads. Among a random bunch of thirty-seven books on aspects of health care published in the early Nineties there was the *Executive Health Guide*, subtitled 'How to Succeed in Business without Sacrificing your Health'.

Similar results could be produced from records of changes in sports, drinking habits, fashions in speech (more complex than other areas); and so on almost endlessly.

*

Group 2 tastes are wider, larger, more amorphous. In television, BBC 1 or, more often, Channel 3 rather than BBC 2 or, even less likely, Channel 4. Not Radio 3 but often Radio 4 if it hasn't been displaced by Classic FM, cable or satellite – though radio plays a smaller part than TV in the daily pattern, especially in the evenings. As to cars, Fords from Escorts up to a few Mondeos, Nissans, some Toyotas and Peugeot 405s, Vauxhalls, the smaller Renaults and Citroëns and VWs; all making part of a wide centre of tastes and expenditures in many things and activities. Shopping at Sainsbury's, Safeway, Gateway and Tesco, largely according to which is most handy. Piat d'Or. Holidays usually in packages from firms such as Thomson's. For recreations, gardening above all (though that is in some respects classless), perhaps fishing, family visiting. Then there are 'hobbies', the historic successors of fretwork; and, increasingly, visits to theme parks, Also, in the upper parts of this group, the assumption that you should take part in voluntary good works. Much lower down, soft-porn videos, flashy new drinks and TV dinners. It is a very large group, and even such a quick look as this reinforces the idea that it probably does need sub-dividing. Its most common quality is, to repeat, still the almost uxorious assumption of the centrality of marriage; though that is being much eroded.

*

Most people in the third group, no matter how poor they are, will have television, the almost universal entertainer. Most sets will be rented. Renting seems more manageable than hire purchase but is, though few work this out, more expensive. Buying is cheapest of all but usually not possible. There are few hobbies or recreations and no disposition to read books (you could say that about many in group 2). Probably fifty or more hours a week are spent watching television. Channel 3 almost entirely, game shows, soap operas and all. During the daytime, the local commercial radio station is most favoured, though occasionally Radios 1 and 2 or Melody Radio. Holidays, foreign or in Britain, figure hardly at all, though some people may follow an old tradition and go to relatives for a few days in the summer. It makes a change, even if the relatives live in an industrial town similar to yours. Most get no holidays at all from year to year.

Of the supermarkets Tesco used to be favoured and, now, the new rock-bottom discount grocery chains. The successors to the old corner-shops in crowded working-class areas are those grocers, usually allied to the Spar operation, on council estates. Dearer than the supermarkets, they are handier and still the centres for very local gossip. Supermarkets develop wider-meshed gossip.

As to clothing, there may be cast-offs from several quarters: family, charity shops (unless their volunteer staff seem off putting), the immortal and much-loved jumble sales (usually handier than car-boot sales and culturally different); and those national chains which cater specifically for the bottom of the clothing market and hence specialise in sweat-shop products, mostly from Asia – but they must be colourful.

iii PIGGYBACKS, PARTIAL PROFILES AND EMOTIONAL ENERGY

Four more general thoughts about the whole slow but tide-like process arise. First, that the richness, level and complexity of provision made for each group goes down as one moves downward; and, given the nature of contemporary technology as it serves the markets, the range of choice is decided less by gross numbers than by level of sophistication.

The provision for people in group 3 is not rich or varied and lacks texture; it was seen earlier that they are hardly worth tempting. The provision for group 2 is wider and to some extent and within defined limits widening all the time. In that large group most members have some 'discretionary spending power'. What a liberator that is to anyone brought up in a home where an effort was needed to reach each weekend still just in balance. Another glance at those magazine racks confirms that this group is provided with the widest range of hobby-and-recreational journals.

Though several times larger than group 1, group 3, is, in terms of individual taste, less well catered for. If he were writing today, Thorstein Veblen would probably be led to substitute, for 'conspicuous consumption', 'rarefied consumption' and 'stratified consumption'.

Two elements ensure this: members of group 1 have more spare money even than those in group 2; and modern technology makes it profitable to cater for relatively small groups, so long as the money is out there. Even more modern technology, through developments such as the information superhighway, may reduce that advantage.

*

Here there enters the piggyback principle. That first became evident in America in the Sixties, when 'egghead' paperbacks appeared. They were often classics by then out of copyright, together with some other, more intellectual books whose hard-cover runs were exhausted. These 'egghead' titles used spare capacity on machines whose main function was to print millions of popular paperbacks, chiefly for the drugstore market. It was profitable to add to production, and to sell at a dollar each, a few tens of thousands of non-popular titles. That exercise was rather like the space shuttle carried on the back of a jumbo jet and released at the right altitude.

This is an extraordinary conjunction. The popular end of the market, through all its agents of persuasion, more and more concentrates itself so that millions are month after month buying the same book, magazine, cassette, disc. In that sense their tastes – this is group 2 – are being all the time more narrowly focused. Those in group 1 profit from the process. Their more refined tastes, their almost minority tastes in comparison with those in group 2, are more and more precisely catered for; they are in this sense partly parasitic on the increasing concentration of the mass market. Better and better provision – more accurately, more and more expensive rather than consistently better provision – is there for those who can pay and have to some extent trained tastes; and is on the way to producing a new kind of imaginative servitude – for others.

*

The third of these more general thoughts is that the different groups in the emerging society are hardly ever addressed as whole human beings. Their members are approached as partial people – as constantly renewed appetites, as consumers of food, of clothing, of leisure and of notions (not of thoughts or ideas); all these are regularly and, because of the nature of technology and of competition, changed, discarded. It is symptomatic that two of the newer fashionable words are 'collectables' and 'disposables'; those two 'things' used to indicate 'attitudes' are inseparable. There is more and more segmented provision for more and more firmly stratified groups. This is the partial approach, not a provision which recognises the varied reality and wholeness of individuals and of small groups, or of 'the community' as a whole.

The computer profiles now being used by those insurance companies which by this means decide with whom they will do business, are the epitome of the 'partial person' approach: if your profile as to age, sex, salary, occupation fits then we will issue a policy over the phone through a VDU operator who is given no room for manoeuvre or negotiation; if not, not; there is neither room nor time nor profit in entertaining deviations – unless you are really very well-off. There is also provision-partiality within the same organisation; as in Forte's firmly and finely devised distinctions and levels of catering service, from the Little Chefs to some of the most expensive hotels in the world. Conversely, some organisations have discovered how to cross most class and status divisions at the same time and place. An example is Argos. Also, to some extent, the largest supermarket chains. They can serve a very wide band, but they differentiate by class their products and the aisles on which they are displayed; the customers differentiate by the times and days on which they shop, and most know the status of each aisle.

The fourth general thought goes to the very roots of the process of change from class to status. Much of the emotional energy which was spent in sustaining the sense of class-divisions has not been dissolved; it is being switched into maintaining the sense of status-differences. Naturally, the icons, the mantras, differ, but they are no less clear. Some remain much the same: different groups have differing access to education, to occupations, to the intellectual and artistic life; and their illnesses and life-expectancies differ. The 'our kind of people' society remains. The marking-out of those differences has to be constantly renewed, or undesirables will push their way in. Differentiations are made through an almost unconsciously known and operated set of signals hardly less strong than the old ones. The exact make and model and registration letter of any car can be read so as instantly to make a sophisticated judgment on where the owners have reached on the status-ladder; or where they may be going. Permutations upon permutations: in clothing, electronic gear, skiing holidays, in all those markers which instantly distinguish those on a similar ladder to oneself from those not on a ladder at all.

Energy of this sort, spent in maintaining class- or group-divisions, still operates. But today more energy is spent on maintaining distinctions between oneself and other people near enough on the same status-ladder as to pose a comparison and perhaps a challenge or threat. Relativism remains, but claims about the existence of an 'open' society are false.

CHAPTER TEN

Patrons and Sponsors

I regard it as an important part of the function of the Department of National Heritage to encourage the development of public support for heritage activity – but as I have said before, public support is not a euphemism for taxpayer support. What we seek is individual commitment by members of a growing audience.

The Secretary of State for National Heritage, late 1994 (There is no suggestion that the government will help that audience to grow, and discover a 'commitment')

It seems at first curious that in so relativist, levelling and, latterly, aggressively market-dominated a society both governments and industrialists should pay at least some attention and a kind of homage to the arts: that support for the arts should be a tiny bit of a spoke in the whirling free-market wheels. Why do the arts, why should the arts, matter to those now in the driving-seat; in particular, certain of the 'high arts'?

One can more easily see why, in spite of that social wide-openness, those in power reinforce the action of the spoke or check, of class into status. It is also to some extent easier to understand their support for the check of censorship, in a society they claim should be freer. Sexual puritanism thrives at the higher social levels as much as in working-class Primitive Methodism; it is here part of the historic fear of 'anarchy' – if They are let loose. The official English disposition towards control by secrecy will not be much diminished by a mere couple of decades of limited relaxation. But, again, why need there be any attention to the high arts?

Partly this attitude is yet another instance of the homage which profit-making pays to something felt to belong to a more disinterested world. Or, less loftily, a grander world. Hence the concentration on selected high arts (unless the Corporate Affairs Director argues convincingly for a more popular image); hence too the tendency to select, for major public positions in official arts bodies, aristocrats or unassailably Establishment figures, meritocrats who have become monumental; or, best of all, Royalty (some of whom can, more than other Hon. Patrons, be relied on to chivvy the Arts Council: 'Her Royal Highness is particularly concerned that . . .').

Here also is that simple culture-vulturedom which reaches its apogee in the crush bar at Covent Garden, where Cabinet Ministers mingle with major corporate sponsors. Their view of the arts may be limited and finely graded socially; and grand opera – especially the best-known dozen or so – is one of the nicer signs of having 'arrived'. The focus on the arts here is a public focus; it illuminates the stage and the auditorium; few such people would be up-to-date on classic or contemporary literature.

Other than such relatively minor impulses there is no clear reason, given the growth of populism over the last century and given the unimaginativeness of recent governments, why the arts should be supported from public funds or by industrial-commercial sponsorship. That they are so supported, for no matter what dubious reasons, is some comfort until better thoughts on the need to support them prevail. The force of Aldous Huxley's pre-war judgment has been tempered by the creation of the Arts Council but in general it remains true, especially about such expensive arts as opera: 'If it were not for the intellectual snobs who pay – in solid cash – the tribute which philistinism owes to culture, the arts would perish with their starving practitioners. Let us thank heaven for hypocrisy'.

Meanwhile, less subtle members of the government look forward to the day when industrial-commercial sponsorship and the National Lottery entirely take over from public funding. More sophisticated members argue the case for public support as though attention to the arts can be a sort of cultural Polyfilla to reinforce and hide the crumbling fabric of society's traditional institutional safeguards. We have grand opera that we may not perish from the truth.

The record of most Local Authorities is little, if any, better. How many have spent anywhere near the sixpenny rate made available for the arts?

i WHY GIVE AT ALL – IN AN 'OPEN' SOCIETY?

The case for public money for the arts can be and is argued passionately and, for some, convincingly. Like so much else in this area it cannot be objectively proved. Discussions are mostly contentious and either self-righteous or dismissive. No wonder the Arts Council itself is nervous about putting its case forcefully; that would smack of self-seeking.

Democratic governments are inherently disinclined to commit themselves to statements of principle outside defence matters; especially the British. For years governments shied away from including the word 'Culture' in the relevant Minister's title. Minister *of* Culture was bad enough; Minister *for* Culture seemed to increase the problem, by sounding more proprietorial. 'Minister with Special Responsibility for the Arts' clumsily avoided the high-toned, or any suggestion of knowing, nationally, what The Arts or Culture are (and is a Cabinet seat really necessary?).

Today that Minister is in charge of 'The National Heritage', which hides the Arts and Culture generally behind its bricks-and-mortar suggestion. Whatever their titles, such British Ministers are likely to declare in international conferences on Culture and the Arts: 'I would not claim to be able to define art or culture. But I think I and my compatriots know and recognise these qualities when we see them.' Nowadays a more glib National Heritage Minister will add: 'Anyway, the definition of such things changes in each generation.' Relativism again, a slippery escape.

*

Dictatorships know what they mean by art: they mean propaganda, *agitprop*, 'socialist realism', Nazi racist heroics. In these definitions, art does not look at experience as though for the first time, freely. It mirrors existing, laid-down expectations and definitions of experience. *Samizdat* art must be rejected since it accepts a qualified, conditional, disordered, flawed, open and unbuttoned world.

At first glance Stalin's banning of pop music and dance seemed no more than an old puritan's dislike of young people making a noise and enjoying themselves in ways good Young Pioneers would never do. There could have been a more subtle but probably unrecognised impulse behind the ban. On those occasions, and whether in the West or in the old Eastern bloc, when young people disobeyed the injunction and let their hair down, that kind of music and dance seemed to express not abandon but an uncommitted freedom and personal confidence, a sense that they took their own bodies and what they did with them, their own behaviour, as indeed *theirs*, not to be pushed around by anyone else. To a Stalinist this could have suggested, no doubt below the conscious level, that anarchy, uncorralled individual free-will, were just about to break out.

*

Commercial democracies are less sure of themselves. They prefer external to governmental sponsorship, not only to save public money but also because State-funded artists can be more rebarbative towards public authorities than they are towards outside donors. Some tend to take such funds as a natural right, as much to be expected as a National Health Service. They are expert at biting the hand that feeds them. That is better than grateful subservience but gives the intervening bodies, notably the Arts Council, continuous harassment; and tempts them to successive buyings-off, according to the nuisance-value of each harasser.

*

Perhaps that paragraph applies chiefly to Britain. Within mainland Western Europe public support for the arts differs from country to country, but in most countries is more confident than here. Germany and France have long and solid traditions. The German approach has come down from the days of the Principalities, and has been carried through to the present *Länder* (though as a result of the cost of East–West unification the largesse is now being reduced: after all, they have 20 orchestras). Today in France Malraux's legacy survives and had been built on by Jack Lang. The French tradition has been strong and centralised for centuries, coming down in particular from Versailles and surviving in successive Republics on the assumption that France is, almost as a decision of God, the home of European and perhaps even international culture. There is some truth in this, much as the British may wish to deny it; the French state does take artistic matters much more seriously than the British state and is prepared to pay accordingly. It shouldn't be regretted that Paris became the home of the UN's cultural and artistic agency, UNESCO. It is pleasant that the *quid pro quo* was that the British provided the first Director-General: Julian Huxley, one kind of classic British intellectual, free-wheeling and eccentric.

It is fashionable to describe the British attitude to public funding for the arts as philistine, grudging and all the rest of the litany. To some extent all that is true; but there is more to be said. When public money for the arts is at last given in Britain it is often given through those Royal Chartered, 'arm's-length' bodies described elsewhere in this book. At least it was until the last decade and a bit. As someone has said, latterly arm's-length has given way to arm-twisting. That is ceasing to be necessary now that most of those who take the Chairs – and their committee members – are avowedly and strongly conservative.

It might be useful to reserve 'patronage' for money given without overt strings, and 'sponsorship' for the string-bearing kind; which is almost all we recognise in Britain. Since 'patronage' is usually only apparently disinterested – the patron looking not so much for treasures in heaven as for a 'gong' – perhaps we need to bring in 'donor' for the totally disinterested and usually anonymous giver.

Sometimes in intellectual and artistic matters the British capacity to surprise themselves, to do something out of character, something unusually imaginative, comes into play. An example is the founding of the Open University, that damned close-run thing. Another is in the rapidly increased public spending on the arts from not long after the end of the last war to the early Eighties; with a great surge in the mid-Sixties and for a while after.

It is always interesting, if difficult, to seek out the play of forces by which at a certain moment such a lively jump is made, to assess the interaction of social changes with the influence of a persistent and influential individual or group: Jennie Lee for both the Open University and the increase in arts funding, say.

The developments in arts funding, mainly funnelled through the Arts Council, from the mid-Sixties to the start of the Eighties, has not yet been fully appreciated. The Arts Council, as we have seen, is disinclined to give serious thought to its own purposes and to make its work known. Many of its achievements have gone by default; it has been derided both by those who object to its existence and by those who are not given as much as they believe they deserve. The Council itself needs a good word.

Apart from the network of Arts Council-supported repertory theatres, the provision of art galleries, concerts, literary events in every large and most middle-sized to small cities is also far greater than it used to be. Behind most performances and exhibitions there is likely to be an Arts Council grant to the painters, the choreographers, the composers, the venues. Many of these also were, by the mid-Nineties, malnourished. That is not the Arts Council's fault, though it is often blamed.

Today the Arts Council (now the Arts Council of England only) is even more uncertain than its former self. This is not due mainly to delegation of the Council's work; the controls on decentralised work are tight. It is due rather to the characteristically imperceptive notions of recent Tory governments on the nature and needs of the arts, and in particular to their illusory wish that some day soon private sponsorship and the National Lottery will make public funding superfluous. The more frank disbursers of commercial sponsorship have pointed out this error but to no effect. These governments have been obdurate in their belief (though it hardly deserves to be called a belief; it is a rooted prejudice) that the market can and will by its own internal mechanism supply all needs, material, intellectual, imaginative, spiritual. It is shameful that at the end of the twentieth century a country with a not negligible record of occasional maturity of outlook should be ruled by such bigots. That they have ruled for so long tells as much about those who voted for them as about the Tory politicians. Still, one remains haunted by the ugly cries of the committed at their annual party conferences when an issue which calls for generosity of spirit rather than lowering of income tax is put before them.

This succession of governments has naturally failed to understand, or rejected as derisory, the nature of the traditional, free, non-political and unpaid Quangos: they have their own types of Quango, packed with paid nominees chiefly of their own persuasion. It follows that the Arts Council must be a bad thing (together with the BBC and the British Council), and must be done away with bit by bit in the cause of privatisation, decentralisation, competition, anti-bureaucracy, anti-free-wheeling intellectualism and anti-artistic licence. Even the Tory politicians who can claim some artistic knowledge tend to speak from what may justly be called a closed-bourgeois perspective; here one can use such a term as just criticism.

ii CLASS, EDUCATION, THE ARTS; AND PUBLIC DUTY

A large selection of the population is completely indifferent to anything that comes under the general heading of 'culture' and they have every right to stay in that state of non-grace . . . the appetite for culture in this country is less voracious than many of us pretend.

Public Patronage and the Arts, 1965

The above passage is from a Political and Economic Planning pamphlet. Trite language used to slide over shallowness – 'every right . . . state of non-grace . . . appetite for culture . . . less voracious . . .' – reminds us that the opposition does not come from one side only.

We are looking now at the indisputable correlations between response to the arts and level of education. Correlations between class and access to the arts will come a little later. 'The arts' here means those expressions of creativity which have been generally admired among those who, whatever their education and social class, have sought to make judgments of quality. There will be no refuge in either writing down such work as 'merely expressions of bourgeois hegemony' or in widening the definition of art to include whatever someone somewhere has enjoyed, including the latest ephemeral hit in the pop charts.

It was noted earlier that if you are highly educated the arts are more likely to be accessible to you. This does not mean that a good education automatically makes you appreciate and respond to the arts, treat them as an important part of your daily life. Your intelligence may be high but may not embrace attention to the arts. Strange as this may seem, the peaks of opera, of drama and of fiction may say nothing to you. Though highly educated and very competent, you may be blind and deaf to the arts.

Education does not ensure appreciation but, from a certain level and for both intellectual and social reasons, is for most people a necessary precondition. There are exceptional people with very scanty educational qualifications – and anyone who has taken adult classes outside formal full-time education has met them – who show a natural responsiveness to the arts. That has led them to seek to go further by enrolling in a class or, like E. M. Forster's Leonard Bast, attending concerts of classical music and seeking single-handed entry to that world. They are making an effort to get out of their enveloping culture. Their existence may well suggest that many others, who for whatever reasons do not make that effort, could appreciate the arts if their educational opportunities and the culture of their class did not work so powerfully against them.

So: an appreciation of the arts involves, first of all, the interplay of natural taste, talent and educational opportunity. The next major factor is social class, the differing physical and financial conditions within each class and, more important, their differing cultural conditions and assumptions. It cannot be convincingly argued today that most working-class people should not be expected to take an interest in the arts, on the grounds that their hours of work are long and arduous; for many, this is no longer true. Generally, executives and managers work longer hours, are under more strain.

To appreciate the arts can be expensive. Classical concerts are not cheap and Covent Garden is beyond the reach of all but a few, the wealthy and the corporate beneficiaries. Prohibitive cost is a favourite argument to explain why many people do not attend. It ignores the fact that a ticket for a pop concert by a famous group at a prime venue can cost at least as much as one for a symphony concert in the Royal Festival Hall.

Once again, more people than ever before have money to spend as they will, and exercise that right; those choices are educationally, socially and culturally conditioned; this is the ground-level of the matter.

The climate provided by class and occupation is much the most powerful element. Recreational habits in working-class districts or in those areas and among those people whom it would be hard nowadays simply to label as working-class, but who have certainly not become middle-class, such habits are heavily conditioned by age and sex. At the first level is the beer-and-bint culture of many young men in pubs and clubs (they have their female counterparts and both have their middle-class counterparts). Conversation after that age focuses on sport, cars, family problems, gossip about neighbours, what's been on the telly, royalty, crime, the cost of living, problems at work, and sex again. They divide also according to participant recreations, with gardening, DIY and fishing predominant. What you would not expect, what it would be ingenuous to expect, is any talk about the arts, about plays or books or music or dance. They are *out*, simply not part of the culture.

It is at the middle-class professional level that an interest in the arts first surfaces, the assumption that some attention might be paid to the professional arts. Before that and ranging from the 'respectable' working class up through the mid-middle class is the astonishingly widespread practice of amateur arts. Hutchison and Feist (*Amateur Arts in the UK*) record that in 1989–90 there were 66,000 performances of amateur opera and drama in Britain, that 1.8 million people were involved in staging them and that they had audiences of 12 million. Presumably those did not include the figures for amateur pantomimes.

All that is a different matter from the appreciation of some professional arts. It is tempting and would be easy to assume that the two interests are interconnected and that one leads to the other (the favoured 'onwards and upwards' hope). It seems more likely that the two interests are not importantly connected, that they meet different psychological needs and aspirations.

The solidly middle-class response to the professional arts is founded in family custom, educational background, the cultural climate of the main professions and, of course, but not most importantly, in imaginative interest as that has been nurtured by those other factors or as it has been granted by nature. It covers a wide range of different approaches, from substantial knowledge of one or more art-forms, a well-informed enthusiasm, across to little more than the acceptance of some attention to the arts as a sign of class or status. It runs from the person who follows a symphony with the score across the knees to those who will accept corporate hospitality at the opera for what it implies of their having 'arrived' or being on the way there; these are usually people who would not think of initiating or paying for their visits. They include the notorious bored chocolate-wrapper rustlers; those are not simply a figment of minds driven by reverse snobbery. But in this the English are amateurs compared with some in the boxes at the Vienna State Opera. There, old-style continental European bourgeois snobbery and new-style executive rock-climbing come together to display themselves in one of the world's two or three most cachet-ridden venues. English people of roughly this kind may well have on the coffee-table, together with a casually placed programme from last month at Covent Garden, large, glossy, illustrated art books – but a mass-market blockbuster at the bedside; if anything. In Vienna, opera house affairs (not only scandals) are discussed by taxi-drivers and in the popular press (especially scandals).

Nothing of what has been said above can reasonably be taken to reinforce the argument, so popular in some quarters, that traditional high arts – let us say, since these are commonly cited in such arguments, the three-volume nineteenth-century novel – were and remain simply bourgeois creations, serving their known audiences, mirroring that way of life, trapped in their cultural box-files and only of meaning to 'the bourgeoisie', yesterday's or today's.

Chapter 3 showed how those who have such convictions often go on to demand the encouragement of 'working-class art' and especially working-class writing. There is a great deal to be done towards increasing the practice and appreciation of the arts among those parts of society where they are at present ignored. There is room for more attention being paid in art to the experiences of other than middle-class people. The North London novel has had an excessively long run; the Sixties working-class novel is no longer in vogue. It would be good to read more about the lives of people in those new social groups based on status described in Chapter 9, who are neither middle- nor working-class. Yet writers must be left to write about what they know or would like to know and, since so many novelists are at present from the middling areas of society, that is another reason why a wider range of people should be encouraged to discover what talents they have. But it is neither necessary nor helpful nor sensible to set up false oppositions, to set the nineteenth-century 'middle-class' novel against what might appear today – and to some extent has already appeared. To all such considerations labels such as 'middle-class' and 'working-class' literature soon prove to be beside the point. Literature, writing, of any quality is always more than that.

By this point we are, then, a long way from labels such as 'bour-geois art' and the rest. They served their turn and had some, quite limited, use. That so much art in the nineteenth century sought a middle-class audience should go without saying; that class of people were not only literate but had the money to buy those long novels. That the novels were three-deckers (usually issued first in monthly parts) was a material consequence of the methods of production, sale and presumed consumption. It would be coarse to assume that such purchases were the equivalents of today's coffee-table books. It was expected by the writers and the purchasers that the books would be read – and read passionately, not only as approving and reinforcing reflections of their own ways of life.

A solid reading of Trollope is particularly instructive here. In some senses he is immured in the class he addresses and writes about, and fascinated by those above that class; sometimes his novels show this uncritically and disablingly. But for much of the time his books rise above and out of these constrictions and become illuminating cri-tiques of the societies they depict, morally penetrating and at the same time exceptionally charitable because so perceptive into human frailty. Doubters might begin with the long task of reading *The Way We Live Now*. To read – one almost has to say 'really read' – a novel of that calibre is to be offered a valuable extension of consciousness; to describe this as offering, vicariously, aspirations towards middle-class styles and values is to lead yourself into an ideological dead-end.

Many ways are practised of resisting the belief that more than those who at present practise and appreciate the arts could do so. When, in the early Eighties, the then Secretary General of the Arts Council, Roy Shaw, proposed that an Education Department be created, some on the Council turned up their noses at the proposal. Masticating the arts for the masses was not to be seriously thought of. On the other, the far, side are those who dismiss as the latest bourgeois trick any suggestion that a much wider range of people should be given the opportunity to practise and appreciate the arts. Why should they have middle-class values foisted on them? Encourage them to create 'their own' art.

Two basic truths need to be repeatedly asserted. First, that the arts are valuable beyond all the arguments about 'hegemony'. Second: that people at present outside do not need to be talked down to.

iii GRASS-ROOTS, 'ETHNIC ARTS' AND THEIR CLAIMS

A recurring theme in this book is the seduction wrought on many people of goodwill by romantic words and phrases, such as 'from the grass-roots' and 'at the coalface'. Those who have been promoted to a managerial from a production job in television are almost always said to have 'deserted the coalface'. The implication is that they will from then on progressively lose touch with the realities necessary for artistic life, will become routine and uninspired bureaucrats. Some do; and some retain their inventive fire and flair, to the greater benefit of all.

The attraction of the call to the grass-roots is particularly tricky, and has a wide range of reference. In dismissing 'desk-bound arts apparatchiks' it is exercising the fairly common English intellectual's and artist's suspicion of all administrators and all committees.

A proud provincialism, in some a rooted amateurism, a form of inverted class snobbery, a machismo which can also be adopted by women, all come together there to demote or reject the 'metropolitan organisation men'.

By now, and this is its widest application, the invocation and self-crediting of grass-roots has come to be regarded as in itself a sufficient guarantee of quality. The claim to be of, to come from, to represent the grass-roots, is taken as a self-evident advantage in applications for public subventions. The claim becomes comical when its spokesman is an aggressive *émigré* New Yorker, with a degree from

Columbia, who assumes that anyone in a suit and tie is a cousin of the Big Apple executives he's escaped from.

Much the same pattern of attitudes, aggressive or submissive, come into play when the claims on public funds of ethnic minorities (not of 'ethnic groups', for sure) are being considered. Anyone who in any way wishes not to dismiss but simply to consider such claims carefully will sooner rather than later be in trouble. Should 'positive discrimination' be practised so as to encourage their particular arts? Perhaps, but the case is not axiomatic and needs to be properly made; it rarely is.

iv CONFUSED ALARMS OF STRUGGLE AND FIGHT

Clearly, the arts-and-the-public-purse debate promises to continue in its confused state. Those politically on the Right stick to what may fairly be called old-style élitist assumptions on to which have latterly been grafted thrusting commercial attitudes. There is no need to spend much time on these attitudes; they are usually simple and misguided. The more extreme left-wing attitudes are both more interesting and complicated (not complex). They usually mix very firmly held political beliefs with unclear assumptions about the nature and the social relations of the arts; the mixture is rarely enlightening. Still: somewhere far back they seem to be drawing on good roots, on Morris if not on Arnold, perhaps even on Wordsworth and Coleridge if not on J. S. Mill, on Orwell if not on Eliot. All this is a much more nourishing sub-soil than those most Tories draw on nowadays. They could draw on a better and more cultivated Conservative ancestry, but few do; few know what wells to tap. Such references as a few make almost always suggest a sclerotic enclosed system of reference and belief.

In this part of the field false arguments and false comparisons abound. Startling contrasts are invoked at every opportunity by the expansionists. Do you realise, we are asked, that the Germans spend x times more on opera than we do? Yes. They also spend x times more on water-cannon to throw back their citizens when they go on the rampage. It is badly misguided to think you can pick up, out of context, one habit of public spending in another country which makes your own seem parsimonious whilst ignoring those customs in which your country shows generosity and inventiveness – in our case, Public Libraries, allotments, Public Parks, voluntary help of all kinds to others in need, the Open University. All cultural habits have tentacular roots; they cannot be handled like cut flowers.

Much the same is true of internal false contrasts. No more money for our theatre company or for others like us! But one Trident costs more than all theatrical claimants in the country. True, but you can't discourage a potential enemy with a line of massed and mixed theatrical troupes. Defence never comes cheap. You may if you wish be an out-and-out pacifist and demand that no money be spent on defence and that all the money saved be given to good causes, starting with drama groups. That is at least consistent.

You would then have to argue with those who assert that money spent on theatrical companies is money wasted and should be transferred to research into the causes of cancer; or a hundred other things. There is nothing like leather, certainly, but there are many different kinds of leather, real and metaphorical; everyone has to make choices between them.

This all merges into the bread-from-children's-mouths argument as put by some outright opponents of public subventions. Why waste money on the arts, which anyway few patronise, when so many children are undernourished, old-age pensioners cold and millions badly housed.

You don't *have* to support the arts. If, however, you would like to, but wait before doing so until all those and many another ill are erased, you will wait for ever. Improvements in penal arrangements alone could use more than the arts would ever claim. Such a delay would satisfy those who care nothing for the arts; people such as those can be found in every society, even the most wealthy. The results of that denuding would not be instantly visible, nor ever visible to those who do not wish to see them. They would nevertheless be there, in many aspects of a starved civility.

At a slightly more ingratiating level some people will say they agree with spending public money on good community activities, including even something for the arts, but that just now they need a new swimming pool or children's playground before this or that artistic item. This was said by some councillors of St Ives when the new Tate Gallery was established there and needed some local money. It will always be so. There is said to be a Chinese epigram – there always is – to the effect: 'If I had only a penny I hope I would spend a ha'penny on bread and a ha'penny on a rose.' The St Ives councillors would not be amused or affected by that; it is not a very British sentiment. Perhaps the dubious 'bringing in tourist money' argument helped.

The economic case for spending public money on the arts is being more and more used. It is increasingly based on sophisticated data: about the power of high-level art to attract foreign tourists, who then spend much money on all sorts of other activities, and so on to the government's revenue from VAT on tickets (unless the argument being offered is that VAT should not in principle be levied in this area). The revenue from VAT can be shown to be more than the public purse gives to support the arts in the first place. No doubt any Treasury tyro could demonstrate the holes in this argument. If the government began to give subventions to all sorts of bodies thought worthy by somebody, on the grounds that those bodies paid a great deal of VAT, we would have a pantomimic, Widow Twankey situation – in which we all took in each other's washing but had no external expenses. It is sounder to argue, not that public subventions should be more generous because of the amount their activities attract in VAT, but that the arts should, as are books at present, be exempted from VAT on the general grounds that they can be educative and civilising.

It can easily seem that any stick is good enough to beat opponents with when one is arguing a case about which one feels strongly and virtuously, on the side of the angels. That is never a good way to argue and can rebound badly. The arts, like any other activity whose benefits are not easily assessed and never entirely proved, should have their case made on the most clear and honest and mature grounds, not by cobbling together dubious claims.

V PATRONAGE AND SPONSORSHIP

The list of products that the do-gooders, the latter-day puritans, will proclaim bad for us is endless. If something is illegal and the government declare it so then we won't touch it. If not, will people please clear off and let us make our own decisions.
A senior representative of a public body concerned with sport

We cannot afford to have ethics like that.
Sponsorship officer of a large national theatre company

Sir, I would take money from the Devil himself if it helped the arts survive.
Highly cultured peer (echoes of Dr Johnson)

Sponsorship [in broadcasting] still has a long way to go before it attains the kind of impact on the viewers of which it is capable. A more sophisticated marriage between programme and product and increased creativity are the key to sponsorship's coming of age.

Broadcasting consultant, market research, 1992 ('sophisticated marriage . . . increased creativity . . . coming of age' – thus more good words become unusable)

Picasso was at the leading-edge of the art world; he pushed barriers back; he thought and saw in an original way. That's very much the Ernst and Young philosophy of leading-edge thinking which delivers . . .

Advertising agency modestly underlining its sponsorship of a Picasso exhibition

On this subject the most useful recent book is *The Spread of Sponsorship* (1993), edited by Roy Shaw (from which most of the above quotations have been taken).

Sponsorship in Britain is, from a weak base and not swiftly, growing stronger; especially after the encouragements of the 1990 Broadcasting Act. Even so, it is important to say again that in the funding of the arts external sponsorship is very unlikely to take the place of public funding even as it now is, and even more unlikely to meet the needed level. In the year 1991/2 Arts Council subsidies to drama were 34.1 per cent; sponsorship produced 4.8 per cent. Literature received 26.2 per cent of its support from the Council, 1.5 per cent from sponsorship. Music received 31.3 per cent from the Council, 11.6 per cent from sponsors. Sponsorship for dance was a fifth of that provided by the Council. Only the visual arts showed fairly strong figures: 30.7 per cent from the Council, 18.2 per cent from sponsorship. It is not difficult to see what cultural conventions were in play in that lot.

In broadcasting, commercial funding could do away with the need for public money; that is, the licence fee. If that time comes, the fabric of the public service idea as we have known it will have been torn to tatters, become fragments on the studio floor, found only in dark, off-peak corners.

Some Directors of Sponsorship or 'Corporate Affairs Directors' (a favourite title) or Community Affairs Directors can be, unless pushed by a no-nonsense Managing Director or Chairman, not excessively demanding as to the amount and kind of acknowledgment they seek for their money. Others turn the screws so that every last drop of advertisement is wrung out of the artistic event.

They have the government on their side. An Office of Arts and Libraries leaflet of the mid-Eighties, meant to encourage firms to sponsor the arts, said that sponsorship is 'a payment by a business firm . . . for the purpose of promoting its name, products or services'. No artistic, high-minded nonsense there, even from the office supposed to help the arts. More explicitly, 'the Inland Revenue regards sponsorship as advertising, and allows expenditure on it to be set against a company's tax liability because it is regarded as money spent "wholly and exclusively for the purpose of trade". Any hint of philanthropic purpose would make the expenditure ineligible for tax relief.' It is difficult to find a metaphor which captures the full Gradgrindery of that position. It is perhaps like saying, to a particularly active hit-man; 'If you advertise your services as free, we will tax you on what you should be charging. But if you advertise your services and charges you may offset the advertising against your receipts.' Governments can make no value-judgments. Put more directly: money given as an act of enlightened philanthropy with no demands on the recipient is not exempt from tax; money given for the purposes of explicit self-advertisement is exempt. That puts weight behind the demands of the Corporate Affairs Directors.

The Foundation for Sports and the Arts, the Business Sponsorship Incentive Scheme and ABSA (the Association for Business Sponsorship of the Arts) make their contributions, though claims as to the amounts given are not always clear. *Culture and Consensus* (1995) by Robert Hewison is helpful here. But these sorts of initiatives are only a kind of patchwork. One has the impression, in the mid-Nineties, that the Treasury is waiting for the lifeboat – the National Lottery – which looks like making competitive mendicants of the arts, sports, museums and so on; as they all squabble for the small percentage of the Lottery takings which are left for distribution after the creaming-off. Small wonder many charities are worrying that, direct donations to them having been diverted, they will be losers in the switch. Many individuals, told that the Lottery will be used to support the arts and other such good causes, pay their pounds to it, not realising how small a proportion will be left for those causes.

Officers in arts companies appointed to seek sponsorship money rarely seem to have so objective and proper a pride in their colleagues' work that they will not sell the company short, even to excessive and ill-judged demands by sponsors. Only one example of resistance comes to mind: the Royal National Theatre, and that was some years ago. Most sponsorship seekers would be startled to think that one of their number might one day say to a predatory Corporate Affairs Director, as politely as may be, something like: 'Thus far and no further. You should take pride in being associated with such a fine company as ours, with such splendid examples of our art – so proud that simply to have your name as sponsor on our programmes should be enough.' Fat chance.

It is rapacious for a commercial company to demand, and pusillanimous for the theatre to agree, that since the commercial firm has put £10,000 into a particular production (against the Arts Council's £100,000) a performance shall be billed in huge letters as 'The Vallambrosa Vermouth's *Traviata*' or 'The Bloodsucker Bank's Season of Popular Classical Music'. Similar instances include a bank's demand for prominent billing in connection with an event to which they had contributed one-seven-hundredth of what the Arts Council gave. Another company demanded exclusive billing where the Council had given thirty-two times more than it had. There are many such examples. The most popular bar in a theatre may be reserved on opening night for the sponsor's corporate hospitality. On such occasions the chocolate-wrapper rustling level in the best seats rises significantly.

Some years ago the Royal Opera House, Covent Garden, permitted an unusually cheeky example of excessive commercial demands: a large banner across Bow Street on which the sponsor appropriated the opera and Verdi got the small print, the crush bar was reserved, and so on. A member of the Arts Council pointed out that the sponsor had given towards the mounting of that production about one-tenth of what the Council had given. The Opera House's spokesmen replied that sponsors must be given virtually anything they asked for in the way of grateful mentions because they did not *have* to give anything whereas the Arts Council did; that's what the Council was there for.

Wrong on both counts. The sponsor was not giving support chiefly out of the goodness of a culturally enlightened heart. He was making a considered commercial decision as to where he could place his advertising money to the best effect, if necessary after some bullying. In this instance he was himself seeking further patronage from the wealthier parts of society. He could have no interest at all in bringing small touring groups to, say, Goole. If sponsoring the Royal Opera House brought him exactly the audience he wanted then *he*, no less than the Arts Council, *had* to offer money to grand opera.

He is therefore no more free than the Arts Council. The Council is free to give much less than the millions of pounds a year it gives to the Royal Opera House. In the extreme, it could stop the grant altogether. Its responsibility is to distribute public money – taxpayers' money – for the greater good of the arts and their audiences as a whole. Its criteria range from judgments about the importance and essential costs of any particular art, the competence at any one time of a company practising it, the needs of all the different parts of the United Kingdom in terms of accessibility to the arts, the encouragement of new forms of art and so on. The Arts Council has to give money to the arts, certainly; it does not have to give money to any particular art-house. Much depends on geography, more on quality, and on success in opening arts and their venues to more varied audiences; that last is at least as important as the other two elements.

The attitude of the spokesman for the Royal Opera House is typical. He and the majority of his colleagues yield too easily. They do not recognise the limitations of commercial sponsorship, even though they have been rehearsed many times. A recapitulation: commercial patronage tends to the safe and established rather than the new and difficult in art. So it can influence the planning of orchestral concerts. A good manager will insert a new piece in between the well-known because it seems fair to the audience and the composer that the piece should be heard (concerts devoted entirely to new music attract only the already knowledgeable, and they are few). A commercial sponsor may well react against planning of that sort, and the new piece is likely to be dropped. Some years ago a major London orchestra received what was described as 'major' sponsorship; within six months the differences in the composition of their programmes was marked; back to the eighteenth or nineteenth centuries. In that event the encouragement of new art falls even more on the Arts Council, thus giving its enemies the opportunity to say that it hands too much money to 'way-out highbrows' and not enough to 'ordinary people's tastes'. The BBC also is often in danger of being put into such a cleft stick.

Commercial sponsorship can exhibit the 'Chairman's wife' syndrome – or that of the Chairman – by which it is fickle and can lead to ill-considered changes in the repertoire or in style. Such changes may be brought about by what the Corporate Manager or the top boss thinks might suit the tastes of the corporate clients. Commercial sponsorship rarely has a long breath, is unlikely to brave the experimental. Five years' sponsorship is regarded as a very long time indeed and is rare; this is too short for a major company in a major art-form to plan ahead adequately.

Some American sponsors do better than British ones. This may be partly due to the vast size of the country and the relative isolation of many of its large centres of population. Inhabitants of a Midwest city of several hundred thousand people, with three or four major industries, may find that some of those industries have allotted their sponsorship funds to improving local provision. A major and inter-nationally respected museum or gallery or orchestra may be adequately and consistently funded. True, voluntary groups of middle-class matrons tend to predominate on the management com-mittees and may talk like culture-vultures. They have their British equivalents but are more prosperous and confident; and no less efficient. The decision to give most sponsorship money to the places where it has been earned has more to be said for it than a self-regarding giving to prestigious national institutions only.

Patronage or, better, the giving of donations can be a civilised activity. Commercial sponsorship rarely is, and the sooner we decide to do without it, the better. That *Boule de Suif* attitude – let us put up with it if it shields our tattered gentilities – is a miserable one. So is the 'I'll sup with the Devil if it helps the arts' attitude. You are giving that 'Devil', feeble though it may be, a mask of apparent virtue, cheap. All arts directors have to juggle several balls at a time; commercial sponsorship introduces another, an irrelevant and large ball which works against the right artistic and audience judgments. That big ball takes the eye off the job of juggling the other balls. A democracy should meet its own cultural needs, not call in tainted support; or only accept it on entirely untainted terms.

vi WHO SHOULD GET WHAT, AND HOW?

Wherever the money comes from, whether from public or private sources, how should it be allocated? That phrasing implies that private sponsors will give money on much the same criteria as public funders, chiefly according to quality and need. That this is not so is plain. Best in this part of the argument to stick to the distribution of public funds.

How to weigh the competing – and they are always competing – claims of large and expensive forms of art (opera, orchestral music, ballet, large exhibitions) against those of new work which may be cheap to mount but will have small audiences, and which constantly throws up new claimants; as against the claims of theatres which are small when compared with the Royal National Theatre and the Royal Shakespeare Company but are spread over the whole country; and those of artists of several other kinds wanting money to buy time; or of expensive galleries in London as compared with struggling but lively new exhibition spaces two or three hundred miles away, or of 'community' arts and 'ethnic' arts?

There will never be enough money. The demands are infinite in the sense that if by a great and unlikely effort all demands in any one year were met in full, that success alone would set off new and escalating demands. The geyser flows for ever and with undiminished force, unless regularly capped and carefully monitored. Choices will always have to be made, judgments-between. Unlucky claimants, those who receive no grant or much less than they asked for, will always object and probably cry foul. Even claimants who might seem to be among the lucky ones will, as a matter of tactics or one-eyedness, complain that their demands were really a minimum so that any other figure – a 5 per cent increase instead of the 15 per cent they asked for – means ruin.

How do you draw up what would no doubt be called 'guidelines' for such decisions? You can, you must, try, but must not expect them to be generally greeted as a Solomonaic solution. Yet it might have been better if the Arts Council had carried out these exercises more transparently and publicly. Or perhaps it wouldn't have helped. In the early Eighties the Council, finding its annual grant smaller than had been anticipated, carried out and made public a rigorous exercise in defining the revised criteria for distributing the money. All entirely to no avail; the explanation of their efforts was ignored and vicious obloquy heaped on them. In conscience it could not have done less.

*

Some fairly simple propositions can be made as a start. That, if people wish for opera of an international standard, they must be prepared to subsidise it publicly and adequately. This is more pressing and inescapable a demand than that posed by the enormous fees some international stars command – which are often cited, erroneously, as the main reason for opera's costliness. The country may decide that it will do without opera at that level; chamber music is much cheaper and so is 'chamber opera'; certainly most people would not notice

232

the loss. Even a country of fifty-odd million people with a substantial historic interest in grand opera can change its mind.

Or it could continue to subsidise that art-form but generously enough to make it available at reasonable prices. Opera is and has long been popular with far more people than can nowadays afford to see it. The pre-war Carl Rosa Opera Company – not of a very high standard – toured the provinces and was very highly thought of. Some of the inhabitants of Hunslet in Leeds (as working-class a district as you would be likely to find) got together the money to go to the Grand Theatre when the Carl Rosa Company was there and knew many of the great popular arias by heart. There is no doubt that those audiences could be found again and widened. This would be quite different an exercise from the Soviet habit of bussing in the women workers from a huge dairy co-operative to sit, unprepared apart from a stodgy introduction, unchoosing and largely uncomprehending, through *Turandot*. The scandal about Covent Garden is, first, the existence of the corporate seats and, second, the huge subsidy behind every one of the better seats. It should be protected but should do more to widen its audiences. Something similar could be said about ballet, major drama productions, classical concerts, and their possible audiences.

The arts are to be kept up if we believe they contain works of the creative imagination of which any mature culture should be proud; and, secondarily, if we believe existing audiences could be greatly widened once we gave proper thought to how to set about it. Against this simple but powerful pair of propositions, dismissals of the arts as 'bourgeois tricks', and relativist claims that all works of art are equal but 'grass-roots' arts probably more equal than others, fall or give no more than limited illumination.

Equally, to argue that all the arts should be able to make their way commercially is to fall into a double error, a double fault of the mind. It is to fail to see that the simple processes of commerce will never make some of these activities profitable; and it is (this time the word is apposite) entirely to ignore the imprisoning force of 'hegemony'. So, left alone, a free market will either price these things out of reach of all but the rich and the corporate clients, or will let them die. In these matters, and in spite of all those of their arts practices which are irrelevant here, France and Germany do have a lot to teach us about respect for the arts and a society's duties towards them. Not, as is still too nearly the case over there, for the sake of élitists and the bourgeoisie, but for fully democratic, non-class reasons.

Other arts, those which do not involve inescapably high production costs, have at first glance smaller claims on public or private funds. The most obvious and in some ways most interesting instance is literature and, more accurately, writing. Direct sponsorship of individual writers, as distinct from patronage (that does exist but is rare these days and not greatly publicised), hardly applies. Dust-jackets do not carry slogans such as 'Mary Winterton is sponsored by Bloggs the Printers'. She may, though this is becoming rarer and tighter, have been given a sufficient advance from the publisher to allow her to concentrate solely on writing for the next two or three years. There are foundations and trusts which may give fellowships, bursaries and the like towards work in progress; the Arts Council gives some and the Society of Authors disposes of a few more. There are the book prizes, from the big ones such as the Booker, the Whitbread and AT&T to the small and specialised. But those tend to be retrospective, the work having been done and published.

In some respects writing is a hedge-industry; you can carry it on at home with little equipment. Publishing is a public industry and increasingly corporate; but still generally it works through face-to-face relations between individuals. It is rooted in people, women and men alone, some putting things down, and others responding to them, also individually, from the publishers' readers to the buyers, and the borrowers at the Public Libraries. Even now, in spite of all those pressures towards amalgamation in publishing, it would be hard to sustain the argument that far too few new books see the light each year in Britain; the loss is in small runs at the edges of genres, themes and subjects.

The problems lie elsewhere; in, for example, the poverty of many serious writers who need several years to complete a major work, or the increasing number of good titles now out of print, or the pressure on Public Libraries to reduce both their opening hours and their buying across a wide range of tastes and levels; they then focus their buying on the already popular.

Since the products of writing do not require large sums if they are to be issued and, more important, since writers are of all artists the most directly vulnerable to political interference, in a perfect world it would be better if writers never needed public support, were never in danger of becoming pensioners.

This is not a commonly held view. Literary claimants on Arts

Council funds are as demanding as any others. Marghanita Laski was pleased to be asked in the early Eighties to be Chairwoman of the Council's Literature Panel, but soon became disillusioned. She then spoke of 'the literary pressure group's total lack of philanthropy'. There appeared earlier the playwright who claimed that he should be paid a regular wage, just as the stagehands, carpenters and box-office staff were. A stagehand does not gain or lose salary according to whether a play succeeds or loses. That would be unjust; his job has been done and presumably properly done, no matter how good or bad the play. He has very much less freedom than the writer; he has to work regular hours, his work may often be repetitive, he is not his own master. If he wants to feed the family he has to do as he is told. By comparison, the playwright is a very lucky person, a sort of gambler but the gamble may pay off well, a free spirit. Nobody can order him to write and no one owes him a living. In a very practical – and unimaginative – sense he is not as necessary as a milkman or a postman. In a larger and more important sense, he is very much needed and free to demonstrate this. If that is not satisfactory the role of *agitprop* writer might better suit such a man.

So what, if anything, can the public disbursers of funds for the arts do about literature? Bursaries can be valuable, for young writers who seem to have great promise but cannot find enough time to write, for others of any age who have committed themselves to books that promise to be valuable over the long term but for which few publishers feel able to give a good-sized advance. Such writers still exist, some of them surviving and bringing up families on much less than the average national income. They need to travel, to sit in distant libraries, to buy new word-processors, to pay the rent. These are not always the people who besiege the Arts Council with their claims.

Book prizes provide money too but, as was noted, retrospectively. Do they encourage the reading of at least the short-listed entries? To some extent, but the phenomenon is similar to the buying of books which have been adapted for television: impulse-driven, short-term; not a serious or lasting gain.

A more important flaw is the claim the prizes directly or by implication make: that four or five people have found the *best* novel or biography or children's book of the year. They have not. Except in the very rarest of cases, they have exercised a compromise; they have found the book which, the judges being almost always unable to

agree unanimously on the 'best' book, is at last and wearily acceptable to all or the majority.

That is bad enough as an example of a mistaken claim. Worse is
the irrelevance of the whole process to the matter of writing and of
literature; and by now, with the big prizes and the publicity, the
event outshines and has come to seem more important than literary
considerations. This applies chiefly and unavoidably to prizes given
across complete genres; it is much less applicable to small prizes for
neglected sub-groups. There was for a few years a modest prize
for the book which best threw light on a social problem: the homeless, child abuse, prisoner rehabilitation, disablement. That was little
noticed in the press but gave great encouragement to people who
worked in those areas.

There are several ways in which public money can be used to
support literature and reading without funds being given directly
to writers. They have not been greatly employed, but some have been
used by the Arts Council, and by occasional Public Libraries and
Local Education Authorities. One seeks in several ways to encourage
the reading of good books, through poetry readings by poets themselves or writers' sessions on their own work or that of writers
they admire, through displays and exhibitions in libraries, schools,
hospitals, prisons. Most of these are cheap to mount and there is
room for many more.

Small publishers struggling to remain independent and to produce
experimental work, especially poetry, may be given subventions for
particular titles. Good books now out of print – the lesser-known
works of major authors, or the works of minor but interesting figures
(especially of the last century) – may be brought back into print.
Foreign embassies and EC groups do sponsor translations, but such
efforts are only a beginning. One remembers Elias Canetti, who had
a British passport and lived for a long time in London; he won the
Nobel Prize for Literature in 1981. Which of his works, other than
Auto-da-Fé, is known here? It is typical that Herman Bang's lucent,
brief novel *Tina* was translated into French and German more than
half a century before appearing in English.

One member of the US Endowment for the Arts had what would
be called today a 'robust' approach to public funding for the arts –
in the USA:

[In this year the Endowment] gave $700,000 in direct fellowship grants
to visual artists. It also provided $640,000 in matching grants to fifty four

art museums. The first of these programs centralized the patronage power within the Endowment; the second dispersed it among fifty four museum directors. The first imposed the Endowment's judgments on the nation at large; the second made participants out of fifty four cities or towns in the raising of matching funds. The first gave the artist a handout and so perpetuated the alienation between the artist and the taxpayer; the second provided payment for a product, and so brought the artist into accord with all other citizens.

If I had my way ... I would offer matching funds to symphony orchestras, chamber ensembles and choral groups to commission and perform new works. In place of direct grants to novelists and poets I would offer to match the sums that publishers pay as advances for works of unusual merit but limited appeal. Thus, I would not shun the experimental, the esoteric, the offensive, but I would remove from the shoulders of government the burden of acting as direct and predominant patron; a role it is ill-equipped to fulfil.

I realize of course that in nations where tax relief is not provided to corporations, foundations, universities, churches, or individuals, the raising of matching funds may not be a practical prospect. Nonetheless, I suspect other ways can be found to disperse the patronage power.

That is very good in parts, inappropriate to Europe and especially Britain in some regards, but all in all well worth thinking about.

vii SPREADING YOUR ARTS ABROAD

There is some danger that this object [establishing a News Department in the Foreign Office] may imperceptibly be transformed into a general desire to spread British culture throughout the world; and they [My Lords of the Treasury] do not think it would be possible to defend in Parliament or in its committees expenditure on such a purpose.
The Treasury to the Foreign Secretary just after the First World
War

The British Council has by now existed for several decades. But in some places and some people attitudes such as those above do not greatly change. Don't try to do good outside Britain with taxpayers' money; anyway, we don't see how exporting British *culture* will do good; and if we start spending money on one thing it will soon spread to another. ('If we give them one, everybody else will want one – where will it all end? They'll *take advantage.*')

These may up to a point be worthily cautious attitudes and no doubt save us from the worst excesses of less fortunate or less well governed nations. Still, one could wish for more letting down of the national hair, occasionally.

Many states have agencies for artistic and generally cultural promotion overseas beyond simple and obvious propaganda, though the enterprises vary greatly in volume and thrust. Since the last war the export of national cultures has become more subtle. The United States characteristically has worked through several bodies, of which the best-known is probably USIS (the United States Information Service). That is the nearest equivalent to the British Council and can be very intelligent, but it is more tied to the State Department than the British Council is to the Foreign and Commonwealth Office. (To some extent that Royal Charter protects the Council from direct interference. It would not accept – or perhaps not explicitly acknowledge – the few lines for action which the State Department gives USIS each year.) The Council would take very seriously what is less than an order; the preferred phrase is 'giving a steer'.

The French have several agencies: the cultural attachés and the Alliance Française, for instance. They are highly competent in many respects, especially as to film; for the rest, they are – we may say – very French. The Dante Alighieri Society nourishes Italian culture overseas and doesn't fuss; it goes straight for the high-culture jugular, whether in Paris or Chicago. The Japanese, being very wealthy, give much money towards the greater understanding of Japanese culture overseas by, especially, subsidising individual scholars and artists. When it was set up after the last war, the Goethe Foundation of, then, West Germany was explicitly modelled on the British Council, particularly in its concern for the Foundation's independence. It is notably strong on interaction, on bringing other cultures into Germany as well as on offering German culture abroad.

Naturally, different ways of behaving reflect the different cultures. The French are very confident and culturally clever with it; the Italians are smart, unshaken by modern postures; the USA is slightly uncertain behind what seems a very confident exterior (Hollywood is the greatest cultural-agenda-setter in modern history), the British are as always mixed, several things at once.

For many countries the British Council is seen as offering in some ways a model. It is a particularly interesting example of an arm's-length Quango but has had to fight that corner repeatedly, even more than the BBC and the Arts Council. It has had to insist on the case for promoting particular programmes and directions, even the case for the independence of a body founded by Royal Charter. It is financed directly by the Foreign and Commonwealth Office (FCO), and in those traditional and loyal halls the independence of a chartered Quango is sometimes not appreciated. Officials in Whitehall and diplomats overseas do not always see a difference between it and the Central Office of Information (COI) – a straight mouthpiece of government. The Council has also been long and viciously attacked by some of the philistine non-broadsheet press (especially Beaverbrook's). It has had to dig up its roots again and again, decade by decade.

*

Why do so many governments nowadays care so much about their external cultural reputations? There is still some direct propaganda, but it varies greatly in sophistication and is lessening except in more authoritarian states. Yet still, especially in this otherwise sophisticated state, Britain, most politicians, and many civil servants and diplomats, have little grasp of artistic matters except in their more conventional and classical forms (younger diplomats might suddenly divert into talking about Pink Floyd). The head of the Civil Service might act as Treasurer to the Royal Opera House. More typically, one recent head of the Foreign Office delivered himself of the statement – in response to the question: Why are the arts so little regarded in official attitudes towards our cultural relations abroad? – that 'The arts aren't sexy just now.' Perhaps he was showing he could talk tough too. An ambasssador in Bonn offered visiting academics a remarkably ingenuous comparison between German and British attitudes to the arts; an ambassador in Washington confidently gave a similarly innocent comparison between American and British attitudes to public patronage. For almost all of them, art as dissent, or even as a critical light, was a rather foreign idea.

Yet governments, or a sufficient number within governments, now feel that the arts do somehow matter, are a sort of gloss indicating civilisation, culture in one narrow definition. Open democracies seem to be more or less all for it these days; so long as it is not too costly or too subversive. They will feel only a few qualms at the export of John Osborne's plays but would have tried to lean on the British Council if Edward Thompson had been invited to lecture in India. So: acceptable if not likely to undermine a fairly simple chauvinism; and nowadays, if at all possible, able to be linked with a commercial drive.

That is not too simple a sketch of attitudes. Give a lecture at the invitation of the British Council in a major European capital, a lecture critical of aspects of British life but also appreciative of its good sides. It may well be that a member of the audience will stand up at question time and ask, 'with the greatest respect', whether you have not been a little hard on the public schools, or the state of some parts of British industry, or commercial broadcasting. Perhaps you have in his eyes, but it is not the place of an FCO or British Council official to imply that visiting speakers from Britain are COI propagandists. That sort of thing is obviously not as blatant as Soviet academics curtailing your lecture in Leningrad because you seemed likely to mention George Orwell. One expected that. The British example, and it is only one of several, is worse because it shows obtuseness by some government officials towards freedom of speech in a democracy.

*

The question, then, still hovers: why should governments and their diplomats bother with all this? Or: how do they justify it to themselves? The short-term and limited view is held by a good number of diplomats: cultural work abroad is an arm of diplomacy, a support to the diplomatic programme of the day; and it will alter as discussions with the FCO ('always recognising the British Council's independence') require. The FCO says, as one of its steers: 'For the next few years we will concentrate on Western Europe.' The British Council is expected to do so; and usually does, but should be more forceful in entering its own cultural and intellectual considerations. In some countries the British Council representative is also the Cultural Attaché of the Embassy, so the presumed relationship is clear, though not easy to square with the rep's status as an employee of a Chartered body. For long historical reasons the Council representative in Poland does not have diplomatic status. In Communist days that was an almost indigestible concept to the Poles but, once they had swallowed it, a great aid to inspiring confidence in the many Polish users of the Council's services, and not unwelcome to the Council's staff in Warsaw.

In the general FCO view the job of the Council is Cultural Diplomacy, culture as an extension of or aid to diplomacy by other means, the minor second side of the coin whose first side is Clausewitz's war as an extension of diplomacy. John Burgh, Director-General of the

Council in the Eighties and himself a refugee from Nazi Germany, argued against that in a fine public lecture in Bonn. A body such as the Council, he said, was best regarded as a branch not of Cultural Diplomacy but of Cultural Relations; and that is a much more long-term, exploratory matter.

Cultural Diplomacy moves easily into linking British culture with the promotion of suitable British commerce and industry. Of the Heritage kind. A sprig of Royalty may be flown to the Midwest to attend a British art and culture festival; a Rolls-Royce is found for the public appearances. If *Macbeth* is being played the programme will certainly advertise Scotch and shortbread; the ushers may even sport kilts.

By contrast Cultural Relations is indirect. It has to do with making friends and influencing people because you think you have interesting things to say and show; it is prepared to trust in long-term and not easily assessed results rather than in the sales-graph. That too is a form of persuasion, but subtler than the other and much more defensible.

This difference of interpretation has been active for the past two decades. The more powerful side is Cultural Diplomacy; they speak traditional British-speak, they have the power and the money. They are not idiots. If they find that a British sculptor whose work they cannot in the least understand is a great success in São Paolo they will say to themselves: 'It can't be bad for our image; so – fine.' But generally they lean towards easily demonstrable economic or political advantages.

The British Council, whose staff are far more devoted and hard-working than the public are led to believe, have to do their best amid all these definitions, redefinitions and straightforward, ill-informed attacks. It is not surprising, therefore, that many of them have taken refuge in a 'hard' definition of their own: that the Council should give priority not to the arts but to language, not to English literature but to English linguistics. That can easily be shown as profitable since it is in great demand all over the world; it can only help British industry and commerce; it is not easily attacked as arty-farty and suede-shoed. It appeases the FCO without seeming to compromise too much. It is a deeply mistaken priority for several reasons, of which the most important is that the bearer of language at its finest is, precisely, literature. Linguistics divorced from literature is cul-turally and imaginatively inorganic.

With the greater export of linguistics went that of information technology. This culminated in the sight one day of the Council library's shelves in a European capital being stripped of their nineteenth-century classics so that room could be made for computer software. A British Council representative in Africa faxed back to London that he did not wish to receive a touring Shakespeare company since he did not have time for 'such marginal things nowadays'. An Indian official faxed to point out that they could get computer technology from lots of places; from Britain they wanted, above all, Shakespeare.

Cultural Relations is not so small-visioned. The more idealistic of those who promote it feel they are working disinterestedly; and if they believe it, they nearly are. Others find this approach a manageable opportunism. One of the more successful initiatives on this side has been in the scholarships offered over many decades to very clever students from territories the donors occupy or formerly occupied. In this, the French are as good as we are, or even better.

Francophone Africans speak even more warmly of their time at the Sorbonne than Anglophones of the LSE. The major aim of French colonial education policy was to make Frenchmen; the British made lawyers. Neither made many engineers or farmers.

If those bursary-holders met with racism, they did not forget. Even if they were treated kindly they often went back, in colonialist days, to fight those who had helped give them the intellectual weapons with which to fight; they then often spent time in prison; and subsequently became leaders of their own new nations. Yet the major, diffused result of these initiatives was to create a body of people who had learned to understand some of the better, the more humane and democratic elements in British and French culture; that sort of thing, when you are young, sticks.

CHAPTER ELEVEN

Effects of Mass Media: Kinds of Censorship – a Baker's Dozen

We speak for convenience about a mass audience but it is a fiction. The audience today is numerically dense but highly diversified ... audiences are specialised by age, sex, hobby, occupation, mobility, contacts, etc ... they reflect and influence the diversification which goes with increased industrialisation.

Lawrence Alloway, 'The Long Front of Culture', in Russell and Gablik, *Pop Art Redefined*, 1969

There are no masses. There are only ways of seeing people as masses.
Raymond Williams

Lawrence Alloway and Raymond Williams can seem to be saying similar things, but the first impression is deceptive. Alloway is writing about the kinds of diversification which are described in Chapter 9, on the movement from class to status, and in that context he is right. Williams is saying something quite different, is making a political statement: people are diversified, but it is in the interests of the various kinds of mass persuaders to see them as parts of large masses. It is a ringing statement, but in the end it blurs. The effort to see people as masses is in some ways successful. People *are* persuaded, on different occasions, to act as masses. They may not be 'prolefeed' then, but are acting collectively under suggestion, not making individual or small-group considered decisions. Advertising, popular music promotions, film hypes, PR, fashions in clothing and food, political propaganda; sheer mass-suggestion – one could go on and on – do create temporary and contingent masses for the purposes of these persuaders. Sometimes, as with football hooligans, the behaviour of the temporary mass is well below what those who compose it would practise as individuals.

That overwhelming fact has to be faced just as firmly as does the existence of individuals and small groups below or, better, outside that level; of individuals and groups which in the end, one hopes, have a firmer hold, are more 'real'. That has to be examined, not assumed. This is the context in which several kinds of censorship are still practised in Britain; and by which they are defined.

Television is particularly interesting here. It is not by nature a mass medium, since it is viewed by individuals and families. If one is examining effects one should not view it in a group. On the other hand one does have the sense, whilst viewing, that millions of others are seeing the same thing at the same time. The ads insist that *you* can have wonderful hair, but you know and they know that the 'you' is millions of you; and the half-thought is curiously comforting, reinforcing, like the hint of a community to which you belong. Otherwise, the ad has failed.

i COUNTERWEIGHTS AND CONTRADICTIONS AGAIN

In discussing the debate about the effects of the mass media and the nature of censorship in Britain, one meets again both a countervailing force and a contradiction. The relativist society contains some of its own counter-forces, of different strengths and likely life. More spokes in the wheels, stones to interrupt slightly the predominant flow. This particular paradox, the continuing strength of censorship, is closest to arts sponsorship and patronage in a non-valuing society. It has to do with countervailing forces within the agents of relativism themselves, rather than with resistances by individuals and groups to social changes.

The recent Conservative governments speak of a liberated society, a free society, a self-regulating society. They have encouraged the more predatory forms of capitalism, 'the Devil take the hindmost', 'on your bike', exploit things and people up to the very limits of legality, and beyond if you can get away with it. They have given a licence to the poachers.

It soon became plain – surprisingly! – that the poachers will take the grossest liberties, especially in those areas which most disturb these governors' sensitive – well, narrow – souls. So they have to set up new bodies of gamekeepers, by which some areas of public life are more tightly controlled than before. They became more like Mary Whitehouse than like Winston Churchill, more prim than 'robust', commonly showing a shrinking gentility. In some ways the market might be self-regulating, with competition holding fairly the market for goods and services (though that is not automatic). The market is in no sense *morally* self-regulating; it will flow into every profitable alley open to it.

Both the BBC and the Independent Television Authority (as it then was) already had their supervisory bodies, the BBC Governors and the Members of the ITA. To this was added the Broadcasting Complaints Commission in 1984. To those was added in 1988 the Broadcasting Standards Council, with a narrow brief and a special focus on sex, violence and rude words (taste and decency). Oh, God! Oh Finchley! If ever there was an instance of the superfluous this was it. Eventually good sense intervened and in 1994 it was proposed that the last two merge.

The British Board of Film Censors was rendered less threatening by being renamed the British Board of Film Classification in 1985. A PR smudge that, since its job remained much the same, to 'classify' films and now videos from the most innocent to those which were in effect banned. Continental Europeans are incredulously amused to learn that you cross the banning line if you show a penis erect rather than limp; even more, if you show actual penetration. This explains why films which remain just inside the banned line display long minutes of grunting, groaning and heaving, plus sounds like those of a suction pump with a faulty washer.

More was to come, to the even greater amazement of foreigners. It must have seemed unfair, a little un-British, to let the BBFC, especially with its new title, have the last word. So a Video Appeals Committee was quickly established to rule finally on any disputed classification. Since videos given an R (Restricted) classification could only be available through licensed sex-shops, and since the sex-shops, as a result of earlier legal action and commercial concentration, were now few, such a classification could mean losses to the film-makers. But people learn quickly and adjust, so there were, after the first years, few appeals.

A pity, for that is one of the more hilarious of British public committees. The Board itself has to be more cautious than the Appeals Committee, especially on matters of Common Law -- blasphemy, for example; or where some dreadful accusation such as 'sado-masochism' may be invoked.

So there was, once again, the attempt at providing counterweights to movements far bigger than the governments had expected but which they had rather blindly encouraged. There was the contradiction at the heart of these people. They set themselves up as rough, tough buccaneers of the wide-open, get-rich-quick society. But when they saw the results of their actions they reverted to their more traditional role as the Guardians of Provincial Propriety; they marched at the head of the shabby foot-soldiers of suburban morality.

ii EFFECTS, BROADCASTING AND ELSEWHERE

From the shelves-ful of research into the effects of the mass media, in particular of television, few firm and generally agreed conclusions can be drawn. This does not mean that there are no effects, only that this kind of effects-analysis is in its infancy.

By comparison, research into the effects of reading is slight. Clearly, television is more attractive, more a current concern (and much more likely to attract research grants). The gap is a pity, though; the study of literature's effects raises some different and culturally trickier questions.

It seems to be assumed that books are less likely to have bad effects than television. You have to go out and buy or borrow a book; you have to know what sort of book will meet your needs; you have to carry out a quite difficult act – reading even an elementary book needs more effort than simply watching what passes before your eyes. You have to translate into pictures in the mind words which may be meant to shock or incite; the screen does that job for you, whatever your age or level of literacy.

The public authorities seem progressively to have given up on their scrutinies of books for sexual obscenities. Perhaps their failures from the early Sixties onwards, starting with *Lady Chatterley's Lover*, have discouraged them. Perhaps they have decided that the likely deleterious effects of reading are rather a recherché matter as compared with those of television. As a result some of the paperbacks now on the higher shelves of shops which belong to what like to think of themselves as 'respectable' chains make one wonder yet again what all the fuss was about in the Sixties. These are sexually explicit masturbatory fantasies but not usually violent.

Perhaps the authorities still look for sex-and-violence paperbacks, with the emphasis on violence, and seize those. If so, that might be a reasonable literary-moral judgment, and economy; but rather sophisticated. To separate those excessively invoked twins might clear the air a bit. There is certainly sex-and-violence in life, in books and on television; there is also violence; and there is sex. It is too often assumed that the two always go together; but that says more about people than about the things they see and read.

Do different people, different kinds of people, receive the same message from the same material, written or filmed? The question is out-of-date by now; there is substantial evidence of different, 'polysemic', readings. Does stylised violence have less effect than the realistic sort? The thought is engaging and proof would be comforting; but there is no certain proof. Is the effect of violence determined or conditioned by the context in which it is found? It would be foolish to think violence is cancelled out by the victory of the virtuous or at least of the powers-that-be. The powers-that-be are, on contemporary television, often as violent as the villains.

Upholders of good literature, whether or not virtue finally triumphs in a text, like to think more complex and mature contexts do corral whatever violence there has been on the way, that they are finally cathartic. For some, perhaps (though that is not sure). But what of those who wrest the violence from its context, who do not respond to the whole mature movement and resolution but only to the violent bits; who distort the work to suit their needs? This recalls the old joke about the man who took the Rorschach Blot test and saw in every blot only what he needed to see; sexual activity. A rich, full life.

*

Now and again, reading yet another British report on the effects of sex-and-violence in books and on the screen, one has the impression that some of the research workers are not as interested as they should be in questions such as the above – and there are dozens more. They are rather too anxious to cock a snook at the traditional sex-and-violence puritans. That may be a temptation but a shallow one. You may fairly challenge simple copycat assumptions about effects. You may ask: Why not cathartic or at least emetic instead of a temptation to copycatting? You may say that children are not such fragile flowers as some seem to think; they have long been used to violence in their own literature.

You don't explore a very deep lake by taking pot-shots at a few lame ducks on the surface. A little more imaginative humility would not be out of place here, a little more of 'At present we don't know much for sure. Our instruments have come apart in our hands, can't cope, have taken us as far as they can, but it's not far enough.' To say, as though rather relieved at being able to spike the National Viewers' and Listeners' Association's guns: 'There's no firm evidence of bad effects,' is to do no more than say: 'We are still in our research childhood,' rather than to give a rebuff.

The most difficult of all is the question of possible long-term effects: not copycatting, nor emetic or cathartic effects, but less obvious, more submerged and in the end perhaps more unpleasant effects. These are almost impossible to assess, at least at present; which does not mean that they can be dismissed.

The question now is of possible long-term 'desensitisation'. Does a daily diet of violence lead most people, not to act out such things, but simply to come to assume that they are normal, a regular and important part of daily life? What is the effect over time of television's tendency to merge everything it touches into one sensory experience, so that one does not always make, internally, a distinct difference between the news – the actual news – and a drama documentary or indeed a drama? Or a soap opera; or a game-show – for it would be short-sighted to assume that television's 'desensitising', if it works at all, affects only matters of violence. To put the matter at its simplest: if there is no effect why are the advertisers wasting their money? Yes, they have to keep renewing the dose; but who says it leaves no sediment? The surrounding culture does have an effect; why shouldn't an environment which has the attention of very many people for thirty hours a week and in which violence – and of course much else, including greed – seems normal, become an influence over time? Why shouldn't all this be, if not a sufficient cause, at least an important contributory cause?

In reply to such questions it is not enough to say: the onus of proof here must rest with those who assume that desensitisation occurs; until then nothing should be done. That conclusion might be reversed, however unwillingly. Again, the question is open and important. It would be more to the point to bring in the latest form of 'uses and gratifications' theory and argue that most people filter out, resist, the process of desensitisation, since television has to take its place within very much wider and deeper cultural contexts. The next question is: what about those who do not have or yet have such a context? If they exist, do others have any responsibility towards them? And what about a process by which desensitisation may turn into reinforcement? If it runs with much in the dominant cultural grain, why shouldn't it reinforce?

Anecdotes can be dragged in to support almost any generalisation; but that does not make all anecdotes non-significant, unrepresentative. Here are two. A nine-year-old boy on a tough council estate was rebuked by his grandmother for mugging a six-year-old. He was unabashed and answered: 'You don't understand. If you don't leather them they'll leather you. You can see it on telly.' On such a rough estate such a boy may have behaved like that before television appeared. His invocation of television as a copycat inducer may have been cute. Or he may have been tuned in to the more violent elements of the culture, which television heartily exploits through its programmes.

Second: a television documentary about extremely violent videos (available under the counter in most towns) and their possible effects is worth recalling. The producers found a family in a Leeds council house who admitted watching very violent videos until very late most nights; father, mother and several young children. The parents were asked whether they thought it might have done emotional harm to the children. 'Nar. Why should it. It never did us any 'arm.' You looked at and listened to the father and mother and your heart sank. It recalled the old *New Yorker* cartoon in which a couple in a comfortable apartment, staring at television, are asked the same question and give a similar answer. 'What nonsense to claim that the constant watching of television will reduce us all to morons.' When you look more closely you see that they have the heads of apes. Whoever admitted to being changed for the worse? We carry our changing world with us all the time, and it always seems normal.

iii KINDS OF CENSORSHIP

When complaints are freely heard, deeply considered, and speedily reformed, then is the utmost bound of civil liberty attained, that wise men look for. . . . Give me the liberty to know, to utter and to argue freely according to conscience, above all liberties. . . . Though all the winds of doctrine were let loose to play upon the earth, so Truth be in the field, we do injuriously by licensing and prohibiting to misdoubt her strength. Let her and falsehood grapple; who ever knew Truth put to the worse, in a free and open encounter.

John Milton, *Areopagitica*, 1644

Eppur si muove. (But it does move.)
The splendidly obstinate counter-recantation attributed to
   Galileo after he had recanted before the Inquisition his claim
      that the Earth moves, in 1632 (probably apocryphal)

That the British are in official matters secretive and given to censorship is part of the common stock of assumptions, but this one is true. There are unusually severe laws about the disclosure of official secrets, and on libel, slander, obscenity; hence, among other attitudes, the current concern with the effects of television; in this context that is only a sub-branch of historic resistances. English authorities have long and deeply mistrusted 'the right to know'; they are nay-sayers by instinct and only yea-sayers when pushed; they are firm in the conviction of rightness in all this and assume similar convictions in others. If the Central Office of Information asks you to write about the condition of British culture they will with no sense of oddity sketch out the lines on which your piece is expected to run: essentially, a few easy admissions of tolerable weakness, and a resounding and complacent assertion of fundamental rightness at the end. At that point you say: 'Why not write it yourself, then.' We need a new phrase for that: censorship by pre-emptive literary takeover. All this runs like a nervous twitch from top to bottom of society; anarchy, it is felt, is just around the corner.

Naturally, there have been changes over the years. A few centuries ago censorship was chiefly political or religious, or both. Those kinds are not dead but work rather differently these days. From the mid-nineteenth century or somewhat earlier sex, sexual censorship, came to the fore – in a society which even in its more 'respectable' groups secretly practised some of the grossest sexual practices and abuses. In the present century sexual censorship has remained strong – even though latterly sexual attitudes have been widely and greatly liberated; here, we really are Two Nations by now – and all the stronger because of that presumed inextricable link between sex and violence. In this, the main destructive agent is assumed to be television.

The cake of censorship spreads far wider than to literature and the other arts. It can be cut in at least a dozen ways: direct official and political; class-based; employers' and market-directed arm-twisting; financially self-exonerated; omission and silence; misguided probity; moral and moralistic (much the most evident); ideological (today including political correctness); and then the most hidden of all, four or five versions of self-censorship.

On contemporary official and political attempts at censorship one need only begin with a partial roll-call: the Falklands War, *Real Lives, Spycatcher, Death on the Rock*, Clive Ponting, *Secret Society*, the Gulf War. Here, justifications range from 'a danger to national security' to 'The people are not ready.'

The Falklands campaign produced some rich and particularly foolish examples. Asked how he felt when he heard for the first time the siren announcing real action not an exercise, a Harrier pilot said something to this effect: 'For a few seconds I was shit-scared. After that, it was all right.' The official censors said this should not be broadcast. Because no British serviceman admits to being scared, if only for a few seconds? Because they don't use bad language? Both broadcasting systems simply went ahead and used the verbatim quotation; no heads rolled

Much worse was the behaviour of a large group of Tory members who called for a meeting with the Chairman and Director-General of the BBC so as to complain in the most abusive way that a BBC reporter had, among other things, referred to 'the British' and 'the Argentinians' instead of using some such phrases as 'our boys' and 'the enemy'. Incidents such as that make you feel like handing back your entrance ticket to English society. Still, it's our society as much as theirs. By contrast censors were more relaxed during the Gulf campaign; the much more open American practice stayed their hands to some extent.

As to broadcasting, official attempts at censorship have recently been worse than they used to be. No matter how much the overseers of the two systems are formally empowered and independent according to the Charter and Act, some governments cannot resist putting their fingers in. Challenged, they are likely to invoke one of their favourite face-saving adages: 'After all, the business of government is to govern,' which is a tautology hiding a disposition to brutality. We did not actually need to see the mixture of embarrassment and anger on the faces of the senior representatives of the BBC and commercial television as they left a meeting at which they had been given a wigging for screening excessive violence by the Home Secretary (at the time a man who had written a number of occasionally violent detective stories). The broadcasting representatives should have done two things: told the Home Secretary to get lost, and issued a public statement vindicating this brush-off by making their own formal rights and duties clear beyond doubt. If the Suez affair of 1956 is compared with the Falklands story and the *Real Lives* imbroglio of a few years ago, the changes become clear.

Real Lives was a TV programme, made in 1985, about the Northern Ireland troubles. It included interviews with IRA leaders and aroused Mrs Thatcher's furious opposition. The Home Secretary, Leon Brittan, wrote a pompous warning-off letter to the BBC Board's Chairman (incidentally, ten of the eleven Governors had been approved by Mrs Thatcher; one wonders who had not been approved). This was another misconceived interference with the Board's role. The letter should have been sent back as, in the technical jargon, 'not receivable'. The Board should then have published the Home Secretary's letter and their one-line rejection of it. It compromised their freedom of action to intervene, if they felt they had to after seeing the programme; any intervention would then have been construed as obedience to the Home Secretary's letter.

The practice is that the Governors do not intervene before a programme has been shown; that would breach the principle that editorial control lies with the Board of Management (full-time executives). The Director-General was away at the time and the Governors decided to preview the programme. They also made a response *of substance* to the Home Secretary and offered to meet him for a discussion. Error piled on error; they had conceded the Home Secretary's right to intervene instead of telling him to push off. The Chairman then made broadcasts of such inadequacy and uneasiness as to suggest he had by now realised that he and his colleagues had set back by years belief in the BBC's independence. The Home Secretary had no such doubts; his smug broadcasts confirmed his and the Cabinet's inability to grasp the arm's-length principle and its relation to intellectual and imaginative impartiality.

The attack on censorship is not always helped by those on the other side. If the Arts Council refuses funds to a body whose work is left-wing they will inevitably be accused of censorship on behalf of the government; even if they have often supported that body before, but feel its latest product is below standard.

It is much the same with the BBC. At a large broadcasting seminar in the late Eighties a playwright argued that a refusal to transmit his latest play was obviously political censorship. He added: 'I knew then what it was like to work in Prague.' Against that self-deceptive enormity, a BBC producer stood up and announced that it was he who had refused the play, with no consultation upwards: 'I wish I could have accepted it, as I had accepted others by X,' he added, 'but it really wasn't good enough this time.'

*

Censorship on social-class grounds is rather less common than it used to be; here again, the *Lady Chatterley* trial of 1960 was probably something of a watershed. Even at that date an objection to publication in paperback, thus making the book available to the workers, seemed old-fashioned. The objectors' fear would have been realised, though, if they had seen the stream of miners, coming off shift at Eastwood on the afternoon of the acquittal, heading for the local bookshop or newsagent's and asking where the really dirty bits were.

The Crown's efforts continued, resisted throughout the 1960s by the newly formed Defence of Literature and the Arts Society. In November 1967 *Last Exit to Brooklyn* was, after long deliberations by the jury, found obscene and banned; but that was a simpler case than *Lady Chatterley*. To begin with, the book was American and its language and situations far more likely to be judged obscene by a British jury than Lawrence's tender sexual situations and one-string verbal fiddle playing on 'that word'. Latterly, the prosecutions have been few. One landmark was the private prosecution of Howard Breton's 1980 play *The Romans in Britain* (the office of Lord Chamberlain having been abolished in 1968). That prosecution failed.

*

Censorship by employers – their versions of the Official Secrets Act – is usually typified by the requirement that employees sign a document agreeing not only to reveal no trade secrets but to make no critical remarks of any sort about their employment, even at any time after they have left that employment. This is increasing. It appears in some parts of the National Health Service, and in some of the Terms of Employment now imposed on teachers in Further Education; an exceptionally illiberal requirement in Public Health and educational institutions. Not surprisingly it is more common in commercial undertakings and is, again, not only meant to deter industrial sabotage but, more subtly, conveys the message: 'Even if we cut corners and produce some dodgy work, don't blow the whistle. Keep your mouth shut. Don't rock the boat. Remember our competitors and your own bread-and-butter.'

This kind of thing can operate in the literary world no less than in the industrial one. A free-lance critic was asked, in the late Eighties, to review a book on public sponsorship for the arts. He said he was unwilling, since a friend had read the book and said it was a mess. The magazine's editor, to his credit, replied that they could not

control what a reviewer said and that he hoped the reviewer would
agree to write the review anyway.

He found the book even worse than he had been told. In the
review he said it was bad without at all doing one of those self-
indulgent hatchet jobs. The editor, now apparently under pressure
from his proprietor, said he hoped the review could be made more
'balanced' (or face-saving words to that effect). Or would the
reviewer be willing to drop the review and have a whole page in
their occasional 'Opinion' series about something which was interesting him at the moment? The reviewer refused but said if they didn't
want to print the review the decision was up to them.

The proprietor then appeared in the correspondence, clearly very
angry. The reason was soon plain and lay in a fact which had been
unknown to the reviewer. The book had been published by the same
firm; magazine and publishing outfit were owned by the one man.
He claimed there was personal animus in the review and went so far
as to telephone the book's author to ask whether he had earlier fallen
out with the reviewer. The answer was no; they had never met either
in person or in print. 'Well, I am not allowing the editor to print that
piece', the proprietor said, adding his own version of 'You don't shit
on your own doorstep.' He then sent a very small fee; it was returned;
the review did not appear; no more was said or done on either side.

*

Another rather tricky form of censorship has, only *partly* as a result
of financial cutbacks, also become more evident recently. The outstanding instance here is in the Public Libraries. Most librarians did
their best in making cuts. Some took the opportunity, whether on
the instructions of their local Council or according to their own
convictions, to make political decisions: not to buy a book which
ran against their ideology, not to buy books which offended their
view of political correctness, not to buy what they decided were
'élitist' books which did not meet their own populist outlook. The
exponents of this form of hidden censorship sometimes deny that it
occurs, and most would mean what they said; self-deception is one
of the major failings in intellectual life as elsewhere.

A traditional British example of indirect censorship is blackballing
by a whisper in someone's ear. A favourite word here is 'unsound'.
'I heard so-and-so give a talk the other night to such-and-such a
society. I formed the strong impression that he's *unsound*.' That will

usually be quite enough. It can cause a near-offer of a job to be hurriedly withdrawn; or the offer of research funds, if purely 'old boy' or 'old girl' objections are raised in high places.

Or consider the effect of the ratings war on television. Only a rare manager, controller, producer, director is going to admit that he turned down a programme-idea which some years ago, because it seemed of good quality, he would happily have accepted. Now, except in selected areas, numbers come early and heavily into the considerations. These are all instances of either pre-emptive censorship or censorship by default; 'keeping your nose clean' as a well-practised skill.

*

These things can happen in the academic world as elsewhere. A writer was asked by a college of London University, in the Eighties, to give an annual memorial lecture which would subsequently be printed. He chose to speak on the nature of 'Censorship by Pressure and Threats' in Britain and discussed a recent gross instance in full. The morning after the lecture was given, the Principal of the college received a letter from the lawyers for the institution criticised (the director of that body had attended the lecture), threatening legal action if it were published. The college solicitor was consulted and reported that in counsel's view the lecture was not actionable but, just to be on the safe side, a few minor amendments might be made. They were made and the college lawyers were entirely satisfied. The Principal, clearly a nervous man, then sent the revised copy to the objector's lawyers. No doubt recognising that they had thus been put in a position of power, those lawyers repeated that they were still prepared to sue. The Principal then capitulated and said that, in the college's interest, he was not prepared to take the risk of publishing, however slight that risk might be. The lecture has not appeared in print.

*

Here now is a not much used type of censorship, but one in its own way more dispiriting than several of the others: censorship by an individual's misguided probity. This occurs when a High Court judge does not wish to have evidence re-examined which seems likely to overturn a conviction; by revealing, for instance, police corruption and the Bench's impercipience. He is deeply uneasy at any move which might show that institutions of justice are as fallible as other institutions and people. His attitude could be taken as implying: 'Better that an innocent individual rot in gaol for a few years than that a re-trial bring the judiciary system into disrepute.' A thing ill-done and done to others' harm which can be taken for exercise of virtue.

*

The most common, evident and wide-ranging type of censorship runs from the sensibly moral through the in-bitten puritanical to the ideological. It begins by assuming that I am my brother's keeper; not an unworthy assumption and not difficult to defend in some closely considered circumstances.

Here we have to come back for a moment to the possible effects of a substantial exposure to violence on the screen. On firm conclusions about that, judgment is, as has been said, still unsure. It would be a pity, even so, if we instituted a great deal of pre-emptive, presumptive censorship; just in case. But what about young children, very old and frightened people, the mentally ill? Is it not the right and duty of an open society to discuss very carefully whether some censorship might apply as a protection for such groups – if only a 9 p.m. 'watershed' on TV? These are neither silly nor punitively narrow notions. If a society decides there are such areas it is not then closing itself but demonstrating its openness to the possible need for some kinds of judgment it wished it did not have to make, a mature judgment to close some doors. It is good that the Broadcasting Standards Council is setting up wide-ranging research into the use of television by children.

Entirely predictably, there was some opposition to the banning of 'horror comics' a few years ago. Many were aimed at quite young people and created a world of violence, of terror and insecurity. Such as the strikingly and horribly illustrated issue in which a little girl grinned from the cover to boast that she had lied in court so as to ensure her parents went to the electric chair. Those comics were meant to give a horrific frisson to young children by presenting very vividly indeed a world without love, compassion or any commitment to truth; a desert. To assume that those magazines all entirely missed their mark is to make ideology override intelligence and recalls the advertisers' ludicrous self-justification – that no one is taken in by their stuff.

The BBFC's guideline that no scene of forced and violent sex should be released until there is reasonable proof that such scenes can have no copy-catting or generally reinforcing effect is also on these grounds justifiable. 'We' can take care of ourselves no doubt and some of us may even know where else we may find our kicks. We have to recognise this terribly unpalatable truth in a democracy: that care has to be taken, even to the extent of limiting our own freedoms, on behalf of some others not so fortunate.

A classic challenge to this argument was posed three decades ago, when Peter Watkins made for television *The War Game*, about the impact of a nuclear strike on Britain. It was a serious, responsible, imaginative and so immensely powerful film which one would wish as many people as possible to see. The Director-General of the BBC, Hugh Carleton Greene, admired the film and would have liked to transmit. He was not by nature disposed to censorship but finally decided it should not be shown on television, even late at night. It has been said that the Chairman, Lord Normanbrook, did not wish it to be shown on political (don't stir up the anti-nuclear debate) grounds, but it would be difficult to find evidence of that.

The resulting brouhaha could have been scripted in advance. In essence, it was said that Hugh Carleton Greene was acting on orders from Downing Street, since the government did not want any increase in the public objection to nuclear armaments. That may well have been the government's wish; but the Director-General denied any such interference. Incidentally, *The War Game* was shown on television years later, but whether that indicated that the British have matured or relaxed is hard to know.

The Director-General said he was willing for the film to be offered for showing in cinemas, and it was shown at the Academy Cinema in Oxford Street. He felt it his duty to be concerned about the possible effect of the film, if shown on TV, on people in a disturbed or distressed mental state. Not that the film exploits horror; its subject is horrible and the film true to that. The Director-General had taken psychiatric opinion and been advised that the film was so horrific, so depressing about what mankind is now capable of doing to itself, that it could reasonably be predicted that some people – a very few, but how few is too few to bother about? – could, if in a very low mental state, be pushed over the edge into suicide. There could be no assurance that such people stopped viewing early, so the

argument that the film could be transmitted on TV late at night was
unsound.

These are unattractive considerations for those of us who count
ourselves among the fighters for the utmost possible freedom of
speech. They were unattractive to the Director-General. Challenged,
he said something like this: 'Even if only two or three people killed
themselves because of this film I would not feel justified in transmit-
ting it on television, using the justification that millions of others
would learn something valuable from it. Television comes into the
home and takes people by surprise; and that can be both a good and
a bad thing. A cinema is another matter (as are books); you make a
distinct personal choice to see a certain film; you leave the house and
pay to go in; you are much less likely to be taken unawares. In such
circumstances my duty, I finally decided, was not to act as an opener
(which I like to be) but as a qualified closer.'

We may call this an instance of censorship; it is. We may also call
it a responsible exercise of democratic freedom of choice and a
recognition of its rare but unavoidable limits. In judging Hugh Carleton Greene it would be right to start by assuming he acted in good
faith, even if not in the way we would have acted in his position.

The point of all this is that civilised societies exist not simply
through the practice of the personal morality of each of their citizens,
but by a set of often unspoken agreements about society as a whole,
about the greatest degree of freedom and the minimum of agreed
constraints. The sum of the agreed freedoms and the agreed constraints makes up part of the accepted texture of the civil society;
they are indissoluble.

That linking of sex-and-violence which was looked at briefly earlier
is, like bacon-and-eggs and fish-and-chips, deeply embedded in the
English psyche. The insistent linking of the two, especially in talk
about TV – 'There's too much sex-and-violence on TV' – plays into
the hands of the more illiberal censors. They are free not only to
suggest like their Victorian predecessors that sex is dirty but to imply
a natural, an inescapable, link with violence.

In a public meeting on censorship, you may deplore this link and
point out that, though sex with violence in any form is terrible, sex
in itself is not, is one of the more pleasant aspects of being human;
that it is a pity so often to link the two. So much might seem self-
evident. Not to everyone, no matter how carefully you speak. For
you may be fairly sure that a member of the audience will rise and
say: 'How dare you claim that sex can be pleasant; violence is never

to be excused.' In such an instance the speaker may simply not have been listening carefully. It is more likely nowadays that she believes sexual activity is always a form of assault.

The fixation on sex-as-nasty is intensely difficult to argue against; there is usually no common imaginative, intellectual or emotional language. Say to a member of the National Viewers' and Listeners' Association that you would not wish to censor a particular play by Dennis Potter on television – shown after the watershed, of course – even though it is explicit about sex; that those scenes are part of a brilliant and moving exploration of our lives today. Add that, if we are considering the drip-drip effect of certain undesirable attitudes as shown on television, you are more concerned about the influence of, say, the glutinous *This Is Your Life*; or that you care less about full frontal nudity on television than about the rampant, immature cupidity of some game-shows. You will be greeted with incredulity. You must be trying to be clever-clever by saying startling but manifestly absurd things. Who could equate Potter's filth with the wholesome, family quality of *This Is Your Life*?

An interesting passage on sex in the Broadcasting Research Unit's booklet *Quality in Television* makes some apposite points here:

> For some, the containment of prurience remains the principal practice of morality. . . . [But] in their approach to the presentation of sex on film and video, staff of the British Board of Film Classification make a distinction between 'manners' and 'morals' – a rough but useful division which could take the heat off some complaints in that area. A matter of 'manners' would be, for example, whether a woman's naked breasts could be shown in the cinema. Up to about thirty years ago, exposure was not allowed there [nor, even more, on TV]; now it is (as it was some centuries ago). 'Manners', 'taste', the frontiers of the acceptable, have shifted. A matter of 'morals' is more fundamental and has to do with, for instance, the abuse of one human being by another through rape, torture or other forms of contempt and assault.

It would still be foolish to say that the depiction of such acts should never occur in creative work; much may depend on context and treatment. This simple preliminary distinction helps to put aside merely narrow-minded, custom-bound and formalistic objections – so that the ground is clearer for addressing more important and difficult questions.

*

Somewhere in this area appears Censorship as Justified Repression. Here, things are ruled out, first, on the grounds that, even if true, they will be used against us by our opponents. Others, mainly linguistic, are proscribed because, again even if true, they will give offence to a certain section of the population. You must not say that two black men carried out a drug-related attack, even though this is in that instance true, and part of the truth about the cultural sub-group you are describing. You must not describe the very superior manner of an Asian surgical consultant, even though part of your purpose is to distinguish between different styles of assumed superiority as they occur in different cultures; and to show how those styles change in some societies but resist change in others; context has to be respected as part of the attempt to be true to experience.

An oft-quoted semantically mistaken instance of this kind of repression was found in the Social Science department of one of the London universities. You were advised not to ask for black coffee but for coffee without milk.

All such prohibitions commit the same offence to the effort at integrity of the mind: they are prepared to distort the truth of events and attitudes on behalf of a no doubt well-meant, but limited, irrelevant and mistaken sense of ideological propriety. They resemble the determination of some student associations, common in the late Sixties but still to a slight degree alive, to prevent from speaking on their campus anyone they think likely to say something of which they disapprove on ethnic, gender or political grounds.

Just below the surface and at all levels racism exists in English society, not only as promoted in the tabloid press or practised in some parts of working-class life. Chauvinism, sexism, racism can be found in all classes and both sexes. Some peers are known to speak of 'wogs', and Cabinet Ministers of 'our curly-headed friends'. Other politicians, especially on the Right and the back benches, will similarly reject all nations over the Channel as well below our level of civilisation (which raises the continuing question of what definition of 'civilisation' some public schools inculcate).

All this should be resisted directly and with intellectual force. To concentrate entirely on a linguistic near-censorship is to miss the point. Special targets have included the Library Association, the Publishers' Association, Local Education Authorities. Some of those have made a few sensible adjustments but generally resisted where they thought right; the Publishers' Association's booklets have on the whole been admirable statements of the issues. Some individual publishers have yielded, being anxious not to damage their American market, since ideological correctness has gone much further over there; or because their editors share the views of the objectors.

The twists and turns can be agonising. One Local Authority has issued guidelines for authors on the need for writing to be designed 'to build up a sense of identity and to promote equal opportunities'. A library authority has pronounced that 'Any old-fashioned books should be destroyed; i.e. any showing the female as the weaker sex and the male as stronger.' Goodbye, O Lady of Shalott. A set of School Library Service guidelines wags its finger: 'Care will be taken to select materials that present positive images of disabled people, especially children.' Truly, we are here in the realms of *agitprop*, and low-level *agitprop* at that. Given those they would dismiss, it is painful to imagine what books such people would admire.

A document addressed to authors advises that 'positive images' of characters from non-British ethnic groups should always be presented. Another advises that authors should always seek to 'reflect' the 'reality' of this now 'multi-cultural society'. On a very quick glance such pieces of advice may seem just about unexceptionable, an appeal to our fair-mindedness. But both of those calls are tricky, Trojan horses. An author who does not write by prescription – yes, some do – seeks to present neither positive nor negative images but rather to see things as they truly appear. That may seem high-flown but is not; it means that an author wishes to explore what seems to be the truth, not to match a prior prescription. The truth may seem different to different people, but that is the arena we live and debate in. It would therefore be as wrong for an author, from outside the text as it were, to seek to present positive images as to seek to present negative images; both are alien to the calling; they belong rather to prescriptive, ideology-driven writing.

A serious writer may hope that his books will in a certain sense prove to 'reflect' aspects of society, but that is not a prior aim. In so far as there is an 'aim', it will be to look, without prejudice, not entirely knowing what will emerge, what things will be revealed which were unknown before, even to the author. An author who is better than he knows may think he has an aim but, in so far as he is gifted, what he writes will take over from him. At its best all this is a path of discovery into often hidden personal attitudes towards society, life and himself. In this perspective the word 'reflect' is inadequate, beside the point – unless you reduce the author to an agent of your, the reader's, prior views of what society is or should be; and of what writing should be.

One need only think of a single book read with admiration and perhaps astonishment at the exploratory power of the human imagination, and then try to apply to that experience sentences such as 'the author has sought to present positive images' or 'the author has aimed to reflect the reality of this multi-cultural/secular/religious society accurately'. The call for *accurate* reflection is then seen as a call for writers to reflect society in a way which a group outside has in advance deemed accurate according to their own definition, as though there is only one true accuracy or, indeed, as if 'accuracy' is a usable word here. At the extreme, then, we are in the presence of pre-censorship, called for by people who seem never to have read a considerable work of literature; or, if they have tried to do that, have not been able to enter it imaginatively.

It will be said that most writing does not live up to that high prescription, that some authors will be 'negative' and will distort rather than 'reflect', out of laziness or the wish to shock – or, perhaps, wickedness. Maybe: in that case they have to be engaged with but not by advance fencings-off which are linguistically and intellectually limited, which foreshorten issues and deny the feel of experience – since they sometimes catch in their nets authors of different and more important kinds; or try to.

Censorship by omission and silence probably runs through all societies, commercially-open or closed-authoritarian; and rabidly through inter-governmental organisations. It is captured in the French aphorism 'Why should I be more royalist than the King?' – another guiding principle of the relativist society. If you are on the liberal or, worse, the left-wing side politically but work for a paper owned by a right-wing tycoon or one whose politics are invisible but whose nose for what sells and what annoys is both finely tuned and taken as the chief guiding rule, then you have to be brave to utter liberal let alone left-wing sentiments in your column; you find it better to stay on safer ground. This is one of the less overt or rarely admitted bad results of the concentration of the press; and not only the tabloid press.

*

Self-censorship takes several forms and is of all kinds the most interesting because most convoluted and morally complex. It is much easier for us to censor someone else, or to censor the censoring of someone else by others, than to catch ourselves in the act of self-censorship.

Self-censorship runs from the fairly outward looking to the deeply internal. It can affect virtually a whole population, as in the blacking-out of the enormity of the Holocaust and even of the threat of nuclear war. Some things are not to be thought of, after this fashion.

It is usually personal. It may be practised as a way of fending off possible and costly litigation. It includes straightforward and fearful deference which leads to guessing well in advance and continuously what you think the boss will like you to say, or will be surprised and pleased to see you say in his name; and hoping nervously that you won't get it wrong. This is a very long way from a responsible civil servant's minute advising the Minister what, in his honest view, circumstances require his boss to say; and being prepared for him not to take the advice. One can still observe that particular propriety in Britain and no doubt in some other countries; it is less practised in the international Civil Service, and for reasons not always due to the pusillanimity of the Secretariat.

Related to that is the sort of self-censorship which is inspired by the wish not too much to displease in public debate – as, today, in that self-censorship which is prompted by the desire not to anger linguistically and politically correct people. The thought seems to be: such people often sound aggressive but may surely be prepared to listen if approached in a very soft-shoed way? In English debate a common preamble to putting the boot in is: 'With the greatest respect . . .'. But in these cases the approach is: 'With the very greatest respect, and having in mind all the factors adduced by those who wish to remove the use of the adjective *x*, it may I suggest also be argued that . . .'.

Self-censorship prompted by misguided loyalty is a rarer type; as when Arthur Scargill refused to condemn two miners who, during the last miners' strike, had dropped a concrete block on a taxi ferrying to work miners who had not joined the strike, and killed the driver. That was obviously an act to be condemned outright, well outside any civilised pale, whatever arguments might be produced in the defence – enormous provocation by the police, fear of the loss of work, over-stretched belief in the overriding importance of soli-darity on such issues. Scargill may have repressed any such condem-nation as the politically expedient course at that moment or – and this is why he appears in these pages on forms of self-censorship –

he may simply not have been able to stomach, *even to himself*, the idea of such an appalling act being committed by some of his 'lads'.

Related is that self-censorship which is meant to protect one's friends from being hurt, even if that omission to some degree distorts what you are saying, and so may protect your friend at someone else's expense.

It is inevitable that all such forms of self-censorship are hugely practised in totalitarian states; but, like persistent bad drains, they can be found in open societies also; especially since they are then private and, except in marginal cases, not an attempt to escape punishment from the public authorities.

We may all – like authors, publishers and booksellers – practise both commercially inspired self-censorship and (probably wobbly) moral self-censorship; or that unholy mélange which calls itself the second but is really the first type, and so sits at ease in Zion. As in those books, so often rewarding to both author and publisher, which expose the ills of capitalist society but in a way which gives the readers a *frisson* yet doesn't quite get under the skin – what Mary McCarthy once described as a Western intellectual disease: 'Like being in a brothel with mirrors in the ceiling: You do it and you watch yourself doing it.'

That professional self-censorship can be so deep that even when it seems to have been brought to the surface it is still resisted because to recognise it would involve a redefinition of both profession and self, which is very hard to bear. This was illustrated at the turn into the Eighties by the reception broadcasters gave to the concept of 'the structuring of reality', especially as it reflects on the shaping of news. Some broadcasters were quite angry. They insisted that the news is 'out there' objectively, waiting for someone with 'news sense' to identify it. The misunderstandings increased between broadcasters and research workers.

The Glasgow dustmen's strike of the early Eighties is relevant here. At its height rubbish was piled high in the streets and rats began to occupy the heaps. A health hazard, the authorities said. The television cameras panned over the scene. A few left-wing sociologists suspected that those scenes had been urged on the television crews by the Local Authority as a way of bringing the dustmen into disrepute. The crews denied this. To them those scenes were self-evidently to be filmed, 'natural for television', pictorial, instant and shocking, real hard news. They needed no mayor or councillors to turn their attention that way. In this instance 'conspiracy theory' deflected the research workers. The more important point was not that the crew were angry because they had been accused of being in the pockets of the Local Authority. It was that they failed to see that they had committed an act of *selective* censorship, had let their professional visual sense lead them to give too much badly needed space to such a startling set of shots at the expense of treating something more important about the strike. They were thus able to brush aside that more significant objection. Self-censorship, unknown to ourselves, helps us to keep on constructing, retaining and as necessary reconstructing, the professional world we know and want to continue to feel safe in.

Hardest of all is the self-censorship meant, consciously or not, to protect you not only from others' criticism but, even more, from yourself, from recognising some failing which you desperately do not wish to recognise, from the pain of self-criticism by revelation; ego-protecting censorship, that. This is even harder to bear than self-censorship to protect oneself from damage to one's professional self-esteem. It strikes at your deepest sense of yourself as an individual, at the sense of your most intimate relations with others and with yourself.

We settle for what Ambrose Bierce called 'A daily record of that part of one's life, which he can relate to himself without blushing'. The most painful part of any attempt at writing autobiography is just here: the realisation that you have unwittingly tapped, drawn up from the depths of memory, incidents not to your credit which you had long kept so well hidden from yourself that you do not at first want to admit they ever happened, and will twist and turn at redefinition until you have finally to concede; and even then not without some flannelling readjustments. Still, 'one damn'd good-natured friend or another' may be relied on to point those out, being clever enough to detect the new uncertainty of tone. You then realise you may have also concealed some things not only from friends but from unsympathetic critics who will use your confessions against you; but by then that is relatively unimportant.

Faced with these kinds of self-censorship one begins to hate, even more, prescriptive censorship by outsiders. There are problems enough sitting at that table trying to avoid self-censorship, to be honest with oneself, fighting off all the face-saving phoney personae which your urge to retain self-respect offers. Direct censorship can be horrible but removes your right to go to Hell in your own way. When we are grappling with the exploding hidden mines of self-censorship that right, those demands, are in front all the time.

For there is a deeper, better and continuing type of self-censorship. The 'self' is a construction, and 'to be honest with oneself' means to honour that construction. It need be neither an escape nor a hiding-away. It is then part of the creative process itself, an aspect of self-respect.

iv 'AM I MY BROTHER'S KEEPER?'

It is important for open Western societies to resist self-righteousness in the matter of censorship. We have plenty of kinds of censorship of our own and, it can be argued, should be more ashamed of that fact than are those who have to endure wider and often more brutal censorships. Our protestations and professions are too assured.

It is of course rather comical if our relativist rulers find themselves, faced with the unpleasant public results of that stance, taking refuge in some old and some new kinds of censorship. Much more important, we should not let that odd fact discourage us from seriously considering where and to what extent censorship may be justified in an open society. Many are too discouraged, deeply disinclined and for reasons far beyond their dismissal of the resurgence of public authoritarianism, to look into that aspect at all.

*

So: to recapitulate. In open societies all freedoms can be exploited and most will be. A very large amount of exploitation must be tolerated, on democratic grounds, even if it stinks to Heaven; as in the mid-Nineties explosion of explicit and no-holds-barred illustrated sex magazines for women and men. But at what point will society say, also on good democratic grounds: 'Enough: this is where we should exercise our freedom to limit our common freedoms'?

That point is reached when there is reasonable cause to think that young children may be damaged and some other particularly vulnerable groups – the very old and the mentally ill – may be put at risk. It should go without saying that such decisions will only be taken after the most careful consideration and will be hedged with qualifications. It would be mistaken to argue that they should never be taken at all. This is not one of those class-infected decisions or authoritarianism-for-its-own-sake regulations. It is a recognition that some members of any societies need a degree of protection, and that it should be the duty of the others to agree that it shall be provided.

In this light the argument that television, because it comes into the home at all hours, needs special attention, has to be taken more seriously than it often is. In the same breath one can also say that it is both over-regulated and over-narrowly regulated today.

To return to the Video Appeals Committee. It was asked a few years ago to adjudicate on a video film in which on a Sunday lunchtime in a West Country pub nearly naked women wrestled in mud. It was not an appetising sight, though it did not seem to disturb or put off the spectators, most of whom were also enjoying a roast and two veg. It seemed sad that so many people – many of them apparently OAPs – could find nothing better to do. But to the Appeals Committee this seemed, in the BBFC's own terms, and as applied to the question of public proscription, a matter of manners rather than of morals, something for the spectators themselves to decide. The Committee had no difficulty in revising the Board's restrictive classification.

What are the best approaches to the often foolish nature of censorship here and the undoubted scruffiness of much that is censored? There are no easy answers. Constant watchfulness, of course – towards excesses on both sides; better education; more scorn, ridicule and laughter, catholicity and tolerance which aren't misnomers for total relativism; responsibility towards those who need that care which nevertheless does not harden into punitive puritanism. These are the only democratic tools.

CHAPTER TWELVE marker

CHAPTER TWELVE

Ancestral Voices: Myths and Mottoes to Live By

*Our opinions graft themselves on to each other. The first serves as stock
for the second, the second for a third. And so we climb up, step by step.
It thus transpires that the one who has climbed highest often has more
honour than he deserves, since he has only climbed one speck higher on
the shoulders of his predecessor.*

(Michel de Montaigne, *Complete Essays*, trans. Screech (Isaac
Newton said: 'If I have seen further, it is by standing on the
shoulders of giants.' Great men think alike; modestly.)

*If I can, I will prevent my death from saying anything not first said by
my life.*

Montaigne again

'Know thyself?' If I knew myself, I'd run away.
Johann Wolfgang von Goethe, in Eckermann, *Conversations
with Goethe*, 1829

i DEEP SPRINGS

The ordinary suffices me.

George Sturt

On a quick glance this chapter might seem to overlap with Chapter
8, since both are about certain kinds of resistance to change, about
'grit on the flywheel'. More accurately, this chapter is complementary
to the earlier one if more difficult to get hold of, at least to the
author; theologians, some kinds of philosophers, and anthropologists
have long grappled with the theme.

Chapter 8 was about the capacity of native phlegm and wily
adaptability to respond to cultural change. This chapter is more
tentative and speculative, since it asks what very deep-seated assump-

268

tions are to some extent – perhaps to a great extent – meeting, resisting and adapting to the relativism of the time; and asks also where such assumptions, such subterranean resistances, may come from.

This is therefore curious territory where one listens to apophthegms, cracker mottoes, hymns, adages, rather than to general statements and less than concrete assertions of belief. Such statements tend to seem banal; which does not mean that what is reached for is at all banal. General statements are sophisticated instruments; traditional speech can point further down, to where sophistication may not exist but where wisdom may still be in play, even if it is what is marked down as 'conventional' wisdom. Consider simply this, from common working-class speech: 'Emily, I do love you, you know.' 'Will you stop saying that word, as if it makes everything all right.' Exact response to tone and precise pinning-down of humbug. A psychologist would quite rightly need a longish paragraph to tease that out; the speaker does not need the analysis, is operating in the clear field – entirely effectively.

It was noted in the previous chapter that some early 'Effects Analysis' in Communications Studies tended to assume that the recipients' (readers', listeners', viewers') minds were more or less blank slates on to which the persuaders bombarded their images. 'Uses and Gratifications' theory followed, and assumed that most people's minds were well-stocked, and therefore engaged with the messages, bent them to their own uses, their own forms of gratification. Within limits, of course, or the persuaders – who have to try to change some forms of uses and of gratifications – would be on the dole. But it was a valuable step forward.

It is nevertheless a rather too mechanical and static approach. The minds of even apparently very 'simple' people are more complex and richer than that. Even though most of them do not handle general or analytic statements, those minds are like vast and deep seabeds, with conflicting currents in play all the time. The present powerful trend towards relativism is undoubtedly affecting those currents, but not in any quick or easy way; total success would make the seabeds all-overwhelming depths.

This deep sea – estuary might be a better word – is the place where sense is made of experience, where shape is given to it and judgments passed upon it. What main streams feed into that estuary? That depends on time and place. For many in the English working-class in the first half of the century or until the last war the main, the overwhelming feeder river, other than the home but probably more than the neighbourhood itself, was church and chapel. For almost all people that direct influence has virtually dried up. It can still be recognised in play, though usually in a qualified form, in people over fifty; it is not easily found in younger people but to some extent lives on in many of those also, though in a more shadowy and unattributed form.

A number of different groups of elderly working-class women in Hunslet, Leeds, were asked, in the late Eighties, what they believed in. They took that to mean: by what beliefs do you guide your daily lives (not: are you Roman Catholic or Baptist or some such)? They all answered, and did not seem to be playing up to the question, with some such common phrases as: 'Doing unto others as you would be done by', 'common decency', 'fair's fair', 'live and let live'. Their minds were structured by a great and still powerful range of rules to live by. Where do those rules come from? Church and chapel, they said at once; and added that they also learned them at their mothers' knees, those mothers being staunch and regular worshippers. Those now elderly daughters didn't much keep up attendance; but they still believed that what is said there is right all the same. There may have been some discrepancy between 'belief' and action, but not always a large one.

At that point they checked themselves and entered a qualification: 'At any rate, that's my opinion.' This is a typical late-twentieth-century, wide-open-world modification. It would not have appeared, or appeared so often (some nervous ones might have employed it), before the last war. Forty years later, they all wanted to avoid seeming 'judgmental'; they knew church and chapel have lost most of their force; and yet they had to say what they still thought, found themselves 'believing' and practising.

Those 'beliefs' seem still to have a hold. If there had not been in their early days those constant precepts of church and chapel – most of them now boiled down to the pragmatic and almost humanist constituents of a secular rather than eschatalogical morality – what would have been there instead? Within what structures for behaviour would they have gone into and passed through the world? How long will that influence continue to provide a frame to guide life by? One more generation? Two? Will 'It's only my opinion' become the universal introduction to any statement which might seem to be going to hint at a value-judgment; which will have by then become entirely the expression of a matter of taste, not a judgment at all?

*

None of those women would know much poetry, if any, except perhaps for a few rhymes remembered from school. But their minds were full of a kind of poetry, a comforting and uplifting poetry on which they could without thinking draw, which they could hear in the backs of their heads. Above all, hymns. As in this quick dip into one memory:

> Jesus shall reign where'er the sun
> Does his successive journeys run . . .

> When I survey the wondrous cross
> On which the prince of glory died,
> My richest gain I count but loss,
> And pour contempt on all my pride.

> Holy, Holy, Holy! Lord God Almighty! . . .
> God in Three Persons, blessed Trinity!

> Praise my soul, the King of heaven;
> To his feet thy tribute bring.
> Ransomed, healed, restored, forgiven
> Who like me his praise should sing?

> He who would valiant be . . .

> Guide me, O thou great Redeemer . . .

> Stand up, stand up for Jesus . . .

> We plough the fields, and scatter
> The good seed on the land,
> But it is fed and watered
> By God's almighty hand . . .

> Spirit of our God descending,
> Fill our hearts with heavenly joy,
> Love with every passion blending,
> Nothing can our peace destroy . . .

> Rock of Ages, cleft for me
> Let me hide myself in Thee . . .

> O God, our help in ages past
> Our hope for years to come,
> Our shelter from the stormy blast,
> And our eternal home.

> Bread of Heaven . . .

> Oh, dearly, dearly, has he loved . . .

> Brightest and best of the sons of the morning . . .
> Lighten our darkness . . .

and of course:

> Abide with me: fast falls the eventide;
> The darkness deepens; Lord, with me abide . . .

It is not difficult to think that memories such as those – and they are only a few from many – will provide a sort of sustaining caul around the personality as it confronts its day-by-day problems, uncertainties and worries, a continuing suggestion that 'there is more to life' than we would otherwise be tempted to think, another dimension.

> He that is down need fear no fall
> He that is low no pride
> He that is humble ever shall
> Have God to be his guide.

That is in the beginning depressing – if you are as low as you can get at least you won't have the shock of falling further. It might seem to fit with much in earlier unexpectant working-class life. But then the words lift and show themselves to be talking about self-conceit not public status.

The same memory produced on a later occasion:

> In vain the surge's angry shock,
> In vain the drifting sands
> Unharmed upon the eternal rock
> The eternal city stands.

It is the bold pictorial rhetoric there which stays with you, as do the haunting images in most of the others; some have the simple force of folk poetry. So does – and this explains its continuing power – Blake's

> And did those feet in ancient time
> Walk upon England's mountains green?
> And was the holy Lamb of God
> On England's pleasant pastures seen?

No other hymn speaks, as does this adopted poem, instantly across so many diverse groups of the English: the pastoralists who hope to speak for the countryman they believe is still in us all, and who know that pastoral is threatened; and the less-and-more gentle patriots, from the Ramblers' Association right through to the British Legion; and the Women's Institute, whose members belt it out across the Albert Hall, louder than any others.

> 'The Church's one foundation
> Is Jesus Christ, her Lord;
> She is his new creation
> By water and the Word . . .

Even a long-time agnostic might go for the melodic beauty of that and a hundred others – if only one could tell what they really mean. Years of Sunday School, of the simple piety of one's Sunday School teacher; the sermons (least of the trio); and most of all those hymns – always interweaving with the simple but straight ethics of a mother or grandmother, would build like a swallow's nest into the lineaments of an always present, even if often fractured, moral frame.

You could escape but you knew you were escaping and from what; it stood always at the back, not like an avenging angel (that would have been too grand) but as a reproving spirit. If instead you had been brought up by and as a 'decent' humanist such precepts might have stuck too; and have had their own memorable echoes. But one would have missed the hymns.

ii SOPHISTICATED MEMORIES

In reading others, one's rejected thoughts return with a certain alienated majesty.

Ralph Waldo Emerson, Self-Reliance, *Essays* 1841

This sets off, as a byway, thoughts on the place of remembered passages in minds stocked with literary memories (hinted at in a rather different way in Chapter 3). Not folk memories but 'well-read' memories. It is odd and interesting how such memories mesh in the same person with the native idiomatic aphorisms from childhood. The later memories have a further character. The early ones were *given*, part of a common stock; the later memories tell something about the particular individual who has retained them, planted them in the memory when so much else has fallen; they tell, no less than the homelier echoes, about hopes and fears and all sorts of hang-ups. Yet the meshing itself is the most illuminating aspect, the great background frieze of retained and shared folk memories, and the idiosyncratic memories picked up and held on to along a more sophisticated route than those who passed on the folk memories ever knew. A strange boiling.

So: Keats's 'Men, I think, should bear with one another', which joins hands with Coleridge's 'Men, I think, should be weighed not counted' (there is a Yiddish proverb from which Coleridge might have taken his lead: 'Words should be weighed not counted'). Both belong to the same charitable spirit as Orwell's 'When it comes to the pinch, human beings are heroic'. As does Hamlet's 'Use every man after his desert, and who should 'scape whipping?'; and Lear's 'Oh, reason not the need'; and Forster's definition of the 'rent' we owe, of the need to trust in the possibility of human honesty; even though we may prove mistaken in that trust (the shopkeeper may have been cheating us or perhaps we were ourselves muddled). Someone from a poor country might comment that you need to be prosperous to have that kind of charitable leeway.

In *A Journey to the Western Islands of Scotland* Dr Johnson joined that company: ' . . . life consists not of a series of illustrious actions, or elegant enjoyments . . . The true state of every nation is the state of common life.' Which, in turn, recalls Chesterton on 'The people of England / That never have spoken yet'; and those not 'well-bespoke' and 'uncounted folk', whom Kipling remembered in 'A Charm'.

On the reverse side of such utterances lie 'Stone dead hath no fellow' one of the most implacable of them all, the tyrant's chill emblematic conviction; and 'simply the thing I am shall make me live'. Somewhere in between are to be found Solon's 'Call no man happy . . .' and Thoreau's 'The mass of men lead lives of quiet desperation', the inconsolable cry 'That it could come to this!' and 'Men

must endure / Their going hence, even as their coming hither: /
Ripeness is all.'

Each of us has special holdings of these kinds of haunting reflections. Among Europeans, Montaigne stands as high as anyone. La
Bruyère craftily and cloudily remarked; 'Aimer Montaigne, c'est
aimer soi-même'; which could be taken to mean that Montaigne so
often says things which, immediately on reading them, we feel (self-
deceptively or not) that we have ourselves arrived at. The exceptional
simplicity of the saying, and sometimes the apparent simplicity and
even playfulness of the thought itself, as well as its often sombre
and honest directness, all contribute to the unique final effect of
moral self-composition. In that sense, Montaigne is a midwife
of thought to all who are captivated by him; probably because of
their own self-preoccupation.

*

'I am not so much worried about how I am in the minds of others
as how I am to myself'; 'There is virtually nothing that I *know* that
I know'; 'We are never at home. We are always outside ourselves';
'When I play with my cat, how do I know that she is not passing
time with me rather than I with her?'; 'Kings and philosophers shit;
and so do ladies' (Swift's 'Celia shits' was a statement of revulsion;
Montaigne is phlegmatically amused); 'Any honourable person pre-
fers to sully his honour than to sully his conscience'; and the wonderfully compact 'Repentance begs for burdens.'

iii THREE TYPES OF APHORISM

Back now to the more everyday saws, aphorisms, tags to live by.
They fall into three main clusters: putting up with things; tolerance,
belonging and charity; the value of honesty and the hatred of cheats.
All three contrast sharply, though some more than others since this
world is never simple, with some aphorisms which are at the forefront
today, with – in shorthand – Thatcherisms.

Putting up with things, being dour and unexpectant, head down but cheerful; and fatalistic

'Don't count your chickens before they're hatched'; 'It never rains
but it pours'; 'A change is as good as a rest'; 'What's done can't be

275

undone'; 'What can't be cured, must be endured; 'No use crying over spilt milk'; 'Keep something for a rainy day'; 'Waste not, want not'; 'Time heals all things'; 'Soonest ended, soonest mended'; 'leave well alone'; 'What must be, must be'; 'Don't foul your own nest'; 'Enough is as good as a feast'; 'Worse things happen at sea'; 'Moderation in all things'; 'Always look on the bright side; 'While there's life, there's hope'; 'No news is good news'; 'It'll all come out in the wash'; 'Everything comes to him who waits'; 'Don't put all your eggs in one basket'; 'You can't put back the clock'; 'You can't have it both ways'; 'You can't have your cake and eat it'; 'We must all eat a peck of dirt before we die'; 'You don't get something for nothing in this world'; 'A stitch in time saves nine'; 'A fool and his money are soon parted' (another in the 'more hope than expectation' group); 'Beggars can't be choosers'; 'All such things are sent to try us'; 'Don't cross your bridges before you come to them.'

Tolerance, belonging and charity

'Never judge from appearances'; 'Every man has his faults'; 'Always mind your own business'; 'It takes two to make a quarrel'; 'The pot calling the kettle black'; 'Never speak ill of the dead'; 'It takes all sorts to make a world'; 'There's no accounting for tastes'; 'There's nowt so queer as folk'; 'One man's meat is another man's poison'; 'Everyone to his taste'; 'Live and let live'; and those others listed a few pages back, in Section i, also on charity and fair-mindedness. 'Lame dogs' and 'Helping hands' figure here too.

The value of honesty and the hatred of cheats

'Tell the truth and shame the Devil'; 'Money isn't everything'; 'Actions speak louder than words'; 'A man is known by the company he keeps'; 'He that touches pitch shall be defiled'; 'Better be a fool than a knave'; 'One good turn deserves another'; 'Honesty is the best policy'; 'Practise what you preach'; 'Do as you would be done by'; 'The Devil finds work for idle hands to do'; 'One law for the rich, another for the poor'; 'Bad news travels fast'; 'Cheats never prosper'; 'Give a thief enough rope and he'll hang himself' (again, more hope than judgment in these two); 'The leopard cannot change his spots'; 'All fur coat and no knickers'; 'A bad penny always turns up again'; 'He knows the price of everything and the value of nothing.'

That last might be one of the key mottoes of the Eighties and Nineties, especially as an indication of some attitudes most promoted by
recent Tory governments; as these are exemplified also in such a
phrase as 'cost-effectiveness'. That sort of phrase, that sort of thinking, would stand like an iron gate against the introduction today of
some institutions which the hard-headed nineteenth century nevertheless created, created as public goods not too narrowly assessed financially, and for the public good: the Public Libraries, the Public Parks,
free art galleries and museums, free universal education, adult education – also often free, from the universities, the churches and
chapels, the local authorities and many voluntary bodies.

Again, that phrase about the price of everything and the value of
nothing is a signpost from a received everyday morality, but not at
all a morally simple phrase. It comes unerringly from its own solid
and workable rules of thumb. It has great 'bottom' and weight; it
suggests a 'philosophy', a way of living, a whole outlook, a network
of beliefs to live by; all in vivid metaphorical terms.

Recalling all this from childhood, one is astonished at the tensile
strength that web can have. Of course, not everyone lived that way;
there are also the brutes and the feckless. But many did so walk, a
remarkable number given the harsh terms of so much in their lives.
'Poor but honest' (the old jokey phrase takes on a new life), but
living by these powerful indicators, not fly or snide, often grindingly
puritanical but not ungenerous in convictions, going on going on,
able to draw on wells of tolerance even towards those who were, if
not the the speakers' enemies, then 'their own worst enemies'. It is
astonishing that so many could live until as late as the mid-century
by such lights; but then, they had earlier been as separated in their
cheap and grimy terraced districts as the Amish of Pennsylvania.

*

Against all that, some other old and new phrases more and more
present themselves today. For example, that limp long-standing
excuse, evasion, justification, for wrong doing: 'If I didn't do it
someone else would.' In different forms that is rolled out in every
debate about arms sales abroad. With it goes the question: 'Do you
want to put *x* thousand men out of work?' A related exculpation,
very common after privatisation – say, to justify refusing to provide

some service to remote communities where the cost is higher than is provision for the cities – is that awful defence noted earlier: 'I have my shareholders to think of first.' This is now often said, in public, on radio and television, with no longer a moment of hesitation; it is taken as an axiomatic fact of life.

Finally, two aphorisms which in related ways typify much in the current mood. The profit-before-everything thruster says: 'You can't make an omelette without breaking eggs', which sounds homely but is cruel because used as the excuse for heedless and probably corrupt attrition towards your competitors, for sacking your workers on the harshest terms which can be got away with, and for cheating your clients and customers.

The second much-intoned motto is even sadder, since it is used by people who should not see themselves as directly driven by market forces. For example, it is pointed out to them (head teachers, directors of museums, NHS executives, local councillors, head librarians, broadcasters) that they are being too easily influenced by the cost-effectiveness doctrine, are being driven into small malfeasances, dubious corner-cutting, self-interested flattery and other accommodations alien to their purposes as originally conceived. The speakers then almost invariably add: 'But you forget, my dear chap, that we live in the *real* world.' Not long after that point, those iron gates clang shut; inside is the chill, dreadful prison of a collective solipsism; Lear's terrible vision has come to pass: 'Unaccommodated man is no more but such a poor, bare, forked animal as thou art.'

iv WALKING ON THE WATER

No: it has not yet come to that vision; to suggest so is a kind of indulgence which can't be afforded. The British do not live in a 'real' world in the sense that many other countries, on mainland Europe and elsewhere, have come to know reality; the British live in a well-cushioned world.

For 'ordinary' people in those other countries assumptions about the nature of society have for a long time been forced to be more Hobbesian than the assumptions of Hobbes's modern compatriots. These others know the thinness of the social order, its fragility, its likeness to a light covering over the abyss, to a stretch of water we walk on by an act of faith, with a continuing, widespread, unconscious and finally unjustified confidence.

It follows that this sort of thought does not occur as much in

English literature as in the literatures of the European mainland. Most of those countries have had more than one evidence of fragility, having been overrun, torn to pieces so that civic order collapsed and the jungle was all around them. Even after the last war no English novelist showed the apocalyptic vision of Kafka or Sartre. Koestler was a foreigner, a mainland European, so did not count for these purposes. Orwell was English and produced *1984*; the English have not ceased to be surprised by that. It is a dystopia, set in a terrible imagined future and so, powerful though its impact is, does not seem to belong to, to re-create the destruction of the world we have known, has little force as documentary or realist fiction.

The twentieth-century writer in English who is most preoccupied with and most brings home the sense of social fragility is Conrad; in book after book and especially in *Heart of Darkness* and *The Secret Agent*. In the first the fragility is seen to arise from a compound of the evils of capitalism and a more fundamental disposition to evil in the heart of man (an old-fashioned phrase, but in this Conrad was deliberately invoking old-fashioned beliefs, so his story should not be reduced, as it has been by some, to a criticism of only one kind of human activity, greed for profit).

Seen from this perspective also, *The Secret Agent* is one of his most intriguing books and a sort of heroic failure. Conrad brings from Central Europe the world of the anarchist who rejects civil society and its ordering, who is committed to the entire destruction of such societies, who does not seek power himself but the removal of all forms of power and authority. He sites all this in turn-of-the-century London, a world of swirling fogs; of congenital shabbiness and squalor surmounted by a thin layer of 'high society' and with a hierarchy of authorities – from the Home Secretary to the police – dedicated to maintaining that order. They are used to dealing with routine crimes such as burglary and murder and are also marginally but edgily aware of what is going in the unreliable and unsteady world across the water, in the name of Anarchy: but they don't really expect it here any more than the English have seriously expected rabies to arrive from across the Channel.

The seediness of London is well caught, like a Sickert painting; the anarchist cell seems superimposed, out of place, precisely foreign, not imaginatively integrated into the life of the novel. It gives a histrionic, a rhetorical quality to the story which suits the anarchists, would suit Conrad's native Poland and Warsaw, but sits uneasily with the realistic documentary quality of the London life of the pornographic bookseller Verloc (about whom the only foreign element is his queer name), and his wife Winnie, who believes that most things don't bear much looking into. A fascinating book, like a part watercolour, part oil painting, part Lowry/part Magritte.

Even in its partial failure, therefore, *The Secret Agent* shows what an extraordinary feat it is that the British can so easily assume so much continuity and security; on the one hand, a feat of sleep walking; on the other founded in a near reality, in the assertion that order will survive. We had a civil war three centuries ago; some major centres of population were badly bombed in the last war, and there have since been some temporary and local breakdowns of order. There can be no suitable comparisons here with, say, Belgium or France or many another West and East European nation. No Holocaust, no Balkan-style disturbances, no Pol Pot, no Vietnam, no atom bombs on the cities, no ethnic cleansing.

PART FOUR

Who Needs a Clerisy?

The number of those who need to be awakened is far greater than that of those who need comfort.
Bishop Wilson, 1778–1858, cit. Matthew Arnold, *Culture and Anarchy*, 1869

We must not accept the wantlessness of the poor.
Gotthold Lessing, 1729–81

'Nor is the People's Judgment
always true:
The Most may err, as grossly
as the Few'
John Dryden, *Absalom and Achitophel*, 1681

CHAPTER THIRTEEN

Democratic Representations and Democratic Spirits

But in each class there are born a certain number of natures with a curiosity about their best self, with a bent for seeing things as they are, for disentangling themselves from machinery, for simply concerning themselves with reason and the will of God, and doing their best to make these prevail; for the pursuit, in a word, of perfection . . . and this bent always tends to take them out of their class, and to make their distinguishing characteristic . . . their humanity. *They have, in general, a rough time of it in their lives.*

Matthew Arnold, *Culture and Anarchy,* 1869

It is often said but rarely substantiated that the British nowadays are not very politically active. There is some slight evidence to the contrary partly at the Local Government level. The weakening in some councils of the traditional party political, Tory or Labour seesaw in favour of the Liberal Democratic interest is a surprising and welcome change; it indicates a wish to attend more effectively to local affairs, not to be chiefly a minor branch of national party political interests. Heartening also is the increased activity, local as well as national and even international, on issues of the day: the Environment, Racism, Human Rights. Not for a majority but for a devoted minority; relativism has not altogether eroded the sense of public responsibility in such fields. Local councillors, members of Amnesty International and the like still devote hours and hours of unpaid activity to voluntary works.

On the other hand, in most council elections the percentage who bother to vote is slight, and many are elected as a matter of routine not on a consideration of their fitness. In these circumstances it is as well, in fact if not in principle, that local councillors have few powers. Their record in decisions on town planning, for instance, has been in many cases deplorable; French and German local councils usually have greater powers; they leave Britain trailing. Here, the specialist pressure groups have often to act, and usually do, as correctives to local council limitations. Such groups exist elsewhere in Europe but usually with more national or international perspectives. The peculiarly British pressure groups are more typically tied into local issues, more homely; but some also have wider horizons. The differences, by countries, are of required emphasis.

As to national authorities there is a growing paradox. In spite of government protestations, their central powers have increased substantially over the last few years; by contrast, the respect in which they – very many politicians and the shadowy civil servants – are held has decreased. As a result, 'grass-roots' opposition, especially in matters about 'rights' (Animal Rights, opposition to the Criminal Justice Act, and so on), finds its national focus and increases.

We have to come back to that elusive and all too often invoked concept of the 'community'; and to that wide range of voluntary work done as a matter of course on behalf of 'the community'. It might on the face of things seem slightly perverse to put that word – 'community' – in inverted commas. In Chapter 6 current misuses of the word were challenged, and with good reason since many were gross. These other uses have to be handled with exceptional care.

Doesn't all this voluntary work spring from a sense of owing something to, being part of, 'a community'? It is tempting to say yes and leave things at that. But there is a niggling doubt. A town can deploy large amounts of voluntary good works and still not seem to have much of a general and widespread sense of community. The main reason for this is that voluntary work is almost entirely a class-recruited thing, done as a matter of duty by the middle-class on behalf of those below them; and generally done with a good heart. So this, oddly enough, underlines that English towns are still so class-defined and divided as to find it hard to be coherent, whole 'communities'.

We have to focus the microscope more finely; until we arrive at 'neighbourliness', and that is practised in but not across all classes. It does not extend across a whole town; its horizons are narrow; its range and composition are too small to merit the word 'community'. It belongs to a 'neighbourhood' and is virtually always single-class. Within those tight bounds its sense of duties owed, to-and-from, is very powerful. One could call it the most powerful single democratic practice in Britain, but those who exercise it would not use the term, would balk if they heard it.

Under authoritarian regimes, local neighbourhood groups also help one another, but that is altogether sadder, because enforced; a threatened and frightened or determined expression of the need to support each other which the secure British do not endure (any more than they endure the need to betray one another). Both types – the British and the less free – useful and often admirable as they are, have this in common: they are separated from the realities and levers of power, have created worthy groupings under the shadow of those realities, or entirely against the thrust of those realities, but are almost entirely without substantial or effective or meaningful connections with 'Authority'. Here is the most troublesome gap of all.

Democratic representation has to be more than that. There are few signs that the larger sense of representation is strengthening; there are several signs that it has been weakening. We have little sense of national democratic – as distinct from totemic – cohesion (we have a good number of myths which purport to describe such a cohesion, beginning with the pinnacle-institution, the Monarchy; the irrelevance of these myths does not prevent them from getting in the way of a growth in more mature cohesion). We have little sense of the democratic integration necessary between the various parts of this society if it is to live up to its name better ('Live at peace with itself'). 'Open democracies' are increasingly more open than democratic; widespread and growing relativism accelerates the process, especially by discouraging serious discussion of the way such societies might best go. There is, once more, neither language nor tone for proper demotic discourse. In such circumstances the cheapjacks, the flatterers, the glib thrive; but 'The best lack all conviction . . .'.

i CONFRONTATION, CONSENSUS AND COHESION

Mrs Thatcher used to declare, with her usual unassailable confidence, that she favoured and practised confrontational government. Her eyes flashed: how else, she asked, does one move forward except through the battle between firmly held opinions and the refusal to compromise? Consensus is assumed to be precisely a smudging word for compromise.

The short first answer is that if we all act like that we will get nowhere, will have a stalemate until someone finally capitulates out of exhaustion, bullying or the pulling of rank, rather than by a process of thoughtful exchanging of opinions. Or the lady's phrasing is doing duty for a clearer expression: 'I let it be known that I will not give an inch, and so I get my way.' Which is not at all the same as truth emerging from the consideration of firmly held opinions; prejudice, short-sightedness, an inadequate grasp may just as well have won. Confrontation can be tonic but, except as a debating device, should be controlled by the overriding wish eventually to arrive at what you will hope to call, if not the truth, then the right course in the circumstances. Otherwise the tonic becomes a heady drug, which can lead to bad judgment.

The incidental but intriguing question arises here: why did so many of the 'Tory grandees' so easily capitulate to the methods and manners of an indisputably domineering, endlessly bossy woman – given their culture, the capitulation before a woman is more surprising than would be that before a man.

Mrs Thatcher is intelligent but not intellectual; narrow-minded, rather; powerfully pushy, like a car with an engine too big for its gears, suspension, steering and brakes; unwilling to admit error because the vision is at bottom limited, and determined to slap you down if you challenge her – unless you are one of the favoured. The steadiness of the half-shut eye or, better, the narrow-tracked determination of the imaginatively one-eyed. 'May God us keep / From single vision and Newton's sleep.' Newton was, of course, Grantham's more famous citizen. The only explanation offered by some people for the lady's dominance of the traditional Tory top-brass would seem to be that she reminded them of the governesses who for so many of their early years controlled their lives; the echo must be hard to resist.

*

The British spirit in government has for long had many elements which have made it more consensual than confrontational. At bottom this is an aspect of the 'we belong to one another' – 'never ask for whom the bell tolls' – spirit. It assumes that we all have some right to be heard, if possible to be accommodated, that compromise can be a mature not a weak-willed attitude, that democracy does not mean forcing our view of the world down other people's throats (least of all under our present electoral system and by governments with small majorities); but means instead trying to make room for as many points of view as possible whilst maintaining a firm grasp on main principles.

We used to be surer and do better. As in inventing and largely honouring that 'arm's-length principle' which most foreigners find inexplicable, a British eccentricity at best, a self-deceit at worst. You make use of the Monarchy by establishing, with the Royal Charter rather than by Act of Parliament, certain bodies on whose briefs direct governmental involvement and intervention could be undesirable; bodies such as the BBC, the Arts Council, the British Council, the universities. Some MPs in all parties do not understand this distinction with a difference, and when it is explained they remain suspicious and antagonistic. They did not like when they raise a question in the Commons about, say, what they regard as bad behaviour by the BBC, to be referred to the Chairman of the Corporation. That principle is now blurred; the Secretary of State may well answer questions instead.

Better times may bring back better practice, for the device is a good one, one of the fences a democracy needs against encroaching parliamentary populism. It need not be a deceit, even though it does not even at its best work exactly according to the book. Politicians have always itched to interfere and to different degrees have done so. When he was Prime Minister Harold Wilson, angered by some critical BBC programmes, sought to harness the broadcasters by appointing a Chairman of Governors who he knew would be unattractive to the Corporation and so a useful instrument for bringing it more to heel.

Manipulation of the membership of the governing bodies of such institutions is the most common form of interference. There is always some, at best a manageable, an absorbable amount; at worst – as progressively in the Eighties and Nineties – a dangerously high and intrusive amount. That shift is another aspect of the rise of confrontational rather than consensual politics. 'Let's not be silly; let's not shilly-shally' (a favourite phrase among confrontationists); 'let's call things by their proper names; let's not admit weak-kneed liberals just for form's sake; let's put in our own kind so that they can bring about the controls and changes they know we want.' At that point the process has become a form of creeping mild corruption.

To come back to them once more; the most mature and, at their best, admirable of the traditional consensual devices are the Quangos (quasi-autonomous non-governmental organisations). They run from Royal Commissions through Departmental Committees to a flood of tributaries. The 'quasi' there is not the most appropriate word, since it can suggest '*soi-disant*' or 'half-way'. Perhaps it is a governmental draftsman's sly semantic ploy, meant to indicate that the 'non-govern-mental' element is more apparent than real; but it can after all this time be lived with. 'Publicly appointed' might have been better, except that 'Pango' sounds like a Latin-American Dance of Frenzied Arma-dillos.

Members of Quangos, who give much unpaid time to this work (or did; many are paid now, and that is a pity) are rightly jealous of their independence. Most of them. From 1979 one could recognise round their tables the British version of the KGB man; listening but not saying much, and tending to have a withdrawn half-smile as though he is hearing hidden programme-music; which he is, though he tends to mishear and misinterpret. Such a politico will interpret any intervention by a committee member, especially on an issue of principle, as politically motivated, meant to serve the interest of an outside body or of the member; that is his world.

There are usually not many members who could be called intellec-tuals, even if that were desirable, nor many who at the start are well-informed on the subject under review. Almost all learn surprisingly quickly; shrewdness and fair-mindedness can make up for lack of intellectuality. Those who decide the composition of the committees usually have the 'healthy' British suspicion of intellectuals and aca-demics; most intellectuals and academics have an unhealthy suspicion of committees.

Most members of Quangos are rather proud of their memberships as well as of their independence. They report to the relevant Minister or Secretary of State; his or her counter-attitude to the Quango's sense of independence is the – correct – insistence that a Quango's report is advice not instruction. That must and should give rise to tensions, especially if a Quango produces recommendations which run against the received opinions, not to say ideology, of the government of the day. You know you have been doing your job properly when the Minister says to your Chairman: 'Please do not try to take over my functions'; to which the Chairman replies: 'And please do not expect us to put in so much voluntary work only to have our findings inadequately considered.'

Politics must intervene and in the most fundamental ways. The Albemarle Committee on the Youth Services of the late Fifties had the fairest of winds because it coincided with, was indeed inspired by, the first wave of public concern about the increasingly dissident behaviour of urban young people. Innocent days, they seem now, in the light of Nineties' violence. Most of the Committee's conclusions were accepted, very quickly; and funds were provided – not as much as the Committee had recommended, but more than it had expected.

By comparison, the Pilkington Committee on the Future of Broadcasting had a more prickly brief and a harder time. Lord Annan's Committee on Broadcasting some years later (1974–7) was differently composed. Noël Annan observed wryly:

> The membership of the committee was certainly not chosen on the principles which are enshrined in the report in 1910 of the Balfour Committee of Enquiry into Royal Commissions. That Committee said 'It is of equal or greater importance that those selected as Commissioners should, as far as possible, be persons who have not committed themselves so deeply on any side of the questions involved . . . as to render the probability of an impartial enquiry and a unanimous report practically impossible. A Commission selected on the principle of representing various interests starts with a serious handicap.

(Noël Annan, Lecture on 'The Politics of a Broadcasting Enquiry', 1981)

No doubt the Chairman had a great deal of resolving and of urging the need for Arnoldian fresh and objective thought on the members. Above all, a chairman in such a position has to try to discourage appendices crammed with interminable 'Notes of Dissent'. In these circumstances, Annan did a formidable job; but he shouldn't have had to work in that way. Generally speaking, a committee largely composed of hard-working and fair-minded intelligent laymen and women is likely to produce better results.

The narrow loading of the brief of the subsequent 'Peacock' Committee on the financing of the BBC (1985–6) was a natural next step for the government. Yet even there habitual fair-mindedness to a good extent prevailed. Having studied the evidence the Committee did not act as Their Mistress's Voice. They had other ideas and said so. But the BBC soon had and for the first time both a Conservative Chairman of the Board and a Conservative Vice-Chairman. From more than one other Quango, Chairmen and their deputies were unceremoniously dismissed in mid-term; it's never too soon to start being confrontational, so long as you have ensured that those with the greatest clout are from your side; peerages to the right people began to fall like confetti.

It is very hard for even the fairest-minded to shrug off their professional inclinations and think in a larger, less interested context. Which is why, to take an example from another Quango, a chairman of the Arts Council used to say that the Council's Drama Panel was much the most difficult to chair; it contained the largest number of specific and sometimes competitive interests, and its members – though not formal 'representatives' of particular institutions – were painfully aware that almost all those institutions were short of money and expected 'their member' to fight for them at the panel's meetings.

It may be useful to look more closely at how members of Quangos are chosen, at the limitations of the method and how it might be improved. Here again we come upon repetitive but not well thought out sloganising: 'This is a democracy; all are equal before the law and all can vote.' So the instruments of a democracy, and the multitudinous committees, must be each within themselves representative. No more stuffed shirts, no more hand-picked-in-Whitehall members of the Brigade of the Great and the Good; representativeness all round and in all things. These slogans especially haunt committees concerned with cultural matters, with broadcasting and with the arts. To attack present methods of selection in the name of democracy has become a specialised branch of anti-racism.

The membership of public committees has indeed been too often drawn from a very narrow range of individuals, a range over-decided by restricted assumptions as to where the most valuable people are likely to be found (still, the traditional method was not quite so screwed down as today's list is – screwed on to that even narrower range of individuals each known as 'one of us'). We can all easily rehearse the case against the old-style class-education-profession-bound list. At its worst this procedure belonged to what Belloc called the rotten boroughs of the mind. Too much was done by centralised but localised string-pulling, through the old-boy network and words in the right ears. It had its inspired moments. At the turn into the Nineties the same man – Graham C. Greene – was Chairman of the left-wing *New Statesman* and a member of the Board of the British Council. There was no harm in that, but many right-wingers must have thought it questionable.

Even more than has been traditionally the case, the 'one of us' test ensures that too many appointments are still given to the same small band. Lord Rees-Mogg may have many committee virtues, but are fifty-odd million citizens so short of that kind of talent that he had to hold at more or less the same time three or four major public posts – Arts Council, BBC Governors, Broadcasting Standards Council and so on? Lord Harewood is no doubt talented too – and what is more an aristocrat – but so are many others (talented, if not aristocrats). Why should Harewood go directly from running The English National Opera to the presidency of the British Board of Film Classification? The questions are rhetorical; the answer is plain; and unpleasant. At their least distorted, managers of these procedures like to talk of 'a safe pair of hands'; and these meritocratic governments still dearly love a lord.

We have seen that the recent sequence of aggressively but only apparently anti-Quango ('the business of government is to govern'), pro-commercial, 'hard-headed' Tory governments nevertheless seem unable to break free from the main elements in this style of thinking and doing. More and more they use Quangos; they even give many of them greater financial and policy-making powers than the old-style Quangos ever had. But they take care that these new but often Johnny Come Lately representatives of the Great and the Good are of their persuasion, solidly Conservative. They have kept the name of 'Quango' but destroyed its best qualities so that it no longer deserves its funny but honourable title. Even worse: 'Executive Quangos' should not exist; they are loaded and not fit for impartial executive powers.

So much is self-evident. Wouldn't a wider and more demotic sweep be fairly easy to devise? That question is not at all easily answered. If you earnestly sought a 'fully representative' committee how would you define the different constituencies from which it would be drawn? Wouldn't you need 'representative constituencies'? It is said that when the Independent Television Authority was being set up the planners were anxious to have an Authority (Board) more democratic in its composition than the BBC's Board of Governors, or General Advisory Council and its Regional equivalents.

The story goes on to say that a market-research report was commissioned to advise on what would constitute a fully representative body: as to age, sex, geographical spread, occupation, ethnic background, religious persuasion, etc. No doubt each proposed member would have to represent several desirable elements – Welsh, female, middle-aged, working-class, perhaps. It is said that one figure who floated to the surface was an early-middle-aged male publican from Carlisle with representative recreational interests but no experience of committees.

In all probability that story is apocryphal; or it may be a comical extension of an exercise carried out with similar purposes but in a less mechanistic manner. *Se non è vero, è ben trovato.* But would even a more sophisticated trawl be by definition 'democratic'? This is after all a much more subtle quest than those by which market researchers test buying habits. It may satisfy the more thoughtless of proponents for 'entirely democratic' methods of committee selection. They tend to invoke here, as a relevant model, jury selection. Even jury selection has some selective criteria, but they are not greatly restricting, as some who serve on a jury illustrate; there are usually a few members who find it difficult to follow an argument of much complexity and are easily swayed by the more histrionic counsels' rhetoric.

What about Members of Parliament, then? They are chosen by ballot. Yes, but before candidates are selected they have been through several powerful scrutinies, none of which could be called widely representational. They have not been drawn out of a hat as typical of this or that. Even so, it is one of the prices of our system that some MPs are elected, on the Left and the Right, who have small brains and large prejudices. The out-and-out democrat will reply; 'So be it.' Odd MPs; odd Quangos; to that, some MPs would also raise no objection.

A 'fully representative' committee, chosen by the kind of criteria which would have produced the Welsh lady and the Carlisle publican, would have sidestepped two important hurdles. The selection system would have failed to introduce these two elements since its proponents would object to them. It would not look sufficiently closely for proven experience and ability in committee work, or for signs of the ability to acquire such skills; that is, a reasonable level of intelligence. We all have to start somewhere, so committees can and should support a few beginners; but we do need at least some natural gifts if we are to take off at all.

In even a small Quango with a limited brief, papers, often complicated, have to be studied with patience and assessed; long, sometimes complex and often *parti pris* arguments have to be listened to and judged. The Great and the Good do not have a monopoly of such skills, but neither are those skills and potentialities evenly or widely spread. If, as we should, we are to consider fully the views of 'ordinary' people, it does not follow that a computer-profiled, fully representative 'ordinary' person can put those views, can effectively express them. A novelist might do better. Equality before God and the law does not mean equal usefulness on a committee, any more than on a football field or in a thousand other situations.

Debates about the composition of the Arts Council were and may still be not so Simon-pure but are no doubt still frequent, inevitably fierce, and paradigms of the present confusion. 'The dozen or so members of the Council should be democratically elected.' All right, but again from what constituencies? 'We would start with members of local government authorities, with those members who have relevant committee experience, with Chambers of Commerce, Townswomen's Guilds, Women's Institutes.' But aren't there others in all centres of population who might have at least as much or even more to bring to such a committee? 'Yes, but they wouldn't have been democratically elected, so to appoint them, no matter how good they were, would be unacceptably *un*democratic. We would also want some actors, producers, writers, painters, musicians, all elected by vote and proposed through their professional bodies: Equity, the Musicians' Union, the Society of Authors. Also some others such as officers from the Regional Arts Associations.'

But wouldn't such a membership run even more than the usual risks that the Council would divide into a number of interested pressure-groups – the theatre people arguing with the musicians and so on? 'Well, there would be a few others representing lay opinion, officials of non-artistic unions (these are always proposed, on the grounds that though they may know little about art they do know what their lads think, are the workers' true representatives); plus the odd head teacher, even a stray MP or retired senior civil servant; but all elected through a properly constituted professional body, not chosen behind closed doors somewhere in Whitehall.'

This is not a parody; it is slightly more measured than many such proposals. It would produce a Council of existing or emerging warhorses, some with much committee experience but not much knowledge of the arts; and of people some of whom knew their own arts and so might well have a single-minded determination to fight their corners for them. At its worst, and this does happen, a union representative feels so much a mandated figure as to be willing to block a new direction or experiment in his members' art-form on the grounds that it runs against some long-standing restrictive practice. Such a largely *parti pris* dog's breakfast of a committee is unlikely to learn the practice of civil discussion and can quickly become the tool of the full-time Secretariat.

Some selective representation can be useful. There is even more value in adding some whose names have come up not because they have the right social or even professional connections but because informed people have come to recognise their merits, skill, knowledge, objectivity – even though they are not by nature 'joiners'. Such people are hardly likely to be proposed by any of the constituencies invoked or invented by those who argue for entirely representative elections – 'fully democratic accountability' is the favourite phrase – to the membership of committees of any and every kind. The old system had more to be said against it than for it; the new systems proposed by some people would be even less fair and effective. There are no easy solutions, just a pragmatic putting together which recognises the claims of democratic election but recognises also that some so elected are likely to be semi-professional place-seekers and that some fine roses prefer to blush unseen, but could be encouraged to come into the light of day for a good cause.

To some extent this happens with the old system. New names are regularly added to the lists critics like to dismiss as consisting solely of the Great and the Good. There are forms of application for those who think they have arrived at the point where they could usefully serve. They have to name referees who, they hope, will speak well of them in confidential opinions; they are sometimes mistaken. What one knows little about is the cultural range and understanding of those who then consider the possible names, new and old, of people to be invited to serve on any particular committee. How often do the old door-opening or door-closing invocations such as 'a safe pair of hands' or its opposite, 'unsound', still come up?

In 1980 the government decided that 'the trawl' could be made more open, through public advertisement. The central idea was that people who would not have thought of putting themselves forward, and were not likely to be known as yet to those who keep the list of possible public appointees, might be suggested by their admiring colleagues. To some extent this happened. There was not, though, much difference between the names proposed in response to the public advertisements and those already thought of in Whitehall. That should not be surprising; in any field most of the competent and emerging people will be known, whatever their politics or existing public profiles.

The more surprising result was that many people suggested themselves. Surprising because such behaviour is generally thought to be un-English. They order these things differently in France. There, a would-be candidate for membership of an important and influential committee will as a matter of normal routine write directly to the Minister concerned if he has a way in; or to a Minister or civil servant he knows, and ask him to have a word with his colleague in the relevant Department of State. There is no feeling of impropriety there; nor would a Minister usually recommend someone who seemed unlikely to bear out his encomiums.

Just as surprising, and slightly ludicrous, is the present government's decision to hire a commercial head-hunting agency to find the names of suitable Quango members. Absolutely no need for that. Members of likely British groups all know intimately the effective and ineffective members among their number; that's one thing which works.

Still, the British sense of greater propriety in these things is at the least a half-myth, and our apophthegms as always betray us; this is the land of the discreet word in the ear (that delicate euphemism for log-rolling). Many people do not hesitate to suggest to their more influential friends that a knighthood would be agreeable; or as second or third best an honorary degree. 'Some people who have titles already regard membership of the Governors of the Royal Shakespeare Company as a desirable further privilege and let it be known, indirectly or even directly, that they would be happy to be elected to the Board' – thus ran the response to one member of that Board who complained to the Secretary of not being given enough to do, of being expected to be a well wined and dined rubber-stamp.

*

As late as the end of the Seventies you might, if invited to lunch at the Athenaeum, overhear fragments of a conversation between some of the great Proconsuls of the Culture: two or three university Vice-Chancellors, for instance, discussing whom they might suggest to Number 10 as a likely Chairman of the BBC; agreeing also that so-and-so from their number might have a word with Sir Humphrey, the Permanent Secretary, or with the editor of *The Times*.

From this distance that looks so out-of-date a way of going on as to be comical. But as always we should, in dismissing it, try to clear our minds of cant. Those people were not plotting. In their enclosed way they thought they were doing their best for their country; they were not illiberal or philistine or feathering their own financial or honorific nests, and they did not live by ideological gobbledegook. They did assume likely agreement on the basis of a common cultural disposition and language; an internalised consensus with tones to go with it. The arm's-length-consensus principle could only be assumed to be a good thing when there was a consensus; there is no longer. Their days are over. Vice-Chancellors now have little public influence, and many of them, as we saw earlier, far from being philosophers or at least statesmen of higher education, have been appointed as good businessmen and raisers of sponsorship money. To appreciate how far things have changed you need only read the press advertisements for posts of Vice-Chancellor (salary not named, of course; that really would be going too far, just at present). Most of those announcements seem to have been drafted by 'Public Appointment Advisory' enterprises – so plastic is their prose, so unintellectual and unacademic, so window-dressing, is their higher-executive-in-higher-education jargon.

Any self-respecting candidate called for interview might begin by telling the committee they should do better, that in its public prose as elsewhere the university ought to show it stands for more than the aims of the consumerist-and-vocational-driven society (and might begin by cleaning or closing its existing Public Affairs operations).

*

A final word about Quangos, old-style and new. It was noted earlier that nowadays the members of Quangos are usually placemen and -women, expected to behave as if mandated by those who appointed them rather than to exercise a patient tolerance before conflicting evidence and arguments; and that the money they spend, often considerable amounts, is largely unaccountable; and that they are now very often paid. It is plain that another name is needed for these instruments: PULCs, perhaps – Plushy Unaccountable Loaded Cabals.

ii JUDE AND HIS KIND

'But remember his education, the age in which he grew up,' observed Arkady. 'Education?' broke in Bazarov. 'Every man must educate himself as I've done, for instance . . . And as for the age, why should I depend on it? Let it rather depend on me. No, my dear fellow, that's all shallowness, want of backbone!'

Ivan Turgenev, *Fathers and Sons*, 1862

For my part I am very sorry for him. It is an uneasy lot at best, to be what we call highly taught and yet not to enjoy: to be present at this great spectacle of life and never to be liberated from a small hungry shivering self.

George Eliot, *Middlemarch*, 1872

Bazarov's briskness and George Eliot's sympathy are only two of the references throughout European literature to what Arnold called the 'aliens' and the 'saving remnant' (his most uplifting phrase among several); and whom others, according to time and place, called the 'anxious corporals', the latest Pelican sticking out of their back-pockets during the last war; and the 'scholarship boys'. The French have many phrases about the role of the undisputed intellectual; the English have many about the search for a role by those who from a standing start seek to be intellectuals.

They are the Jude the Obscures, the Leonard Basts, the Gordon Comstocks and several characters, especially women, from H. G. Wells. They were looked at much earlier, in the section on Adult Education. They call for special attention here because they are unacknowledged members of such a 'clerisy' as we have. As Arnold says in the passage at the head of this chapter, they have tended to have a hard time of it, as they tried to climb out of perhaps bookless environments, and certainly environments which did little or nothing to nourish a nascent questioning of their own and others' lives, of the terms within which their experience is predicated.

They include the bachelor in the terrace house opposite, living with his mother, who had a shelf-ful of encyclopaedias, who lent you books and told you what Pelmanism was and something of Esperanto. They are members of classes run by the Workers' Educational Association and the University Extra-Mural Departments. They are among those who enrol with the Open University. They are those among committed young teachers, men and women of course, who by choice work in tough schools in deprived districts.

There are still many of them, scattered across the country, though it is unfashionable to say so and their very existence will be denied by many. Relativism is indeed making them more isolated than ever, but it would have been against nature if they had disappeared. They are a certain *kind* of person, not determined by any particular age or class; and they will continue to exist.

Just before it was dissolved in the early Eighties the national Advisory Council for Adult and Continuing Education surveyed the size and nature of the demand for that kind of education. There was a much greater demand than was recognised or catered for, even though over a million were students in adult classes at the time.

So those who find reasons for postulating the disappearance or decline of the 'aliens' are making a hypothesis not looking at facts. The hypothesis says: most of the 'aliens' were bright people trapped in their class through lack of opportunity (true, of many); now that opportunities abound for any bright person to move on and up educationally all those have been to grammar school, or sixth-form college or the upper forms of comprehensives and then been absorbed by other social groups. Many Access courses are on offer for those who fell away earlier. Anyone so inclined can buy good paperbacks cheaply, books which cover the whole span of human knowledge, or records and cassettes. 'Aliens' are or can be well-nourished, no longer starved. We need no 'aliens'; there are no 'aliens'.

This is to confuse intelligence with what Arnold called 'a curiosity about their best self . . . a bent for seeing things as they are', to confuse 'brains' with a speculative intelligence. By no means all who move out of the working class are or will become aliens. Some of those who do move out and some from other classes will remain in certain important senses aliens all their lives. That is their cast of mind, thank God.

The argument can be taken further and then stood on its head. Whilst the above new advantages may be admitted, it can also be argued that today's aliens have a harder job in escaping into a questioning uninhibited air than did their predecessors. The physical and financial and to some extent the social class constraints on intellectual and imaginative development are fewer, certainly. That progress need no longer feel so much like cliff-climbing, hand over hand, is not so plainly a wrenching business, this pulling away from a home environment which, for all its limitations, may be shrewd and loving in its own ways. A pull-away remains, though of a psychologically different kind. Hitherto your nearest and dearest might have thought you were getting above yourself, or been bemused by you, or done their best to help you along out of a traditional if uncomprehending respect for knowledge.

Today the surrounding culture, the enveloping levelling fog, is harder to break out from, insistent that its way of looking at the world should be sufficient for anyone, that there is no need to look further, to break out, to go all queer and different. The hindrances, the disinclinings, now come from the whole ambient air. The enemies, the discouragers, are no longer those forces which tried to insist and certainly assumed that you should know your place and stay there, that you belong to the lower orders, that critical judgments are not for you, that it is an impertinence to reach after those intellectual opportunities open to 'your betters'. It is good, naturally, that all such attitudes have been much weakened.

Today's discouragers are those voices which suggest that even to seek more knowledge and understanding is an unjustifiedly snooty idea (the better word, 'aspiration', would hardly pass their lips); that it is an uppity betrayal of the 'lads' and 'lasses' all around you who know a satisfying life when they see it, and follow it, whether as teenagers in pubs and discos night after night or as husbands and wives staring for three hours a night at the telly. Completely sufficient unto themselves, creaturely worlds where every persuasive voice, and there are very many, insists on the fullness, the total adequacy of this life for everyone in their right mind.

To come back to the 'saving remnant'; or, to use Auden's less grand phrase, to those 'Ironic points of light [which] Flash out wherever the Just / Exchange their messages ... [and] Show an affirming flame'. People such as these are among the leading-edges, or nerve-ends, of a democracy; of any society which has not been reduced to or let itself become an industrious ant-heap; or in thrall to a dictatorship. These people are air-holes, antennae sensitive to quality changes; irritants in the oyster.

CHAPTER FOURTEEN

Diverse Voices, and Opinion-Formers

Not the great nor well-bespoke,
But the mere uncounted folk
Of whose life and death is none
Report or lamentation

Rudyard Kipling, 'A Charm'

Moreover, whom are you writing for? The scholars whose concern it is to
pass judgment on books recognise no worth but that of learning. . . . Souls
which are commonplace and ordinary . . . cannot perceive the grace and
the weight of sustained elegant discourse. And these two species occupy the
whole world! Men of the third species . . . composed of minds which are
rare and well-adjusted, are so rare that . . . to try to please them is time
half-wasted.

Michel de Montaigne, Collected Essays (trans. Screech)

It is or should be axiomatic that a democracy needs diverse voices;
diverse and overlapping voices. It should also be axiomatic, but today
is not, that some voices are better worth listening to than others. It is
not by accident that Jules Benda's *The Treason of the Clerks* (1927)
is frequently referred to in England; it both puts off and fascinates.
It puts off because it suggests the unacceptably French notion of a
'clerisy' active in public life – Sartre marching on the Left Bank at
the head of the students in the late Sixties. We had Bertrand Russell
at the head of a CND march, but that was uncharacteristic. Here,
from demagogues in the popular press to some of the most scrupulous
intellectual voices, French assumptions about the public commit-
ments of intellectuals are mistrusted and certainly not thought transferable. The tabloid demagogues would switch to their populist
mode: 'Who do they think they are, laying down the law for us?' –
which comes ill from people who lay down the law in their editorials
every day. For the more intellectual the French style suggests the big

public bow-wow, the stuffed shirt dabbling in 'vulgarisation', in English a term of dismissal. Yet Benda's book fascinates, perhaps because it suggests over here a neglect by intellectuals, those who 'should know better', of a critical public role.

Virtually no one in England today would speak of 'the clerisy', let alone of the need for a clerisy. Among much else, it suggests 'clerics' and so the parsonical or finger-wagging. Dictionary entries on the word are thin; they tend merely to tell us that Coleridge used it in 'On the Constitution of the Church and State' and add the minimum of description. Colmer remarks that Coleridge said that the task of the clerisy was to guide 'The intellectual and moral development of the nation and disseminate learning'. In *Table Talk*, Coleridge could even speak of, simply, 'The clerisy of a nation'. In America, both Emerson and James Russell Lowell used the term but, after them, there is little or nothing.

In the country of the blind not even the one-eyed man is king. Yet the idea of justified distinction lingers, outside those areas where it has not been abandoned; as in sport or accepted styles of beauty. Even Raymond Williams, surprisingly, was led to say that 'Paternalism is power with Conscience'.

People tell themselves they do not 'believe in' clerisies or gurus or gatekeepers, being of the English, who stand on their own two feet, make their own decisions and trust the good sense of ordinary people. There they tend to leave it. But they ought to take at least two further steps. First, to recognise that a society such as this needs, not what it largely has today, an inadequately literate, comprehensively abused majority, but a critically literate majority. Second, and the harder to recognise – indeed, even to utter it is regarded as heinous by the populists – that a small minority of people will never be able to live up to the demands a democracy makes of its citizens. One has to go on acting as if they can be so educated; and to go on trying to help them all their lives – so far as one can in a free society, to protect them.

It suits the persuaders to deny both the above considerations; it is dangerous blindness for the rest not to accept them and their implications. One has all the time to be working towards an open society capable of respecting and using its openness in the right ways, able to quarrel intelligently with itself and able to conceive that there are mutual dues.

The Way We Live Now

i A MIXED BUNCH, MAINLY OFFICIAL

Against all this background, what diverse voices may be discovered nowadays, ruling out the unabashedly interested voices, the more perversely self-regarding commentators, the unreconstructed authoritarian lay priests?

The first group are both little thought of and little respected. One of the less well-aimed *obiter dicta* of George Bernard Shaw was that 'those who can, do; those who can't, teach'. Naturally some people enter teaching by default; not for the money, for there's little there, but for what might be thought a cushy, not greatly demanding, life with long holidays. But go into school classrooms at all levels, or visit those multitudinous voluntarily enrolled groups of adults learning in the evenings or university seminars and tutorials, and you will be impressed by the spread and strength of the dedication – by the belief in the worthwhileness of the pursuit of knowledge for its own sake, and the respect due to those who seek it; all this often pursued in their own time and sometimes after a day's work. For some teachers, inevitably, the sense of commitment fades with middle age, especially where the work is exceptionally taxing (and stress has increased in the last decade). It does not fade for all; and is often recovered. These are not a clerisy, neither the teachers nor the taught – the idea would startle them – but they are an essential part of the necessary, fundamental texture of a democracy: a quietly dignified group of people who are trying to live up to rare demands they come to believe are made on them, including the just demands from outside.

*

What of the official, the titular, the at least in part elected official voices of society, the Commons and the Lords? There are some thoughtful, intelligent, imaginative and devoted Members of Parliament. But some are not worth the space they are given in which to speak on behalf of the community. They are party placemen protecting their posts, or big mouths uttering banalities and prejudice which they imagine will make them admired spokesmen for the bulk of their constituents. Listen to them pronouncing on public or private morals in general, or on particular important issues – the nature of education, the role of broadcasting or the case for the arts to be publicly supported (or on foreigners) – and you will be as often as not shocked at the low level of their discourse. We are not as well served here as we should be, as we have a right to be.

Still, they can as a body do better from time to time on major issues: on capital punishment or racism; on some such matters they have by a majority rightly resisted referenda, which might well have revealed some very unpleasant attitudes normally kept fairly well hidden by or from most of us. Two surveys in the early Nineties revealed that three-quarters of the population are in favour of the return of the death penalty. At these points Parliament is exhibiting one of the basic truths of a working democracy: that its elected spokesmen will sometimes do better than most of their constituents.

In certain respects the House of Lords does better nowadays than the Commons. To some extent it is carrying on the best in the traditions of the Proconsuls, who felt that *noblesse oblige* in social responsibility.

Before saying any more about the virtues of the Lords it is essential to say – obvious though it is – that the hereditary element in the Lords is overwhelmingly the biggest single undemocratic device we still accept. This case is not weakened by the fact that some hereditary peers work hard and intelligently; it would be surprising if all were absentees except when whipped in, or rural backwoodsmen, or slick types trading their titles for seats on City boards. But all in all the system has nothing to be said in its favour, and those – there are a few – who seek to defend it are trading in flannel.

There are also some landed gentry, with inherited titles below the rank needed to qualify for the Lords, whose assured membership of the Commons is still almost hereditary; the family have held that seat for generations. They are not always the brightest of people, but deference, vicarious snobbery, ensure the succession. One of them recently objected to any enquiry into allegations that British para-troops in the Falklands campaign had deliberately killed their pris-oners; we had more important things to do than being punitive towards our lads. So much for the Geneva Convention, which charity suggests he may not have read in spite of being a member of the House's Committee on Defence. Had he read it the case would be worse.

As the years pass and as, very slowly, the nominated life peers increase their percentage (here is another instance in which the demand for 'a fully elected peerage' would be a mistake, unless a most subtle definition of a 'constituency' were arrived at) the Lords' ability in serious and informed debate increases too, as does the comparison with debates in the Commons. The case for a second chamber, with no hereditary element, becomes stronger; a chamber composed of people not dependent, as are Euro-MPs, on regular re-election by a huge geographical constituency – though reappointment might be a possible element – but people nominated/appointed for their talent and application; as a limited and controlled backstop to the Commons.

*

To echo Chapter 5: from the beginning of broadcasting in Britain it was taken for granted by its practitioners that the new form of communication would become a valuable and respected voice in the country, a force for unbiased comment on all aspects of the common and the individual life. To some extent that good hope was fulfilled. The idea of the public service here was at bottom admirable; and its increasing weakness today should be a matter of concern to governments of all persuasions.

The press, the Fourth Estate, long regarded as one of the primary democratic organs of communication, can still occasionally live up to that honorific. But the pressures against are great and increasing. A good deal has already been said about the popular press, about how its claims to speak for the 'ordinary man and woman' are ill-founded or at best both partial and distorted.

The broadsheets, the 'quality' press, are not in much better shape. They still pay attention to issues which matter, and some of their writers – oddly, the political journalists more than the literary ones – are, though some trade in instant opinionation, weighty and well-considered. But the armies of 'commentators' of all kinds go on multiplying.

The competition is fierce here too and these newspapers are led ineluctably down the populist paths – for example the hectic, fashion-conscious weekend magazines – presumably for competitive reasons. If increased circulations result from following them, those routes will be taken, and regarded as self-justifying.

*

What, then, of the (usually weekly) 'journals of opinion'? Many have died, their places taken by journals centred on professional interests; though some of those – for example, *The Economist* – give attention to more general, citizen's issues. None of them has as good a spread as *New Society*, an early specialist-focused weekly, had. They have also been damaged by the broadsheets' interest in investigative journalism, usually on important issues; that did some good but is by now too often dressed up as spirited crime detection. As compared with the weekly magazines, the broadsheets, daily or Sunday, have the money to lead in this, at least in paying for access to sources and in column inches.

The increasing weakness of the journals of opinion has therefore been due to the increasingly narrow professionalisation of the lives of those who might have been readers and who now feel they haven't the time to think about general things, or to read the literary or arts pages. More important has been these weeklies' difficulties in finding a sense of direction, whatever their politics. Relativism works like dry rot. When you try to stand on a board it gives way under you. So you take refuge in either narrow-minded haranguing or snide smart-Alec-ism; or the successive fashions of your readers' professions.

ii REVIEWERS; AND SOME CRITICS

The more you startle the reader, the more he will be able to startle others with a succession of smart intellectual shocks. The most admired of our Reviews is saturated with this sort of electrical matter... The intrinsic merits of an author are a question of very subordinate consideration to ... supplying the town with a sufficient number of grave [those are in decline now] or brilliant topics for the consumption of the next three months.
    William Hazlitt, 'On Criticism', repr. in *Table Talk*, 1821

The prospect of having to read them [the latest batch of ill-assorted books], and even the smell of the paper, affects him like the prospect of eating cold ground-rice pudding flavoured with castor oil... The great majority of reviewers give an inadequate or misleading account of the book that is dealt with ... That kind of thing [having a much bigger team of reviewers so that more are knowledgeable across a wider range of subjects] is very difficult to organise. In practice the editor always finds himself reverting to his team of hacks – his 'regulars', as he calls them.
    George Orwell, 'Confessions of a Book Reviewer'

One cannot review a bad book without showing off.
    W. H. Auden, *The Dyer's Hand*, 1962

The situation has not improved since Hazlitt wrote in the nineteenth century and Orwell in the mid-twentieth. In some ways the pressures are worse. Within some newspapers and weeklies, straightforward literary pages have been reduced and the pressure on reviewers to be bright, to be 'brilliant' in Hazlitt's sense and to 'show off' in Auden's, have increased. Literary editors are under pressure and look quirky if you are ingenuous enough to send a book back and suggest they try someone else who knows more about the subject than you do. Life is too short and anyway the 'regulars' can be trusted to turn in something readable and on time. Regular reviewing is still a way of paying the bills until your own big book appears, so those hacks deserve sympathy.

Looking at the books which are reviewed you have to conclude that there are still too many, or too many from too few and too narrow ranges – say, a range of currently fashionable novelists – and that even when a book does deserve more attention it will be lucky to be given more than the usual eight hundred words.

There are still some good reviewers, whether they be hack regulars or academics trusted not to be dull, who will not put brightness before every other quality. The *London Review of Books* (subsidised by the Arts Council) has to be read: it chooses books for review without much attention to current fashions or an insistence on short deadlines; it gives space to its writers and moves outside Britain for many of them; most are extremely well-informed. Yet somehow it seems enclosed as though produced only for a very small number of extremely intelligent and well-informed people – which it is – and as though it is not aware or does not believe that there might be a wider but still intelligent, if not so well-informed, audience out there; who could be helpfully reached. The *Times Literary Supplement* has some very good things but hasn't a particular intellectual centre and may not seek one; as is its right. *New Statesman and Society* no longer gives the importance to the arts and literature which it once did, as in the days of V. S. Pritchett's Books Page, but is much better today than the small change of current opinion usually suggests. *Granta* is very good in its way but is a different kind of magazine, a solid and usually single-issue compilation. The most intellectually taxing journal is *New Left Review*, but that does not have or seek other than a predictably very small and closely focused readership.

In the broadsheets, daily or Sunday, the best reviewers from wherever they hail can give the impression of intelligent and scrupulous catholicity whilst acknowledging their own limits. They are not too much beset by the fear of being thought dully expository. The worst among them are the up-market equivalents of the 'rent-a-mouth' columnists in the popular press and those who appear in the increasing number of low-level chat-programmes on radio. Radio 4 in particular is beset by the fear of seeming solemn or highbrow, so that, as was noted earlier, its book programmes, such as *A Good Read*, are almost all now just unrestrained enthusiasm with rarely a limiting judgment made and virtually every book hailed as 'brilliant', 'lovely' 'super', 'enthralling'. That soon becomes, whether in broadcasting or in the press, a further undervaluing, and certainly understretching of their readers.

Sydney Smith declared: 'I never read a book before reviewing it; it prejudices a man so.' He has his modern descendants. One academic, a successful Sunday reviewer, heard with surprise that a colleague had declined to review a book of five hundred pages because he hadn't time to read it through and so do justice to it. The seasoned man replied, as to an earnest but uncomprehending-of-the-realities-of-life novice: 'You surely don't expect to a read a book for review all the way through if it's very long? You dip and skip and taste. That should give you enough ideas to fill the eight hundred words.'

There are many devices for disguising this skating on the surface. You may, for example, pick on one weakness in a book – it may be one of few relatively slight weaknesses in an otherwise good book – and hammer at it until it seems like a major flaw running right through the text; good qualities can be ignored or only briefly mentioned. A strange process has taken place, rather similar to what happened if, as a child, you begin to spin violently in one direction and then cannot pull out of the spin, change direction or slow down: you spin till you drop; or reach that eight hundred words. You hadn't meant to go on like that but can't stop yourself until your space is used. There should be a name for that mental process: Inescapable Distorted Spin, or something like that. It is also another form of 'showing off', applied to good books as to bad; a low trick but quite common – more common than malevolent reviews inspired either by personal animus or because the editor has suggested a 'hatchet job', since someone 'is due to be taken down a peg'; those do exist.

Or a reviewer may pick on one slight element in the author's manner, tone or style and make an *ad hominem* remark about it so as to produce what looks like a carefully honed dismissal of the book and its author.

Everything must seem to have the ease of someone who writes simply and fluently, without effort; relaxed, knowing, conversational, from the deeps of a well-nourished mind, one whose judgment is totally assured and to be trusted. Lightness is all; 'not to get caught, not to be left behind', at all costs not to seem earnest, labouring, uncertain in the face of a book which, in most cases, you could not have written yourself. This whole style is, especially with academics taking time off, a way of signalling to your peers that, even though you do a lot of newspaper reviewing and may even have an annual contract, you would not dream of taking it seriously. The 'common man' and those who think the broadsheets the pinnacle of intellectual life might – you comfortably think – learn a little from it; and the money is good. In scholarly journals, house-rules usually inhibit this light style, and so does the wish to demonstrate that you are at bottom as straightforwardly scholarly as your peers.

Whether in the newspapers or the scholarly journals and whether from Oxbridge or elsewhere, some academic reviewers have one particularly bad habit: they pinch ideas and do not give their sources. Once an unattributed theft has been made by one person, later users can hardly be blamed for adopting it as part of the public stock of knowledge, a public right of way or common land.

*

All the foregoing has been about literary reviewers. Reviewers of the other arts, not in specialist journals but, again, in newspapers, seem just as lightweight; and some are routinely anti-Establishment; so that one comes to expect little in the way of good judgment. At the turn into the Eighties the Arts Council decided not to renew its grant to the D'Oyly Carte Opera Company (which for many years had held the copyright in performances of Gilbert and Sullivan's work). The company was in a boring, ill-produced and poorly performed seam. The reviewers then predictably savaged the Arts Council for its 'élitist' attitudes, didn't consider the level of the performances at all, but demanded that this 'much-loved institution' have its grant restored.

BBC Television prepared a short feature to expose this butchery. The commentator presented the issue as one simply attributable to Arts Council snobbery. His introduction was followed by a scene from one of the company's regular performances. It thoroughly vindicated the Arts Council's decision. What kind of judgment had made the BBC go ahead with so clear an exposure of its own critical ineptitude? Perhaps the show was live and the performance not seen in advance. There's charity for you, or face-saving; but the pattern is typical. Gilbert and Sullivan are now out of copyright, much better performances have been given by different companies and the D'Oyly Carte Company has had a useful reform – even those reviewers say so; but they have not acknowledged their injustice to the Arts Council.

There was a similar conventionally anti-Establishment uproar when the Arts Council, in 1984, its grant badly cut by the government, decided that the butter could no longer be spread more and more thinly over every client but that at last (after hesitating to do so for years) it had to make judgments of quality. It had been saved from having to do so by annually increasing grants. The uproar was enormous and again predictable; as though this had been mayhem on a grand scale. The Council had proposed to cut two out of forty recipients. None of the protestors addressed the question of those two companies' standards of work.

In spite of the air of sophistication there is overall in English reviewing an intransigent parochialism and domesticity. Hence the treatment across part of the literary field of Edward Said's Reith lectures in the early Nineties, 'Representations of the Intellectual'. He was speaking about the responsibilities of intellectuals (that alone would be enough to put him in the firing line) and clearly trying to reach what he thought of as the ideal Reith lecturer's audience, not all of them scholars but many intelligent lay-readers. He aimed at a demotic style for that presumably very British audience; that is not easy at any time. For a Palestinian who teaches in New York, it requires a considerable act of sympathetic adaptation.

He was well received in some places but condescendingly reviewed in several newspapers and journals. His style was mocked, by some because he had not been able to remove all professional language, by others because he had dared to attempt *haute vulgarisation*. Even more, he was criticised because he had dared – or been foolish enough – to look into the question of whether intellectuals had public duties outside their professional and creative lives and if so in what terms. He had plainly hit a tender spot. At the lowest level one reviewer became 'racist': how could a Palestinian understand these essentially Western concepts?

Something similar happened in the reviews of Said's *Culture and Imperialism* (1993). A few gave the impression, their authors bouncing up and down with dismissal, that Said had attacked Jane Austen and Charlotte Brontë on the grounds that they had paid virtually no attention to the fact that Britain was in their time an imperialist power, its middle and upper classes grown rich on the subjugation of millions, especially of coloured millions.

That would have been crude in any critic and unthinkable in one of Said's subtlety. He was saying something different, more interesting and well worth pursuing: he made well, the – after all, obvious – point that, to a degree not always recognised, all writers are culturally conditioned. 'To a degree not always recognised' because nowadays one often comes across the argument from 'cultural materialism' and, with that, 'cultural determinism', whereby cultural conditioning is elided into, precisely, determinism. Said does not and would not do that. He does not say that Jane Austen and Charlotte Brontë *ought* to have described the evils of Empire. He observes that they and many another writer did not discuss such things, did not feel drawn to or disposed to or called upon to do that; this is a different approach from the one his critics fathered on him. He knows conditioning is not determining and that Jane Austen and Charlotte Brontë rise out of their times – think only of Charlotte Brontë's 'feminism' (to use a favoured word but one cruder than is properly needed) – and become great novelists about aspects of the human condition at all times and places. Said also reflects, as he has the right to do, on the extent to which the culture of any time exercises a largely unconscious self-censorship, a selective steering on almost everyone; perhaps on everyone. A very worthwhile argument. One felt like apologising to Said. The metropolitan reviewer can also be very parochial.

And domestic, as in Auden's 'English Literary Happy Family' where some things are not much talked about and where a theme which runs throughout the present book is again illustrated: the thinness of most public debate on cultural matters; as with the lack of serious discussion about the Broadcasting Act of 1990; and there are other instances.

Academics do not do well here. They would rather not acknowledge the terms of their comfortable lives. Most kept their heads down during the troubles of the late Sixties or acted as though the students were saying nothing of importance but only acting like children. They did not question their own servicing role in the new meritocratic society; they saw no larger or more challenging role; they did not ask where their students come from, socially; they ignored remarkable opportunities offered by expansion, especially in rethinking the definitions of subjects and thinking for the first time how best they could approach the many more and new kinds of students. Either they just did not want to know or the questions did not occur to them.

If as an academic, or as any other kind of professional with intellectual interests, you enjoy such a mixture of attitudes, you are likely to accept, unthinkingly and almost innocently (though with an innocence well honed by sophistication), the principle that 'the great mass of people' are best left to their own devices, have nowadays what they want in most things, know what interests them (that old familiar mixture of myths), and may have some wisdoms which serve them well and are not in the ken of more intellectual people.

This may be at bottom, but is not always, fed by a sense – again hardly recognised – of superiority. When that is in play it usually takes cover under a mask of flippancy, a 'lightness of touch', a playing around, a demonstration that you would never be solemn about such things in the way the French or the even heavier German intellectuals can be. Within that protective frame you are allowed to be, as seems needed, aggressive in your showing off. This kind of smart Alec can have a hard carapace; it is all part of the ineffable air of privilege and superiority.

The late Richard Crossman, philosophy don from Oxford and Socialist politician, once announced that he 'stood up for the common man's right to be trivial if he pleases'. He said that with the apparently outward smile which is really inturned, the mark of being quite pleased with what one is about to utter. Of course 'the common man' has that right. Don't we all? It provides, incidentally, the perfect space for the commercial television and tabloid press and advertising exploiters. We all have the right to say that; and whoever may hear us has the right to ignore us.

iii NO COMMITTEES, PLEASE, WE'RE ENGLISH

A few writers, artists and intellectuals, have been willing to give time to committee service they thought might be valuable; generally, the full-time administrators find them useful because they may bring new insights into work which easily becomes routine. But for most, no. One sees why they have been dubbed 'the chattering classes'; that tells a great deal both about them and about the English attitude to such people. Not 'the talking classes' or 'the discussing classes' or 'the intellectual classes' or (Heaven forfend on their behalf) 'the intelligentsia', or even 'the arguing classes'. 'The chattering classes' suggests rooks, magpies, starlings – chattering in the eaves – nattering away endlessly but weightlessly, very much for its own sake and for self-display. The phrase makes a harsh and philistine judgment but one sufficiently well aimed to be embarrassing. Not power without commitment, but talk – opinions, views, attitudes, postures – without commitment.

Those who do accept – but never seek; only those aspiring to be Vice-Chancellors and the like do that; and they are identifiable – public committee service usually do so on the 'be willing to walk the plank for the public good' principle. It would be so much more comfortable for an academic to stay in that pleasant Chair. One has to become used to responses from colleagues on the lines: 'I do wonder what prompts you to give so much time to that sort of thing.' They are right to surmise that to undertake 'that sort of thing' will delay or extinguish the book you have been planning; you too know that. But their disinclination is more deep-seated.

Such attitudes have been growing since at least the turn of the century, as the rise of relativism and populism gradually made proconsular activities or even modest activities *pro bono publico* seem patronising or pompous. Yet they survived fairly well until at least the Sixties. It has been shown that in the last couple of decades the rejection of them has been strengthened, as consensual political attitudes turned into the confrontational.

The limiting labels stick, so that if you wrote the 'Ode on the Intimations of Immortality' but also served on a few committees you would first be described, suspiciously, as 'a committee man' or even 'a congenital committee man'. This is a pity because outside these islands the British are thought to be exceptionally good committee members; where 'good' means fair-minded and dedicated; often eccentric but unstuffy and independently minded. Such as Julian Huxley, John Maud, Joseph Needham, Mary Warnock, Edward Boyle, Lionel Robbins, John Fulton, Diana Albemarle, Fred Dainton, Arnold Goodman and many another.

iv JOBS FOR INTELLECTUALS?

Culture has always been in minority keeping . . . the minority is being cut off as never before from the powers that rule the world.

F. R. Leavis

Who Needs a Clerisy?

[Those concerned for cultural improvement are best] led, not by their class
spirit but by a general humane *spirit, by the love of human perfection.*
Matthew Arnold

Gramsci among others noted the tremendous increase in the number
of and the importance given to intellectuals in modern society. It is
an importance accorded because of their *uses* to modern society, not
for their role as critical voices within such a society. They help to
service that society; and for the rest they talk among themselves.

Both Leavis and Arnold are not much called in evidence today.
Leavis is criticised for insisting that culture is in the hands of a
minority and always will be; that the rest are in the hands of the
mass persuaders. That the maintenance of 'high culture' (not simply
the high arts) has been almost entirely the province of a few is true,
and has been historically inevitable for the social and educational
reasons already discussed. But one cannot consign everyone else to
the mass world outside; there are wider responsibilities and they
remain, however society changes. In not sufficiently stressing this
Leavis was open to criticism. But in the passage above he makes,
quite early, a different, important and accurate point: that the 'powers
that be' pay decreasing attention to the highest cultural reach and
being and quality of a nation; they are in that sense unfit to rule a
civil society.

Some passages from Arnold seem to go in different directions, to
be more class-bound than he knew or to be full of inflated rhetorical
gestures. The one above – though we may think the phrase about 'the
love of human perfection' excessive, we can translate it adequately for
our own unrhetorical manners – is neat, puts 'class' to one side,
where it should belong, and concentrates on what should be the very
heart of these debates, 'a general *humane* spirit'.

*

Time to sum up, though without the expectation that a generally
acceptable comprehensive definition of the 'role' of intellectuals (even
if such a phrase is accepted in the first place) will be arrived at. What
such a role is *not*, is much more easily stated. 'Clerisy' not being
available, its possible meanings are not caught in phrases such as
'gatekeepers' (too bossy, instrumental and social-scientific), 'opinion-
formers' (much the same; and smart-Alecky), 'gamekeepers' or
'poachers' (crude, and suitable only for discussions on public

censorship), 'taste-setters' and 'trend-setters' (ugh! both straight from the status-conscious area where the awful voices live).

Charles Frankel, a magisterial teacher who insisted on taking first-year classes as well as post-graduate, was Distinguished Professor of Philosophy at Columbia and believed that people such as himself, and others as lucky as he was, should have two main duties: to be like the 'maggots in the soft cheese of modern society' and to listen politely, not to force your views down the throats of others. He was shot dead in bed whilst trying patiently to convince a pair of drug-crazed burglars of the error of their ways. He would not have thought his end in any way invalidated his life.

Colmer on Coleridge goes wider, on this role and these duties: 'To preserve the stores and to guard the treasures of past civilisations and thus to bind the present with the past ... but especially to diffuse through the whole community ... that quantity and quality of knowledge which was indispensable both for the understanding of those rights and for the performance of the duties correspondent.' Gramsci comes in here too, surprisingly sounding like both Coleridge and Arnold. He writes of the need for 'critical self-consciousness – the creation of an élite of intellectuals' – to go out and teach.

Every one of these attempts at a job-description points towards a duty which is habitually pushed aside or even rejected today. They imply the making of judgments, of what an American academic – criticising the overwhelmingly shallow-rooted opportunism he found in much American university life today – saw as the obligation upon university teachers to 'bear witness', not automatically to accept majority opinion as a value-judgment in itself. This is to recognise, in Irving Howe's phrase, the demands of 'substantive morality'; which is not easy to define but should be impossible to ignore, at the least as a continuing commitment and search.

So whatever other qualities may go towards the definition of intellectuals, given their proposed 'role', a crucial element must be a self-aware consciousness, the unwillingness to be swayed by either public fashion or self-interest. Neither membership of a particular social class, no matter how well-educated that may have made you, nor admission to Mensa, are sufficient grounds for entry. Membership is trickier, but constantly renewed, and its brief retuned but not redefined.

By no means all intellectuals obey the above precepts, but they should know when they are falling down on them. These are the only grounds on which intellectuals may presume to speak outside their own circles with some sort of measured confidence; as, to quote Auden again, 'ironic points of light' seeking after 'sane affirmative speech'; which nowadays may often be very rude speech indeed.

It all begins in that critical sense of self. Statements here come more often from the French than from the English. Montaigne talks about the need for a sense of watching yourself from outside. Camus has a similar remark: 'An intellectual is someone whose mind watches itself' (*Notebooks 1935–42*). One does not expect to hear remarks such as those from the English. They would seem slightly embarrassing, self-conscious rather than self-aware, portentous and self-important. But we should have our own language for the idea. Perhaps we have, but it is not easy to find. The inhibitions are considerable; this is the society whose standard reductive phrases towards putative intellectuals include being 'too clever by half', 'a clever Dick', 'an intellectual eunuch', 'clever to a fault', someone who has 'swallowed the dictionary' and who 'talks like a book'.

*

These common attitudes may partly explain the enclosed nature of so much in our intellectual life, the sense that many writers in particular seem to think their parishes extend no further than the reception of their latest book and conversations with their own kind at receptions, launches, dinners. They rarely engage in serious and sustained public debate even on issues which greatly concern both the condition of the general culture and their own freedom to work as they wish.

Some have campaigned recently on behalf of the beleaguered Public Libraries, but that is about all. In the Sixties the conversion of the Third Programme into Radio 3 provoked a considerable public protest led by T. S. Eliot and Peter Laslett. The plight of the BBC in the Eighties and the passing of the 1990 Broadcasting Act were witnessed in almost total silence by the universities, the opinion-formers, the Great and Good, and even by virtually all those who have most profited from the BBC's catholic programming. They continued to go to Broadcasting House to 'chatter' on Radio 3 as though they were a protected rather than, now, a threatened species. Much more important than their own fate (and it could be argued that they had long enjoyed an excessively privileged broadcasting existence) was the unavoidable fate of the whole public service idea. That too escaped almost all of them.

That is only one instance, obvious because it bears directly on the

intellectual health of the culture. One could also mention the removal
of minimum wage regulations, the relaxation of the rules governing
old people's homes, especially those run privately. Beyond any doubt
the one will lead to further exploitation of women, who desperately
need some extra money and many of whom do not know when they
are being robbed. The other relaxation will cause even more old
people to be ill-housed, ill-fed and ill-treated; for profit. But this is
the freedom which 'market forces' need and will be said finally
to justify. The governments' role in all this and similar matters is
inexcusable; to a somewhat lesser extent so is 'the intellectuals'' lack
of the assumption of a function in such matters. In some ways they
prefer to think of themselves – another self-gratifying fiction – as
'internationals' rather than nationals. They will more readily write
to the press about abuses in Latin America than about those nearer
home. In other respects they can be deeply domestic, even suburban.
To have this characteristic confirmed, you need only observe the
combination of back-scratching of friends, and short-term memory,
in the broadsheets' annual lists of Books of the Year.

Even worse are the positive decisions. How can so many graduates
deliberately go into advertising copywriting? The intention is usually
said to be to use the period so as to become 'a serious writer'. That
is like seeking training in a thieves' kitchen for a job which demands
honest practice. How can you justify using what you believe are your
emerging powers of perception and expression on behalf of low-level
propaganda, verbal trickery and intellectual short-changing? Better
to go out to teach, devotedly, in the more remote provinces, and
write by night.

*

The debate about The Condition of England did not die after the
mid- to late nineteenth century: a few decades after *Culture and
Anarchy*, say. At its weakest it is a continuing grumble under
the surface. Much in the mood of the 1890s did not encourage it,
though, as always, there were counter-currents: Shaw, the Webbs,
the Fabians, Wells, working-class novels and documentaries. After
them came R. H. Tawney, the Coles, Richard Titmuss and Michael
Young.

The First World War had given creative writers a narrow range of
deeply felt themes about the changing nature of Britain, but that
partly faded with the Twenties. Yet Lawrence and Forster played

their part in both fictional critiques of society and to some extent – Forster more than Lawrence – as active direct spokesmen. Thereafter, Orwell is the outstanding and archetypal name among novelists and essayists; but one could now honourably add Raymond Williams and Edward Thompson.

By the Seventies, for reasons still not entirely clear, the Left seemed to lose its creative impulse, become directionless, to lack contact with its own heart. The initiative, a rather heartless kind of initiative, passed to the Right. That phase is not quite over.

*

Much of the immediately foregoing has been, as has much throughout this book, about divisiveness rather than about difference and variety; one bad, the other good. It has been about the urge to compartmentalism, and that is a human not a specifically British inclination. There is always the urge for 'a hierarchy of specialisations', a tripartite division of society (for some: scientists and industrialists, labourers, and artists-poets-philosophers). That doesn't smell right. Nor do other eighteenth-, nineteenth – and twentieth-century prescriptions of the sort.

Above all, one needs to hold not only to the idea that some people in a society must 'bear witness' but, even more, to the belief that they are not a special caste, that a society should be fluid and that that fluidity allows for very many – more than are habitually assumed – to bear witness, to be among the intelligent lay people who are as important as the recognised intellectuals, whatever their origins. Such a sense of responsibility depends on a certain spirit and cast of mind; and those may exist or be elicited in many people and all parts of society. This is the major counterforce to the pressures of hegemony.

But even as one says this the problem indicated by Leavis, quoted at the head of this section, rears up to pose itself as one of the major problems of the day. Hegemony does exist and its powers do not seem to be diminishing. Perhaps they are increasing because supported nowadays by all those mighty engines of communication in whose nature and interest it is to uphold the system, to increase the grip. 'The intellectuals' have now joined 'the masses': in being virtually cut off from the sources of power. The ideologues, whether in politics or the City, and their mates, the commercial publicists, and the self-appointed populist opinion-formers, do not exactly rule; they do have their plump hands somewhere near most of the important levers of power.

PART FIVE

A Summing-up; and a Very Qualified Prospectus

The permanent distinction and the occasional contrast between cultivation and civilisation . . . The permanency of the nation . . . and its progressiveness and personal freedom . . . depend on a continuing and progressive civilisation. But civilisation is itself but a mixed good, if not far more a corrupting influence, the hectic of disease, not the bloom of health, and a nation so distinguished more fitly to be called a varnished than a polished people, where this civilisation is not grounded in cultivation, in the harmonious development of those qualities and faculties that characterise our humanity.
Samuel Taylor Coleridge, 'On the Constitution of the Church and State', 1830

[A nation is not free when] one class of person has greater liberty than another or liberty is less extensive than it should be.
John Rawls, *On Liberty*

CHAPTER FIFTEEN

Where are We, and Where Do We Go from Here?

I perceive we have destroyed those independent beings who were able to cope with tyranny single-handed . . . the poor man retains the prejudices of his forefathers without their faith, and their ignorance without their virtues; he has adopted the doctrine of self-interest as the rule of his actions . . .
Alexis de Tocqueville, *Democracy in America*, 1835–40

You shall not crucify mankind upon a cross of gold.
William Jennings Bryan, speaking to the Democratic National Convention in Chicago, 1896

i RELATIVISM RAMPANT

To live is itself a value judgment. To breathe is to judge.
Albert Camus, introduction to *The Rebel*, 1951, trans. A. Bower. (This remarkably anticipates a comment by Iris Murdoch quoted in Chapter 3; and also Charles Taylor, later in this chapter.)

That girls are raped, that two boys knife a third,
Were axioms to him, who'd never heard
Of any world where promises are kept,
Or one could weep because another wept.
W. H. Auden, 'The Shield of Achilles'. (On compassion and the keeping of promises, two of the chief markers of progress towards Coleridge's 'cultivation'. Relativism could, if not faced, move from emptiness to disenchantment to this heartlessness.)

Very much earlier (in Chapters 2 to 7) the effects of relativism in several important areas were examined. In education (Chapter 2) there emerged, as has happened so often, a strange set of paradoxes: vocationalism was stressed in itself and as an unconscious support to relativism; you don't discuss critical values if your education is predominantly practical. But life can't be left to be as loose as that, especially for 'ordinary' people, so authoritarianism reappeared: as an insistence, not of course on specifically denominational practices, but in the demand for an undefined 'act of worship'. And in the resurrection of the importance of sport as a stiffener of the national backbone; Dr Arnold watered down for the mass of people, a clean practical mind in a moderately healthy body. The clean mind impulse then appeared in the call for 'a return to basics' – which no one at government level would or could define. Most 'ordinary' people thought it had to do with personal morality, predominantly in sexual and financial matters. In which case large numbers of MPs, especially on the government side, were soon proved to have run away from basics. So one wondered what the 'basics' were – and was left only with vocationalism, an obligatory act of worship, and sport; no moral considerations or considerings. A little earlier the call for a return to 'Victorian values' had blown up even more violently in its propounder's face; it was so plainly an example of picking out from a mish-mash the bits which suited, and burying the rest. The hidden authoritarianism of the marshmallow state was revealed. The circle was complete.

On the approach to art (Chapter 3), as an activity of great value in itself and as an illuminator of society and its meanings, all was plainly another muddle. No change so clearly illustrates the damage wreaked by relativism – except the decay of language (Chapter 6). But that is itself central to the creation of some arts. Language is the battleground, the arts among the major casualties.

'Popular culture' and 'mass culture' (Chapter 4) – these terms are less confusing and rightly give less away than 'mass art' and 'popular art'. Mass culture was seen as predominantly a branch of the consumer society. It emerged as entirely devoted to telling people that theirs is the 'real' world, to defining people for and to themselves (since no one else will do it nowadays, and to do it for ourselves is too much to bear).

The evidence is all around, painfully. One need recall only one simple but sad and exact pointer to the collapse of considered choice, choice considered as a matter of personal judgment: virtually every actor and actress, singer, championship winner, star of any kind will take money for making insincere professions, especially on TV, as to the virtues of the goods produced by whoever will pay them most. It is bad that they do this; they are exploiting the affection built up in the viewers by their appearances in television programmes. It is worse that they affect this 'sincerity' without a qualm; especially the already successful, who command the highest fees. Add the growing exploitation of children as targets for and participants in television advertising; another shameful exercise. Perhaps even worse is the constant succession of smart articles in the press which profess to debunk all aspects of this whole consuming process; but do so without breaking the skin, and thus become a sustaining part of the process itself.

Broadcasting offers the most striking evidence of change for the worse in cultural institutions today, even more striking than the educational changes, though likely to be less profound over the long term. It is worth saying again that in spite of all the damage done in recent years British broadcasting can still deliver first-rate programmes. Positive – 'thou shalt' – liberating legislation tries to make sure this applies to commercial broadcasting as to the BBC, though the former is increasingly chafing at the constraints on profit-making.

On the other side, programmes made for the mass market have gone downhill to a new low. One need mention in the mid-Nineties only the new commercial 'talk' radio stations which mean to attract listeners by being abusive and as obscene as may be permitted. This illustrates yet again the theme of Chapter 9, the division of society into the meritocrats and the rest. The meritocrats are still quite well provided for; the mass audiences now have programmes of such low quality that they make early versions of *Double Your Money* seem if not innocuous at least innocently incompetent. Broadcasting is therefore more and more pushing along the process which was discussed earlier – dividing, hardening, extending – and reinforcing.

Again, as with the actors making ads, such things can always be justified. It is in the nature of all societies (as of individuals) to be self-vindicating; today's society is as if organically built for self-evasion and self-vindication. Hence the BBC's programmes presenting the ignoble National Lottery; and its yet more disgraceful ads; and recall that the Controller of BBC 1 called those programmes great national occasions. Against so egregious a misjudgment one might even defend the Queen's Speech on Christmas Day. To cap that sequence one needed only hear the Secretary of State for the National Heritage defend the Lottery on the sole ground that it will help charities. Did he think no one out there could do simple arithmetic, or was he blinded by his own government's rhetoric?

In case any reader is inclined even at this late stage to claim that the case made earlier against the trend of broadcasting since the mid-Sixties, with an acceleration in the last few years, has been at bottom a denial of the value of competition, it is necessary to repeat in the simplest form a rebuttal. Competition in broadcasting is to be welcomed; it can and did usefully loosen the BBC (and in some things degraded it, but that was because competition was for the wrong reasons). This argument is as sound now as when it was first made thirty years ago: competition can be valuable but must have the right aim; all parties must share one unqualified purpose: to produce good broadcasting. A system which introduces competition but in which one network has its eye on increasing advertising revenue, and so wants mass audiences as often as possible, produces a squint in that network. Thinking of what will attract the advertisers takes the eye off the real ball. Then the other network, the BBC, has to fight dirty so as to capture some mass audiences, and to fight its way out of the slipstream of the commercial channels so as still to make some programmes it respects. Both rapidly begin to squint.

The study of society today, generally but by now rather confusedly called 'cultural studies' (Chapter 7), in its turn reflects much relativism of thought whether it is discussing 'high' art or mass or popular culture. It exhibits the widespread confusion of language not only in its fondness for abstract jargon but more widely, as a distemper of convictions and, in some parts, even as a tendency towards some very particular kinds of censorship.

*

The following notes are codas to some of these specific areas.

Most of the qualities and consequences here identified flow in the long run from the secular, long-term changes which have been discussed throughout the book. The present sequence of governments has exploited and extended them. Yet one needs to avoid laying too much influence at their door; that could be unjust to them and make them seem more important than, in the last analysis, they are.

As to the first quality, a quotation about the Canadian economist and historian Harold Adams Innis is apt: 'For Innis, the oral tradition representative of man's concern with history and metaphysics had to be preserved if we were not to fall victim to a sacred politics and a sanctified science' (cit. J. Carey, *Harold Adams Innes and Marshall*

McLuhan, 1968). That is apt because it sets the concern for meaning and value against what Innis saw as a newly sacred and sanctified belief in the operations of politics and the assumed 'truth' of science. It points to the advent of a merely factual and operational world. What Innis could not be expected to see was that half a century later politics would no longer be sacred or science sanctified, that even those partial stays against flux would have been discarded.

The end-of-the-century world of the developed societies has, increasingly, no sanctities, no firm holds. All is successive, momentary, two-dimensional, with little background in a recognised, a recovered, a usable past; no roots. It can therefore have no future or vision of a future. It exhibits what Burckhardt called 'the sense of the provisional'.

Not much more than a generation back the idea of progress, of a progressive amelioration of the human condition, lay somewhere at the backs of most people's minds, even at the backs of many poor people's minds. It is there no longer. Yet that does not imply a fatalism or disappointment; it implies a living in the successive-present. In that sense there is a movement but one similar to going the wrong way on an escalator or round and round on a carousel; it is not felt to be going anywhere; its movement is sufficient unto itself; it does not require a gradually opening future into 'a better world for us and our descendants'. There is not felt to be any 'better' except in successive tastes. As has been said: 'the lawless flood of our greed outstrips everything we invent to try to slake it'. This mood pervades everything from the endless re-creation of artificial wants to the emphatic concentration on 'youth' and youth's always insistent taste for pleasures and satisfactions; the concept of a 'dignified old age' is not comprehensible. 'Senior citizens' are not dignified old men and women; they are patronised cardboard creations.

A relativist society is only apparently an open society; it is closed in its own way. It is solipsistic, collectively solipsistic; it encourages a self-generating and self-defining individuality. At a lower level it recognises no society at all but, in that phrase of Mrs Thatcher's, 'only family' – and, presumably, close friends. It is therefore encouraging people to think only of themselves and their nearest and dearest. It honours the democratic trio, but in its own way: Liberty – as the freedom to make money by trampling on those in your way; Equality – but only at the very start of the rat race and with no allowance for the initial disadvantages of others; after that, it's everyone for themselves; Fraternity – as the false bonhomie of the disc-jockeys but not as an attitude and a duty which would disturb the advantages the opportunist society can offer to the bright, nimble and sharp. This society is kind to those smart enough to move and feed high on the hog; they do not grumble, nor do they move over. They then combine *sauve qui peut* with pursed-up suburban morality, a most comfortable and unattractive middle-range position and one much reinforced latterly.

It follows that relativism encourages a type of conformity which, because it is going nowhere, eventually becomes indifferentism; and that, to adapt Tawney, is more perilous to the soul than wickedness. At that point, only one kind of morality can be recognised: 'functional morality'; if it works in terms of numbers, it's OK.

Conformity-with-indifferentism goes right to the uneasy soft heart of relativism: its deep-seated disinclination to judge anything outside a very few gregarious and at bottom insignificant areas. As in the two false guiding-phrases mentioned earlier: that knowing all means to forgive all; and that any disgreement may be due not to a difference of opinion or belief but to 'a breakdown in communication'.

Such phrases are part of the stock of the ubiquitous hired persuaders, those who are capable of uttering such sentences as 'Your common man is a pretty shrewd bird after all'; the bland – or the pseudo-spicy – leading the bland; those who also, like so many politicians, are confidently riding the prevailing waves, the flattering populists in a world where too few contradictory voices are to be heard.

Is it difficult to be even more specific about all these changes, their effects, and perhaps the counter-movements if any, they invoke? Not at all, though the evidence is inherently unpleasant. The main social effect is the emergence or continuation of a society most of whose members are insufficiently educated for its complexities, educated only to the level at which they may be exploited. Down with sub-literacy, up with critical literacy. How strange it is that that banner has even by this date to be run up. At this point Dostoevsky's Grand Inquisitor always comes to mind: 'Yes, we shall set them to work, but in their leisure hours we shall make their life a child's game . . . we will save them from the great anxiety and terrible agony they endure at present in making a free decision for themselves.'

In asserting that this inadequacy exists one is not saying that it equates with, say, all those below the middle-classes. Middle-class homes are not in general articulate centres of sweetness and light;

they can be as prejudiced as anywhere else, as susceptible to toadying gossip about Royalty; to the TV game-shows which exploit that semi-literacy; to the acceptance with hardly a murmur of the award of a peerage to Jeffrey Archer. 'For services to literature,' one wag said.

At one of the lowest levels of all we have the sight of provincial working-class adolescent youths on a package holiday to the Costa Brava. In the cheapest hotels, the hoteliers are used to hosing out the rooms after each week's visitors. The provincial working-class equivalent, at bottom, of young City stockbrokers' larks.

Above all, this sort of society leads to and appears to condone both the emergence and the ignoring of that apparently permanent 'underclass'. The sense of a coherent 'belonging' dissolves, that sense eloquently described by Alasdair MacIntyre in *After Virtue* (1981):

> I am someone's son or daughter ... a citizen of this or that city ... as such I inherit from the past of my family, my city, my tribe, my nation, a variety of debts, inheritances, rightful expectations and obligations. These constitute the given of my life, my moral standpoint. This is in part what gives my life its own moral particularity.

Local wisdom, MacIntyre is saying, is essential as a grounding, but will no longer do in the global market-place.

And the reactions against? These are more difficult to identify, since they are usually movements in the mind rather than firm facts and actual events. They had best be offered as a set of suppositions. They seem to arise from the feeling that life is hardly supportable in a void, an uncomfortable large space. This is different from the sense that 'the unexamined life is not worth living', for that is a very sophisticated position. It does not say: 'I must seek certainties,' but rather it responds to the inner, inchoate, unarticulated feeling: 'I must question the ways of my life and that at the least may make it seem worth going on.'

So: why is television so much given to nostalgic re-creations? Because it reanimates the sense that life was once manageable, human-sized, to be held in the hand, not so agoraphobic? And might be again?

Why are those museums which try to re-create the way of life of earlier times so popular, especially those concerned with no more than about a century ago? Nostalgia again, it is said; and there may be truth in that. But listen to people as they walk around; you will find not so much nostalgia as a now focused but inarticulate regret and sense of loss.

Here is reached the worst supposition of all. Hannah Arendt posited that she could just see the decline of the nationalist state. That was, at the time, understandable; and very cheering. What she could not have foreseen is the increase, especially in some other countries, of nationalism, of the coarse nationalism, the xenophobia, which does not deserve to be equated with patriotism; and of its cousin, racism (not the respectful and respectable case for minorities but narrow ethnic closures of the mind). Of that the worst example is religious extremism and fundamentalism. We seem once again to be in the presence of the fear of mental agoraphobia, of the need of some people – neurotics of any class or age or country, disaffected young people, artery-hardened old people – for certainty, preferably a narrow and immovable certainty which leaves the rest of humanity outside, not belonging, which inhabits an enclosed world, a self-righteous enclave, to hold on to and remain within. 'Human kind/ cannot bear very much reality.'

The English working class, both Bevin and Bevan noted, have long suffered from 'a poverty of ambition', an inability or reluctance to 'lift their eyes'. That was due as much as anything to lack of opportunity and stunted education.

What we are seeing today is a more general and diffused poverty of the spirit, a society increasingly lacking at the heart at all levels, especially the governmental, the ghost of what was once, at least, a partially civilised (better, Coleridge's 'cultivated') society, being succeeded by a morally maimed society. A writer in *Blackfriars* captured the case:

> [This vision does not contain] a conception of society as encompassing a plurality of functions, groupings of interests, or of a public, political realm as a place where these different elements are accommodated to each other in a principled and rational way ... The freedom [this] state protects is the only freedom it knows: the freedom to have what I want, not the freedom to be what I choose; the freedom to have precisely what I want precisely when I want it, not the freedom to be associated with others in giving up what I want (e.g. immediate treatment by the Health Service) for the sake of something else which seems important (e.g. accessibility to health care for all). In [this government's] view there is nothing else, beyond the satisfaction of desires. There is not even identity; government does not express it and individuals do not possess it.

A Summing-up; and a Very Qualified Prospectus

ii OLD STRENGTHS

Reflecting upon the magnitude of the general evil, I should be oppressed with a dishonourable melancholy, had I not a deep impression of certain inherent and indestructible qualities of the human mind.
William Wordsworth, Preface to *Lyrical Ballads*, 1798

It has rich relations who are to be kow-towed to and poor relations who are to be sat upon . . . It is a family in which the young are generally thwarted and most of the power is in the hands of irresponsible uncles and bedridden aunts. Still it is a family. It has its private language and its common memories, and at the approach of an enemy it closes its ranks. A family with the wrong members in control – that, perhaps, is as near as one can come to describing England in a phrase.
George Orwell, 'The Ruling Class'

Some of that, thank God, no longer much holds; and some of it, thank God again, survives.

> *. . . One would have said beyond a doubt*
> *That was the very end of the bout,*
> *But that the creature would not die.*
Edwin Muir, 'The Combat'

Chapter 8 looked at the slowness of accepting change among the English, and their capacity to wrest change to their habitual purposes. Chapter 12 looked at related characteristics, the deeper swells at work to and fro in the English character.

First, the idea of the family, in spite of the accepted opinion, survives to a considerable degree, often in stable partnerships which do not necessarily lead to marriage.

Neighbourliness survives among middle-class as much as in working-class people. It is narrow in the sense of being confined to a restricted neighbourhood. Within that area it is all-pervasive (and can cohabit happily with 'keeping yourself to yourself'). It can be restricting since it is by nature not an agent for change; it works according to firm and long-standing rules and can seem stifling to young people looking for a freer air. At some levels it emerged chiefly though not entirely as a reaction to common hardship. Nowadays its remarkable continuance is based more on the sense that an on the whole agreeable style of life is not likely to be overturned by riot, revolution or invasion and is well worth keeping. It is also the single most sustaining communal practice in English society, in both admirable and pettifogging ways. The window-watching, curtain-twitching neighbour lives on, was never a comic fiction. Yet on balance neighbourliness is more helpful than harmful; there are worse habits.

Wider than the sense of neighbourhood is that of the duty to do voluntary work for 'the community'. It is a long tradition. From the early nineteenth century it showed its main strength especially among the professional middle-class and upwards, in the promotion of that long sequence of major socially beneficial Acts. Some of those initiatives, especially those on education, drew on reformers from all classes. But inevitably the main promoters were from the socially concerned among the already educated and well-to-do. The line from them to the active middle-class voluntary workers of today is continuous but transformed, like a great river flowing into a wide and multi-streamed delta.

Added to those scores of voluntary bodies in small and larger towns are at least as many collectives given to spare-time activities, which to some extent often cut across class or, if still divided by class in their membership, have a common enthusiasm. The variety and spread of 'leisure activities' is huge, another for the short-list of amiable English preoccupations. The surprise is, once again, that in a society changing so rapidly, so much of the old manner remains.

So one arrives, in this recalling of some traditional qualities which seem largely to have resisted main present trends, at attitudes to others outside the immediate circle. One arrives at last at that dodgy word 'tolerance'. Chapter 12 argued that to a good degree tolerance survives, tolerance properly so called, not its neutered simulacrum 'indifference'. In some people it has been cast aside, as rabid nationalism and racism take hold; but those are still a minority.

In such matters comparisons are odious, and cross-national comparisons resented. They do not have to be made and, if attempted, would need a book on their own. One can say, though, that – all usual and obvious exceptions admitted – the general demeanour in English life, the general assumption about how one should behave towards others outside, is that cheerfulness should insist on breaking in. Everyone has horrid stories about obstructive shop assistants, minor officials and the rest; they enrage us so much because they are against the dominant style. Yes, you can also find people of both styles in many countries; and no, the assertion about their strength in England cannot be proved. But we have to tell what we think we see; others can contradict us. Orwell's bold and unapologetic 'When it comes to the pinch, human beings are heroic' might have been complemented by: 'When it comes to the pinch the English insist on being cheerful.' 'It's being so cheerful that keeps me going.'

'Bloody-mindedness' has two main faces. The first is the one mentioned above, which is plain rudeness for its own sake, because you've got out of bed on the wrong side, had a row with your partner, are worried about money or just not very well. The other bloody-mindedness is an aspect of self-respect, a refusal to be pushed around or put down; sometimes a minor cousin of moral courage. Another one for the short-list of respectable resistances – together with taking the mickey out of pretension.

*

All such attitudes come together to form what has been called 'the creativeness of ordinary everyday life'. They are aspects too of that English sense of belonging to one another, to – Orwell again – being part of a family, warts and all. They do not imply you should assume you are in some senses called to be your brother's keeper; they do imply you should be prepared to be his helper as needed. All these things form a delicate but tough spider's web of relationships, some admirable, some not, which make up the largely shared sense of the society we live in. They contain many elements of a remarkable moral decency, at all social levels.

Is this what some people would greatly like to call 'a common culture'? Probably not: it is, rather, an elaborate pattern of common qualities – qualities which in some respects and at some times (wars outstandingly) do bring the British together; at other times and in other regards they remain divided. But, as has already been said more than once here, that divisiveness is not to their credit; they are better in those parts where they are, instead, diverse. Like other nations the British have for centuries fed themselves and their children partial, self-regarding and divisive histories; in state schools as much as in public schools. It is time to do better. A more open and relativist society is not all bad; whatever its giddinesses and agoraphobia, it may also lead towards getting rid of some of the worst legacies of the authoritarian-deferential state.

iii NEW OPPORTUNITIES

*This type of society also has many unattractive traits, and its virtues are
open to doubt. On balance, and with misgivings, we opt for it; but there
is no question of an elegant, clear-cut choice.*
Ernest Gellner, *Tractatus Sociologico-Philosophicus*, 1984

*Take for instance the question how far mankind has gained by civilisation.
One observer is forcibly struck by the multiplication of physical comforts;
the advancement and diffusion of knowledge; the decay of superstition; the
facilities of mutual intercourse; the softening of manners; the decline of
war and personal conflict; the progressive limitation of the tyranny of the
strong over the weak; the great works accomplished throughout the globe
by the co-operation of multitudes ...*

John Stuart Mill

Raymond Williams, who quotes this passage (in *Keywords*), goes on
to list some negative effects noted by Mill, such as 'loss of independence, the creation of artificial wants, monotony, narrow mechanical
understanding, inequality and hopeless poverty'. It would have been
thoughtless when Mill wrote and would be no less thoughtless today
to assume that a profit-and-loss account over all those elements
could be easily drawn up. Some of Mill's positives have proved quite
illusory; few of his negatives have lost force.

In modern life there is much to admire and be glad about, from
the simply gratifying to much more important elements which make
for better lives; yet most need qualifications. It is good that food is
abundantly and quite cheaply available; a pity, though, that many
people buy badly, under constant pressure. It is good that so many are
far better housed than their predecessors. Those who grew up before
the war can call up this advance simply by saying: 'Thank God for
a warm bedroom in the morning'; or 'No more low-wattage bulbs.'

Clothing, particularly for working-class people, has lost its pre-
war drabness; brightness can be afforded by many. Just look at a
class of seven-year-olds coming out of school on a council estate.
Travel to almost anywhere in the world is available to numbers
hitherto undreamt-of (but has proved to be, for some, simply a source
of cheap drink and easy sex).

There is much still to improve in education; but in comparison
with the cruelties and intellectual rigidities of many public schools
before the war, or with the low-grade teaching at many 'elementary'
Board Schools, a gain is there. But we have not always caught up

with our own best challenges. As shown in the report of the Glasgow comprehensive-school teacher who asked her pupils each to write down the job they hoped to gain. She misread one boy's aim as 'carpet layer'. He corrected her; he wanted to be a 'corporate lawyer'. The revolution of rising expectations seems to have been well fed by courtroom television dramas there. Equally, though the National Health Service is not at all what it should be by now, no one in their senses, especially people from the working-class, would wish to go back to the days of the 'Panel' doctor, the local 'Fever Hospital', the old people's 'workhouses' – though kindness and dedication could reveal themselves even in those people and places.

The existence of spare money for an immensely wider range of people is one of the great dissolvers. It is easy, but not improper, to recognise that many choices are ill-made, responses to hard sells, or forms of self-indulgence. But if you went to, let us say, the Soviet Union and met there a different kind of drabness even from that of pre-war working-class England, the rejection of the idea of the *homme moyen sensuel* and his wife choosing for themselves even to the point of self-indulgence and beyond, the dull hortatory slogans instead of the ads for food and sexy underwear and every kind of personally decided taste – if you saw all that your most powerful response would be likely to be: 'As compared with this, thank God for some parts of capitalism. At least it sees me at the start as a freely choosing creature.'

*

Which leads to the direct consideration of freedom. It is common, and as easy as criticising features of contemporary society, to tip the other way and accuse such critics of being afraid of freedom, of the unpleasant things freedom can bring, of the costs of that lessening of authority and deference.

There may be such people. For others the ghetto-blasters, the endless Muzak-syrup – and all those intrusions which you cannot escape in modern society (you don't have to share television programmes or newspapers; you do have to share much else, especially the never-ending 'loudspeakers' in public places) – all such intrusions are a small price to pay for the spread of freedom and its potentialities.

So when someone says that a person who is concerned about aspects of television as they appear today is afraid of life (since, it is added, TV is only a medium and will show us as we are, and this is the price of democracy and well worth paying) – such a riposte sounds at first smartly epigrammatic.

On a second thought it is wrong. Television is not simply a medium. It is used according to the freedoms and constraints each particular society allows it; against its own good intentions at the start, British society by now allows it to patronise through selection and distortion; and so to despise. It does not show people as they are; it shows us as, encourages us to think of ourselves as, the kind of creatures who will serve the cajolers' turn. And since – another unpleasant truth to face – many of us are much less sophisticated than the advertisers, they have considerable success.

These are elements of the total equation which it is wrong to ignore. If offered junk one has a right to accept it, even junk which gets junkier all the time as the pressure between competitors increases. It is to some extent true that people are better informed than ever before; they are also more comprehensively conned, unthinkingly. After a set of deliberately ugly and provocative ads appeared for a soft drink, sales went up by 40 per cent. A society most of whose citizens fall, say, for the 'tie-breaker' device in pro-motions which offer mountainous prizes needs to educate itself better.

In the face of such things, anyone also has the right to says: 'Junk is junk'; and, following Chekhov: 'You live badly, my friends. It is shameful to live like that'; rather than to announce smugly: 'I stand up for the common man's right to choose junk if he pleases.' So do some others – but they also exercise their right to do more, to say more, to describe exploitation when they see it. What they see is not the unqualifiedly cheerful face of a free and largely prosperous democracy; it is what – to use that much-misused word – the 'hegemony' has decided shall be made of it.

It would be a pity to end this part on such a note. Freedom is indeed, as Barbour said in 1376 a noble thing. If one wished to name one change in British attitudes which this freedom has encouraged over the last few decades, it should be the lessening of that damp, unexpectant, niggling puritanism in which so many families, so many communities, used to live. Some still do; but many do not and their numbers increase. That is one place where one can raise a cheer.

Another instance is the increase in common action on behalf of good social causes – to protect the environment, to reduce cruelty to animals, and so on. They attract at present many in the middle and some in the lower middle-classes only; but that is to be expected.

A Summing-up; and a Very Qualified Prospectus

They are not party-political or simply self-seeking or entirely class-bound; they can have a truly communal quality.

iv WHAT TO DO ABOUT IT?
OR: LET'S PUT OUT THE LIGHTS AND GO TO SLEEP?

So now there are a great many couriers; they post through the world and, as there are no kings left, shout to each other their meaningless and obsolete messages.

Franz Kafka

It would be easy to be depressed by many of both the long- and short-term trends and apparent prospects in modern life: by that constant flattery which is really contempt, by the 'stay as sweet as you are' chorus, by the movement out of old-fashioned class but towards a new and hardening two-part (or two-and-a-bit parts) division by status, by the triviality spawned by persuasion on relativism, by the increasing separation of the citizens of this democracy from the sources of power, national or, more and more now, international, by the increasing failure to connect privately and publicly, or the private-with-the-public.

In his time Burkhardt was grim, though perhaps his last three words here hold out a hope: 'A party which is not afraid of letting culture . . . and welfare go to ruin completely can be omnipotent for a while.' In *Nostromo* Conrad was just as depressed: 'The popular mind [an unusable phrase today but at least it is not one of the cant phrases of Left and Right] is incapable of scepticism; and that incapacity delivers their helpless strength to the wiles of swindlers and the pitiless enthusiasms of leaders inspired by visions of a high destiny.' That last line at least, the English are no doubt inclined to say cheerfully to themselves, is not our style. Not leaders with visions of high destiny, but cheerful chums with low horizons.

Herbert Read was most plangent of all: 'It will be a gay world. There will be lights everywhere except in the minds of men and the fall of the last civilisation will not be heard above the incessant din' ('Atrophied Muscles and Empty Art', 1965). One must respect Herbert Read's gloom; he had earned the right to voice it. One should also remember at such times, though not with Herbert Read in mind, Dr Johnson on cant, on the crucial distinction between public and private grief. Neither hard-nosed nor soft-centred, then.

This is, again, a largely sub-literate society, if literacy means more than the ability simply to read and write, not to assess. Democracy is always more an intention than an achievement. A semi-literate society suits well some of the main forces now at work. An achieved democracy must work for critical literacy, must believe that very many more in all parts of society can be encouraged towards that level; must bank on their own and others' potentialities. Those who have 'newly entered society' must, especially, be neither exploited nor patronised. It is equally a betrayal to rest content, out of a misreading of democracy (by, yet again, standing up for 'the common man's right to be trivial'), not to regret and resist the fact that so many should be trapped in this frozen and aborted kind of literacy.

As always, Tawney was eloquent on this:

> The purpose of an adult education worthy of the name is not merely to impart reliable information, important though that is. It is still more to foster the intellectual vitality to master and use it so that knowledge becomes a stimulus to constructive thought. Also it is partly, at least, the process by which we transcend the barriers of our isolated personalities and become partners in a universe of interest which we share with our fellow men, living and dead alike.

That is one good definition of a community.

Tawney was one of the founding fathers of adult education regarded as essential for democratic life. He knew and proved in his own practice that good adult classes, meeting week after week and year after year, patiently trying to weigh evidence, to learn openly without benefit of privilege, can become civil and civilising societies in themselves. Such people, such groups, are an essential yeast, a small leavening, to any country which dares call itself a democracy. A large, self-run centre for continuing education is a model of that incorrigible voluntarism, of determined amateurism (in the sense of 'for its own sake'), of an almost intuitive understanding of how unofficial groups can best work, a coming together uncompetitively and respectfully.

These may truly be called communities; they recall that one cannot create those so often invoked 'close-knit communities' simply by calling loudly and repetitively for them, using words as a surrogate Aladdin's lamp. 'Community' best emerges as a by-product of some other activity, from the pursuit of a craft or skill or of intellectual training, or of working hard for others not as fortunate. In engaging in any of these kinds of activity people are implicitly refusing to be type-cast in the way modern society increasingly seeks to do – as 'consumers', as units in agglomerated figures delivered to the advertisers and all the other self-interested word-mongers, as 'customers', as 'voters', as 'senior citizens'; as, in short, merely a succession of partial creations, stick figures made to suit other people's books.

There is a good deal to build on, as has become clear. There are plenty of sound indicative phrases to enlist: 'What sort of people do they think we are?'; 'We're not as daft as all that'; 'Who do you think you're kidding?'; 'How do I know what I like till I see what's possible?' (a good motto for broadcasters' audiences). The much-quoted lines from Chesterton are again to the point: 'We are the people of England / That never have spoken yet'; and for whom 'nothing but the best' should be good enough. When 'the people of England' do speak they can confound the persuaders. Tempted by the market researchers to agree that the broadcasting licence fee is an imposition, a majority refused to agree and insisted that it is very good value. Residents of a Midlands working-class suburb, in which a huge majority bought the *Sun* daily, resisted the imputation that they took their political information from that rag: 'Of course not. We go to the radio and TV for that.' Against the cries of the newspapers they read, a majority were tolerant towards Channel 4.

Strangely, that uprooted figure Auden invoked the sense of neighbourliness lyrically: 'O every day in sleep and labour/Our life and death are with our neighbour.' He goes on to recall how love, that other-regarding impulse, illuminates our experiences in larger, external contexts, including 'the world's great rage, the travels of young men', ('New Year Letter'). The mental travels of many young men and women today, illuminated by love, bear that out: their suspicion of national and largely class-based party politics, their attraction to more than national good causes such as anti-racism, Human Rights – the rights of women in particular – and the protection of the environment. The British can in these ways and at whatever age still be compassionately creative: Amnesty International, PEN and Article 19 were all born here, in this century.

*

So one goes on, must go on. 'Going on going on' – a very unpretentious claim – is also true to the British grain. When all the pros and cons have been entered one has to accept the fact that on the road towards (to resurrect a phrase which has been wrongly mocked out of easy use) 'a better quality of life' there are no easy answers, no quick fixes. That way lie mirages, or new forms of authoritarianism whether of the Left or Right. One has to resist being 'screwed into virtue', however well-intentioned the screwer.

Orwell hit the right qualified note:

> Capitalism leads to dole queues, the scramble for markets, and war. Collectivism leads to concentration camps, leader worship and war. There is no way out of this unless a planned economy can be somehow combined with the freedom of the intellect, which can only happen if the right and wrong are restored to politics.

There are some long-term and continuing steps. Education first, of course; an education not bemused by vocationalism to the detriment of education as the development of the humane critical spirit.

Broadcasting, if it remembers its old high purposes, can be almost as important. British broadcasting transmits some excellent specifically educational programmes. Probably more to the point today is the generally educative nature of many other programmes: on current affairs, the arts, recreational interests and a vast range of social issues. They are at least as effective as the explicitly educational programmes and reach much larger audiences.

Commercial broadcasting has to be tender towards those who pay for it. The BBC need have no such inhibitions. So it could do even more towards – to take only one example – becoming the Consumers' Association of the air; not only in the very good existing programmes which expose corrupt practices, but in giving comparative judgments on goods and services, almost all of which make excessive claims for themselves. A much more classless CA.

Urgent practical steps include, for example, sorting out the problem of cross-media ownership of mass communications (more effectively than the Green Paper of 1995 does); legislation of the press which curbs the worst excesses but doesn't infringe freedom; and above all finding a better balance between private commercial interests and the State's care for the public interest.

Then scorn, wit and contempt, mockery and debunking, for all the hollow and would-be seductive voices. Even partial literacy is an aid here: Caliban is the model: 'You taught me language; and my profit on't / Is, I know how to curse. . . .'

Plainly, to hint at the need for some sort of 'clerisy' would be to invite instant dismissal. A word or two now, though, for those many who, however much they may back away protesting, do see themselves as licensed voices, legitimate commentators on the condition of society, among its opinion-formers. Not to have a position you are prepared to make explicit and defend is to go with the stream, to reinforce present tendencies many of which you would not be willing actually to approve. It is to join and support the already self-reinforcing tendencies of this as of all centralised systems of power; it is to drop if not into populism then into a sort of sophisticated but anxious, indifferentist knowingness.

A classic instance by a regular columnist in *The Times*. A. S. Byatt had said about Jeffrey Archer's novels, in a discussion on literary records: 'There are books that need to be preserved and his are not among them.' The columnist dismisses this as 'A. S. Byatt's irritable knee-jerk snobbery, that'. Wrong on all counts. A. S. Byatt is not irritable just dryly measured, not making a knee-jerk reaction (oh, the exhausted cliché) but a well-considered response; and not snobbish but simply recognising wide differences of quality in fiction.

Such people may dislike on sight Coleridge's qualifications about democracy, but they point straight at them and at many of the dominant myths they operate with:

> It has never yet been seen, or clearly announced, that democracy, as such, is no proper element in the constitution of a state. The idea of a state is undoubtedly a government . . . or autocracy. Democracy is the healthful life-blood which circulates through the veins and arteries, which supports the system, but which ought never to appear externally, and as the mere blood itself.

Better connections have to be made with those of whom Lessing and Bishop Wilson spoke in the passages quoted at the beginning of Part IV. But not at the cost of a commitment to the idea of quality, of standards, of those things – in ideas, arts, beliefs and practices – which are better than others. A hundred and seventy-odd years ago, Goethe was asked by Chancellor von Müller why he had stopped reading Sir Walter Scott. He replied: 'I have time only for the most excellent.' Such beliefs, tough as they are and pompous-sounding today, are not relative nor amended by history. Here is Charles Taylor in our own time: 'To be a full human agent, to be a person or self in the ordinary meaning, is to exist in a space defined by distinctions of worth.'

Yet once again: all societies seek to deform, and to defend their deformations. Working democracies will nevertheless support genuine antibodies against their own diseases, not simply legitimated-but-neutered protests. A well-running democracy will constantly quarrel with itself, publicly, about the right things and in the right way. A good many antibodies and healthy irritants have been noted throughout this book, especially when practical resistances and deeper ethical anchors (such as the three forms of aphorism: about putting up with things, charity and honesty), come into play. A fair number of people know how to blow the gaff on the worst of the new and to turn the best to their own purposes.

To quote again the writer from *Blackfriars*:

> Things that are insignificant in the infinitely flexible market – things such as political liberties, a collective purpose, a sense of morality, tradition or responsibility – are not necessarily insignificant to the voting citizen armed with the power of choosing an alternative to [a particular government's style] if the political parties will offer him one.

Out of that, a true sense of community, diverse but not divided, might emerge.

That'll be the day.

INDEX

accents, 170, 180, 199, 203
Adams, Henry, 69, 184–5
Adorno, Theodor, 184
ADT, 31
adult education, 49–54, 219, 297, 336
Adult Literacy Unit, 51–2
advertising: arts as commodities, 70; broadcasting financing, 114–15; career choice, 316; language, 157; mass media, 243–4; television, 99, 244, 322–3, 334; US broadcasting, 114–15
Advisory Council for Adult and Continuing Education (ACACE), 297
agitprop, 215, 235, 261
Albemarle, Diana, 312
Albemarle Report, 40, 288–9
Alice in Wonderland, 121
Alliance Française, 238
allotments, 224
Alloway, Lawrence, 243
American Cultural Studies Conference, 177
American Express, 202
Amnesty International, 283, 337
Animal Rights, 284, 334
Annan, Noël, 289
Anouilh, Jean, 81
aphorisms, 275–8
Archer, Jeffrey, 327, 339
Archers, The, 129
Arendt, Hannah, 198, 328
Argos, 211
Army Bureau of Current Affairs, 50
Arnold, Matthew: concept of 'culture', 108; Englishness, 14; influence, 224; on mass culture, 97;

quoted, 13, 21, 72, 90, 92, 281, 283, 297–8, 313–14; 'touchstones', 72
Arnold, Thomas, 322
art galleries, 225, 232
Article 19, 337
arts: allocation of funding, 231–7; amateur, 220; as commodities, 70–2; broadcasting and, 138–44; ideologies of, 69–70; public funding, 216–18
Arts and Entertainment Training Council (AETC), 39–40, 64, 167–8
Arts Council, 56–61; arts funding, 214, 216, 217–18, 232, 234–6, 252, 306, 308–9; composition, 290, 292–3; conferences, 55, 138; creation, 214; discussion papers, 60)1, 74, 146; Drama Panel, 290; Education Department proposal, 223; influences on, 214; Library Association collaboration, 55, 68; Literature Panel, 235; Royal Charter, 118, 238, 287; subsidies compared to sponsorship, 227, 229–30
Ascot, 199
Assisted Places Scheme, 22, 30
Association for Business Sponsorship of the Arts, 228
AT&T Prize, 234
Auden, W.H.: education, 41; quoted, 63, 64, 75, 80, 82, 94, 96, 160, 305–6, 310, 315, 321, 337
Austen, Jane, 87, 140, 310
Avon County Council, 31
Ayckbourn, Alan, 140

Bacon, Francis, 19, 41

Bagehot, Walter, 139–40, 200
Bakhtin, Mikhail, 62
ballet, 56
Bang, Herman, 236
Baptists, 5
Barbour, John, xiii, 334
Barnes, George, 131
Baudelaire, Charles, 157
Bauman, Zygmunt, 3
BBC: Charter, 116, 118, 238, 287;
    censorship issues, 119, 251–2;
    Falklands coverage, 251; future,
    149, 338; government attitudes,
    116, 118–19, 218, 287; Gilbert and
    Sullivan, 308–9; Governors, 245,
    251–2, 287, 289, 290, 291;
    independence, 116, 118–19; licence
    fee, 117–18, 337; new art, 230;
    National Lottery, 323; PR office,
    102; Presentation Unit, 135; public
    service broadcasting, 114–26,
    135–6, 304; radio, 126–33; radio
    drama, 140; ratings war, 255, 324;
    recruitment patterns, 122–3,
    204–5; Reith's achievement, 23;
    role, 118, 120, 124; World Service,
    116–17
Beardsley, Aubrey, 89
Beatles, 112, 175
Beaverbrook press, 239
Beckett, Francis, 31, 32
Beckett, Samuel, 81, 95
Belloc, Hilaire, 290
Bellow, Saul, 55
Benda, Jules, 300–1
Bennett, Alan, 142
Bennett, Arnold, 76
Berelson, Bernard, 182
Berger, A.A., 85–6
Bergonzi, Bernard, 88
Beria, Lavrenti, 93
Bevan, Aneurin, 17, 328
Beveridge, William, 17
Bevin, Ernest, 136, 328
Bierce, Ambrose, 265
Birkbeck College, London, 42
Birmingham University, 174
Blackfriars, 328, 340
Blackmur, R.P., 103
Blake, William, 14, 75, 273
Bleak House, 62

Bleasdale, Alan, 142
Board of Guardians, 5
Boat Race, 120
book prizes, 234, 235–6
book reviewing, 253–4, 305–8
Booker Prize, 234
booksellers, 17, 71, 264
Boule de Suif, 231
Boy George, 131
Boyle, Edward, 26, 312
Braden, Su, 55
Bradley, Alfred, 140
Brain of Britain, 133
Brenton, Howard, 253
British Airways, 169
British American Tobacco, 31
British Board of Film Censors, 245
British Board of Film Classification
    (BBFC), 245, 257, 259, 267, 291
British Council, 118, 218, 237–42,
    287, 290
British Gas, 14
British Legion, 273
British Telecom, 14
Brittan, Leon, 251
broadcasting, 114–56; arts and,
    138–44; commercial, 118, 120,
    126, 145–6, 150–1, 323, 338;
    competition, 324; decline, 323;
    future, 338; legislation, 144–8,
    323; licence fee, 117–18, 337;
    market forces, 17; news, 264;
    professionalism, 122, 155; public
    service, 7, 114–26, 135–6, 146,
    304; recruitment patterns, 25,
    204–5; sponsorship, 227
Broadcasting Act (1990), 141, 144–8,
    310, 315
Broadcasting Complaints
    Commission, 245
Broadcasting Research Unit, 119,
    126, 153–5, 259
Broadcasting Standards Council, 245,
    256, 290
Brontë, Charlotte, xiii, 310
Brontë family, 53
Brother to the Ox, 58
Browning, Robert, 92
Bryan, William Jennings, 321
BSkyB, 118
Burckhardt, Jacob, 325, 335

Burgh, John, 2401
Burial Societies, 108
Burroughs, Edgar Rice, 174
Business Sponsorship Incentive
 Scheme, 228
Butler, Samuel (1835–1902), 53
Byatt, A.S., 339
Byron, Lord, 89, 92

Callaghan, James, 36
Cambridge University, 41, 49
Camus, Albert, 315, 321
Canetti, Elias, 236
Cannadine, David, 34
Cantona, Eric, 123
capital punishment, 303
Carey, John, 324–5
Carl Rosa Opera Company, 233
Carlyle, Thomas, xii, 53
cars: makes, 207, 208; use of, 194
Cartland, Barbara, 67
censorship: kinds of, 244, 249–66;
 supervisory bodies, 245–6
Central Office of Information (COI),
 239, 240, 250
Chambers of Commerce, 293
Channel 3, 151, 208, 209
Channel 4, 151–2; advertising policy,
 150; audience, 207; broadcast arts,
 138; Maupin dramatisation, 139;
 quality, 124; status, 149, 151–2
chapel, 4–5, 197, 270
charity shops, 183, 209
Charles, Prince, 98
'chattering classes', 311–12, 315
Chaucer, Geoffrey, 52–3, 121, 186
cheerfulness, 331
Chekhov, Anton, 334
Chesterton, G.K., 174, 274, 337
Childe Harold's Pilgrimage, 89
Children in Need, 121
church: going, 4, 197; rules of
 conduct, 270; training for, 25
Church of England, 4, 27, 120
Churchill, Winston, 50, 119, 120, 244
Cicero, 65
City Technology Colleges, 22, 31
Civil Service, 25, 122, 239, 263
Clarke, Kenneth, 49
class, attitudes to, 198–212; accents,
 170, 180, 199, 203; *Dad's Army*,

124; education system, 24, 35;
 status and, 202–12; *see also* middle
 class, working class
Classic FM, 131–3, 136, 208
Claudel, Paul, 63
Clausewitz, Karl Marie von, 240
clerisy, 297, 300–1, 313, 338–9
Cleverdon, Douglas, 131
Cline, Patsy, 108, 112
Co-ops, 64, 108, 186
Cobbett, William, 13, 14
Cole, G.D.H. and Margaret, 316
Cole, Nat King, 112
Coleridge, Samuel Taylor: Colmer on,
 301, 314; quoted, 166, 274, 301,
 319, 321, 328, 339; values, 14, 224
Colleges of Advanced Technology, 43
Colleges of Art, 37, 44
Colleges of Further Education, 37–8
Collins, Norman, 114
Colmer, John, 301, 314
comedy, 121
Committee of Vice-Chancellors and
 Principals (CVCP), 46–8
committees, 288–95, 311–12
Communications Studies, 269
communitarian art, 61–5
community, 164–5, 284, 330, 336,
 340
comprehensive schools, 32–3
confrontation, 285–6
Congregationalists, 5
Conrad, Joseph: *Heart of Darkness*,
 174, 279; *Nostromo*, 76, 335;
 origins of works, 76, 78; quoted,
 76, 78, 182, 189–90, 335; *Secret
 Agent*, 76, 189, 279–80
consensus, 285–6
Conservative governments, 3–4, 11,
 26, 30, 45
conspiracy theory, 187–8, 264
consumer choice, 147
consumerism 8–9, 56, 70, 97
Consumers' Association, 338
Contemporary Cultural Studies, 144,
 172–7
Continuing Education, 50
Coomaraswamy, Ananda, 64
Cooper, Giles, 140
Council for National Academic
 Awards (CNAA), 43

council-house buying, 14, 16, 195
Country and Western, 108–9
Covent Garden *see* Royal Opera
  House
Coventry University, 42
Coward, Noël, 109
Criminal Justice Act (1994), 15, 284
Crossman, Richard, 311
Cultural Diplomacy, 240–1
Cultural Relations, 241–2
Cultural Studies, 172–7
culture: English, 108, 329–31; mass,
  97–102, 322; popular, 102–13,
  322
Culture and Anarchy, 21, 281, 283,
  316
cummings, e.e., 126
Cunningham, Valentine, 88
Cup Final, 120
Czechoslovakia, broadcasting, 115

Daalder, Hans, 45
Dad's Army, 124
Daily Mirror, 98
Daily Telegraph, 207
Dainton, Fred, 312
Dante Alighieri Society, 238
Darwin, Charles, 89–90
de Gaulle, Charles, 136
Death on the Rock, 250
deconstructionism, 83
Defence of Literature and the Arts
  Society, 253
defence spending, 225
democracy: antibodies, 340;
  capitalist, 25; literacy and, 336;
  open, 239, 285; precepts, 7; Radio
  3, 130; share-holding, 16;
  television, 334
Department of Education and Science
  (DES), 45, 47, 52, 53, 68
Department of Employment, 169
Department of National Heritage, 69,
  213, 215
Dickens, Charles, xiii, 64–5
Disraeli, Benjamin, xiii, 21, 198, 199
Docker, Sir Bernard and Lady, 201
domesticity, 196–7
Donnellan, Philip, 140
Dostoevsky, Feodor, 62, 78, 87, 326
Double Your Money, 323

Douglas, J.D., 182
D'Oyly Carte Opera Company, 308–9
Dryden, John, 281
du Pre, Jacqueline, 142–3
Dyke, Greg, 145
Dylan, Bob, 59

East Anglia, University of, 168
EastEnders, 126
Easthope, Anthony, 55
Economist, 304
Eden, Anthony, 116
education, 21–54; adult, 49–54, 219,
  297, 336; climate, 22–6; further
  education, 37–40; future, 338;
  quality, 332–3; response to arts,
  219–20; schools, 26–37;
  sponsorship, 31–2; universities,
  40–9
Education Act: (1870), 21; (1902),
  29; (1944), 21; (1992), 52
'Education and Training for the
  Twenty-first Century' (White
  Paper), 52
effects analysis, 246, 269
Elementary Education Act (1870),
  21, 34
Elgar, Edward, 61, 108, 142
Eliot, George: judgments of work,
  57–8, 140; *Middlemarch*, 65,
  84–5, 88, 141, 296; quoted, 65,
  84–5, 296–7; 'touchstone', 87
Eliot, T.S.: influence, 81, 93, 103,
  224; on culture, xii, 107–8;
  quoted, 107–8, 114, 191; Third
  Programme campaign, 315
Emerson, Ralph Waldo, 273, 301
Empson, William, 88, 93
English National Opera, 291
'Englishness': BBC's role, 120–1, 129;
  censorship, 250; cheerfulness,
  330–1; committees, 294; culture,
  108, 329–31; housing, 14;
  literature, 279; nature of, xi, xii
enterprise culture, 32
environmental issues, 334
Equity, 293
ethnic arts, 164, 224
Eton, 29, 199
Euro-MPs, 304
Ewart, William, 67

Experiment in Criticism, An, 103

Fabian Society, 316
Falklands War, 116, 250–1, 303
Fascism, 27
Fathers and Sons, 87, 296
Faure, Edgar, 44–5
Federal Communications
    Commission, 115
Federation of Writers and
    Community Publishers, 62
Feist, Andrew, 220
Fire Service, 10
First World War, 316
Fish, Stanley, 83
Flaubert, Gustave, 27
Fleming, Ian, 97
Flower, Fred, 38
Fordism, 8
Foreign and Commonwealth Office
    (FCO), 116, 238, 239, 240, 241
Forster, E.M.: influence, 316–17;
    Leonard Bast, 219, 297; on
    character, 65, 78; *Passage to India*,
    181; quoted, 65, 181; values, 14
Forte's, 211
Foucault, Michel, 179, 184–5
Foundation for Sports and the Arts,
    228
Four Quartets, 72
France: arts, 216, 233, 238; clerisy,
    300–1; colonial education policy,
    242; committees, 294–5;
    intellectuals, 297, 300–1; local
    government, 283; trade unions, 50;
    universities, 44–5
Francis of Assisi, St, 14
Frankel, Charles, 314
Fraser, Sir Robert, 145
freedom, 15, 266, 333–5, *see also*
    liberty
Friendly Societies, 64, 186
Fuller, Roy, 57
Fulton, John, 312
Further Education, 37–40, 52
Furtseva, Yekaterina, 93

Galileo, 249
Gaskell, Elizabeth, xiii
Gateway, 208
GCSE results, 38–9

Gellner, Ernest, 332
General Strike (1926), 119
Geneva Convention, 303
Germany: arts, 216, 233, 238, 239;
    local government, 283;
    universities, 45
Gilbert and Sullivan, 308–9
Gill, Eric, 63
Gilliam, Laurence, 130
Giotto, 62, 77
Gissing, George, 70
Glasgow: dustmen's strike, 264–5;
    education, 333
Glasgow School, 332–3
Glyndebourne, 199
Goethe, Johann Wolfgang von, 62,
    96, 97, 268, 339
Goethe Foundation, 238
Goldmann, Lucien, 177
Good Read, A, 307
Goodman, Arnold, 312
Gourmont, Remy de, 71
Grade, Michael, 124, 145, 150
Graham, Cunninghame, 78
Gramsci, Antonio, 69, 185, 313, 314
Granada, 124, 142
grant-maintained schools, 22
Granta, 306
grass-roots, 164, 223–4, 233, 284
Gray, Thomas, 85
Great and Good, 290, 291, 292, 294,
    315
Greene, Graham, 38, 78, 168
Greene, Graham C., 290
Greene, Hugh Carleton, 257–8
Grossberg, L., 177
Guardian, 207
Gulf War, 250

hair-styles, 196
Haley, Sir William, 153
Hall, Stuart, 185
Hamlet, 64, 96–7, 274
Hardy, Thomas, 41, 75, 87, 181, 297
Harewood, Lord, 290–1
Havel, Vaclav, xiii
Haworth, D., 104
Hazlitt, William, 185, 305–6
health, 16–17, 333, *see also* National
    Health Service
Heart of Darkness, 174, 279

Index

Hebdige, Dick, 112
Heeks, Peggy, 68
hegemony, 69, 186, 223, 233, 317, 334
Hemingway, Ernest, 158
Henley, 199
Henry, Clarence 'Frogman', 112
Heppenstall, Rayner, 130
Herbert, George, 92
Hewison, Robert, 228
Higgins, Jack, 67
Hitler, Adolf, 28, 92–3, 119
Hobbes, Thomas, 278
holidays, 207, 208
Holocaust, 263
Horowitz, I.L., 179
horror comics, 256–7
Horsbrugh, Florence, 50–1, 52
House of Commons, 302–4
House of Lords, 302–4
housing, 14–15, 16, 195
Housing Associations, 15
Howarth, David, 140
Howe, Irving, 314
Hungary, broadcasting, 115
Hurd, Douglas, 160
Hutchison, Robert, 220
Huxley, Aldous, 214
Huxley, Julian, 216, 312
Huxley, T.H., 49
hymns, 271–3

Independent, 207
Independent Television Authority (ITA), 118, 145, 151, 245, 291
Inland Revenue, 228
Innis, Harold Adams, 324–5
Institutes of Higher Education, 44
intellectuals, place in English life, 297, 300–18
IRA, 251
ITMA, 129

Jackson, Michael, 127
James, Eric, 41
James, Henry, 76, 141, 182
Japanese culture, 238
Johnson, Samuel, 65, 81, 226, 274, 335
journals of opinion, 304–5
Joyce, James, 81, 109, 168

Jude the Obscure, 41, 297
judgment, judgmental, 3, 36, 58, 161–2, 270, 322
Juvenal, 96, 197

Kafka, Franz, 95, 279, 335
Kaleidoscope, 138–40
Karloff, Boris, 167
Kay-Shuttleworth, Sir James, 21
Keats, John, 274
Kellogg Foundation, 24
Kelly, Edith and Tom, 67
Kent, University of, 42
Kermode, Frank, 95
King, Cecil, 98
King Lear, 72, 81, 87, 278
Kingsley, Charles, xiii
Kingsway College, 38
Kinnock, Neil, 13
Kipling, Rudyard: Auden on, 63; critique of work, 69; quoted, 12, 71, 274, 300
Kitchen, Fred, 58, 70
Koestler, Arthur, 279
Kraus, Karl, 157

La Bruyére, Jean de, 275
Labour governments: education policy, 43, 45; (1979), 11, 14, 45
Labour Party, 30, 62, 64
Labour-run councils, 12
Labov, William, 185
Lady Chatterley's Lover, 135–6, 246, 252–3
Lambeth Council, 12
Lang, Jack, 216
language: and ideology, 163–6; changes in, 158–60; 'correct' speech 9–10; decay, 322; misuses, 157–71
Laski, Marghanita, 235
Laslett, Peter, 315
Last Exit to Brooklyn, 253
Lawrence, D.H.: influence, 87, 316–17; Lady Chatterley's Lover, 135–6, 246, 252–3; on characters, 78; on English culture, xii; patronage, 168; quoted, 79, 82, 83, 181; Sons and Lovers, 181; values, 14; Women in Love, 64, 72
leadership, 27–8

Leavis, F.R.: Lewis's broadside, 103;
    quoted, 86, 160, 312–13, 317;
    values, 74–5, 313
Leavis, Queenie, 103
Lee, Brenda, 112
Lee, Jennie, 217
Left, 7, 9, 35–6, 56, 224, 335, 338
leisure, 197, 220–1, 330
Lerner, Laurence, 88
Lessing, Gotthold, 281, 339
Levellers, 186
Lewis, Clive Staples: *Experiment in
    Criticism*, 103–4; influence, 103,
    108, 109, 110; quoted, 103–4,
    105, 108, 143
Liberal Democrats, 283
liberty, 319, 325, *see also* freedom
libraries, *see* Public Libraries
Libraries Act (1850), 67
Library Association, 55, 68, 260
Listener, The, 130
literacy, 21, 179, 326, 336, 338
literature: academic responses, 82–8;
    Arts Council, 56–61;
    communitarian art, 61–5; effects,
    246–8; funding, 234–6; literary
    essences, 75–82; literary influences,
    88–95; reading, 65–75
Little Chefs, 211
Liverpool Council, 12
Llewellyn, Richard, 102
Local Education Authorities, 236,
    260
Local Government, 5, 17, 214, 261,
    283–4
London Review of Books, 306
London School of Economics (LSE),
    242
London University, 42, 255
Lottery, National, 214, 218, 228, 323
Lowell, James Russell, 301
Lowry, L.S., 280

Macbeth, 62, 241
McCarthy, Mary, 264
McDonald's, 196
McGill, Donald, 105
MacIntyre, Alasdair, 155, 327
McIntyre, Ian, 23
McLuhan, Marshall, 324–5
MacNeice, Louis, 130

McRobbie, Angela, 172, 197
magazines, 208, 266
magistrates, 5
Magritte, René, 280
Mahler, Gustav, 57
Malraux, André, 100, 216
Mansbridge, Albert, 35
market, 16–18, 244–5
Marley, Bob, 61
Marsh, G.P., 157
Martin Chuzzlewit, 65
Marvell, Andrew, 53
Marx, Karl, 69, 84
mass culture, characteristics, 97–102,
    322
Masterman, J.C., 23
Mastermind, 133
Maud, John, 312
Maupin, Armistead, 139
Maxwell, Robert, 13
Means Test Inspector, 5
Measure for Measure, 64
Media Studies, 178
Melody Radio, 209
Melville, Herman, 87
Members of Parliament (MPs), 287,
    292, 302–3, 322
Mencken, H.L., 98
Mengham, Rod, 157
Mensa, 314
Meredith, George, 79
Methodists, 5, 171, 179
middle class: authority-consciousness,
    6; life-style, 194–6, 326–7;
    membership, 205–6; myth, 16;
    response to arts, 220–1; social
    causes, 334; taxation, 15
Middlemarch, 65, 84–5, 88, 141, 296
Mill, John Stuart, 90, 224, 332
Millar, Ronald, 14
Mills and Boon, 64, 129
Milton, John, 53, 59, 96, 249
Mitchell, Denis, 142
Monarchy, 27, 30, 285, 287
Montaigne, Michel de, 182, 268, 275,
    300, 315
Moral Maze, The, 129
Moravia, Alberto, 21
Morning in the Streets, 142
Morris, William, 224
Muir, Edwin, 329

Müller, Chancellor von, 339
multi-cultural society, 165, 261, 262
Murdoch, Iris, 74, 321
Murdoch, Rupert, 24, 204
museums, 196–7, 327
music, 66, 109–12, 220, 232, 333
Musicians' Union, 293
Myrdal, Gunnar, 184

Napoleon III, 100
National Curriculum, 36
National Health Service (NHS), 10,
    12, 16–17, 216, 253, 333
National Heritage, 196; Department
    of, 69, 213
National Viewers' and Listeners'
    Association, 247, 259
National Lottery, 214, 218, 228, 323
National Vocational Qualifications
    (NVQs), 39–40, 64
National Youth Orchestra, 98
nationalism, 328, 330
Needham, Joseph, 312
neighbourhood, 284–5, 329–30, 339
neighbourliness, 329–30
Neighbours, 111, 126
Netherlands, art, 80
New Left Review, 306
New Society, 305
New Statesman, 290
New Statesman and Society, 306
New Yorker, 249
Newbolt, Sir Henry, 27
Newman, John Henry, 41
news broadcasting, 264
Newton, Isaac, 41, 268, 286
Nicholas Nickleby, 65
Nichols, Peter, 140
Nietzsche, Friedrich Wilhelm, 82, 166
1984, 110, 163, 279
Nixon, Richard M., 136–7
Nobel Prize for Literature, 236
Normanbrook, Lord, 257
North and South, 58
nostalgia, 196–7, 327–8
Nostromo, 76, 335
novels, 222

Office of Arts and Libraries, 228
Official Secrets Act, 253
Old Wives' Tale, The, 76

Open University, 21, 52, 217, 225
opera, 56, 221, 232–3
opinion, 270
Orwell, George: Eton performance,
    28–9; influence, 38, 103, 105, 224,
    317; *1984*, 110, 163, 279; on
    English culture, xii, 105–7, 108,
    121; on reviewing, 305–6; quoted,
    102, 106, 143, 163, 274, 297, 305,
    329, 331, 338; 'Ruling Class', 329;
    Soviet attitude to, 240; values, 14,
    224
Osborne, John, 239
Oswald, Lee Harvey, 136
Othello, 64, 81
Our Mutual Friend, 65
Ovid, 65
Oxbridge: BBC, 118, 204; education
    system, 24; future, 49; reviewers,
    308; selection system, 41, 49; social
    calendar, 200
Oxfam, 183
Oxford University, 24–5, 41, 49

Paradise Lost, 59
Parker, Charles, 140
Parliament, 302–4
Passage to India, A, 181
patronage, 217, 231
Peacock, Thomas Love, 171
Peacock Committee, 147, 289
PEN, 337
Performance Measurement, 38–9
Pern, Eva, 111
Persuasion, 176
Picasso, Pablo, 227
piggyback principle, 210–11
Pilkington Report, 40, 114, 125, 151,
    289
Pink Floyd, 239
Pinker, Steven, 157
Pinter, Harold, 81, 140
Pirandello, Luigi, 83
Plater, Alan, 142
Poland, British Council, 240
police, 5, 199
Political and Economic Planning
    (PEP), 218
Polytechnics, former, 43–4, 48
Ponting, Clive, 250
Pope, Alexander, 53

popular culture, 102–13, 322
populism, 4, 8, 56, 312
post-modernism, 10
postal services, 17–18
Potter, Dennis, 122, 137, 142, 145, 259
Potter, Stephen, 140
Pound, Ezra, 158–9
Prelude, The, 90
Presley, Elvis, 127
press: Beaverbrook, 239; legislation 338; popular, 17, 187, 200, 304; quality, 304; training, 25
Primitive Methodists, 5, 213
Pritchett, V.S., 306
Proust, Marcel, 79
Public Libraries, 66–9; aims, 148; campaigns for, 315; censorship, 254; funding, 224; pressures on, 17, 234, 315; public service, 10, 277; support for literature, 236
Public Libraries Act (1964), 68
Public Parks, 224, 277
Public Patronage and the Arts, 218–19
public schools, 24, 26–30, 200
public service, 7, 10, 114–26, 135–6, 304
publishers, 17, 236, 264
Publishers' Association, 260
Punch, 167

Quality in Television, 153, 155
Quangos, 15, 116, 118, 218, 287–96
Queen's Speech, 323

racism: colonial education policy, 242; increase in, 328, 330; multi-culturalism, 165; Parliamentary response, 260, 303; prevalence, 260, 328
radio, 126–33; generic, 127; talk, 323
Radio 1, 126, 209
Radio 2 (Light Programme), 126, 138, 209
Radio 3 (Third Programme), 130–1; audience, 127, 151, 153, 208; book programmes, 140; broadcast arts, 138–9; campaign for Third Programme, 315; effects of Classic FM, 132–3, 136

Radio 4 (Home Service), 128–30; arts programme, 135; audience, 127, 208; book programmes, 138, 307; *Kaleidoscope*, 138–40; news, 178
Radio 5, 127–8
Ragged Trousered Philanthropists, The, 58
Ramblers' Association, 273
Rawls, John, 319
Read, Herbert, 335
reading, 65–6, 72–5, 246
Real Lives, 250, 251–2
Reed, Henry, 130
Rees-Mogg, Lord, 290
Reith, Lord, 23, 114, 119, 147, 153
Reith lectures, 309
relativism, 3–10, 321–8
religion: chapel, 4–5, 197, 270; church, 4, 27, 120, 197, 270; fundamentalism, 328
Remembrance Day, 120
reviewing, 253–4, 305–11
Ricardo, David, 13
Richards, I.A., 79, 91
right-wing, 7, 56, 224, 335, 338
Ring and the Book, The, 92
Robbins, Lionel, 312
Robbins Report, 40–1
Rogers, W.R., 130
Roman Catholic Church, 3, 4
Romans in Britain, The, 253
Round the Horne, 129
Rorschach Test, 247
Royal Charter, 116, 118, 238, 287
Royal Family, 120, 199, 200–1, 214, 241
Royal Festival Hall, 220
Royal National Theatre, 228, 232
Royal Opera House, Covent Garden: 'corporate' seats, 71, 214, 233; cost of tickets, 220; funding, 56, 229–30, 233; status, 199, 214, 221
Royal Shakespeare Company (RSC), 232, 295
Ruskin, John, 82, 83, 158
Russell, Bertrand, 300
Russell, Ken, 135

Safeway, 208
Safire, William, 83–4
Said, Edward, 309–10

Sainsbury's, 207, 208
St Ives, 225–6
Salmon, Pierre, 45
Sandys, Duncan, 136
Santayana, George, 11
Sarnoff, David, 119
Sartre, Jean-Paul, 279, 300
satire, 121
Saturday Night and Sunday Morning, 186
Scargill, Arthur, 263
Scarlet and Black, 72
Schiller, Johann Christoph Friedrich von, 69
Scholes, Robert, 173
School Attendance Officer, 5
School Library Service, 261
schools: comprehensive, 32–3; grant-maintained, 22; independent, 22; public, 24, 26–30
Scotland, education, 34
Scott, Sir Walter, 339
Secret Agent, The, 76, 189, 279–80
Secret Society, 250
sex magazines, 266
sex-and-violence, 245, 246–9, 258–9
Shakespeare, William, 52–3, 64, 69, 96, 242
Shaw, George Bernard, 66, 302, 316
Shaw, Roy, 31, 57, 223, 227
Shelley, Percy Bysshe, 69
Shils, Edward, 4, 45
shopping, 207–9
Sickert, Walter, 279
Sillitoe, Alan, 186
sixth-form colleges, 29, 33, 37
Smith, Sydney, 307
Social Security, 5; 'scroungers', 13
Social Services Department, 5, 10
Socialism, 14
Society of Authors, 40, 234, 293
Solon, 274
Solzhenitsyn, Alexander, 94
songs, pop and mass, 109–12
Sons and Lovers, 181
Sorbonne, 242
South Bank Show, 120
Soviet Union, 93, 94, 148, 240, 333
Spar, 209
sponsorship, 31–2, 150, 214, 217–18, 226–31

sport, 29, 322
Spread of Sponsorship, The, 31, 150, 227
Spycatcher, 250
Stalin, Joseph, 215
Start the Week, 138
state, 'nanny', 15
status, 202–12
Sterne, Laurence, 79
Stock Exchange, 203
Stoppard, Tom, 140
Strangeways, 142
student revolts (1968), 44–5, 310
student-teacher equivalents (STEs), 45
Sturt, George, 268
Suez crisis (1956), 116, 119, 251
Sun newspaper, 21, 99, 102, 337
Sunday papers, 9
Sunday School, 4, 273
Surprised by Joy, 103
Sussex, University of, 42
Swift, Jonathan, 11, 275

Tagore, Rabindranath, 64
'talk' radio stations, 323
Tawney, R.H.: influence, 34, 52, 316, 336; quoted, 125, 326, 336; values, 14, 50, 52
Taylor, Charles, 321, 339
Tchaikovsky, Piotr, 93
teachers, 10, 35–6, 297, 302
Technical Colleges, 37
television, 133–8; advertising, 99, 244, 323, 334; American, 115; class attitudes, 195; effects, 246–9; impact, 333–4; Iron Curtain countries, 115; nostalgia, 327; producers, 187; ratings war, 255, 324; rented sets, 209; viewing patterns, 207, 208, 209; violence, 248–9; watershed, 256
Temple, William, 34, 50
Tesco's, 32, 208, 209
Tess of the Durbervilles, 62, 87
Tester, Keith, 172
Thatcher, Margaret: confrontational government, 285–6; election (1979), 14; quoted, 1, 325; *Real Lives* affair, 251–2; Thatcherism, 10–11, 68
Thatcherism, 10, 275

theatres, 56, 225, 232
This Is Your Life, 259
Thomas, Dylan, 130
Thompson, E.P., 70, 137, 239, 317
Thoreau, Henry, 274
Through the Keyhole, 126
Tiller, Terence, 130
Times, The, 207, 339
Times Literary Supplement, 306
Titmuss, Richard, 14, 17, 316
To the Lighthouse, 203
Tocqueville, Alexis de, 11, 70, 72, 97, 99, 321
Torquay, dancers, 108–9, 197
Townswomen's Guilds, 293
Toynbee, Arnold, 35
Trade Unions, 5, 11, 64, 108, 186
Trades Union Congress (TUC), 50
Training Councils, 39
Traviata, La, 143, 229
Treasury, 51, 117, 146, 228, 237
Tressell, Robert, 58, 70
Trevelyan, G.M., 19, 34–5
Trilling, Lionel, 1
Trollope, Anthony, xiii, 13, 64, 81, 103, 198, 222
Tupperware, 61
Turgenev, Ivan, 87, 94, 172, 296

Ulysses, 109
underclass, 206–7, 327
UNESCO, 216
United States: arts funding, 239; broadcasting, 114–15; cultural studies, 59; Endowment for the Arts, 236–7; Information Service, 238; sponsorship, 231
universities, 40–9; American, 314; extra-mural departments, 21, 50, 297; Oxbridge, 24, 41, 49, 118, 200, 204, 308; student revolts, 44–5, 310; Vice-Chancellors, 46–8, 295–6, 312
'uses and gratification' theory, 248, 269
Ustinov, Peter, 166

Valery, Paul, 145, 157
value-judgments, 36, 58, *see also* judgment
VAT, 226

Veblen, Thorstein, 40, 210
Verdi, Giuseppe, 229
Victorian Values, 322
Video Appeals Committee, 245, 267
video recorders, 195
Vienna State Opera, 221
violence, 245, 246–9, 256–7
Viz, 72
vocationalism, 22, 25, 30–1
Voltaire, 74
voluntary work, 224, 330

Wagner, Richard, 92
Waitrose, 207
Wales, education, 34
Wallace, Nelly, 121
Waller, Fats, 112
Walpole, Horace, 65
Wandsworth Council, 31
War Game, The, 257–8
Warnock, Mary, 312
Warwick University, 42
Waste Land, The, 181, 191
Watkins, Peter, 257
The Way We Live Now, The (Trollope), xiii, 103, 222
Webb, Beatrice and Sidney, 316
Weber, Max, 180
Wedgwood china, 61
Wells, H.G., 297, 316
West, W.J., 67
Wheldon, Huw, 123–4
Whitbread Prize, 234
Whitehead, A.N., 81, 91
Whitehouse, Mary, 244
Wilkinson, Ellen, 153
Williams, Raymond: influence, 317; on working-class creativity, 64, 186; quoted, 83–4, 108, 243, 301, 332
Williams, Shirley, 45
Willis, Paul, 112–13, 185
Wilson, Bishop, 281, 339
Wilson, Harold, 287
'winter of discontent', 11–12
Woman's Hour, 127
Women in Love, 64, 72
Women's Institute, 273, 293
Wordsworth, William, 14, 53, 90, 224, 329

Workers' Educational Association
(WEA), 21, 297
working class: arts appreciation,
219–20; creativity, 64, 186; culture
after Second World War, 193–7;
culture before Second World War,
4–6, 333; poverty of ambition, 328;
recreational habits, 220, 327
Working Men's Clubs, 64, 108
World Service, BBC, 116, 148

Yeats, W.B., 63
Young, Michael, 49, 316